PUBLIC RELATIONS AND COMMUNICATION MANAGEMENT

Public Relations and Communication Management serves as a Festschrift honoring the work of public relations scholars James E. Grunig and Larissa A. Grunig. Between them, the Grunigs have published 12 books and more than 330 articles, book chapters, and various academic and professional publications, and have supervised 34 doctoral dissertations and 105 master's theses. This volume recognizes the Grunigs' contributions to public relations scholarship over the past four decades.

To honor the Grunigs' scholarship, this volume continues to expand their body of work with chapters from renowned colleagues, former students, and research associates. The chapters discuss current trends in the field as well as emerging issues that drive the field forward. Sample topics include theories and future aspects of the behavioral, strategic management approach to managing public relations, and its linkages and implications to related subfields and key field issues. Contributions stimulate academic discussion and demonstrate the relevance of applied theories for the practice of public relations and communication management with up-to-date concepts, theories, and thoughts.

Krishnamurthy Sriramesh is Professor and Distinguished Faculty Scholar in the Brian Lamb School of Communication, Purdue University, USA. Dr. Sriramesh is recognized for his scholarship on global public relations and has published over 150 books, articles, book chapters, and conference papers. He is on the editorial boards of a number of scholarly journals.

Ansgar Zerfass is Professor of Communication Management at the University of Leipzig, Germany, and Professor in Communication and Leadership (Adjunct) at BI Norwegian Business School, Oslo, Norway. He has published 30 books and numerous journal articles and chapters, and serves as Editor of the *International Journal of Strategic Communication*.

Jeong-Nam Kim is Associate Professor in the Brian Lamb School of Communication at Purdue University, Indiana, USA. He has published 50 journal articles and book chapters, and is working on 4 books, including a book on situational theory, *Situational Theory of Problem Solving: Communicative, Cognitive, and Perceptive Bases*.

PUBLIC RELATIONS AND COMMUNICATION MANAGEMENT

Current Trends and Emerging Topics

Edited by Krishnamurthy Sriramesh,
Ansgar Zerfass, and Jeong-Nam Kim

Routledge
Taylor & Francis Group

NEW YORK AND LONDON

First published 2013
by Routledge
711 Third Avenue, New York, NY 10017

Simultaneously published in the UK
by Routledge
2 Park Square, Milton Park, Abingdon, Oxon OX14 4RN

Routledge is an imprint of the Taylor & Francis Group, an informa business

Library of Congress Cataloging-in-Publication Data
Public relations and communication management : current trends and
emerging topics / edited by Krishnamurthy Sriramesh, Ansgar Zerfass,
Jeong-Nam Kim.
pages cm
1. Public relations. I. Sriramesh, Krishnamurthy. II. Zerfass, Ansgar, 1965–
III. Kim, Jeong-Nam.
HD59.P7843 2013
659.2–dc23
2012037411

ISBN: 978–0–415–63089–4
ISBN: 978–0–415–63090–0
ISBN: 978–0–203–07925–6

Typeset in Bembo
by Keystroke, Station Road, Codsall, Wolverhampton

CONTENTS

LIST OF FIGURES

LIST OF TABLES

ABOUT THE EDITORS

Krishnamurthy Sriramesh, Ph.D., is Professor and Distinguished Faculty Scholar at the Brian Lamb School of Communication at Purdue University, Indiana, USA. He is recognized for his scholarship on global public relations. For over a decade he has advocated the need to reduce ethnocentricity in the public relations body of knowledge. His research interests also extend to public relations for development, corporate social responsibility and public relations, and the use of new media for public relations. His rich teaching experience includes teaching at 10 universities on 4 continents. He has won several teaching and research awards and was awarded the prestigious Pathfinder Award from the Institute for Public Relations (USA) in 2004. Dr. Sriramesh has co-edited *The Handbook of Global Public Relations: Theory, Research, and Practice* and *Public Relations Research: European and International Perspectives, Culture and Public Relations*, and edited *Public Relations in Asia: An Anthology*. Between these books, he has contributed to chronicling, for the first time in the field, information about public relations in about 50 countries and regions of the world. He also has presented over 80 research papers, seminars, and given talks in over 30 countries. In addition to authoring over 30 book chapters, he has published over 30 research articles in refereed journals. He serves as the Assistant Editor of *Public Relations Review*, Associate Editor of the *Journal of Communication Management*, and as a member of the editorial board of several international journals.

Ansgar Zerfass, Ph.D., is Professor of Communication Management in the Institute of Communication and Media Studies at the University of Leipzig, Germany. Moreover, he is Professor in Communication and Leadership (Adjunct) at BI Norwegian Business School, Oslo, Norway. Prior to taking up these positions Ansgar Zerfass worked in management positions at various companies and institutions for more than ten years. He has a degree and doctorate in business administration and a habilitation (second doctorate) in communication science. He has received several awards both for his academic work and his communication campaigns, among them the Ludwig-Schunk Award for economic science, the German Public Relations Award, the German Multimedia Award, and the Jackson-Sharpe Award, and he was elected "PR Head of the Year 2005" in Germany. Dr. Zerfass serves as Executive Director of the European Public Relations Education and Research Association (EUPRERA), Brussels, is Editor of the *International Journal of Strategic Communication*, and Head of the Jury for the International German Public Relations Award, Berlin. He is the Lead Researcher of the annual European Communication Monitor, the largest empirical study on strategic communication worldwide in more than 40 countries. He has authored and edited 30 books as well as 170 articles and book chapters on corporate communications, online communication, investor relations, evaluation and measurement.

Jeong-Nam Kim, Ph.D., is Associate Professor at the Brian Lamb School of Communication at Purdue University, Indiana, USA. He received his doctorate in Communication (Public Relations) from the University of Maryland, College Park, in 2006 and joined the faculty at Purdue in 2007. His specialties are communication theory, strategic management of public relations, public behavior and its social consequences, information behaviors and problem solving. Jeong-Nam Kim has constructed a communication theory called the *situational theory of problem solving* with James E. Grunig, which explains causes and processes of information behaviors in problematic life situations. Situational theory has been applied to public relations, public diplomacy, health communication, risk communication, science communication, and employee communication. Another area of Jeong-Nam Kim's research is the integration of causes and processes of organizational relationships, reputation, and brand through the behavioral, strategic management paradigm in public relations. He has published 50 journal articles and book chapters, and is working on 4 books, including a book on situational theory, *Situational Theory of Problem Solving: Communicative, Cognitive, and Perceptive Bases*.

CONTRIBUTORS

Günter Bentele, Ph.D., is Professor of Public Relations at the University of Leipzig, Germany. He has held the chair of public relations, the first for any German-speaking country, at this university since 1994. Previously, he was Professor of Communication Science and Journalism at the University of Bamberg. Dr. Bentele has served as visiting professor at several European and American universities. He has authored, co-authored and edited 45 books and written more than 230 scientific articles in the fields of public relations, communication theory, journalism, and semiotics.

Bruce K. Berger, Ph.D., is Reese Phifer Professor of Advertising and Public Relations at the University of Alabama, USA. His research specialties are employee communications, power relations, and leadership in communication management. He is a trustee of the Institute for Public Relations and founding director of the Plank Center for Leadership in Public Relations. Previously, he was VP of public relations at Whirlpool Corporation and worked on communication projects in more than 30 countries.

Shannon A. Bowen, Ph.D., is Associate Professor in the School of Journalism and Mass Communications at the University of South Carolina, USA. She won the Jackson Jackson & Wagner Behavioral Science Prize for her program of research on ethics and dominant coalition participation in ethical decision-making. Her doctoral work with the Grunigs studied issues management in the pharmaceutical industry and posed models combining the Excellence Theory with Kantian deontological ethics.

Yi-Ru Regina Chen, Ph.D., is Assistant Professor in the School of Communication at Hong Kong Baptist University, Hong Kong. She won the 2006 Bob Heath Top Paper Award for her ICA public relations division paper on multinational corporations' governance and management of government affairs for business issues in China. In addition to strategic government affairs, her research specialties include issues management, corporate social responsibility, governance and communication, and online rumor management.

Estelle de Beer, M.A., lectures in the Communication Management Division of the Department of Business Management and is a founding member of the Centre for Communication and Reputation Management at the University of Pretoria. She served on the research team for the King Report on Governance for South Africa, 2009 (King III). She is also past President of the South African Communication Association (SACOMM) and worked in practice for more than 17 years. Her research interests are strategic communication, stakeholder relationships, sustainability, corporate governance, strategy, and reputation.

Nigel M. de Bussy, Ph.D., is Associate Professor and Head of the School of Marketing at Curtin University, Perth, Australia. He gained more than a decade's experience in the public relations profession in the United Kingdom and Australia, consulting to major private sector and government clients. He is a Fellow and past State President of the Public Relations Institute of Australia. His current research interests include corporate social responsibility and organizational identity, stakeholder dialogue and its impact on business performance, and credibility in new communication media.

David Dozier, Ph.D., is Professor in the School of Journalism and Media Studies, San Diego State University. He has written over 100 books, book chapters, journal articles, and conference papers in public relations and mass communication. With James and Larissa Grunig, he co-authored the three Excellence Study books. The Public Relations Society of America (PRSA) named Dozier outstanding educator, a national award. He received the Jackson Jackson & Wagner Behavioral Science Prize and the Pathfinder Award for Excellence in Scholarly Public Relations Research. The Institute for Public Relations named him a Research Fellow.

Sandra Duhé, Ph.D., is Associate Professor and Head of the Public Relations Program in the Division of Communication Studies at Southern Methodist University's Meadows School of the Arts, Texas, USA. She has an extensive background in public affairs management for three multinational corporations, with experience in merger communications, media relations, corporate branding, community outreach, risk/crisis communication, and philanthropy. Her research investigates political, economic, and social influences on how organizations build and maintain relationships with their stakeholders.

Mohan J. Dutta, Ph.D., is Professor and Head of the Department of Communication and New Media at the National University of Singapore and the Founding Director of the Center for Culture-Centered Approach to Research and Evaluation (CARE). He holds an adjunct appointment with the Brian Lamb School of Communication and with the Center on Poverty and Health Inequities (COPHI) at Purdue University, USA. His research specialties are grassroots activism for social change, the culture-centered approach to global public relations, Marxist theories of social change, new media and social change, and postcolonial and Subaltern Studies approaches to communication.

Maria Aparecida Ferrari, Ph.D., is Associate Professor and Researcher at the School of Communications and Arts of the University of São Paulo, Brazil. Between 1987 and 2009 she was Director of the School of Journalism and Public Relations as well as Coordinator of the undergraduate program in public relations at The Methodist University of São Paulo. Her research interests include intercultural communication, organizational communication, and global public relations. She is the co-author *of Relações Públicas: teoria, context e relacionamentos* with James E. Grunig and Fábio França (2009, 2011), and of *Relaciones Públicas: naturaleza, función y gestión en las organizaciones contemporáneas* (2011) and *Gestión de Relaciones Públicas para el éxito de las organizaciones* (2012), both with Fábio França. Dr. Ferrari is currently Editorial Director at ABRAPCORP, the Brazilian Association of Research on Organizational Communication and Public Relations. Additionally, Dr. Ferrari has taught Communication and Public Relations in different Graduate Programs in several Latin American countries.

Tiffany Derville Gallicano, Ph.D., is Assistant Professor in the School of Journalism and Communication at the University of Oregon, USA. She studied under James and Larissa Grunig at the University of Maryland. Her recent scholarship has focused on social media, as well as Millennial public relations practitioners. She is a Page Legacy Scholar and two-time winner of the Jackson Sharpe Award.

Anne Gregory, Ph.D., is Professor of Public Relations and Director of the Centre for Public Relations Studies at Leeds Metropolitan University, United Kingdom. She was President of the Chartered Institute of Public Relations, is Chair-Elect of the Global Alliance for Public Relations and Communication Management, and holds the Sir Stephen Tallents Medal for her outstanding contribution to public relations. Her research specialisms are the strategic role of public relations in organizations, leadership, and practitioner capability. Dr. Gregory is Editor-in-Chief of the *Journal of Communication Management*.

Derina R. Holtzhausen, Ph.D., is Professor of Strategic Communication and Director of the School of Media and Strategic Communications at Oklahoma State

University, USA. Previously, she worked as a communication practitioner in South Africa and as Associate Professor at the University of Southern Florida. She was co-founder of the *International Journal of Strategic Communication* and received the Pathfinder Award from the Institute of Public Relations for her original research agenda on postmodern public relations.

Yi-Hui Christine Huang, Ph.D., is Professor in the School of Journalism and Communication at The Chinese University of Hong Kong. She received her Ph.D. in mass communication from the University of Maryland, USA. Yi-Hui Huang's research interests include public relations management, crisis communication, conflict and negotiation, and cross-cultural communications and relationship. Her research awards include the Best Article Award in Public Relations Scholarship awarded by the National Communication Association, USA, the Distinguished Research Award given by the National Science Council, R.O.C., and a Top Paper Award given by the International Communication Association.

Chun-ju Flora Hung-Baesecke, Ph.D., is Associate Director of the Center for Media and Communication Research and Assistant Professor of the Public Relations & Advertising Option in the Department of Communication Studies at Hong Kong Baptist University. Her research interests are relationship management, strategic management, reputation management, crisis communication, conflict resolution, and corporate social responsibility. She is a member of the Academic Committee of the China International Public Relations Association.

Emanuele Invernizzi is Professor of Corporate Communication and Public Relations Management and Director of the Institute of Economics and Marketing at IULM University, Milan, Italy. His research specialization is strategic public relations and organizational and entrepreneurial communication. He is past President of the European Public Relations Education and Research Association (EUPRERA).

Fraser Likely, M.A., is the Director of Likely Communication Strategies in Ottawa, Canada, a management consultancy founded in 1987 to provide Chief Communication Officers and their departments with strategic direction, organizational design, operational and service improvement, and performance measurement counsel. He is a member of the Institute for Public Relations' Commission on Measurement and Evaluation, USA, and has been an Adjunct Professor at the University of Ottawa.

Joanne Chen Lyu is a Ph.D. candidate in the School of Journalism and Communication at The Chinese University of Hong Kong. Her research interests include public relations, crisis communication and management, relationship/*guanxi* management, and Chinese communication. She was selected to present in the Top Student Papers in the Public Relations Division of the International Communication Association. Her research work has been published by *Public Relations Review* and Chinese scholarly journals. Previously, she worked for several years in the public relations department of a transnational media corporation.

Lan Ni, Ph.D., is Associate Professor in the Jack Valenti School of Communication at the University of Houston, USA. Her research specialties are strategic relationship management, identification of publics, and intercultural public relations. She has published in the *Journal of Public Relations Research*, the *Journalism and Mass Communication Quarterly*, *Public Relations Review*, the *International Journal of Strategic Communication*, the *Journal of Public Affairs*, and the *Journal of Communication Management*.

Kenneth D. Plowman, Ph.D., is Associate Professor at Brigham Young University, Utah, USA. Specializing in strategic communication and conflict resolution in public relations, Dr. Plowman earned a doctorate in journalism from the University of Maryland and an MPA from George Washington University. He spent 15 years in the professional field, the majority of them on Capitol Hill. He is also the author of over 40 publications and is a retired public affairs officer from the U.S. Army Reserve.

Bryan H. Reber, Ph.D., is Professor in the Department of Advertising and Public Relations at the Grady College of Journalism and Mass Communication, University of Georgia, USA. His research areas include public relations management, public relations and activism, and crisis and risk communication. He practiced nonprofit public relations for 15 years in a college setting.

Ronél Rensburg, Ph.D., is Professor in the Communication Management Division of the Department of Business Management at the University of Pretoria, South Africa. She served in several management positions at the University and is currently Director of the Centre for Communication and Reputation Management; is past President of the Public Relations Institute of South Africa (PRISA); and is a board member of the Global Alliance for Public Relations and Communication Management. Her current areas of research are the role of reputation management, managing country reputation, and the role of sustainable communication.

Yunna Rhee, Ph.D., is Associate Professor in the Division of Communication, Hankuk University of Foreign Studies, Seoul, South Korea, where she teaches public relations. Her research on employee communication, public relations outcome measurement, and social media public relations has been published in the *Journal of Public Relations Research*, the *International Journal of Strategic Communication*, and many Korean scholarly journals.

Stefania Romenti, Ph.D., is Assistant Professor of Public Relations and Corporate Communication at IULM University, Milan, Italy, where she teaches Public Relations Management. She is Vice-Director of the Executive Master in Corporate Public Relations at IULM. Her research centers on strategic public relations, stakeholder dialogue and engagement, communication measurement, and evaluation.

Benita Steyn, APR, MCom, presently lectures in the web-based Master's program in Public Relations Management at the Cape Peninsula University of Technology in Cape Town. Before entering academia, she spent 13 years in the South African diplomatic service (the US, Europe and South America) and speaks five languages. She also practiced Public Relations for 14 years (South Africa and New York) and lectured at the Department of Marketing and Communication Management, University of Pretoria, from 1996 to 2003. She was twice awarded "Educator of the Year" by PRISA (1999/2001) and has received a Quill Award from the IABC for her research on communication strategy development in 1999. She received the President's Award from PRISA in 2012 in recognition of outstanding services to PRISA and the profession. Benita has delivered 50 international and national conference papers on strategic PR/communication management and authored more than 20 academic publications including the textbook *Corporate Communication Strategy*.

Minjung Sung, Ph.D., is Associate Professor and Chairperson of the Department of Advertising and Public Relations at Chung-Ang University, South Korea. Her main research interests include strategic management of public relations, global public relations, issues management, and corporate communication.

Ana Tkalac Verčič, Ph.D., is Professor at the University of Zagreb, Croatia. She is also a Visiting Professor of Internal Communications at the Universita della Svizzera Italiana, Lugano, Switzerland. Dr. Tkalac Verčič has authored, co-authored, and co-edited numerous papers and books in the fields of marketing, public relations, and research methodology. She was recently awarded the PR PRO award as a significant recognition for her professional contribution to the development of the public relations profession in the region.

Dejan Verčič, Ph.D., is Professor at the University of Ljubljana and a co-founder of a communication consultancy, Pristop, in Ljubljana, Slovenia. In 2001, he was awarded the Alan Campbell-Johnson Medal for outstanding service to international public relations by the Chartered Institute of Public Relations in the United Kingdom, of which he is a Fellow. Dr. Verčič has served, *inter alia*, as the chairman of the Research Committee of the IABC Research Foundation and as the President of the European Public Relations Education and Research Association (EUPRERA). He co-organizes the international public relations research symposium known as Bledcom, and has authored, co-authored, and co-edited over 150 articles and books.

Robert I. Wakefield, Ph.D., is Associate Professor at Brigham Young University, Utah, USA. His research interests are global public relations, activism, culture, and strategic public relations. He is Assistant Editor of the *Public Relations Journal* and serves on the Global Public Relations Committee of the Institute for Public Relations.

Tom Watson, Ph.D., is Professor of Public Relations in the Media School at Bournemouth University, United Kingdom. He has led PR functions and agencies both in the UK and Australia. Tom Watson has completed research and written extensively on public relations measurement and evaluation and is the Chair of the annual International History of Public Relations Conference, held in Bournemouth.

Louis C. Williams, Jr., ABC APR, is Chairman of the Lou Williams Companies, Inc., and was a senior vice-president of the international public relations firm of Hill & Knowlton, Inc. (H&K). He has conducted hundreds of research-related seminars for practitioners and authored the best-selling IABC book *Communication Research, Measurement and Evaluation: A Practical Guide for Communicators*. He is past Chairman of the International Association of Business Communicators and was elected a Fellow. He is an Honorary Trustee and Fellow of the Institute for Public Relations and currently a member of the Institute's Commission on Measurement and Evaluation. As chairman of the IABC Research Foundation, he was instrumental in the creation and development of what has come to be known as the Excellence Study and was awarded the PRSA Foundation's Jackson Jackson & Wagner Award, and inducted into the PR News Measurement Hall of Fame.

Donald K. Wright, Ph.D., is the Harold Burson Professor and Chair in Public Relations at Boston University's College of Communication, USA, the world's first degree-granting institution in public relations. He specializes in social and emerging media, communication ethics, and employee communication. In addition to teaching, conducting scholarly and applied research, and lecturing in more than 30 countries on 5 continents, Dr. Wright has worked full-time in corporate, agency, and university public relations, and has been a corporate communications consultant for more than three decades.

NOTES ON THE GRUNIGS

James E. Grunig

PROFESSOR EMERITUS, UNIVERSITY OF MARYLAND, USA

James E. Grunig was a faculty member at the University of Maryland for 36 years before retiring in 2005. He rose through the ranks as an assistant, associate, and full professor in the College of Journalism from 1969 to 1999 and served as a full professor in the Department of Communication from 1999 to 2005. Prior to joining the faculty at the University of Maryland, James Grunig was an assistant professor for a year in the Land Tenure Center at the University of Wisconsin while conducting research under a U.S. Agency for International Development grant in Bogota, Colombia. In the summer of 2004, he was the Wee Kim Wee Professor in the School of Communication and Information at Nanyang Technological University, Singapore.

James Grunig was awarded a Ph.D. in mass communication from the University of Wisconsin in 1968. He received his M.S. degree in agricultural economics from Wisconsin in 1966, passing his M.S. exam in economic theory with distinction. He also graduated with distinction from Iowa State University in 1964, earning a B.S. degree in agricultural journalism. James Grunig received awards from Sigma Delta Chi, the society of professional journalists, as the outstanding male graduate in journalism and for most significant contribution to campus journalism for his co-editorship of the student magazine *The Iowa Agriculturalist*. He was selected for Phi Kappa Phi, Kappa Tau Alpha, Cardinal Key, Alpha Zeta, and Gamma Sigma Delta honorary societies.

He has been awarded four honorary doctorates (*Honoris Causa*) by universities outside the United States: the Universidad San Martin de Porres of Lima, Peru, in

2006; the University of Bucharest in Romania in 2008; Istanbul University in Turkey in 2009; and, with Larissa Grunig, the University of Quebec at Montreal in 2011.

James Grunig began his career as a researcher and theorist by publishing one of the first *Journalism Monographs* in 1968, entitled "The role of information in economic decision making," while he was a doctoral student at Wisconsin. He extended that theory into two studies of decision-making by large landowners and peasant farmers in Colombia, which became the basis for his doctoral dissertation and several articles in communication and economic development journals. James Grunig's theory of communication and decision-making evolved into his situational theory of publics, which has been the subject of many of his articles and his students' theses and dissertations, as well as the framework for research by other communication and public relations scholars.

In 1976, James Grunig began his research on how organizations practice public relations by applying the situational theory of publics and organizational theories to the communication behavior of organizations, publishing a second *Journalism Monograph* entitled "Organizations and publics relations: Testing a communication theory." That program of research resulted in his well-known four models of public relations and his research and theorizing on employee communication, the organization of the public relations function, the relationship between public relations and marketing, and the role of public relations in the strategic management of organizations. During the 1970s and 1980s, James Grunig also published research on evaluation of public relations, science writing, and public relations for scientific organizations, media relations, and communication theory.

From 1985 until 2002, James Grunig served as project director for the $400,000 research project on excellence in public relations and communication management, which was funded by the International Association of Business Communicators (IABC) Research Foundation. James Grunig and a team consisting of Larissa Grunig, David Dozier, William Ehling, Jon White, and Fred Repper conducted a program of research on 327 organizations in the United States, Canada, and the United Kingdom. The research combined a number of middle-range theories of public relations and showed that public relations creates value for organizations and society through relationships and that public relations is most valuable when it is managerial, strategic, symmetrical, diverse, integrated, socially responsible, ethical, and global. Today, the Excellence Theory has evolved into a strategic management theory of public relations, which James Grunig contrasts to the symbolic-interpretive paradigm that he believes characterizes many theories and practices of public relations.

After completing the IABC project, James Grunig and his students and colleagues extended the Excellence Theory into a global theory of public relations. This global theory specified that there are generic principles of public relations that can be applied in different cultural, political, and economic situations, but also maintained that these principles must be applied differently in different contexts. In recent years, he has also worked on theories of organization–public relationships, reputation, public relations as an intangible asset, evaluation of public relations, and the contribution of new digital media to the practice of strategic, symmetrical public relations.

James Grunig has edited, authored, or co-authored 6 books and 242 other publications such as book chapters, journal articles, reports, and papers. His articles have appeared in the *Journal of Public Relations Research*, the *International Journal of Strategic Communication, Journalism and Mass Communication Quarterly, PRISM, Journalism and Mass Communication Monographs, Journalism Studies, Communication Research, Human Communication Research, Public Relations Review, Public Relations Research & Education, Public Relations Research Annual*, the *Journal of Communication Management*, the *Academy of Management Journal, Economic Development and Cultural Change*, the *Journal of Communication*, the *Journal of Technical Writing and Communication*, and *American Behavioral Scientist*.

James Grunig's co-authored books are *Relações públicas: Teoria, contexto e relacionamentos* [Public relations: Theory, context, and relationships], *Excellent Public Relations and Effective Organizations: A Study of Communication Management in Three Countries, Managing Public Relations, Public Relations Techniques*, and *Manager's Guide to Excellence in Public Relations and Communication Management*. He was also the editor of *Excellence in Public Relations and Communication Management*. The book, *Excellent Public Relations and Effective Organizations* received the 2002 PRIDE award of the Public Relations Division of the National Communication Association as the best book on public relations.

James Grunig was named the first winner of the Pathfinder Award for excellence in academic research on public relations by the Institute for Public Relations Research and Education in 1984. In 1989, he received the Outstanding Educator Award of the Public Relations Society of America. In 1992, the PRSA Foundation presented him with the Jackson Jackson & Wagner Award for outstanding behavioral science research. He won the most prestigious lifetime award of the Association for Education in Journalism and Mass Communication (AEJMC) in 2000, the Paul J. Deutschmann Award for Excellence in Research. In 2002, he was awarded the James W. Schwartz Award for Distinguished Service to Journalism and Communication by an alumnus of the Greenlee School of Journalism and Communication, Iowa State University. In 2005, he received the highest award of the Institute for Public Relations, the Alexander Hamilton Medal for Lifetime Contributions to Professional Public Relations, and the Dr. Hamid Notghi Prize for Career Achievement in Public Relations from the Kargozar Public Relations Institute, Tehran, Iran. In 2006, he delivered the annual distinguished lecture of the Institute for Public Relations. In 2008, the Arthur W. Page Society awarded him its Distinguished Service Award. Also in 2008, he was named a Research Fellow by the U.S. Institute for Public Relations. In 2011, *PRNews* inducted him into its Public Relations Measurement Hall of Fame.

James and Larissa Grunig received the Lloyd Dennis Award for Distinguished Leadership in Public Affairs from the Public Affairs and Government Section of the Public Relations Society of America in 2005. They also received the 2010 Presidential Award from the International Public Relations Association for outstanding contribution to better world understanding at the Embassy of Indonesia in Washington, DC.

In addition to his career as a scholar and teacher, James Grunig has worked professionally in public relations and as a science writer for the National Science Foundation, the International Harvester Company, the U.S. Department of Agriculture, the University of Wisconsin, and Iowa State University. He has also served as a research consultant to AT&T; the Edison Electric Institute; the Maryland State Department of Education; Black & Decker; the American Alliance for Health, Physical Education, Recreation, and Dance; the U.S. Department of Energy; Edelman Public Relations Worldwide; and many other organizations.

James Grunig is a member of the Arthur W. Page Society, the Public Relations Society of America (PRSA), the International Association of Business Communicators (IABC), the International Public Relations Association, the Association for Education in Journalism and Mass Communication (AEJMC), the International Communication Association (ICA), and the National Communication Association (NCA). He served as head of the AEJMC public relations division and the ICA public relations interest group. He is an honorary member of the Slovenian Public Relations Society and the Public Relations Institute of Australia.

James Grunig was Associate Editor of *Public Relations Review* from 1975 to 1981. He founded the journal *Public Relations Research & Education* in 1984 and served as its editor for two years. He then arranged the transition of this journal to a new publisher, and it became the *Public Relations Research Annual* and then the *Journal of Public Relations Research*. With Larissa Grunig, he was co-editor of *PRRA* and *JPRR* from 1989 to 1994. He has also served on the editorial boards of *Journalism and Mass Communication Quarterly*, the *Journal of Public Relations Research*, *Health Communication*, *World Communication*, *Public Relations Review*, *Corporate Communications: An International Journal*, *Corporate Reputation Review*, and *Human Communication Research*. He has reviewed manuscripts for *Communication Research*, *Journalism Monographs*, *Management Communication Quarterly*, *Communication Theory*, *Communication Yearbook*, *Journalism Educator*, and other journals in communication and management-related disciplines. He also served as an advisor to Lawrence Erlbaum Publishers (and its successor, Routledge) for its series of books on public relations.

James Grunig has been an invited speaker at conferences, universities, and professional societies around the world. He has presented talks and seminars to approximately 400 professional and educational groups in 45 countries. Among these appearances, he was Visiting Eminent Practitioner of the Public Relations Institute of Australia from July to August 1996. At that time, he delivered two named lectures to the Public Relations Institute of Australia: the Noel Griffith Lecture in Sydney and the Donald Dyer Oration in Adelaide. He was also the Excellence-in-Communications Lecturer for the University of Lugano Executive MScom Program in Zurich, Switzerland, in 2006.

At the University of Maryland, James Grunig has advised 75 Master's theses, 25 doctoral dissertations, and many other non-thesis M.A. papers.

James Grunig has devoted his life to his family and community as well as his profession. Larissa Grunig and he are parents of four children and five grand-children. He also has served as a scoutmaster for the Boy Scouts of America, a youth basketball coach, a church school teacher, and a volunteer for many church and community organizations.

Larissa A. Grunig

PROFESSOR EMERITA, UNIVERSITY OF MARYLAND, USA

Dr. Larissa A. Grunig, retired professor in the Department of Communication at the University of Maryland, College Park, taught public relations and communi-cation research from 1979. In 1996, the public relations graduate program at UMCP was ranked #1 in the United States by *U.S. News & World Report* and in 2002 by a study done at Marquette University. In 1996, she and James Grunig received a *Resolution of Congratulations* passed by the Senate of Maryland and a recognition ceremony in honor of the top ranking of that graduate program.

In 2002, Larissa Grunig was appointed University of Maryland representative to Lt. Gov. Kathleen Kennedy Townsend's Maryland Work-Life Alliance. She then chaired the University of Maryland President's Commission on Women's Issues and, shortly before her retirement in 2005, served as Special Assistant to the President for Women's Issues.

Larissa Grunig received her doctorate in public communication from UMCP in 1985. She taught in both the College of Journalism and in the Department of Communication there. She was an affiliate faculty member of Maryland's School of Public Affairs and its Women's Studies Program. In 1992, she was a Title III Visiting Scholar at Eastern Washington University; she also taught for one year, 1984–1985, at Washington State University. In 1991, she won the Phi Kappa Phi Faculty Mentor Award from the University of Maryland System. During her years in the classroom, she advised 30 master's theses and more than 70 master's degree students who selected the non-thesis option, for a total of about 100 MA students and 10 doctoral dissertations. She also mentored and taught numerous visiting international graduate students, including several Fulbright scholars. In 1996, she was named Outstanding Educator by the Public Relations Society of America.

In a 1990 Survey of the Profession, conducted by *pr reporter*, Larissa Grunig was one of seven educators nationwide named most often as a role model and mentor who has helped shape and share the body of knowledge in public relations. In 1999, she was listed in *PR Week*'s 100 most influential public relations people of the 20th century and one of the country's Top 10 educators. In 1995, she was elected to the Honor Roll of Women in Public Relations.

Larissa Grunig is a member of both the National Capital and Maryland chapters of the PRSA and was an original board member of PRSA's Body of Knowledge project. Together with colleagues, she was commissioned to conduct a series of "glass ceiling" studies for the Public Relations Society of America. From 1985 to 1988, she served as adviser to her campus' chapter of the Public Relations Student Society of America. From 1988 to 1997, she was adviser and co-founder of the chapter's Public Relations Student Society of America Graduate Council. In 1999, she was named to the Hall of Fame of the National Capital Chapter of the PRSA.

Larissa Grunig, formerly a public school teacher and subsequently a reporter and editor of a community newspaper in Colorado, has served as a consultant in public relations since 1969. She has designed and conducted major professional development programs in public relations for the USDA Forest Service, Powell Tate Public Affairs, Fleishman-Hillard Public Relations, and Goddard Space Flight Center. She participated as a faculty member in professional development programs directed by the Institute for Public Relations, United Technologies, Mobil Oil, American Airlines, IBM, Marriott, Ragan Communications, the National Rural Electrical Development Corporation, the Public Relations Society of America, the International Association of Business Communicators, Erlich-Manes Advertising and Public Relations, the Defense Information School, Colorado State University, the U.S. Navy, Eastern Washington University, Buena Vista College, the Center for Foreign Journalists, the National School Public Relations Association, the Texas Public Relations Association, Baltimore Public Relations Council, the Religious Public Relations Council, the Korean Public Relations Society, the Association of Teachers of Preventive Medicine, Women in Communication, the Robert Wood Johnson Foundation, the University of South Carolina, the Ohio State University, Henry J. Kaufman and Associates Public Relations, Continental Telephone Service Corporation, Allstate Insurance, and the Department of Energy Office of Science and its National Energy Technology Laboratory.

Her research interests center on public relations, development communication, communication theory, gender issues, organizational response to activism, organizational power and structure, ethics, philosophy, scientific and technical writing, and qualitative methodology. In 2003, *The Measurement Standard* named her a "measurement maven." She is the 1994 recipient of the Jackson Jackson & Wagner Behavioral Science prize, sponsored by the PRSA Foundation, for her public relations research. In 1989, she received the Pathfinder Award for excellence in research, sponsored by the Institute for Public Relations Research and Education.

In the 1980s, Larissa Grunig served as a consultant with the U.S. Department of State's Historical Office. At that same time, she developed the public relations curriculum for the Washington Center for Internship and Academic Seminars, an international program. Late in that decade, with James Grunig, she conducted a program of research for the UMCP International Development Management Center and the Development Project Management Center, OICD, USDA, on

"Strategies for Communicating on Innovative Management with Receptive Individuals in Developing Organizations" (published in various outlets, including books and journals).

In the late 1980s and early 1990s, Larissa Grunig conducted studies of the U.S. Foreign Service, focusing on women in development communication and subculture and diplomatic communication (published as a book chapter and in conference presentations). She received grants from the Sea Grant College, the Environmental Protection Agency, and UMCP's Institute for Philosophy and Public Policy to study community attitudes toward, knowledge of toxic pollutants in, ecological restoration of, and sense of place in the Chesapeake Bay. At that same time, she established a program of research on the stigma of chronic mental illness for the Montgomery County (MD) Department of Addiction, Victim and Mental Health Services. These projects, in particular, led to her career-long interest in the focus group method, both as a research topic and as a communication tool.

She has chaired external reviews of a number of public relations programs around the world, including a proposal for a BAA degree program at Conestoga College in Kitchener, Ontario, Canada; Hong Kong Baptist University's proposal for a master's degree program in integrated marketing communication; the Department of Marketing and Communication Management at the University of Pretoria in South Africa; and the Department of Communication Studies at Eastern Washington University in Cheney, WA.

In 1996, Larissa and James Grunig were named in the Larissa and James Grunig Scholarship, funded by Korean scholar HoChang Shin. They also were named in the Grunig Dissertation Award of UMCP's Department of Communication and in the Grunig PRIME Fellowship, sponsored by PRIME Research and the Institute for Public Relations. In 2005, they received PRSA's Lloyd B. Dennis Award for Public Affairs.

In 2003, Larissa Grunig was honored with the Alumni Achievement Award of North Dakota State University, her undergraduate *alma mater*. Together with James Grunig, she later taught a graduate seminar in public relations management at NDSU. She was the Public Relations Institute of Australia's 1996 Visiting Eminent Practitioner and the 2006 Hooker Distinguished Visiting Professor at DeGroote School of Business, McMaster University, Hamilton, Ontario, Canada. In 2011, she and James Grunig received an honorary doctorate from the University of Quebec in Montreal and the Presidential Award of the International Public Relations Association for "outstanding contribution to better world understanding."

Larissa Grunig has written well over 200 articles, book chapters, monographs, reviews, and conference papers on public relations, science writing, feminist theory, focus group methodology, communication theory, and research. Over her career, she has served on the editorial advisory boards of 13 refereed journals. She continues to review manuscripts for more than two dozen scholarly journals and book publishers.

From 1987 to 1990, Larissa Grunig was founding co-editor of the *Public Relations Research Annual*, which then became the *Journal of Public Relations Research*. Volumes 1 and 3 of the *JPRA* won the PRIDE award for outstanding innovative, developmental, and educational research sponsored by the Commission on Public Relations of what was then the Speech Communication Association. From 2000 to 2002, she was a quarterly contributor to *PR Herald* and from 1998 to 2003, co-editor of the quarterly Research in Public Relations supplement to *pr reporter*. In 1988, she was guest editor of a special issue on women in public relations in *Public Relations Review*; from 1984 to 1989, she was Associate Editor of the *PRR*.

She is lead author of the first book about women in public relations, coauthored with Elizabeth Lance Toth and Linda Childers Hon: *Women in Public Relations: How Gender Influences Practice*. It was a finalist for the Frank Luther Mott/Kappa Tau Alpha Research Award for the best book in journalism/mass communication published in 2001.

Larissa Grunig has lectured to campus, corporate, government, and professional audiences in South Africa, Slovenia, Spain, Italy, Canada, Denmark, Bermuda, Brazil, Scotland, England, Egypt, Germany, Finland, Austria, the Bahamas, Mexico, New Zealand, China, Hong Kong, Ireland, Croatia, Taiwan, Chile, South Korea, the Netherlands, Iran, Poland, Peru, and Russia as well as the United States. She is an honorary member of three professional associations in public relations: the Guangdong Public Relations Society, Guangzhou, China; the Public Relations Institute of Australia; and the Slovenian Public Relations Society.

Larissa Grunig is a former president of the Association for the Advancement of Policy, Research and Development in the Third World and past head of the Educators' Advisory Committee of the Institute for Public Relations, the Public Relations Interest Group of the International Communication Association, and the Public Relations Division of the Association for Education in Journalism and Mass Communication. Since 1985, she has been a charter member of the Advisory Council of the International Public Relations Association's Educators Advisory Council. From 2000 to 2004, she was a member of the Executive Board of PRSA's Educators Academy. From 1994 to 2000, she served two terms as a member of the Executive Committee of the Board of Directors of the Institute for Public Relations.

Beginning in 1985, Larissa Grunig served as a member of an international grant team, sponsored by the IABC Research Foundation, investigating excellence in public relations. The Excellence Study resulted in three books; she was first author of the third volume: *Excellent Public Relations and Effective Organizations: A Study of Communication Management in Three Countries*. This book, written with James Grunig and David M. Dozier, won the 2002 PRIDE book award of the Public Relations Division of the National Communication Association for innovation, development, and educational achievement in public relations research.

In the year the Excellence Study began, Larissa and James Grunig were the parents of four teenagers. Larissa Grunig considers her most important and gratifying role to date to be the grandmother of five.

INTRODUCTION

*Krishnamurthy Sriramesh, Ansgar Zerlass,
and Jeong-Nam Kim*

Public relations scholarship is relatively young with efforts to build a body of knowledge having their origins only in the mid-1970s even though public relations practice has a much longer history. The Excellence Study, which was initiated in the mid-1980s under the leadership of James E. Grunig with major contributions by Larissa A. Grunig, among others, has been one of the main pillars of the current public relations body of knowledge. In the past two decades there has been a significant growth in public relations scholarship that has included an increase in research emanating from several regions of the world (a significant portion of it using the Excellence Theory), thereby reducing the ethnocentricity in the body of knowledge to some extent. It is indisputable, however, that despite the welcome growth of the past decades, the field of public relations is poised for, and needs to focus on, further growth that broadens its horizons.

On the one hand, communication is becoming more and more important to organizations of all types that are increasingly being forced to communicate across national and cultural borders, and scholars need to offer perspectives that help practitioners in this challenging, and important, task. On the other hand, public relations is expanding beyond media relations to encompass a broad set of communication activities with a clear link to organizational goals and relationship management. The increasing popularity of the term *strategic communication* to refer to public relations and other planned communication activities is a direct result of these developments. For example, six chapters in this volume use the terms "strategic public relations" or "strategic communication" in their titles. Another significant development is the increased efforts toward establishing academic programs and professional training opportunities in public relations and communication management, both in developed economies and increasingly in emerging markets.

As heartening as these developments are, by its very nature, knowledge is not static. Only constant churning of knowledge will help extract cream. The churning process has begun where paradigms such as the system theoretic, managerial, rhetorical, and critical approaches are competing with paradigms such as organizational, corporate, and strategic communication. The opportunities and challenges posed by globalization require public relations practice and scholarship to strive to work together to find optimum solutions to communication problems or risk becoming even more marginalized, or worse, obsolete. When a group of former students and colleagues of the Grunigs decided to honor them, it was decided that the best way of recognizing their contributions of more than four decades was to produce this compilation of essays that builds on the past and assesses where we go from here as we look to the future. We recognize that the 2006 book edited by Elizabeth Toth (*The Future of Excellence in Public Relations and Communication Management*) was a Festschrift for the Grunigs. In our view, the primary difference between the two Festschrifts is that this volume does not focus only on the Excellence Theory but intends to initiate discussions on several topics that, we hope, will lead us to a holistic body of knowledge that eclectically harnesses wisdom from several perspectives.

James and Larissa Grunig have been recognized by many around the world for their contributions to the field of public relations, primarily through the Excellence Study and what is popularly known as the Excellence Theory that they developed, along with David Dozier and other associates, in the 1990s. Many scholars around the world, especially in emerging countries, have been building upon the Grunigs' work by assessing the relevance of this theory in other cultural contexts. There has also been debate with differing perspectives offered by rhetorical, critical and interpretivist scholars, among others. Good theories provide the seeds and a fertile soil for debate without which knowledge cannot grow and therefore we acknowledge the important contributions of the Grunigs to the development of the field, thus far and to come, in multiple ways.

The Grunigs have developed the field by introducing a number of key questions and concepts such as publics, relationships, symmetry, power, measurement, and ethics. The Excellence Theory incorporates these and other concepts to provide one normative approach for analyzing and optimally practicing public relations. In addition to theory building, the Grunigs have contributed to the spread of public relations scholarship in many regions of the world by mentoring the next generation of scholars from five continents. This Festschrift contains a collection of chapters that deal with the key concepts propounded by the Grunigs, while also exploring future directions and alternative ways of thinking. A large number of renowned scholars from all over the world have contributed to this effort, among them several former students of the Grunigs. Due to their other commitments, several others could not adhere to the strict deadline we were forced to set. In spite of that, the authorship is indicative of the deep esteem for James and Larissa Grunig from colleagues around the globe.

As stated earlier, this Festschrift aims to simultaneously celebrate the past and look to the future. The Grunigs, and we, collectively chose the first three essays (sole-authored by each and one co-authored by them) as representative of the primary contributions by these two stalwarts of public relations research. In Chapter 1, James E. Grunig uses the first-person narrative to give us an overview of 40 years of his advocacy aimed at making public relations practice and scholarship achieve wider recognition as a strategic management function rather than a publicity function based on media relations. He also addresses the conceptual foundations of his theorizing, leading up to the Excellence Theory that he refers to as the "edifice." The chapter also challenges scholars to strive toward making strategic public relations accepted by the majority of organizational senior managers while furnishing and refurnishing the edifice.

Larissa A. Grunig has been recognized in public relations circles as a passionate advocate for according women equal status and recognition in public relations practice and scholarship. She also uses the first-person narrative in Chapter 2, her sole-authored essay, to enunciate the need to address the marginalization of women in public relations. She uses phase analysis to propose that "[E]xcellent public relations departments and effective organizations develop mechanisms for helping women gain the power they need to advance from the technician to the manager role and to implement their understanding of two-way symmetrical public relations."

Chapter 3 (jointly authored by the Grunigs) uses a piece of the evidence gathered for the Excellence Study to discuss the relationship between public relations and marketing. As they have done over the past decades, in this piece the Grunigs contend that effective organizations will see the conceptual separation between these two disciplines and therefore also maintain them as separate functions in organizational settings. Further, the authors advocate the integration of advertising and marketing-oriented public relations as Integrated Marketing Communication that is coordinated by the broader public relations function.

In Chapter 4, Nigel de Bussy discusses the formidable challenge identified by James Grunig (in his "edifice" essay of Chapter 1) of institutionalizing strategic public relations as a bridging rather than a buffering activity, so that strategic public relations management becomes standard in most organizations and most people think of public relations that way. De Bussy contrasts the concept of strategic public relations management with strategic communication, stakeholder management and corporate social responsibility and concludes that strategic public relations management (when properly understood) is the responsibility of organizational leaders at all levels and from a variety of disciplines—not just public relations specialists alone.

In Chapter 5, Sandra Duhe and Donald Wright extol the foresight of James Grunig by stating that the four models of public relations practice he offered with Todd Hunt predated the emergence of social media platforms by nearly three decades, and yet his concept of symmetrical communication remains both relevant and timely in a rapidly expanding online environment. The authors trace how his work has influenced current scholarship in social media and discuss ties between symmetry and the evolving concept of interactivity. They also offer insights into how social media have impacted the practice of public relations and provide examples of how a strategic mindset (or lack thereof) affects the outcomes of social media use.

The current era of globalization has increased the significance of public relations, especially at the cross-national and cross-cultural levels. Chapter 6 by Krishnamurthy Sriramesh, Yunna Rhee, and Minjung Sung reviews the impact of globalization on public relations practice and scholarship, and shows how current public relations scholarship has attempted to prepare the industry for an increasingly global practice. The generic principles and socio-cultural variables that should be taken into consideration while applying the principles are reviewed by the authors. The chapter also reviews the studies based on these two streams of thought and how those studies have helped reduce the level of ethnocentricity in the body of knowledge of public relations. Looking to the future, the chapter contends that many more empirical studies from around the world are needed to confirm the theorizing that has evolved from the Excellence Study.

In Chapter 7, Jeong-Nam Kim and Lan Ni discuss the underpinnings of the situational theory of publics, especially in its role as the situational theory of problem solving (STOPS). The authors then discuss theoretical concepts and public relations research originating from the situational theory of problem solving. Based on the discussion, the authors outline and discuss several new and developing research agendas triggered by the situational theory of problem solving. They call for more theory building not only in public relations, but also in other applied fields of communication research related to problem solving and communication.

Conceptualizing public relations as a management function contributing to overall organizational success inevitably seeks answers to the question how one should measure effectiveness and efficiency of communication. In Chapter 8, Fraser Likely and Tom Watson take an innovative approach to this ongoing discussion among scholars and practitioners. They reconstruct debates, progress and setbacks in public relations measurement and evaluation research over the course of 40 years. Starting with early publications in the 1960s, the debate was brought forward by a Maryland conference chaired by James Grunig in the late 1970s, and culminated in the Excellence Study's aim to explain the value of public relations on a general level. The authors show how research in the field has been broadened and deepened since then, and how the search for financial metrics has led to dead ends such as universal formulas for calculating ROI (Return on Investment) as well as promising concepts such as applying value links and scorecards to communication management.

The (re)institutionalization of the public relations function within organizations has been identified as an important task and challenge for the profession. If public relations practitioners try to institutionalize public relations, those efforts can help organizations become more strategic and can generate greater value for the organization. In their essay on the topic, Chapter 9, Kenneth Plowman and Robert Wakefield discuss the conceptual meaning of institutionalization and then its link to strategic communication and public relations. They discuss the two factors, leadership and organizational complexity, and their effects on the institutionalization process of public relations. In doing so, they highlight the contributions of conflict resolution expertise in strengthening the leadership and legitimacy of public relations necessary for (re)institutionalization.

Power and influence are key concepts in any discipline. In Chapter 10, Bruce Berger and Bryan Reber provide an overview of the managerial, rhetorical, sociological, and critical perspectives that are used to explore multiple facets of the struggle for dominating meanings, constraints, and actions in organizational and communicative relationships. They argue that new questions beyond the realm of dominant coalitions and influences of communication professionals have to be asked, and that new theoretical and methodological approaches to explain power are much needed. Along these lines, systemic power rooted in the structures of the profession and educational system can be identified as relevant aspects that shape the future of the field. Researching the majority of professionals and not only those organized in associations might bring about new insights that will advance our knowledge of public relations and its impact on society.

Ethics and corporate social responsibility are two sides of the same coin, at least in public relations. This is the key argument made by Shannon Bowen and Tiffany Derville Gallicano in Chapter 11, when discussing the model of "reflective ethical symmetry." They argue that different approaches of ethical reasoning, namely deontology, rule utilitarianism, and act utilitarianism, may result in well-considered and morally acceptable decisions, and that applying such principles allows organizations to foster trust and gain excellence in stakeholder relationships. Research on the motivation structure and knowledge of the next generation of public relations professionals shows that the requirements for ethical decision making should be available in the field soon.

Mohan Dutta offers in Chapter 12 a critical perspective on the role of public relations in crafting and reproducing frames that shape public attitudes and opinions embodying the individualistic values of neo-liberalism in the globalization process. He points to what he calls the "problematic role" that public relations plays in creating vast inequalities produced by neo-liberal forms of governance and top-down forms of power by transnational companies. Dutta contends that culture-centered public relations could help develop relationships of solidarity with the people in developing nations. He highlights the potential of public relations to help challenge and change inequitable global policies through the creation of communication spaces, rules, and processes that serve as avenues for unheard voices from developing countries to speak.

Research into the structure and dynamics of relationships between organizations and their publics are at the core of Organizational–Public–Relationships

(OPR) theories. In Chapter 13, Chun-ju Flora Hung-Beasecke and Yi-Ru Regina Chen add to this knowledge by exploring how an organization's relationship formed before a crisis may affect the public's evaluation of an organization's behavior in crises and their attribution of responsibility to organizations. In doing so, the authors extend the relationship management research into the crisis context and provide an empirical test of the effect of OPR types and OPR quality dimensions on crisis perceptions. Their test of the relationships of types and quality of relationships provides interesting findings and further questions the relationships between crisis attribution and relational quality.

Public relations history has emerged as a dynamic area of research in recent years. The discussion of anecdotes (describing facts and events) often found in textbooks has long been replaced by a theory-driven approach (model building). Moreover, as Günter Bentele explains in Chapter 14 on public relations historiography, scholars and the way they explain the past are shaped by the specific social contexts. James Grunig made this point in his unpublished draft of the second edition of *Managing Public Relations* before the turn of the century. Bentele, building on this idea, explains how the evolution of public relations can be explained as a process of functional-integrative stratification in which various layers of interpersonal communication, public communication, organizational communication, public relations as an occupation, and public relations as a structured social system complement one another to build the understanding of public relations in modern societies.

The Excellence Theory explains how public relations contributes to organizational success and which organizational contexts enable that contribution. In Chapter 15, Dejan Verčič and Ana Tkalac Verčič link this theory to theories of the networked society, communication power (Manuel Castells), and mediation of everything (Sonja Livingstone). They contend that the situational theory of publics offered by James Grunig is in sync with Castells' mass self-communication theory, with both theories underlining the power of symmetry in communication. Excellent organizations nurture symmetrical internal communication to cultivate organic, inclusive cultures. They nurture symmetrical external communication to cultivate trusting relationships with groups and organizations in their environments. Similar to an agora in Old Greece, a forum in Old Rome, a coffeehouse and a reading club in the Habermasian 18th-century European public sphere, communication is the public space for social media. Public relations is where management and communication meet, according to the authors.

The link between institutionalization and public relations is mostly discussed along the lines introduced by the Excellence Theory—how PR as a practice and a function is rooted in organizational settings. However, as Anne Gregory, Emanuele Invernizzi, and Stefania Romenti show in Chapter 16, additional perspectives help to shed a brighter light on this relationship as well as on the role of public relations at large. The authors introduce analytical principles of traditional and neo-institutionalism to explore empirical studies from Europe and the United

States, which show similar trends about the ongoing proliferation of professional PR in modern organizations. This leads, as the authors argue, to a stronger institutionalization of the organization itself in its external environment and in society. Various ways which foster this development can be analyzed by using the basic concepts of institutionalization theory: internal communication helps to advance organizational culture, professionalization can be explained by the processes of normative isomorphism, and institutional pressures stimulate new ways of sense-making as well as innovations that can create business opportunities.

While public relations research and the managerial approach deeply rooted in the work by James and Larissa Grunig have proved to be a fruitful framework for researching communication and stakeholder and public relationships, alternative paradigms are now evolving in different parts of the world. In Chapter 17, Derina Holtzhausen and Ansgar Zerfass argue that strategic communication, which is used both as a concept for analyzing professional communication in, and between, organizations and their stakeholders and as a label for integrated programs at universities, may be a useful approach that resolves some inherent limitations of public relations research. The authors argue that a clear focus on purposive communication enacted by communication agents in the public sphere to reach the set goals of an entity helps to understand the structures and processes shaping relationships in modern societies. This approach opens the field for theoretical and empirical insights from health communication, political communication, public diplomacy, advertising, and consumer behavior without giving up the link to organizational goals and excellence. Holtzhausen and Zerfass review the status of strategic communication on the macro, meso, and micro levels of practice and suggest new applications to advance the field.

In Chapter 18, Estelle de Beer, Benita Steyn, and Ronél Rensburg contend that over the past two decades South Africa has contributed to the global search for excellence in communication management following in the footsteps of the Excellence Study. They describe these efforts as the "Pretoria School of Thought," whose foundation is based on the differentiation between "strategic com-munication management" and "communication management." Theoretical pillars for this school of thought include the corporate communication "strategist" role at the top management (macro/environmental) level, contributing to the development of the organization's enterprise strategy; and the redefinition of the historic "manager" as a role played at the middle management (meso/functional) level, focusing on the development of corporate communication strategy linked to enterprise strategy. The next wave of thinking in the Pretoria School of Thought makes the assumption that the most value is added on the strategic level, taking into account the changing environment within which organizations operate.

Maria Aparecida Ferrari in Chapter 19 provides the historical development of Latin American academic and professional practice of public relations, highlighting the impact of James and Larissa Grunig's scholarly works over the years. She outlines the views about public relations prevailing in Latin American societies until the 1990s, and the subsequent advancement in education and theoretical research programs of Latin American public relations after introducing the Grunigs' theoretical works such as models of public relations and the Excellence Theory, and describes the Grunigs frequent visits to Latin America.

Chapter 20 by David Dozier and Lou Williams provides a behind-the-scenes review of the Excellence Study. We considered this to be very important, given the frequent references almost every contributor in this book has made to this study. The authors provide a personalized and subjective review of the interplay of personalities and organizational cultures as this massive research project unfolded between 1985 and 2002. Dozier and Williams contend that James Grunig's leadership was essential to the successful execution of the project. In addition, the authors identify a number of challenges that James Grunig had to overcome in order to lead the three-nation collection of survey data, as well as conducting the 25 follow-up case studies, not to mention the publication of three widely cited books.

In Chapter 21, Yi-Hui Christine Huang and Joanne Chen Lyu present the results from an in-depth study of the citations of the Excellence Study over two decades, thus presenting a comprehensive and systematic picture of the influence of the Excellence Study on scholarship. In doing so, they covered a total of 1,862 citations to the study, including 1,477 English works and 385 non-English works in 24 languages. Their findings showed the wide impact of the Excellence Study evidenced by the study being cited in journals from 15 countries and books published in 14 countries. Another key finding is that the study is not cited only in public relations. Other disciplines citing the Excellence Study include advertising, business and economics, communications, public administration, sociology, law, and philosophy.

In conclusion, we feel this Festschrift does the two primary things it set out to do: celebrate the contributions by the Grunigs to public relations scholarship and practice while also building on the past to expand the body of knowledge and make it relevant to the challenges of the future. Globalization mandates that the body of knowledge cannot continue to be ethnocentric or adopt a one-size-fits-all approach. The authors in this volume have highlighted many of the useful contributions by the Grunigs and have also provided many ways in which the field can expand its horizons. We hope these thoughts will reverberate among scholars and practitioners alike and the result will be a more holistic body of knowledge and practice. Anything less will marginalize the field even more. Greater numbers of cross-cultural and cross-national research efforts driven by diverse theoretical approaches and methodologies are the need of the hour.

A project of this magnitude would not have been possible without the cooperation of many friends and colleagues. At the outset, we offer our sincere thanks to James and Larissa Grunig for agreeing to share the first three essays reprinted in this volume. We next thank the contributors for agreeing to work to a very strict deadline. Our thanks and appreciation are also extended to Dejan

Verčič and Ana Tkalac Verčič and their colleagues at PRISTOP in Slovenia for organizing a special session to honor the Grunigs during the annual BledCom symposium in Slovenia in July, 2012. We extend special thanks to His Excellency Dr. Danilo Türk, President of the Republic of Slovenia, who attended and addressed the special session where the manuscript of this Festschrift was presented to the Grunigs. Dr. Türk made very insightful comments, not only recognizing the contributions by the Grunigs but also challenging communication scholars to find communication solutions to several of the world's current problems.

We also thank Linda Bathgate of Routledge for publishing this volume. Finally, we thank all our students and colleagues who over the decades have nurtured our own scholarly pursuits by providing insights and constructive feedback. We all are in this quest together and will continue to strive together to make the field of public relations more meaningful to societies around the world.

1

FURNISHING THE EDIFICE

Ongoing Research on Public Relations as a Strategic Management Function

James E. Grunig

Abstract

This chapter traces the origins and continuing development of a research tradition that conceptualizes public relations as a strategic management function rather than as a messaging, publicity, and media relations function. The tradition began serendipitously with the development of the situational theory of publics in the late 1960s, followed by the application of organization theory to public relations, the symmetrical model of public relations, and evaluation of communication programs. The Excellence Study, which began in 1985, brought these middle-level theories together and produced a general theory, a theoretical edifice, focused on the role of public relations in strategic management and the value of relationships with strategic publics to an organization. Since the completion of the Excellence Study, scholars in this research tradition have continued to improve and furnish the edifice by conducting research to help public relations professionals participate in strategic decision processes. This research has been on environmental scanning and publics, scenario building, empowerment of public relations, ethics, relationships, ROI, evaluation, relationship cultivation strategies, specialized areas of public relations, and global strategy. I conclude that the greatest challenge for scholars now is to learn how to institutionalize strategic public relations as an ongoing, accepted practice in most organizations.

Key Words

edifice, Excellence Study, organizations, public relations, symmetrical

Throughout the 40 years of my academic career, I have used the literature of philosophy of science and of cognitive psychology to inform my attempts to build public relations theory. Early in my career, I rejected logical positivism—the idea that theories are "true" because they reflect an underlying order in the universe. From Kuhn (1970), I learned that theories are subjective because the theory itself defines what evidence should be used to "prove" a theory. From Suppe (1977), I learned that theories are semantic structures: ideas in the minds of researchers. This cognitive nature of theory is supported by research in cognitive psychology, which shows that thought takes place in the form of abstract cognitive representations (see, e.g., Anderson, 2000). From Carter (1972), I learned that order is not inherent in reality. Rather, scholars construct theories to make sense of reality—to supply order to it (see J. Grunig, 2003, for further explanation of Carter's views).

We can judge a theory to be good, therefore, if it makes sense of reality (in the case of a positive, or explanatory, theory) or if it helps to improve reality (in the case of a normative theory). Public relations scholars need to develop both positive and normative theories—to understand how public relations is practiced and to improve its practice—for the organization, for publics, and for society. As researchers develop theories and integrate them, a research tradition, as defined by Laudan (1977), develops around a comprehensive conceptual framework, which Kuhn (1970) originally called a "paradigm" and later called a "disciplinary matrix" in the second edition of his book.

Kuhn conceptualized a paradigm as a rigid pattern of thinking that limits the ability of scientists to think outside the paradigm. Once scientists develop a paradigm, Kuhn said, they devote most of their time to solving puzzles identified by the paradigm. If they cannot solve a puzzle in the way the paradigm predicts, the puzzle becomes an "anomaly." If researchers repeatedly cannot solve this anomaly, a scientific revolution occurs and the paradigm is discarded and replaced by a new one. Other philosophers of science (e.g., Brown, 1977; Lakatos, 1970; Laudan, 1977; Shapere, 1977; Suppe, 1977; Toulmin, 1972), conceptualized these comprehensive cognitive structures to be more malleable and changeable than did Kuhn. In their view, scholars are similar to architects or engineers who design a structure originally for one use and then revise and add to that structure for other uses or as they see problems with the structures they designed once they are built. As Popper argued in 1970:

> I do admit that at any moment we are prisoners caught in the framework of our theories; our expectations; our past experiences; our language. But we are prisoners in a Pickwickian sense: If we try, we can break out of our framework at any time. Admittedly, we shall find ourselves again in a framework, but it will be a better and roomier one; and we can at any moment break out of it again.

(pp. 56–57)

Kuhn's concept of puzzles also now seems to be too narrow. Rather than "puzzles," for which the solutions are known but the means of reaching them are not, other philosophers substituted the terms "relevant questions" or "characteristic problems" (Suppe, 1977, p. 498). A theoretical structure suggests solutions to these questions or problems, but the solutions often vary from what is expected— therefore leading researchers to refine or enlarge the structure based on their experience in using it to solve theoretical and empirical problems.

Theoretical structures, therefore, resemble the concept of a schema in cognitive psychology: a comprehensive knowledge structure that includes many related cognitive representations and that retains its structure even as it is refined and enlarged. In this chapter, I will call the comprehensive theoretical structure that I and many students and colleagues have developed for public relations over the last 40 years an "edifice"—a structure that can be used positively to explain public relations practice and normatively to guide public relations practice. An edifice provides a framework for public relations practice, but I do not believe that a structure alone is enough. Like the structure of a building, a theoretical edifice must be furnished as it is built. Each time the plan for an edifice is used as a structure for a new building, it can be improved and furnished in different ways. The same is true for the comprehensive general theory of public relations that I have developed.

This general theory does not attempt to explain everything in public relations, as Holtzhausen and Voto (2002) have asserted. Rather, it is a comprehensive way of thinking that can be used to solve many positive and normative public relations problems. Other edifices may solve these problems in different ways. However, it is not necessary to destroy this edifice to justify the value of another edifice, as critical and postmodern scholars (e.g., Curtin & Gaither, 2005; Durham, 2005; Holtzhausen & Voto, 2002; Leitch & Neilson, 2001; L'Etang & Pieczka, 1996; McKie, 2001; Motion & Weaver, 2005) have tried to do. Rather, multiple edifices can exist side by side; and all can be useful for solving the same or different problems. (An example of how different perspectives can be useful can be found in Hatch's (1997) discussion of the concurrent value of modern, interpretive, and postmodern approaches to organizational theory.)

This chapter, therefore, will focus on the origins, continuing development, and new directions for research of the theoretical edifice I call the strategic management role of public relations. I believe this edifice has played a central role in the development of public relations theory and research during the past 40 years. As I will show, the research tradition that has produced this edifice continues to generate new ideas for theory, research, and practice in public relations. Other research traditions may join it, and critics will try to destroy it; but I believe this one will continue to guide the public relations discipline for years to come.

Serendipitous Development of the Edifice

The theoretical edifice, as it stands today, both describes and prescribes the role of public relations in strategic management. It is a general theory that explains how the public relations function should be structured and managed to provide the greatest value to organizations, publics, and society. Specifically, the edifice does the following:

- Explains how public relations contributes value to organizations, publics, and society.
- Explains how an empowered public relations function makes a unique contribution to strategic management and distinguishes its role from that of other management functions, especially marketing.
- Prescribes techniques that public relations managers can use to fulfill their role in strategic management.
- Explains the critical role of relationships in the planning and evaluation of public relations programs.
- Identifies different models of communication and explains which models are the most effective strategies for cultivating relationships with publics.
- Incorporates ethics into the strategic role of public relations.
- Explains how to apply the theory globally.

Each of these components of the general theory is logically related to the others. Together, they produce a strong structural edifice that can be applied both in research and practice. Forty years ago, however, I did not envision that my research eventually would produce this structure. Instead, I worked on pieces of the structure serendipitously without realizing until I began work on the Excellence Study how they would fit together.

Situational Theory of Publics

I begin the discussion of the edifice, therefore, by tracing the origins of some of its critical components. The first piece of the edifice was the situational theory of publics. When I entered the doctoral program at the University of Wisconsin in 1965, communication scientists were focused on the effects of the media and messages on attitudes and behavior. Cognitive dissonance theory attracted a great deal of attention because it seemed to explain why effects generally were limited to reinforcing existing attitudes. According to the theory, recipients of messages were most likely to accept messages that were consonant with their attitudes. More importantly for a theory of communication behavior, the theory explained that people were likely to selectively expose themselves to messages that supported their attitudes.

This second focus of dissonance theory on information seeking eventually led me to what I now call the situational theory of publics. In a course taught by the pioneering mass communication scholar Bruce Westley, I reviewed both rational and behavioral theories of economics to develop an understanding of why people seek information when they make economic decisions. This paper, which was published as one of the first *Journalism Monographs* (J. Grunig, 1966), which Westley then edited, suggested that people are more likely to seek information that is relevant to decision situations in their lives than to seek information that reinforces their attitudes. Under the mentoring of Richard Carter, a pioneering scholar of communication behavior (see J. Grunig, 2003), I developed this theory into a study of how and why Colombian farmers seek information in decision situations, which became my doctoral dissertation (J. Grunig, 1968).

At the time, I did not foresee that the theory of communication behavior developed in this study would continue to develop through many studies over 40 years and become a critical component of today's theory of public relations and strategic management (for a review, see J. Grunig, 1997). At the time, I simply wanted to know why people seek information to explain why messages have effects. Eventually, I realized that the situational theory provides a tool to segment stakeholders into publics, to isolate the strategic publics with whom it is most important for organizations to develop relationships in order to be effective, and to plan different strategies for communicating with publics whose communication behavior ranged from active to passive.

Organizational Theory

The situational theory also provided a framework when I switched my attention from the communication behavior of individuals and publics to the communication behavior of organizations (J. Grunig, 1976). When I returned to the United States from Colombia in 1969, I was convinced that most of the failures in the communication programs of agricultural agencies in Colombia resulted not from the backwardness or resistance of farmers but because of the nature of the communication programs that organizations developed to communicate with them. Organizations that I studied were more likely to give information than to seek information. They also were unlikely to listen to or engage in dialogue with their publics. Organizations, in other words, seemed to engage in the same types of communication behavior identified by the situational theory for individuals and publics. This one-way information giving typically resulted in policies and programs of agencies that did not work well for farmers in the situations they faced.

My 1976 monograph and a great deal of subsequent research (reviewed in J. Grunig & L. Grunig, 1989) extended this research to all kinds of organizations doing public relations in the United States. First, I identified *independent variables* from organizational theory that varied in the extent to which they would produce problem recognition, constraint recognition, and level of involvement, the independent variables of the situational theory, at the organizational level. These variables included organizational structure, environment, technology, size, age, culture, worldview, and power structures. The first *dependent* variables were simply one-way and two-way communication, but I further conceptualized them as synchronic and diachronic communication, following Thayer (1968). Eventually, I revised these two communication behaviors into the now well-known four models of public relations: press agentry/publicity, public information, two-way asymmetrical, and two-way symmetrical (J. Grunig, 1984).

For the most part, this program of research failed to identify organizational variables that explained why organizations practiced public relations as they did, although top management's worldview about the nature of public relations and organizational culture seemed to explain the most variance in public relations behavior. The knowledge of public relations practitioners also had a major effect. For example, even though practitioners should have been most likely to practice two-way and symmetrical public relations when the structure was organic, the environment was turbulent, management valued collaboration with publics, and the culture was participative, they did not practice public relations in that way because their knowledge of public relations was limited to one-way methods, publicity, media relations, and marketing support.

The research, therefore, suggested that the relationship among the models of public relations and these organizational variables was normative rather than positive. Logically, in other words, practitioners should have been most likely to practice two-way symmetrical public relations in certain favorable conditions. They did not do so, however, because of their lack of knowledge to do so.

Symmetrical Model of Public Relations

The next stage of my research, therefore, was an intensive program of research on the two-way symmetrical model of public relations. The idea for the symmetrical model was mostly mine, although the symmetrical model elaborated on the simple idea of two-way communication and incorporated Thayer's (1968) idea of diachronic communication. The symmetrical idea also was stimulated by Carter's (1965) and Chaffee and McLeod's (1968) conceptualization of coorientation. Coorientation represented a movement away from theories of attitudes held by one person and research on how to develop messages to change the *orientations* (attitudes) of a person. Instead, *coorientation* focused on how two people, or two higher-level systems (such as organizations and publics [see, J. Grunig & Stamm, 1973]), oriented jointly to each other and to objects in their environment.

The symmetrical model and its parent, the coorientational model, proposed that individuals, organizations, and publics should use communication to adjust their ideas and behavior to those of others rather than to try to control how others think and behave. Although there is still a great deal of naysaying in the public relations literature about the symmetrical idea, there is so much logical, empirical, and ethical support for it after 20 years of research and theoretical development that its value seems axiomatic to me (see L. Grunig, J. Grunig, & Dozier, 2002,

Chapter 8, for a review of the criticisms, theoretical development, and empirical evidence in support of the model). There are many similar theories in the literature, including theories of conflict resolution, dialogic communication, relationships, rhetoric, and postmodernism. To a large extent, I have used these theories as I developed the symmetrical model; but I believe that much more work can be done to bring these theories into the public relations domain where they can be used to elaborate on the simple, but powerful, idea of symmetrical communication.

Evaluation Research

In the late 1970s, at the same time that I was working on the theories of publics, public relations behavior of organizations, and the symmetrical model of communication, James Tirone of the AT&T Corporation asked me to work on a project to develop measures for and means of evaluating the effectiveness of public relations. As described in Tirone (1977), we decided to approach this problem at the level of public relations programs rather than for the entire public relations function.

Tirone and his AT&T team developed measures and methods to evaluate media relations, community relations, employee relations, educational relations, and advertising. Coorientational theory provided the framework for conceptualizing the effects of public relations programs. My research for this project concentrated on community relations (see J. Grunig & Hunt, 1984, pp. 277–279) and employee relations (see J. Grunig, 1977). This research on the evaluation of public relations provided another critical element of the theory of public relations and strategic management. Public relations could not have a role in strategic management unless its practitioners had a way to measure its effectiveness. It is interesting that the public relations trade press today continues to debate how to evaluate public relations—a problem that I think we solved in the late 1970s with the AT&T research.

At this point, the year was 1984 and several crucial middle-range theories were in place: publics, the role of public relations in organizational decision-making, the symmetrical model of public relations, and concepts to define objectives of public relations programs and measure their accomplishment. The Excellence Study then provided the means for unifying these concepts and adding other theoretical building blocks to the edifice.

The Excellence Study: Putting the Edifice Together

When the International Association of Business Communicators (IABC) Foundation, now the IABC Research Foundation, issued a request for proposals in 1984 for research on "How, Why, and to What Extent Communication Contributes to the Achievement of Organizational Objectives," I first thought of the opportunity to move beyond the program level of evaluation, where we had worked in the AT&T research, to construct a theory of the overall value of the public relations function to the organization. I had read some of the literature on organizational effectiveness when I wrote my 1976 monograph, and my Maryland colleague, Mark McElreath (now at Towson University), had alerted me to the difference between evaluating public relations programs and evaluating the overall contribution of the public relations function to organizational effectiveness. Thus, the Excellence Study offered the possibility of constructing a grand theory of the value of public relations.

At the same time, my collaborators on the project (David Dozier, William Ehling, Larissa Grunig, Fred Repper, and Jon White) pointed out that the project also would make it possible to integrate a number of middle-range concepts that explained how the public relations function should be organized to increase the value of the public relations function to the organization. I brought my concepts of publics, organizational theory and decision-making, models of public relations, evaluation of public relations, and research on employee communication to the project. David Dozier contributed his and Glen Broom's roles theory. William Ehling contributed his knowledge of operations research (Ehling, 1992) and his views on the controversy over public relations and integrated marketing communication (IMC). Larissa Grunig brought her knowledge of gender, diversity, power, and activism. Jon White contributed his ideas about public relations and strategic management. To this mix, Fred Repper, our practitioner member, added his understanding of how our theories worked in practice. The package became what we now know as the Excellence Theory.

The Return on Investment (ROI) of Public Relations

IABC's emphasis on explaining the value of public relations stimulated us to put measurement and evaluation into a broader perspective than the program level. Although program evaluation remained an important component of our theory, we realized that it could not show the overall value of the public relations function to the organization. Our review of the literature on organizational effectiveness first showed that public relations has value when it helps the organization achieve its goals. However, the literature also showed that it has to develop those goals through interaction with strategic constituencies (stakeholders and publics). We theorized that public relations adds value when it helps the organization identify stakeholders and segment different kinds of publics from stakeholder categories. Second, we showed that public relations adds to this value when it uses symmetrical communication to develop and cultivate relationships with strategic publics. If it develops good relationships with strategic publics, an organization is more likely to develop goals desired by both the organization and its publics and is more likely to achieve those goals because it shares those goals and collaborates with publics.

Today, the public relations profession is focusing a great deal of attention on showing that an investment in public relations has a positive financial return on investment (ROI). Much of this effort has been devoted to research at the program level: For example, many commercial research firms are trying to show that investment in marketing communication sells products—or, at least, sells more products than a comparable amount spent on advertising. Other professionals are focused on showing that public relations messages have effects on cognitive concepts such as reputation, brand, image, or identity, which they believe increase the value of an organization beyond its tangible assets (an argument also made by business scholars such as Fombrun [1996] and Fombrun and Van Riel [2004]). For the most part, I believe these explanations of ROI rationalize the enduring belief among practitioners and their clients that traditional publicity-oriented public relations creates value though a change in one of these cognitive concepts.

The Excellence Study revealed a more complicated, but logically more satisfying, explanation of the value of public relations. For an organization to be effective, we argued, it must behave in ways that solve the problems and satisfy the goals of stakeholders as well as of management. If it does not, stakeholders will either pressure the organization to change or oppose it in ways that add cost and risk to organizational policies and decisions. To behave in socially acceptable ways, organizations must scan their environment to identify stakeholders who are affected by potential organizational decisions or who want organizations to make decisions to solve problems that are important to them. Then, organizations must communicate symmetrically with the different kinds of publics found within these stakeholder categories to develop high-quality, long-term relationships with them.

Although we concluded that it is difficult to place a monetary value on relationships with publics, in order to measure ROI exactly, our interviews with CEOs and senior public relations officers revealed numerous examples of how good relationships had reduced the *costs* of litigation, regulation, legislation, and negative publicity caused by poor relationships; reduced the *risk* of making decisions that affect different stakeholders; or increased *revenue* by providing products and services needed by stakeholders. Those examples provided powerful evidence of the value of good relationships with strategic publics.

Best Practices in Public Relations

In addition to explaining the value of public relations, the Excellence Study provided solid theory and empirical evidence of how the function should be organized to maximize this value. The reasoning flowed logically from our general premise about the value of public relations: Public relations must be organized in a way that makes it possible to identify strategic publics as part of the strategic management process and to build quality long-term relationships with them through symmetrical communication programs.

First, following Jon White's (White & Dozier, 1992) lead, our research showed that involvement in strategic management was the critical characteristic of excellent public relations. We found that public relations must be empowered through representation in the dominant coalition or from having access to these powerful members of the organization. Unless it is empowered to be heard, public relations will have little effect on organizational decisions. The importance of involvement in strategic management expanded our knowledge of the managerial role to include strategic managerial and administrative managerial roles (see Chapter 6 of L. Grunig, J. Grunig, & Dozier, 2002)—the strategic manager being the essential role for excellence.

Second, the debate over integrated marketing communication helped us to focus on how the public relations function should be organized both vertically and horizontally in an organizational structure. We learned that if public relations is sublimated to marketing or other management functions, it loses its unique role in strategic management. Sublimation to another management function typically resulted in attention only to the stakeholder category of interest to that function, such as consumers for marketing or employees for human resources. Sublimation to marketing also usually resulted in asymmetrical communication, which our research has consistently shown is not an effective strategy for cultivating relationships.

In the vertical structure, public relations programs for different stakeholders were gathered into a single department or coordinated through a senior vice president of corporate communication or similar title. In the horizontal structure, an excellent public relations function worked with other management functions in a matrix type of arrangement to help those functions build relationships with the stakeholders with which they interact. Thus, public relations, marketing, and other functions collaborated more than they competed for resources when the public relations function was excellent.

Third, because of IABC's traditional interest in employee communication, we used theories of organizational communication, sociology, and psychology in the Excellence Study—adding the concepts of organizational structure, culture, and systems of internal communication to the theoretical edifice (see J. Grunig, 1992; L. Grunig et al., 2002, Chapter 11). We also measured two types of employee satisfaction: satisfaction with the job and with the organization. This made it possible to build a bridge to the study of relationships, in research subsequent to the Excellence Study, because satisfaction was one of four key characteristics of relationships we identified (see, e.g., J. Grunig & Huang, 2000; H-S. Kim, 2005).

Fourth, we focused on gender in the Excellence Study because of the growing number of women in public relations and because of evidence that women had difficulty entering managerial roles—thus limiting the number of knowledgeable public relations professionals available for a strategic role. We found that organizations with excellent public relations valued women as much as men for the strategic role and developed programs to empower women throughout the organization.

The emphasis on gender, however, also focused our attention on diversity of race and ethnicity—a fifth part of the Excellence edifice. This focus, along with the international nature of the project, helped us to expand the edifice to make it appropriate for use outside the United States—in diverse cultural, political, and economic contexts. Our replication of the research in Slovenia (Verčič, L. Grunig, & J. Grunig, 1996; L. Grunig, J. Grunig, & Verčič, 1998) made it possible to conceptualize the Excellence Theory as a theory generic to many contexts, as long as the theory is applied differently when contextual variables are different.

Although we had discussed ethics in the books that resulted from the Excellence Study, our subsequent research in Slovenia called attention to the need for an ethics component of the edifice (see Chapter 12 of L. Grunig, J. Grunig, & Dozier, 2002)—a sixth component. We began to develop such a theory in a conference paper (J. Grunig & L. Grunig, 1996), and as I will discuss below, our students have filled in the gap.

Since completing the Excellence Study, my colleagues, doctoral students, and I have developed concepts and tools needed to furnish the edifice for a theory and practice of public relations and strategic management. Our recent research has focused on the three segments of this process: (1) identifying and segmenting stakeholders and publics and the issues they create; (2) developing communication strategies and programs to cultivate relationships with publics; and (3) evaluating communication programs and the public relations function by their success in producing quality relationships with publics. In the rest of this chapter, I will summarize this research and suggest how other researchers can help in solving what I earlier called the "characteristic problems" (Suppe, 1977, p. 498) that this edifice addresses.

Developing Tools for Public Relations to Participate in Strategic Management

In the Excellence Study, we asked CEOs and heads of public relations the extent to which public relations contributed to strategic management in six specific ways: (1) regular research activities; (2) research to answer specific questions; (3) other formal approaches to gathering information; (4) informal approaches to gathering information; (5) contacts with knowledgeable people outside the organization; and (6) judgment based on experience.

All but the last of these six contributions consist of methods of scanning the environment of the organization for information relevant to strategic management. All six contributions increased dramatically when we compared the organizations valued least by CEOs with those valued the most. We followed up the survey by conducting in-depth qualitative interviews of the CEOs whose organizations had the most-excellent public relations functions. We asked them, specifically, what contribution their communication function made to organizational goals. One of the most frequent responses was the value of hearing external voices in the strategic management process—voices amplified by public relations professionals who scan the publics in the organization's environment.

At the same time, we found that participation in strategic management meant different things to public relations professionals. Even in some organizations with excellent public relations departments, participation meant only providing media relations or information campaigns to support strategic goals chosen by others. The most excellent departments participated fully in strategic management by scanning the social, political, and institutional environment of the organization to bring an outside perspective to strategic decision-making. Most did not participate fully in strategic management, however, because of lack of knowledge and the tools to do so.

Chang (2000) found much the same thing in a Delphi study of senior public relations executives in U.S. corporations. Only a few of them reported having a sophisticated system of environmental scanning in their public relations department. Most also were skeptical that public relations professionals had the skills to do environmental scanning. And, most said they believed senior management did not have confidence in the ability of public relations professionals to be environmental scanners. Some did not even understand the term "environmental scanning," believing that it had something to do with reacting to pollution and other natural environmental issues.

Environmental Scanning and Publics

One of our major research programs, therefore, has been devoted to developing tools and concepts that public relations executives can use in environmental scanning. Chang (2000), for example, found that personal sources of information are more useful than impersonal sources such as media, public opinion polls, or published information. The communication executives in her study said the most useful external personal contacts were customers, activist groups, journalists, and government officials. The most useful internal personal sources were supervisors, cross-division staff, and employees. Based on Chang's research, J. Grunig and L. Grunig (2000) developed an ideal process of environmental scanning that included monitoring strategic decisions of management to identify consequences on publics, monitoring web sites and other sources of information from activists, using the situational theory to segment publics, developing a database to analyze information, and monitoring media and other sources to track the process of issues management.

Environmental scanning requires a theory and method of identifying stakeholders and segmenting publics from categories of stakeholders. Yet, few public relations professionals use tools more sophisticated than demographic breakdowns to identify publics. When it is used, the situational theory of publics provides a sophisticated method of identifying different types of publics and for planning strategies to communicate with them. Few public relations scholars have developed a theory of publics other than the situational theory. With the exception of Price (1992), who developed a similar theory of public opinion, mass communication scholars also have ignored the behavior of publics and how it tempers the effects of media on them.

Recently, a few public relations scholars have jumped into the breach either to add concepts to the situational theory or develop an alternative theory. Hallahan (2000, 2001), for example, called for more attention to what he called "inactive publics"—the passive publics that, according to the situational theory, seldom respond to messages related to the problems that created the publics. Others (Cozier & Witmer, 2001; Vasquez, 1993; Vasquez & Taylor, 2001) have disputed the assumption of the situational theory that publics develop about problems in the life situations of people, which often result from the consequences of organizational behaviors, and called for a more social theory of publics.

Research on the situational theory already has moved to accommodate these suggestions. For example, Aldoory (2001) identified conditions that led women to perceive a greater level of involvement in health problems; and Sha (1995) showed how cultural identity affects problem recognition—both of which suggest antecedent variables explaining why inactive publics become active. J-N. Kim (2005) is adding a comprehensive set of new independent and dependent variables to the theory based on theories of social psychology and social movements. His expanded conceptualization of the theory will show the conditions that actively encourage communicating individuals to join with others socially to become collective publics. His conceptualization also includes the active and passive giving of information to others (explaining the social nature of publics) and active and passive cognitive processing (explaining communication effects or lack of effects) as new dependent variables explained by the theory.

In addition to this fundamental work on the situational theory itself, new research continues to demonstrate the value of the theory in its original formulation. Yang (2005) included the independent variables of the theory in a study of the interaction of an organization's relationships with its publics and its reputation. Applied researchers studying reputation often have found a correlation between familiarity with an organization and the favorability of its reputation. This correlation often is cited as support for the idea that favorable publicity improves reputation. By using the situational theory, Yang was able to show that this correlation could be explained by how actively an organization communicates with its active publics. When active communication was controlled, publicity by itself had little effect on reputation, except for low-involvement, inactive publics— which are unimportant to the organization.

Scenario Building

Once a public relations professional who participates in strategic management identifies strategic publics related to a decision, he or she needs tools that can be used to show other managers what those publics might do and what issues they might create if different decisions are made. Management scholars have used scenarios for some time as a way of visioning the consequences of different decisions, but the technique has seldom been used in public relations.

Sung (2004) reviewed the literature on scenarios and integrated it with our theories of the role of public relations in strategic management, the situational theory of publics, and issues management. She then conducted a case study in which she worked with public relations professionals at a major insurance company to identify publics and construct scenarios related to issues. The professionals with whom she worked concluded that scenarios improved their ability to contribute to strategic organizational decisions.

The Empowerment of Public Relations

The relationship of public relations to an organization's dominant coalition was a key characteristic of excellent public relations identified in the Excellence Study. Pieczka (1996), a critical scholar, and Holtzhausen and Voto (2002), postmodern scholars, have criticized this idea and argued that public relations executives should avoid being in the dominant coalition so that they can be an activist voice for publics in decision-making. Power, in their view, would corrupt the public relations function to the detriment of publics.

This criticism, however, is based on an incorrect interpretation of the Excellence Theory and of the concept of a dominant coalition. The dominant coalition does not necessarily consist of those in formal positions of power. The dominant coalition is an informal coalition, whose members can be both inside and outside the organization and who can come from different levels of an organizational hierarchy. It also can be enlarged by empowering larger numbers of people. Public relations does not have to have "authoritative power" or "power at the top of the hierarchy" (Holtzhausen & Voto, 2002, p. 61) or be at a "centre of power" (Pieczka, 1996, p. 154)—the ways in which these critics misconstrued the dominant coalition and the Excellence Theory.

In the Excellence Study, we conceptualized power as empowerment, the expansion of power throughout the organization and to its external stakeholders. In fact, the study showed that the more people inside and outside the organization that were included in the dominant coalition, the more likely it was that the head of public relations and outside stakeholders and activists were included. In contrast, Curtin and Gaither (2005) even coined the "Grunigian fallacy," which they claimed "excludes power as an integral and defining concept in public relations" (p. 96). This criticism is so far removed from the actual assumptions of the Excellence Study that I question whether the critics even read the work they were criticizing.

The Excellence Study, the situational theory, and our previous research on activism focused on empowering the public relations function and through it empowering publics to have a voice in organizational decision-making. Logically, the public relations function cannot serve as an in-house activist, as Holtzhausen and Voto (2002) recommended, if it is not empowered. It would be a fringe managerial function without any influence on decision-making. Power does influence public relations, and its major role is to empower those with less power.

In a recent study of power and the public relations function, Berger (2005) added to our understanding of how public relations influences decisions. Like Mintzberg (1983), Berger found that there is no single dominant coalition in an organization. Rather different coalitions of strategic managers develop for different decisions. Public relations, therefore, typically was a member of these coalitions when its expertise was relevant to a decision. This finding again reinforces the necessity for public relations to have the expertise needed to scan the environment, construct scenarios, and build relationships with strategic publics—the key roles of public relations in strategic management.

An Ethics Framework for Decision-Making

If the role of public relations in strategic management is to bring the voices of publics into the decision-making process, public relations should be able to improve the ethics and social responsibility of organizational behaviors. The public relations function should not be the sole advocate of ethics in management, but it should provide an important framework for ethical decision-making. Research is needed, however, to provide a framework, from a public relations perspective, that practitioners can use to apply ethical criteria to strategic decisions.

Bowen (2000, 2004) has made a major contribution to the development of such a framework. She used Kantian principles of ethics to develop an ethical decision model and explored its use in two corporations. She is continuing this research (Bowen, 2005), working with a grant team funded by the IABC Research Foundation, to determine the extent to which public relations professionals play an ethical role in decision-making and the obstacles to such a role. However, similar research is needed to expand our knowledge of the ethical contributions of public relations to an organization and the publics it affects.

Relationships, ROI, and Evaluation

Since the completion of the Excellence Project, public relations researchers have studied relationships more than any other topic in the discipline (see, e.g., the volume edited by Ledingham and Bruning, 2000). Relationships provide a means for evaluating both the long-term and short-term contributions of public relations programs and of the overall function to organizational effectiveness. Eventually, I believe we will be able to show that the total value, the ROI, of public relations develops through the intangible asset that relationships provide to organizations.

Huang (1997) and J. Grunig and Huang (2000) began this work by identifying trust, control mutuality, satisfaction, and commitment as key components of high-quality relationships that can be measured for both planning and evaluation of public relations. Huang (1997) developed and used a survey instrument to test these concepts in a study of relationships between the executive and legislative branches of the Taiwanese government. Hon and J. Grunig (1999) further developed this index and tested its reliability. The Strategy One research affiliate of Edelman Public Relations has adopted the instrument and used it for numerous clients.

Hon and J. Grunig (1999) also identified two types of relationships to go along with these attributes of the quality of a relationship: exchange and communal relationships. Although we believe an organization needs both types of relationships, we argued that public relations makes a unique contribution to strategy when it helps organizations develop communal relationships with publics—relationships that benefit publics but not necessarily the organization. Based on a study of the relationships of multinational companies in China, Hung (2002, 2005) added several additional types of relationships to this list. They included mutual communal (which is less one-sided than a pure communal relationship), covenantal (where both parties benefit), contractual, symbiotic (where each gains something different), manipulative, and exploitive relationships. She found that covenantal relationships helped reach a win–win ground and that mutual communal relationships benefited multinational companies most.

In addition to conceptualizing these qualities and types of relationships and using them in evaluation research, we have moved forward in showing the value of relationships to an organization. J. Grunig and Hung (2002) began this work by examining the literature on reputation to show how it is affected by relationships. They developed a definition of reputation as a cognitive representation in the minds of different stakeholders and showed that reputation can be explained by the behavior of the organization and the quality of its relationships with publics.

Yang (2005) and Yang and J. Grunig (2005) extended this research and developed structural equation models showing that the reputation of an organization develops from the type and quality of relationships it has with its publics. This research indicates that the value typically attributed to reputation should, instead, be attributed to relationships and that public relations can help to "manage" reputation by cultivating relationships with publics and encouraging management to make socially responsible decisions.

I am continuing to work on the ROI of relationships as the chair of a task force of the Measurement Commission of the Institute for Public Relations, which is studying how nonfinancial indicators of value are influenced by public relations. This task force was initiated by the late Patrick Jackson—the renowned public relations professional. Nonfinancial indicators of value, or intangible assets, are a hot topic in management and accounting circles. I believe that relationships are the most important of these intangible assets and that if we can show that public relations creates value in addition to financial value, we can show the overall ROI of the function. The British public relations practitioner and scholar, David Phillips (2005), also has studied the literature on intangible assets and argued that relationships are the most important of these assets. I believe this approach to ROI eventually will show the value of public relations and encourage public relations scholars to join in the study of intangible assets.

Cultivation Strategies as the Heir to the Symmetrical Model

The new concepts and tools we have developed to help public relations professionals contribute to strategic management will be used mostly by senior-level public relations executives as they interact with other executives. Most of the day-to-day work of other practitioners, however, takes place at the level of the public relations department where they design, execute, and evaluate communication programs for specific publics—ideally publics identified as strategic by the senior public relations executives using the tools just described.

The relationship perspective on public relations suggests that the purpose of these programs is to manage relationships with publics. Yet, logic suggests that it is not really possible to "manage" relationships—or reputation, images, or brands. All of these concepts are the outcomes of processes. It is possible to manage processes but not outcomes. The best we can do is influence outcomes by managing processes. Thus, we need a term to describe the relationship processes we are managing. Relationship scholars in interpersonal communication have used the term "maintenance strategies" (e.g., Stafford & Canary, 1991) to describe what people do when they try to influence their relationships with other people. However, this term does not seem quite right.

In her dissertation work, Hung (2002) discovered and applied Baxter and Montgomery's (1996) dialectical approach to relationships. This approach, based on the writing of the Russian rhetorician Bakhtin (1981), assumes that relationships are in a constant state of flux and, therefore, that they seldom can be "maintained." After searching for an alternative concept, I chose the term "cultivation" for the strategies used in ongoing relationship processes—perhaps because of my agricultural roots. During a growing season, for example, crops are cultivated according to the conditions that affect them. They are not simply maintained. I believe the same is true for relationships.

Hon and J. Grunig (1999) identified several of these cultivation strategies in the literature on interpersonal communication and conflict resolution and classified them as symmetrical and asymmetrical strategies. Hung (2002, 2004) explored these strategies and identified several more in her study of multinational companies in China. Rhee (2004) identified still other cultivation strategies in a study of relationships between the Brookhaven National Laboratory and its community publics. The list of cultivation strategies now is too long to explain in this chapter. However, the strategies can be classified as either symmetrical or asymmetrical.

I now believe that the concept of relationship cultivation strategies is the heir to the models of public relations and the two-way symmetrical model, in particular. Cultivation strategies identify specific ways in which symmetrical communication can be used to cultivate relationships. For example, the strategy of "sharing of tasks" is a symmetrical strategy in which the organization works to solve problems of concern to stakeholders as well as problems it is concerned with. The strategy of "executive involvement in community relations" (Rhee, 2004) shows the importance of contact with a CEO for cultivating relationships with publics.

In developing the concept of symmetrical communication, I believe it is necessary to acknowledge that publics often are not willing to collaborate with organizations and often behave in ways that are destructive to the relationship and to society in general. In a study of the NATO mission in Bosnia, Van Dyke (2005) examined how organizations can use coercion ethically together with symmetrical communication. In general, Van Dyke concluded that coercion must be preceded by and followed by symmetrical communication in order to be ethical.

It is also important to recognize that symmetrical communication, alone, is not enough for public relations to contribute to social justice. H.-S. Kim (2005), for example, found that symmetrical internal communication had no effect on organization–employee relationships unless it also helped to produce organizational justice as perceived by employees. Roper (2005) studied the use of symmetrical communication by the World Trade Organization, the World Bank, the International Monetary Fund, and Shell Oil. She found that these organizations did engage in dialogue with their publics and made concessions to publics in their behaviors. However, she also argued that they changed just enough to maintain social order and to preserve their own hegemony. This argument calls to mind the need for what the European school of public relations scholars (Van Ruler & Verčič, 2002) have called the "reflexive" approach to public relations—in which professionals think not just about the effects of organizational behavior on publics but also on society as a whole. In the future, I believe we need to study how symmetrical communication can be combined with coercive behaviors, the possible misuses of symmetrical communication, and variables that mediate the effects of symmetrical communication on organizational policies and behaviors.

Extending the Edifice to Specialized Areas of Public Relations

Public relations scholars have paid a great deal of attention to the excellence of the overall public relations function, and they now are beginning to apply this theoretical edifice to several specialized areas of public relations. The Excellence Study identified the eight most common categories of stakeholders for which organizations developed specialized programs: employees, media, investors, community, customers, government, members of associations, and donors.

Of these, researchers at the University of Maryland have conducted research to apply the Excellence principles and our new relationship concepts to all but media, customers, and members of associations. Kelly (1991) confirmed, first, that the Excellence principles explained effective donor relations. Schickinger (1998) found concepts similar to those of the Excellence Theory in the literature of investor relations and also found that use of new, electronic media facilitated symmetrical communication with investors.

H.-S. Kim (2005) replicated the employee communication parts of the Excellence Study and added our relationship concepts and concepts of organizational justice from organizational psychology to the Excellence model. She used sophisticated methods of multi-level analysis to sort out whether concepts such as organizational structure, the system of communication, organizational justice, and organization–employee relations are organizational or individual concepts. Her research showed organizational justice to be a critical mediating variable between symmetrical communication and relationships.

Rhee (2004) studied the effect of the Excellence characteristics as exemplified by the Brookhaven National Laboratory on relationships between the organization and community publics. In particular, she found that interpersonal communication between employees and community members had a greater effect on organization–public relationships that mediated communication. Interestingly, she found that involving employees in community relations also improved employee relationships with the laboratory. Chen (2005) studied the relevance of the Excellence principles to government relations programs developed by multi-national corporations in China. In doing so, she found support for the principles in this specialized area and also developed recommendations for government relations in this authoritarian political system.

The Excellence principles and the relationship concepts obviously apply also to media relations, consumer relations, and member relations. I urge researchers working in the tradition of the Excellence Study to also study these areas. In particular, I believe it is time for public relations scholars, in addition to those in the IMC camp, to conceptualize marketing communication principles. Marketing scholars have developed concepts of relationship marketing—literature that Huang (1997) incorporated into her conceptualization of relationships. I believe public relations scholars can make an important contribution to marketing if we move beyond the messaging, publicity, and asymmetrical communication common in marketing communication and use our theories to develop symmetrical principles of cultivating relationships with consumers.

Expanding Public Relations Role in Global Strategy

The last chapter of L. Grunig, J. Grunig, and Dozier (2002) described our research in Slovenia and similar research by Wakefield (1997, 2000) that was designed to extend the Excellence principles to a global basis. We developed a theory of generic principles and specific applications that falls midway between an ethnocentric theory (that public relations is the same everywhere) and a polycentric theory (that public relations is different everywhere). The theory holds that in a broad, abstract way, the Excellence principles can be applied in different cultures, economic systems, political systems, media systems, levels of development, and degrees of activist activity.

The postmodern scholars, Bardhan (2003) and Holtzhausen, Petersen, and Tindall (2003) have challenged this theory, maintaining that postmodern conditions require different forms of public relations in each setting. In particular, they have questioned the utility of the symmetrical model in nonWestern settings. Although I agree that public relations cannot be the same everywhere, I find it easier to interpret Holtzhausen et al.'s data from South Africa as showing that symmetrical communication took different forms in that setting, supporting the theory of generic principles and specific applications, rather than that symmetrical communication did not exist, which was their interpretation. Similarly, Bardhan (2003) used positive data suggesting that most practitioners in India do not practice symmetrical communication as evidence against the theory. Such positive data do not falsify a normative theory, such as our theory of generic principles and specific applications. A normative theory maintains that the effects of the principles would be as conceptualized if they are practiced in another country. They can be tested only by studying the work of practitioners who have actually applied the principles to see if they have the effects conceptualized in the theory.

At the same time, evidence continues to mount supporting the usefulness of our theory of generic principles and specific applications. In addition to the research cited in L. Grunig, J. Grunig, and Dozier (2002), Rhee (2002) found support for the strategic management and symmetrical principles in the work of a sample of Korean practitioners. Hung (2002) and Chen (2005) found evidence for several of the principles in the work of multinational companies in China. Van Dyke (2005) found that NATO applied the principles in the public affairs work of its mission to Bosnia. Finally, Yun (2005) found similar principles in the literature of public diplomacy and extracted the same Excellence factor from research on the public diplomacy efforts of 113 of the 169 embassies in Washington, D.C. that we extracted in the Excellence Study and in our research in Slovenia.

Our research now is moving beyond confirmation of the utility of the generic principles of the Excellence Theory. Ni (2006) is studying how the relationship-building role of public relations contributes to the global strategies of multinational corporations. She has studied the management literature on global strategy to extend our understanding of the strategic role of public relations from national to global settings. Her research, in particular, will help us learn how different global strategies require different kinds of relationships with local employees.

Toward Institutionalization of Public Relations as a Strategic Management Function

In this chapter, I believe I have shown that the theoretical edifice of public relations as a strategic management function that my colleagues, students, and I have constructed and furnished over the last 40 years is not an ossified, deteriorating structure. Rather, researchers are continuing to refine the structure and apply it to new research problems. In addition, we have steadily added rooms to the structure by identifying and studying concepts and tools that public relations professionals can use in their strategic management role.

A major task remains, however, in institutionalizing strategic public relations as actual practice in most organizations. Yi (2005) examined the sociological literature on institutionalization—of how practices and activities come to be standard and generally accepted in organizations. He learned that institutionalists, for the most part, think of public relations as a buffering activity—as something that organizations use to protect them from change. Public relations as a buffering activity fits the common view that its role is to use messages and symbolism to create images and reputations that justify the organization as it is. Other institutionalists think of communication as a bridging activity, in which organizations build linkages with stakeholders in their environment in order to transform and constitute the organization in new ways. Public relations as a bridging activity seems to be equivalent to our theoretical edifice of public relations as a strategic management function.

Unfortunately, public relations has become institutionalized as a buffering function in most organizations and in the view of most people. As a buffering activity, the effect of public relations usually is detrimental to society. Our research, in contrast, has shown the value of public relations as a bridging activity—of value to organizations, publics, and society. The Excellence Study and subsequent research have shown that many organizations around the world practice bridging public relations. It is not just a normative ideal. Our next research challenge, I believe, will be to study how public relations can be institutionalized more broadly as a bridging activity so public relations as a strategic management function becomes standard operating practice in most organizations and that most people think of public relations in that way.

Acknowledgments

This chapter previously appeared in the *Journal of Public Relations Research*, 18(2) (2006), 151–176.

References

Aldoory, L. (2001). Making health communications meaningful for women: Factors that influence involvement. *Journal of Public Relations Research, 13,* 163–185.

Anderson, J. R. (2000). *Cognitive psychology and its implications* (5th ed.). New York: Worth.

Bakhtin, M. M. (1981). *The dialogic imagination: Four essays.* Austin: The University of Texas Press.

Bardhan, N. (2003). Rupturing public relations metanarratives: The example of India. *Journal of Public Relations Research, 15,* 225–248.

Baxter, L. A., & Montgomery, B. M. (1996). *Relating: Dialogues & dialectics.* New York: Guilford.

Berger, B. K. (2005). Power over, power with, and power to public relations: Critical reflections on public relations, the dominant coalition, and activism. *Journal of Public Relations Research, 17,* 5–28.

Bowen, S. A. (2000). A theory of ethical issues management: Contributions of Kantian deontology to public relations' ethics and decision making. Unpublished doctoral dissertation, University of Maryland, College Park.

Bowen, S. A. (2004). Expansion of ethics as the tenth generic principle of public relations excellence: A Kantian theory and model for managing ethical issues. *Journal of Public Relations Research, 16,* 65–92.

Bowen, S. A. (2005, June). Schism in public relations ethics: Overview of grant research findings. Paper presented at the meeting of the International Association of Business Communicators, Washington, DC.

Brown, H. I. (1977). *Perception, theory, and commitment: The new philosophy of science.* Chicago: University of Chicago Press.

Carter, R. F. (1965). Communication and affective relations. *Journalism Quarterly, 42,* 203–212.

Carter, R. F. (1972, September). A general system characteristic of systems in general. Paper presented to the Far West Region Meeting, Society for General Systems Research, Portland, OR.

Chaffee, S. H., & McLeod, J. (1968). Sensitization in panel design: A coorientational experiment. *Journalism Quarterly, 45,* 661–669.

Chang, Y-C. (2000). A normative exploration into environmental scanning in public relations. Unpublished M.A. thesis, University of Maryland, College Park.

Chen, Y-R. (2005). Effective government affairs in an era of marketization: Strategic issues management, business lobbying, and relationship management by multinational corporations in China. Unpublished doctoral dissertation, University of Maryland, College Park.

Cozier, Z. R., & Witmer, D. F. (2001). The development of a structuration analysis of new publics in an electronic environment. In R. Heath, & G. Vasquez (Eds.), *Handbook of public relations* (pp. 615–623). Thousand Oaks, CA: Sage.

Curtin, P. A., & Gaither, T. K. (2005). Privileging identity, difference, and power: The circuit of culture as a basis for public relations theory. *Journal of Public Relations Research, 17,* 91–116.

Durham, F. (2005). Public relations as structuration. *Journal of Public Relations Research, 17,* 29–48.

Ehling, W. P. (1992). Estimating the value of public relations and communication to an organization. In J. E. Grunig (Ed.), *Excellence in public relations and communication management* (pp. 617–638). Hillsdale, NJ: Lawrence Erlbaum Associates.

Fombrun, C. J. (1996). *Reputation: Realizing value from the corporate image.* Boston: Harvard Business School Press.

Fombrun, C. J., & Van Riel, C. B. M. (2004). *Fame and fortune: How successful companies build winning reputations.* Upper Saddle River, NJ: Financial Times Prentice-Hall.

Grunig, J. E. (1966). The role of information in economic decision making. *Journalism Monographs*, No. 3.

Grunig, J. E. (1968). Information, entrepreneurship, and economic development: A study of the decision-making processes of Colombian latifundistas. Unpublished doctoral dissertation, University of Wisconsin, Madison.

Grunig, J. E. (1976). Organizations and publics relations: Testing a communication theory. *Journalism Monographs*, No. 46.

Grunig, J. E. (1977). Evaluating employee communication in a research operation. *Public Relations Review, 3*(4), 61–82.

Grunig, J. E. (1984). Organizations, environments, and models of public relations. *Public Relations Research & Education, 1*(1), 6–29.

Grunig, J. E. (1992). Symmetrical systems of internal communication. In J. E. Grunig (Ed.), *Excellence in public relations and communication management* (pp. 531–576). Hillsdale, NJ: Lawrence Erlbaum Associates.

Grunig, J. E. (1997). A situational theory of publics: Conceptual history, recent challenges and new research. In D. Moss, T. MacManus, & D. Verčič (Eds.), *Public relations research: An international perspective* (pp. 3–46). London: International Thomson Business Press.

Grunig, J. E. (2003). Constructing public relations theory and practice. In B. Dervin, & S. Chaffee, with L. Foreman-Wernet (Eds.), *Communication, another kind of horse race: Essays honoring Richard F. Carter* (pp. 85–115). Cresskill, NJ: Hampton Press.

Grunig, J. E., & Grunig, L. A. (1989). Toward a theory of the public relations behavior of organizations: Review of a program of research. *Public Relations Research Annual, 1*, 27–66.

Grunig, J. E., & Grunig, L. A. (1996, May). Implications of symmetry for a theory of ethics and social responsibility in public relations. Paper presented to the International Communication Association, Chicago.

Grunig, J. E., & Grunig, L. A. (2000, February). Research methods for environmental scanning. *Jim and Lauri Grunig's research: A supplement of PRR Reporter,* 7.

Grunig, J. E., & Huang, Y. H. (2000). From organizational effectiveness to relationship indicators: Antecedents of relationships, public relations strategies, and relationship outcomes. In J. A. Ledingham & S. D. Bruning (Eds.), *Public relations as relationship management: A relational approach to the study and practice of public relations* (pp. 23–53). Mahwah, NJ: Lawrence Erlbaum Associates.

Grunig, J. E., & Hung, C. J. (2002, March). The effect of relationships on reputation and reputation on relationships: A cognitive, behavioral study. Paper presented to the International, Interdisciplinary Public Relations Research Conference, Miami, Florida.

Grunig, J. E., & Hunt, T. (1984). *Managing public relations*. New York: Holt, Rinehart & Winston.

Grunig, J. E., & Stamm, K. R. (1973). Communication and coorientation of collectivities. *American Behavioral Scientist, 16*, 567–591.

Grunig, L. A., Grunig, J. E., & Dozier, D. M. (2002). *Excellent public relations and effective organizations: A study of communication management in three countries*. Mahwah, NJ: Lawrence Erlbaum Associates.

Grunig, L. A., Grunig, J. E., & Verčič, D. (1998). Are the IABC's Excellence principles generic? Comparing Slovenia and the United States, the United Kingdom and Canada. *Journal of Communication Management, 2*, 335–356.

Hallahan, K. (2000). Inactive publics: The forgotten publics in public relations. *Public Relations Review, 26*, 499–516.

Hallahan, K. (2001). The dynamics of issues activation and response: An issues processes model. *Journal of Public Relations Research, 13*, 27–59.

Hatch, M. J. (1997). *Organization theory: Modern, symbolic, and postmodern perspectives.* New York: Oxford University Press.

Holtzhausen, D. R., & Voto, R. (2002). Resistance from the margins: The postmodern public relations practitioner as organizational activist. *Journal of Public Relations Research, 14,* 57–84.

Holtzhausen, D. R., Petersen, B. K., & Tindall, N. T. J. (2003). Exploding the myth of the symmetrical/asymmetrical dichotomy: Public relations models in the new South Africa. *Journal of Public Relations Research, 15,* 305–341.

Hon, L. C., & Grunig, J. E. (1999). *Guidelines for measuring relationships in public relations.* Gainesville, FL: The Institute for Public Relations, Commission on PR Measurement and Evaluation.

Huang, Y-H. (1997). Public relations, organization–public relationships, and conflict management. Unpublished doctoral dissertation, University of Maryland, College Park.

Hung, C-J. (2002). The interplays of relationship types, relationship cultivation, and relationship outcomes: How multinational and Taiwanese companies practice public relations and organization–public relationship management in China. Unpublished doctoral dissertation, University of Maryland, College Park.

Hung, C-J. (2004). Cultural influence on relationship cultivation strategies: Multinational companies in China. *Journal of Communication Management, 8,* 264–281.

Hung, C-J. (2005). Exploring types of organization–public relationships and their implications for relationship management in public relations. *Journal of Public Relations Research, 17,* 393–425.

Kelly, K. S. (1991). *Fund raising and public relations.* Hillsdale, NJ: Lawrence Erlbaum Associates.

Kim, H-S. (2005). Organizational structure and internal communication as antecedents of employee–organization relationships in the context of organizational justice: A multilevel analysis. Unpublished doctoral dissertation, University of Maryland, College Park.

Kim, J-N. (2005). Communicant activeness, cognitive entrepreneurship, and a situational theory of problem solving. Unpublished doctoral dissertation prospectus, University of Maryland, College Park.

Kuhn, T. S. (1970). *The structure of scientific revolutions,* rev. ed. Chicago: University of Chicago Press.

Lakatos, I. (1970). Falsification and the methodology of scientific research programs. In I. Lakatos & A. Musgrave (Eds.), *Criticism and the growth of knowledge* (pp. 191–196). Cambridge: Cambridge University Press.

Laudan, L. (1977). *Progress and its problems.* Berkeley: University of California Press.

Ledingham, J. A., & Bruning, S. D. (Eds.). (2000). *Public relations as relationship management: A relational approach to the study and practice of public relations.* Mahwah, NJ: Lawrence Erlbaum Associates.

Leitch, S., & Neilson, D. (2001). Bringing publics into public relations: New theoretical frameworks for practice. In R. L. Heath (Ed.), *Handbook of public relations* (pp. 127–138). Thousand Oaks, CA: Sage.

L'Etang, J., & Pieczka, M. (Eds.). (1996). *Critical perspectives in public relations.* London: International Thomson Business Press.

McKie, D. (2001). Updating public relations: "New science," research paradigms, and uneven developments. In R. L. Heath (Ed.), *Handbook of public relations* (pp. 75–91). Thousand Oaks, CA: Sage.

Mintzberg, H. (1983). *Power in and around organizations.* Englewood Cliffs, NJ: Prentice-Hall.

Motion, J., & Weaver, C. K. (2005). A discourse perspective for critical public relations research: Life sciences network and the battle for truth. *Journal of Public Relations Research, 17,* 49–67.

Ni, L. (2006). Exploring the value of public relations in strategy implementation: Employee relations in the globalization process. Unpublished doctoral dissertation, University of Maryland, College Park.

Phillips, D. (2005, March). Towards relationship management: Public relations at the core of organisational development. Paper presented to the Alan Rawal CIPR Academic Conference 2005, Lincoln, United Kingdom.

Pieczka, M. (1996). Paradigms, systems theory and public relations. In J. L'Etang & M. Pieczka (Eds.), *Critical perspectives in public relations* (pp. 124–156). London: International Thomson Business Press.

Popper, K. R. (1970). Normal science and its dangers. In I. Lakatos & A. Musgrave (Eds.), *Criticism and the growth of knowledge* (pp. 51–58). Cambridge: Cambridge University Press.

Price, V. (1992). *Public opinion.* Newbury Park, CA: Sage.

Rhee, Y. (2002). Global public relations: A cross-cultural study of the Excellence theory in South Korea. *Journal of Public Relations Research, 14,* 159–184.

Rhee, Y. (2004). The employee–public–organization chain in relationship management: A case study of a government organization. Unpublished doctoral dissertation, University of Maryland, College Park.

Roper, J. (2005). Symmetrical communication: Excellent public relations or a strategy for hegemony. *Journal of Public Relations Research, 17,* 69–86.

Schickinger, P. (1998). Electronic investor relations: Can new media close the symmetry gap? Unpublished M.A. thesis, University of Maryland, College Park.

Sha, B-L. (1995). Intercultural public relations: Exploring cultural identity as a means of segmenting publics. Unpublished M.A. thesis, University of Maryland, College Park.

Shapere, D. (1977). Scientific theories and their domains. In F. Suppe (Ed.), *The structure of scientific theories* (2nd ed., pp. 518–565). Urbana: University of Illinois Press.

Stafford, L., & Canary, D. J. (1991). Maintenance strategies and romantic relationship type, gender and relational characteristics. *Journal of Social and Personal Relationships, 8,* 217–242.

Sung, M-J. (2004). Toward a model of strategic management of public relations: Scenario building from a public relations perspective. Unpublished doctoral dissertation, University of Maryland, College Park.

Suppe, F. (1977). *The structure of scientific theories* (2nd ed.). Urbana: University of Illinois Press.

Thayer, L. (1968). *Communication and communication systems.* Homewood, IL: Irwin.

Tirone, J. G. (1977). Measuring the Bell System's public relations. *Public Relations Review, 3*(4), 21–38.

Toulmin, S. (1972). *Human understanding,* Vol. I. Princeton, NJ: Princeton University Press.

Van Dyke, M. A. (2005). Toward a theory of just communication: A case study of NATO, multinational public relations, and ethical management of international conflict. Unpublished doctoral dissertation, University of Maryland, College Park.

Van Ruler, B., & Verčič, D. (2002, July). The Bled Manifesto on public relations. Paper presented to the Ninth Public Relations Research Symposium, Bled, Slovenia.

Vasquez, G. M. (1993). A *homo narrans* paradigm for public relations: Combining Bormann's symbolic convergence theory and Grunig's situational theory of publics. *Journal of Public Relations Research, 5,* 201–216.

Vasquez, G. M., & Taylor, M. (2001). Research perspectives on the public. In R. Heath & G. Vasquez (Eds.), *Handbook of public relations* (pp. 127–138). Thousand Oaks, CA: Sage.

Verčič, D., Grunig, L. A., & Grunig, J. E. (1996). Global and specific principles of public relations: Evidence from Slovenia. In H. M. Culbertson & N. Chen (Eds.), *International public relations: A comparative analysis* (pp. 31–65). Mahwah, NJ: Lawrence Erlbaum Associates.

Wakefield, R. I. (1997). International public relations: A theoretical approach to excellence based on a worldwide Delphi study. Unpublished doctoral dissertation, University of Maryland, College Park.

Wakefield, R. I. (2000). World-class public relations: A model for effective public relations in the multinational. *Journal of Communication Management, 5*(1), 59–71.

White, J., & Dozier, D. M. (1992). Public relations and management decision making. In J. E. Grunig (Ed.), *Excellence in public relations and communication management* (pp. 91–108). Hillsdale, NJ: Lawrence Erlbaum Associates.

Yang, S-U. (2005). The effect of organization–public relationships on reputation from the perspective of publics. Unpublished doctoral dissertation, University of Maryland, College Park.

Yang, S-U., & Grunig, J. E. (2005). Decomposing organizational reputation: The effects of organization–public relationship outcomes on cognitive representations of organizations and evaluations of organizational performance. *Journal of Communication Management, 9,* 305–325.

Yi, H. (2005). The role of communication management in the institutionalization of corporate citizenship: Relational convergence of corporate social responsibility and stakeholder management. Unpublished M.A. thesis, University of Maryland, College Park.

Yun, S-H. (2005). Theory building for comparative public diplomacy from the perspectives of public relations and international relations: A macro-comparative study of embassies in Washington, D.C. Unpublished doctoral dissertation, University of Maryland, College Park.

2

FEMINIST PHASE ANALYSIS IN PUBLIC RELATIONS

Where Have We Been?
Where Do We Need to Be?

Larissa A. Grunig

Abstract

Feminist phase theory provides a classification system for analyzing any evolution in our thinking about women across the disciplines. The two-fold purpose of this chapter is, first, to suggest further avenues through which to apply Tetreault's (1985) groundbreaking work and, second, to propose a sixth stage relevant to public relations research. Feminist phase theory defines five phases of such research: male scholarship, compensatory, bifocal, feminist, and multifocal. Now, I would propose adding a sixth, integrative phase. That stage, I would argue, will conceptualize women and men who work in public relations not only as communication professionals, but also as human beings often struggling to integrate their work, their family, and their community lives.

Key Words

feminism, integration, organizations, phase analysis, women

> The past cannot be changed,
> the future is still in your power.
>
> *Hugh White (1773–1840)*

Introduction

Feminist phase theory provides a classification system for analyzing any evolution in our thinking about women across the disciplines. It dates from the work of Mary Kay Tetreault (1985)[1] and has been applied primarily to women in the academy.[2]

In 2000, I went beyond the extant literature to apply phase theory in a new domain, public relations.

My goal in 2000 was to approach transformation of our knowledge along the lines suggested by one of this field's leading feminists, Pamela J. Creedon (1991):

> When [the] individual's research program, course, textbook, or lecture reflects the multiple realities that exist in a diverse culture, it gives energy to the process that moves the boundary line of knowledge in the entire field closer to something that works.
>
> *(p. 81)*

I used the five stages of Tetreault's (1985) theory to analyze the literature of public relations, as published in the two leading scholarly journals in the United States, from 1976–1995.

The two-fold purpose of this chapter is, first, to suggest further avenues through which to apply Tetreault's (1985) groundbreaking work and, second, to propose a sixth stage relevant to public relations research. Feminist phase theory defines five phases of such research: male scholarship, compensatory, bifocal, feminist, and multifocal. Now, five years into the new millennium, I propose adding a sixth, *integrative* phase. That stage, I argue, will conceptualize women and men in public relations not only as communication professionals but as human beings often struggling to integrate their work, family, and community lives.

Phase analysis is an important means of identifying how women have been conceptualized to date in public relations. Like Twombly (1993) in higher education, I believe that changing what is studied and known about women has the potential for changing women's—and men's—lives.

The value of this kind of systematic analysis is its potential first for dissecting "the errors underlying patriarchal thought" (Minnich, 1990, p. 10) and subsequently for changing the existing patterns of gender relations. However, I argue that not all research is equally beneficial. We know that research findings often help maintain the division of our world by sex. Creedon (1991), for example, pointed out that the important roles research begun by Broom (1982) and developed by Dozier (1987) and countless scholars over the last two and a half decades has the potential for the self-fulfilling prophecy of inherent differences between women and men.

Scholarly research constitutes the body of knowledge in our field. It reflects the values and the subjectivities of those who design and conduct the research. Although to some extent it may reflect the values of the larger society out of which it developed, a theoretical body of knowledge is intended to *lead* the relevant institutions of that society. At the same time, the literature of the field contributes to social constructions of gender—what and how we think about gender. Thus, by studying twenty years of published research on public relations in the United States, I reasoned in 2000 that we should be able to ascertain the dominant modes of thinking about women in this field.

The only previous effort at characterizing the status of feminist research[3] in public relations was undertaken by this author in 1988. As guest editor of a special edition of *Public Relations Review* (Vol. 14, No. 3), I proposed a research agenda for women. In so doing, I attempted to evaluate the gender research that had been done to date. I concluded that feminist analysis in public relations was at the preparadigmatic stage of inquiry. Little theorizing had been done. I considered the extant research to be "piecemeal stabs" that resulted only in small-scale gains in gender consciousness—progress that hardly began to address women's concerns. I applauded the high-quality work that scholars such as Elizabeth Lance Toth, Pamela J. Creedon, and David M. Dozier had done on women's issues. At the same time, I had to acknowledge that "their studies have been more solo voices than a chorus that echoes the mainstream of public relations research and education" (p. 55). My plea in the discussion of that article was for a commitment to a strong program of research that would help channel female scholars' frustrations at their powerlessness into the agency necessary for productivity in research. Despite my zealousness, my approach to reviewing the relevant literature then was far more impressionistic than systematic.

Tetreault's (1985) classification scheme imposes rigor on what otherwise may become a boundaryless, atheoretical look at a rapidly growing body of knowledge. Her framework is not intended to represent rankings or hierarchies. Instead, it reflects the evolution of thought about women's incorporation into any field. It begins simply by adding women to the equation. It progresses through more fundamental reconstructions (if any exist) of key concepts in the following ways.

Tetreault's (1985) Five Phases

1: Male Scholarship

The first of Tetreault's (1985) five phases is *male scholarship*, wherein the male experience is assumed to be universal and the absence of women is not noted. It is, in essence, womanless. In public relations, a first-phase article may describe corporate vice presidents of public relations without commenting on the fact that few (or none) of the executives profiled are women.

I consider this approach both patronizing and hostile to women. Others may believe that the problems investigated, the theories that frame those investigations, the methodologies employed, and the findings that result are "transcendental truths" that are humanly inclusive. Harding (1986), one of the leading feminists in science, has shown male scholarship to be far less than that. Any scholarship is the product of its collective and individual creators. The creators are marked by their gender, along with class, race, and culture.

However, research conducted before the 1960s often made assertions about women but typically failed to include women in the population studied (Caplan, 1985; Carlson, 1985). U.S. studies about all aspects of organizational life have tended to be gender (and race) neutral. Scholars across the relevant disciplines have generalized from one group—white males—to all (Nkomo, 1992; Allen, 1995). The dominant or male group becomes the reference group (Minnich, 1990). As a result, gender research is marginalized at best. Over time, it may become a domain for feminist scholars, much as race and ethnicity developed as research domains for minority scholars (Moses, 1989; T. Cox, 1990; Nieves-Squires, 1991).

Women's silence in this first phase does not reflect any absence of women's contributions to the field or to its intellectual base. Instead, it is my contention that what is assumed to be the life of the mind—as published in the scholarly literature—merely reflects the political ideology of the mind. But just as there are no all-male research universities in this country and just as public relations never has been a totally masculine preserve, the scholarship of the field should not be all male.

Of course, gender may be less relevant to some studies than to others. Thus in my initial (2000) feminist phase analysis, I construed male scholarship as that which fails to address gender issues when such issues are central. These significant omissions have served to deprive women of their history and their group identity.

2: Compensatory

The second feminist phase is *compensatory*. Literature in this phase seeks to overcome the previously unquestioned absence of women by searching for and profiling impressive women. In essence, it provides an alternative history of the field. It is the first phase to approach the accomplishment of Rakow's (1987) goals for feminist research *per se*: "research that challenges old methodologies and assumptions and openly asserts its politics" (p. 79).

Compensatory scholarship has been alternatively labeled "women in" (McIntosh, 1983), the "search for missing women" (Schuster & Van Dyne, 1985), and "women worthies" (Lerner, 1990). However, the standards used to determine which women are worthy are those of the so-called "great men." This is the "beta bias" described in much feminist scholarship (e.g., Hare-Mustin & Maracek, 1988)—assuming a male norm for human behavior.

In this stage of the literature, we would expect to find two main types of articles. First would be identifications and descriptions of "women who had made it" into top-level positions. Such articles either celebrate individuals' lives or profile the characteristics of successful women (but typically in relation to successful male colleagues). They may document women's obstacles to advancement or the frustrations they experience along the way. The risk here is in the "cult of personality" that raises people to the power of "stars."

Even if our journals chronicled the lives of famous females who headed professional associations or shaped the destiny of Fortune 500 companies, we would need to look beyond these icons. The field needs the history of the legions of women who labor in public relations without fanfare. As I (L. Grunig, 1988) argued in my previous description of feminist research, successful women should be regarded not as the norm. Instead, these highly visible women are examples of those who through their abilities and indomitable optimism have managed to overcome. They are high on agency.

The second aspect of the compensatory phase is counting, or census-taking. Studies of this nature tend to be demographic. They are useful in tracking women's progress in the field, although the implications of women's numbers or percentage of the work force typically are ignored. Still, by their growing numbers alone, women have created opportunities for themselves beyond what fields traditionally considered "female," such as teaching and library science, could have offered. On the other hand, any field suddenly shifting to a female majority[4] as public relations has done faces the realities of dwindling salary, regard, and power. Thus the census type of compensatory scholarship seems a necessary first step.

Unfortunately, both aspects of compensatory scholarship accept male standards as the universal. When women do not "measure up," their differences are translated as deficiencies (Twombly, 1993). The potential risk for women cannot be overstated. As sociologist Reskin (1988) explained, defining a subordinate group as inferior (and thus deserving inferior treatment) helps the dominant group maintain its hegemony. Nevertheless, the risks of compensatory scholarship seem worth taking: In addition to the socialization that may cause women to feel like outsiders in public relations, they may doubt they belong there if they read about few others like themselves in their field.

3: Bifocal

In the third or *bifocal* phase, women and men are conceptualized as separate and equal sexes. Neither is better; they are just different. Here we see the beginning of a "sensitivity to difference" model. At the same time, this notion of inherent, complementary difference helps account for the oppression of women (and their attempts to overcome discrimination) detailed in this phase. Thus bifocal studies go beyond merely including formerly neglected groups, such as women, in the research. We might find comparative studies suggesting that women and men have different ways of knowing, different moral judgments, or different career motivations. We also would expect to read of women's efforts to overcome sexism or other forms of discrimination that have disadvantaged them. This phase often emphasizes strategies for overcoming oppression.

Typically, sex is used as an independent variable in bifocal research that goes on to compare men and women on some variable or variables. Twombly (1993) found, however, that many such studies fail to report results of their studies by sex. More interesting is her finding that few articles using sex as a control variable included any theoretical explanation for why there might be differences between women and men. Camden and Witt (1983) described one problem inherent in this approach:

> Sex per se is not an effective variable in understanding sex-role behavior [...]
> True insight into sex-role behavior requires a use of psychological sex rather
> than biological sex as an independent variable [because] socialization processes
> may be so varied that gender uniformity for social roles is no longer present.
> *(p. 265)*

This type of research may be characterized by "alpha bias," or the exaggeration of differences. Alpha bias occurs when research treats members of any minority group as more homogenous than members of the dominant group. Hare-Mustin and Maracek (1988) pointed out that "Men are viewed as individuals, but women are viewed as women" (p. 459). However, as I have said before (L. Grunig, 1988), there is no "we" of feminism.

To illustrate the problem of alpha bias, Rakow (1986) charged that the two-role mindset of the manager/technician typology has succeeded in dichotomizing the meaning of work in public relations. She explained that roles research has reduced practitioners' functions to a hierarchy of two seemingly dissimilar sets of activities. This not only establishes what she and others (e.g., Creedon, 1991) considered a false dichotomy (because of the overlapping nature of work in public relations), but it also homogenizes the field (because it assumes that the work of all technicians is similar and that the work of all managers is similar). The result, these scholars believe, is that the work of women—clustered disproportionately in the technician's role—is trivialized and devalued. Instead, they would argue (and I would agree) that we need to respect the preferences that become reflected in the career choices of individual women in this postmodern era.

Despite my own commitment to the importance of the managerial role for public relations, I would not denigrate women who choose to remain technicians. Thus I acknowledge that although the roles typology helps us understand, describe, and then teach about public relations, the work women do in public relations actually transcends such facile categorization. More fundamentally, Johnson (1984) explained the problem of comparing women to men as "to reaffirm and perpetuate rather than to question the normative value of male behavior" (p. 80).

Recall that the objective of bifocal scholarship is to overcome the previous notion that women are deficient by valuing alternative models equally.[5] Unfortunately, new stereotypes often replace the old because the research tends to treat women as a homogeneous group. Women are seen as having universal characteristics that differentiate them from men.[6] However, sifting through literally hundreds of studies on gender has convinced me that there is more variation within one sex than there is between women and men.[7] These studies show that most hypothesized distinctions between masculinity and femininity are either unsupported or weakly supported. At most, the evidence is equivocal.

Thus despite the goal of this phase, Tetreault (1985) decried the resulting tendency to end up seeing women, once again, as "inferior and subordinate" (p. 373). As Bryant (1984) described it, "There is women's work, and there is men's work—and men's is better" (p. 47). Stereotypes that speak to masculinity and femininity have assigned power and dominance to men and subordination to women. Traditional sex roles have cast women as caregivers and nurturers (Frieze et al., 1978).

I belabor the description of the bifocal phase for two main reasons. First, Twombly (1993) found that this approach to women in the literature of community colleges was the most common of the five phases. My sense is that, beyond male scholarship, bifocal scholarship predominates in the literature about women in public relations as well. Even before conducting my phase analysis, I was aware that male and female practitioners have been compared on such variables as their styles of management, communication, and even dress; their career aspirations; and their levels of pay, responsibility, and job satisfaction.

The second reason for taking special care to elucidate this third phase is that Twombly (1993) also found it to be most in need of modification if feminist phase theory is to reach its potential as a tool for examining the ways in which women are conceptualized in the literature. She found the somewhat disparate types of bifocal research to be problematic. Thus, she suggested breaking the bifocal stage into two categories. The first would encompass recognition of and attempts to overcome oppression. The second would develop separate, equal, and complementary spheres for women and men. Because I find this refinement theoretically and methodologically pleasing, based on my anticipation of what I would discover in the literature of public relations, I incorporated Twombly's two subcategories of bifocal research into my (2000) analysis.

4: Feminist

The fourth phase, *feminist*, conceptualizes women on their own terms. Women's experiences are valued in and of themselves. Women's activities become the focus. As Dervin (1987) described feminist research in communication, it makes "female experience central. It focuses on the articulations of women; it brings to awareness experiences of women previously denied or suppressed" (p. 109). In this phase we might see a study of women who own and operate home-based businesses or an exploration of women's definitions of public relations. We might find a depiction of intragroup differences, rather than the between-group differences teased out of the third, bifocal phase.

This important development helps preclude stereotypes about the communication or other behaviors and motivations of "all women." As a result, of course, we would not expect to find prescriptions geared to solving such problems as women's promotion in the work force or male managers' interactions with female technicians. As Tong (1989) reminded us, no single perspective on a problem provides the answer to the "woman question."

Consistent with this fourth phase would be a methodological approach that gives women voice.[8] That is, participants speak in their own voice; the perspectives of researchers who study them are not privileged over insights of the participants themselves.

Although qualitative research allows for the contextualization necessary for participants' social construction of their reality (Herndon & Kreps, 1993), any methodology with sufficient depth and what Allen (1995) called "quality of input" may be appropriate. Certainly survey research and experimental design could offer participants voice. However, scholars (e.g., L. Grunig, 1986, 1994; Allen, 1995) have recommended the combination of qualitative and quantitative methods for research on diverse participants. Such complex triangulation may be the only adequate way of observing how gender contributes to the "complicated web of socially constructed elements of identity formation" (Nkomo, 1992, p. 488).

Whatever their methodological approach, feminist scholars (e.g., Keller, 1985) refute assumptions of objectivity and neutrality. Gould (1981) considered these mythical norms. He explained that researchers are so embedded in their surrounding culture that they often fail to identify the assumptions of that culture. Perhaps most relevant to the fourth phase, feminists propose *noncomparative* approaches (Gregg, 1987; Spitzack & Carter, 1987). At most, they would support research that questions the causes of any differences between genders, rather than continuing to try to establish that differences exist (Pearce & Freeman, 1988).

5: Multifocal

Multifocal, the fifth and final phase, is the most difficult to describe because it remains largely unrealized. It is characterized by exploration of the relationship between women and men and by reconceptualization of the human experience as a continuum (rather than dichotomy) between the masculine and feminine. Multifocal research has the potential to redefine a field. Its more immediate goal is to develop an understanding of both women's and men's experiences.

The Sixth Phase: Integrative

Women represent a substantial majority of public relations practitioners (and students), both in the United States and in many other countries of the world. In spite of the decades since the most recent women's liberation movement in the 1960s, women continue to do more than their share of the household chores and child- and eldercare. This results in what has been called the "triple shift" for women who work outside the home: their paying job; the housework; and the nurturing of family members, young and—increasingly with the graying of the population[9]—the elderly. We could add a fourth dimension to the lives of women: that of their community.[10] Organizational initiatives that help workers integrate all these dimensions have become critically important in light of this nation's workforce demographics: increasingly female, with 85% having daily family responsibilities, less than 7% of U.S. families fitting the "traditional" mold of husband as sole wage earner and wife and children at home, and the number of single working parents having jumped nearly 50% in the last two decades (U.S. Census Bureau, as cited in Maryland Work-Life Alliance PowerPoint, n.d.).

Excellent public relations departments and effective organizations develop mechanisms for helping women gain the power they need to advance from the technician to the manager role and to implement their understanding of two-way symmetrical public relations (L. Grunig, J. Grunig, & Dozier, 2002). They also work toward the kind of flexibility that allows employees, men and women alike, to achieve their personal as well as professional goals. The *integrative* phase of feminist theory I propose would acknowledge the holistic nature of workers' lives—their commitments not only to the employer and to the profession but to their partners, their children, their parents (and their partners' parents), and to their neighbors. Ideally, they might even have time for themselves.[11] Further, integration worthy of inclusion in this sixth phase would go beyond the minimum of government regulation such as the U.S. Family and Medical Leave Act.

For example, we on the Excellence team exploring effective practices in public relations (L. Grunig, J. Grunig, & Dozier, 2002) developed 22 such "discretionary" items. We measured policies and programs related to sex discrimination and harassment, pay equity, parental leave, leadership opportunities, mentoring and other advancement programs, organizational climate, multiple employment centers for maximum flexibility, and perks (such as all-male clubs or executive dining rooms) that divide employees based on their gender or tenure. We hypothesized that organizations taking positive steps to affect women's careers would produce a culture conducive to excellent public relations practice. This guiding hypothesis was supported. Effective organizations did indeed allow for flex time, established successful programs to handle problems of discrimination and harassment, paid equal salaries for comparable work, and (to a lesser extent) provided child-care services.

Thus, research fitting in the sixth, new phase would include studies that, first, show understanding of the issues—either the business rationale for family-friendly and flexible policies or the moral responsibility of treating employees as worthwhile individuals rather than merely means to an organizational goal (or both). Studies may focus on the existence of policies, programs, or practices that fit both the practitioners' needs and those of the company. They would explore workplace culture, understanding that participatory—rather than authoritarian—culture is conducive to the most-excellent public relations practice as well as to individual satisfaction on the job and at home. They also would document the outcomes and outflow of programs that help public relations practitioners integrate all aspects of their lives.

Of course, integration of work and family and community life is not a guarantee of balance. It means more than entitlements; and it extends beyond human resources to organization-wide cooperation. As Kathy Burke (2002, pers. comm., Nov. 18), work–life consultant to Hewlett-Packard and professional effectiveness coach, put it, "Work/life *is* a framework—a set of policies, programs, management philosophy, services and practices—that provides employees and managers with what they need to be fully engaged and produce great results . . . without sacrificing their health or family." It does not just pay lip service to the notion of employees with lives outside the organization; it encourages them to achieve their goals at home and in the neighborhood as well as on the job.

Types of research I would expect to include in the integrative phase include culture or organizational audits, employee needs surveys, and targeted-issue focus groups. These cultural assessments are all categories of employer best-practices, part of the Maryland Work-Life Alliances' (MWLA) "Workplace Excellence" Seal of Approval program.[12] They deal not only with the organizational context for excellent public relations practice but with the following family-oriented policies: support for elder care and child care (including backup, emergency help), parental leave, adoption assistance, resource and referral services, pretax dependent care spending accounts, after-school programs, summer camp, lactation services, planning and support for milestone life events (such as birth, death, marriage, or illness of a loved one), scholarships for dependents, bring-your-kids-to-work day, and health–insurance subsidies for domestic partners.

Flexible work arrangements and time off are central to helping women integrate their multifaceted lives. Such arrangements include flextime, telecommuting, job sharing, compressed work schedules, part-time employment, sabbaticals, leave sharing and leave pools, phased retirement, post-retirement job placement, summer hours, and emergency leave. *Learning and development* also are pivotal. Such programs include mentoring, tuition reimbursement, career counseling, a policy of internal job posting, safety and emergency preparedness, and a flexible schedule for education. A third category of programs and policies designed to help employees integrate their family and professional lives deals with *fitness and mental wellness*: health insurance, CPR and first-aid training, Employee Assistance Programs (free outside counseling on issues related to all aspects of life), transportation subsidies, sports and fitness programs, stress-management programs, wellness workshops, on-site health screening and health fairs, support groups, smoking-cessation programs, programs on domestic and workplace violence, ergonomic work stations, casual dress policies, on-site or telephone concierge services, personal financial planning, personal loans, personal travel-planning, subsidized cafeterias, and referral programs that reward employees for recruiting newcomers to the workforce. Finally, integrative practices include opportunities for *civic involvement*: philanthropic support, time off for volunteerism, youth employment, school-to-work initiatives, public–private partnerships, and matching of employees' contributions.[13]

Together these programs help create an environment at work that supports the Holy Grail of balance between the job and the rest of one's life. A study by Work in America, abstracted by *pr reporter* ("Work in the Balance," 2001), called this approach a "dual agenda strategy" that boosts performance while improving employees' lives. Without attention to integration in organizations, employees are likely to seek meaning in their lives—and make their best contributions—elsewhere. *With* such attention, according to Pagani-Tousignant (2003), reputation capital increases. She found that a people-friendly environment helps create a sense of "best place to work," higher-than-average stock returns, better operating performance, and higher return on average assets.

Methodological Approach to the Initial Study

Data for my initial research (1995, 2000) came from the U.S. literature of public relations published between 1976[14] and 1995. I concentrated my analysis on the two scholarly journals of the field, *Public Relations Review* and the *Journal of Public Relations Research* (formerly the *Public Relations Research Annual* and, before that, *Public Relations Research and Education*).

I excluded the professional or trade press because although such publications may report on research, they typically encapsulate the data for their non-academic readers. Likewise, I did not analyze the treatment of gender in public relations textbooks because at best these sources typically report on previously published research.

Also absent from my phase analysis was research published as chapters in books because no comprehensive list of such books could be imagined. I further omitted conference papers, which may present cutting-edge research in public relations but for which no comprehensive data-base exists.[15] Because no books on women in public relations had been published, none could be included in the initial analysis.

Because a feminist phase analysis of any one of the publications that *was* included in this (1995, 2000) study would represent a major undertaking, my overview was meant to be suggestive rather than definitive. A second important caveat was that the very notion of "phases" suggests a systematic development in gender-based research that analysis of the publications may not support. However, we know that little programmatic study actually takes place in public relations, as in the wider scope of communication research. Research in communication has been characterized as "particularly unsystematic" (Lowery & DeFleur, 1995, p. 5). Instead, scholars may become interested in and then—as quickly—lose interest in a topic. Or, external demand may lead to funding for research in an area whose relevance then declines for the funding agency. This may have characterized the "glass ceiling" project (Wright et al., 1991) sponsored by the Public Relations Society of America. PRSA committed itself to a longitudinal study, begun in 1989 but stalled when funding was withheld at the four-year point. Fortunately, the interest of the researchers on the project prevailed and PRSA's Research Foundation (rather than the Society itself) assumed responsibility for financing the second stage in late 1994. Still other findings may result almost serendipitously from what Lowery and DeFleur (1995) called "byproducts of ongoing and continuously funded research programs originally designed for other purposes" (p. 4). Such is the case with the gender dimensions found to be central in the roles research of Broom and Dozier (1985).

These reasons help explain the lack of systematic progression in *most* research in public relations, not just gender-based studies. However, I believe early studies such as the delineation of technician's and manager's roles or the Velvet Ghetto compendium (Cline et al., 1986) funded by the Foundation of the International Association of Business Communicators *have* influenced later initiatives. Thus the phases of this feminist analysis may reflect at least in part an accumulation of concern for and knowledge about women's experiences in public relations. The work of scholars such as Cline, Broom and Dozier, and Toth undoubtedly provided a starting point for feminist scholars such as Hon (1992) and Jones (1991) who came later.

I "coded" the data,[16] considering date, authorship, topic, and length (as a potential indicator of significance). I often determined "male scholarship" by the absence of consideration of gender issues where I thought such attention was warranted. (As I pointed out in 2000, this added to the complexity of the analysis, of course, because it meant analyzing what was not there.) Most important, of course, was treatment of the topic that would place it in one or more of the five phases. I relied on my own understanding of Tetreault's (1985) classification system in this, the only feminist phase analysis of the literature of public relations to that point.

In 2000, I described my subjectivity in this way:

> My determination of which phase a study fits into was inherently subjective but born of a solid quarter-century of study, teaching and research in the field. I did remain aware of the partiality resulting from my having written or edited much of the research reviewed here. I also acknowledged that as a white American woman, my gender helps explain why I consider this feminist analysis so important. At the same time, I granted that through my nescience of other races and cultures, I may inadvertently have distorted or even omitted issues of equal concern to other ethnicities.
>
> *(pp. 95–96)*

Adding to this complexity was my understanding that, as Twombly (1993) had done, I could place texts reviewed into more than one category.[17] In most cases the primary focus of the article easily determined its placement. Still, the occasional overlap in categorization may indicate a very real state of transition that characterizes postmodern scholarship in public relations.

Finally, classifying the literature according to its place in one of the five feminist phases cannot explain why each article belongs there. Explaining the absence of feminist scholarship, in particular, remains problematic. A dearth of research about women in public relations cannot be equated with lack of interest in their experiences or concern for their prospects. Just as Allen (1995) traced the reasons for *race*-neutral research in organizational communication, so must we consider alternative explanations for the initial, gender-neutral or "male scholarship" phase in public relations. Allen listed such impediments as journal editors and doctoral advisers who consider this kind of non-mainstream research a "ghetto," lack of funding from the corporate world, concern about reinforcing stereotypes or prejudices, unwillingness to become a spokesperson for the racial-ethnic group, and other worries about one's academic or professional reputation. Disclaimers aside, can I "prove" that I had interpreted each article correctly, placing it in the same category as, say, Tetreault (1985) would have? No. My only pledge was to make a strong case that could be argued for.

Results of the Initial Study

The most comprehensive report of results of my phase analysis can be found in L. Grunig (1995).[18] Like Twombly (1993), I reported on findings by phase. Although this approach to data analysis may suffer from a false assumption of linearity, it does exploit the value of phase theory as a conceptual framework.

Summary of Analysis of Public Relations Review (1976–1995)

I assessed 531 articles from the *PRR* in the twenty-year period under review. The first mention of women came in 1979, the fourth year of publication. That compensatory scholarship was followed by fewer than two dozen articles that mentioned gender issues. Of these, most were bifocal, comparing women and men primarily in terms of the roles they played. One fit the feminist phase and two, the multifocal. The remaining half-dozen of the 23 articles mentioning women or gender concerns combined the different phases.

Over time, there was a shift from the totally compensatory toward feminist and multifocal research. However, male scholarship remained the norm—to an extent that astonished even me as a regular reader of the *Public Relations Review*. The move from compensatory through bifocal and on to at least some feminist and multifocal research shows development in the depth of our understanding of feminism and public relations, if not linearity in the research of this field.

Survey research alone seems inadequate for understanding the problems women may face and the advantages they may bring to their work. When gender was included as a demographic variable in survey research published in the *PRR*, it often was tossed in with little explanation of how or why it should make a difference. Combined methodologies were rare in public relations research of any type, gendered or gender-neutral. Most—but not nearly all—feminist research was conducted by women or by women and men together. Many of the (few) studies that went beyond the early phases were based on graduate student research.

Despite the preponderance of male scholarship, then, readers at least would understand the following:

- Women have been active in public relations since we began to study its history. They have played a part, as wives of famous men and also, in their own right, as social activists, publicists, and corporate communicators. They study and practice public relations in countries throughout the world.
- Despite this involvement, women are disadvantaged by their gender, much as minorities are by their race. They also are subjugated by public relations role—which is gender-biased as well. As a result, women are paid less than men and enjoy fewer opportunities to advance and thus to affect their organizations at the highest levels of decision-making. Understandably, they express less satisfaction with their work.
- Public relations has become a female-intensive field. Within the last fifteen years, women have come to represent the majority in both the classroom and in the office. Public relations cannot be considered "female dominated," however, because women typically lack the autonomy, power, and influence of men in the field.
- Women tend to fulfill different roles than do their male colleagues, although women's relegation to the technician's role seems to be diminishing over time. They may play a role reserved for the female gender, that of "glamour" public relations. "Lookism" appeared as early as the first mention of women in an article published in *PRR* and as recently as the decade of the 1990s.
- Women express more value than do men for research in public relations; they do more research of all kinds; and at least two scholars writing in the *Review* suggested that environmental scanning, in particular, may be women's ticket from the technical to the managerial role. Women also may practice public relations more ethically.
- Other supposedly inherent differences between men and women were not supported by much of the research reviewed here. Thus these studies, taken together, debunk a number of gender-based myths and explode an equal number of sexist stereotypes. Any real differences seem to result from social-ization rather than biology.
- Women's activity and acceptance in public relations are determined in part by industry. Non-profits, government, and travel/tourism seem especially receptive to the new female majority.
- Over time, the language used in the literature of public relations has become gender-inclusive. So, too, has the language of annual reports and other organizational publications. The depiction of women in company art seems to remain more sexist, although this has been studied very little.
- Systems theory, one prevailing paradigm for the field, denies women's contri-butions from a feminist perspective. The addition of concepts of dissymmetry,

which acknowledges the value of differences, and the infrasystem, which explains organizational norms, could add value to this paradigm.

- Early research on women, with the best of intentions, typically suggested ways in which women could change to become more competitive at work. However, at least some scholars have determined that these "blaming the victim" remedies devalued women. They were also unrealistic. Even women who were willing to relocate, who put job before family (or at least on a par with personal relationships), who dressed for success, and who were ambitious and skilled in public relations failed to advance at a rate equal to men's. The literature reviewed in *PRR* reveals a growing realization that society and its institutions need to change every bit as much as do women. In particular, feminist scholars have called for a transformation of culture so that women alone are not forced to choose between family responsibilities and high-powered careers.

Summary of Analyses of Public Relations Research Annual *(1989–1991) and* Journal of Public Relations Research *(1992–1995)*

I examined 7 reviews and 24 research reports from the *Public Relations Research Annual*. In 1992, the *Annual* became the quarterly *Journal of Public Relations Research*. Of the total of 75 articles published in the 6½ years since the *Journal* began as the *Annual* and my analysis in 1995, there was a predominance of male scholarship. Little research focused on women. Gender issues were ignored even when such issues should have been relevant (as in studies of power, the dominant coalition, culture, roles, job satisfaction, and professionalism).

More of this research is qualitative than research typically published in the *Review*. Qualitative study, or a combination of methods, lends itself to feminist research. Of the nine major studies about women in the *JPRR* before 1996, only one was even somewhat compensatory. It combined elements of "adding women" with comparisons between women and men and feminist theorizing as well. Feminist phase research was obvious in six of the articles; only one was truly multifocal. Insights from the *Annual* and the *Journal* about gender issues that add to the literature already reviewed in the *PRR* include the following:

- Women, unlike men, tend to play the dual role of manager and technician—doing it all, and still for less pay and with less satisfaction. However, the roles research has been advanced considerably. We have been helped to understand, for example, that dichotomizing between the craft and counseling aspects of this field may devalue the people who choose this work or trivialize the work itself. The roles hierarchy, and the assumption that women are subjugated in the technician's role rather than choosing it, both deny women's established agency in public relations. Further, old patterns of role and salary discrimination seem to be decaying. At the same time, a new and distinctly feminine role has been described empirically: that of corporate conscience.

- A new and powerful explanation of the problems women encounter has been proposed. Marginalization of the function, rather than overt sexism, keeps women out of positions in which they can contribute most to their organizations and to society.
- For this and other reasons (such as engaging in less scientific program research than men do), women tend to be excluded from the dominant coalition.
- Dominant culture and the subcultures that coexist within organizations also have been shown to influence women's agency in public relations.
- The most extensive set of recommendations to date for transforming society (and, by association, the work lives of women in public relations) has been proposed. Transformative strategies include affirmative action, political involvement, re-negotiating gender roles at home, and education.

The single article most central to this feminist phase analysis is Hon's (1995) development of a feminist theory of public relations. Her depiction of combined methodology[19] alone warrants a close reading of this text. She delineated major obstacles for overcoming the discrimination her participants had faced; she also proposed solutions, from a radical feminist perspective, for dealing with them.[20] In fact, her work qualifies as postfeminist in the sense that she took care to acknowledge the differences within her group of women (rather than contrasting any differences between women and men). It approaches the multifocal phase by suggesting societal transformation and placing women's issues in this larger context: "Discrimination against women in public relations cannot be separated from the organizational and societal systems that produce gender biases" (p. 65).

Other Sources to Analyze

Analyzing the two major scholarly journals in the field tells only part of the story of how women have been conceptualized in our body of knowledge. Future work, in my view, also should explore major grant projects that deal with gender and public relations. Three massive studies—the *Velvet Ghetto* (Cline et al., 1986), *Beyond the Velvet Ghetto* (Toth & Cline, 1989), and the *Glass Ceiling* (beginning with Wright et al., 1991)—have established the value of (1) combined qualitative and quantitative methodology; (2) teamwork on the part of researchers; (3) support from the industry as well as the academy; and (4) establishing benchmarks in such areas as women's numbers, salaries, roles, and job satisfaction. We know from my initial phase analysis (L. Grunig, 1995, 2000) that merely comparing women and men on these dimensions may not fully explore or explain how women experience public relations.

A cursory look at this comparative or bifocal approach, even when framed in feminist theory, exposes its inadequacy for understanding the numbers and ratios and for proposing the requisite social agenda we can see in the work of less-established scholars: the graduate students whose research we also need to analyze. I propose as a future direction for feminist phase analysis in public relations a review of doctoral dissertations and master's theses that are framed by feminism. A brief assessment of six master's theses (Wetherell, 1989; Humphrey, 1990; Jones, 1991; Doonan, 1993; Pien, 1994; Kucera, 1994) and a doctoral dissertation (Hon, 1992) completed at the University of Maryland in the same years as the journal articles I analyzed is, of course, too narrow to generalize to the larger population of graduate students. It does suggest, however, that at least some female students are concerned about the situation women face in public relations and they are determined to both understand and overcome the problems their research exposes. In each case, they went beyond male scholarship and beyond compensatory scholarship. Some comparison between men and women in the field may be necessary for understanding any uniqueness about women's experiences. Only one study (Wetherell, 1989) was bifocal; all of the others focussed on women alone. However, because each study cited the one before, we can see a pattern of incorporating relevant theorizing and data and then going beyond the previous work to break new ground—whether methodological, theoretical, or empirical (or all three). The pattern, then, does suggest a growing sophistication in scholars' depth of understanding of sexism—its roots, its effects, its implications, and the most promising and ethically acceptable solutions for overcoming gender-based oppression.

We also need to study the works of public relations pioneers such as Edward L. Bernays that refer to (or ignore) women in the field. In this last way, in particular, we may recapture much of the history of our field. Finally, a comprehensive phase analysis would include any books written about women or gender issues in public relations.

Discussion

Analyzing the treatment of women in the scholarly literature of public relations reveals only a part of the status of women. At the same time, it does offer important indicators of the degree of receptivity to full participation in such critical aspects of the field as managerial decision-making. The data indicate some progress in our thinking and writing about women in public relations. Complicating this feminist phase analysis is the understanding that assessing any real progress requires the following computation. We must consider any increases in women's valuation in light of any decrease of their presence in the field, through entrepreneurship or dropping out. Taken together, then, the studies analyzed here only have begun to reconstruct our understanding of public relations by bringing gender fully into the center of our body of knowledge.

If the literature I reviewed had remained constant at the male scholarship phase, or even the compensatory of Tetreault's (1985) phases, I would have to conclude that that reflected lack of improvement in the status of women in public relations. Instead, undeniable strides have been made through incredible energy expended both individually and in team research.

Surprisingly, I found little compensatory scholarship. Although we have counts and amounts of women and their salaries, we remain in the dark about their earliest contributions to and agency in the profession. More inclusive biographical or autobiographical accounts would add considerably to our historical body of knowledge. So, too, would the inclusion of women globally, as more and more post-totalitarian societies begin to practice sophisticated models of public relations.

The most common phase I found, bifocal, may be warranted even though it risks stereotyping women and devaluing them when compared with their male colleagues. This kind of neat compartmentalization can be misleading. Not all women are technicians; not all women do more (or less) research than do men. However, studies that continue to compare salaries, in particular, seem justified since women's wages still lag behind men's. More important, financial self-sufficiency is a prerequisite for autonomy and personal fulfillment.

Encouragingly, I also found a gradual move (albeit it inconsistently) toward the feminist phase. At the feminist phase, women are not ignored nor mentioned in a token way or even measured against a male norm. Instead, the entire profession becomes elevated as the women within it are empowered, rather than undermined. The mid-1980s represented a major turning point away from neglect or tokenism and toward substantive research about and for women. We may date these efforts from 1985, when the field's awakening interest in women's issues led to studies, often using qualitative or combined methodology, that showed women to be richly productive.

This feminist research also showed female practitioners to be doing more with less. The politicized concept of agency that helped frame my analysis does not deny women's ability to combine their caring nature (largely a product of sex-role socialization) with their managerial responsibilities. This is precisely what analysis of the literature established. Women in public relations succeed in marrying agency with communion. In fact, by any measure but their wages and job titles, women often "do it all" by blending their roles as counselor to senior management, conscience of the corporation, expert technician, and nurturer of the family.

Teasing out the interrelationships among these roles and between women and men in public relations remains for the multifocal phase. What little scholarship of this nature I found came primarily from graduate students. Many, but not all, of them are women. Like suffragist Elizabeth Cady Stanton, speaking to the International Council of Women in 1888, I feel "a peculiar tenderness for the young women on whose shoulders we are about to leave our burdens" (as cited in Schneir, 1972). My own academic burdens are lightening as I have retired. Former graduate students have become professors, mentoring a new generation of ambitious woman and men. These young scholars have an advantage. They have the legacy of our published research. They will find the readers of contemporary journals more enlightened about women's issues than were we, much less *our* faculty advisers. Thus they will not be "mere echoes of men," as Stanton said of women in her generation.

This retrospective—reconstituting women's role in public relations—is not meant to discomfort or discredit those who wrote and practiced a generation ago. Rather, it should energize those who look to the future. It conceives of difference in a new way, challenging male–female binary opposition. For women, it means setting aside their former way of reading the already-written with a double consciousness—both as women and as the masculine reader they have learned to be.[21] Most important, this analysis has established structural theory as a more powerful explanation than individual behaviors of women for women's circumstances in public relations.

The time has come to rethink fundamentally in our minds and in a substantial body of both scholarly and professional literature what the influx of women means to public relations practice and education. I hope my (1995, 2000) analysis provides insight into whether the state of female practitioners is likely to improve or worsen. We know that the growing number of women in public relations, largely reported in compensatory scholarship, may conceal the fact that there are few in senior positions. But trends are not destiny.

Adding to the significance of this study is our understanding that what works to enhance the careers of women also may help people of color, gays and lesbians, older workers, those with physical disabilities, or any other nontraditional practitioners of public relations. Thus this research may be valuable to people everywhere who want a better understanding of how women and others associated with disadvantaged groups work and how their bosses, organizations and societies work against them.

In fact, the study of women in public relations provides a superb model of women in the workplace as a whole. Not only does it encompass a field entered by an increasingly large number of nontraditional workers, it is a field in which every conceivable abuse is manifest. Public relations is, in essence, a microcosm of the workplace—an experiment for the protection of women's sense of self and their incorporation into the public sphere. That experiment even may include the so-called reverse discrimination, to help ensure equality of attainment as well as opportunity.

Achieving political or social solutions is extraordinarily difficult. Suggesting the range of possible remedies is, again, beyond the scope of this chapter—for many reasons. For instance, even when the goals for incorporating women into the public relations workforce are agreed on, the emphasis or the means to reach them may differ. Also, the "guilty party" is not always a faceless government or corporation. It can be each of us.

"Blaming the victim," endemic in seemingly well-intentioned public relations research of the compensatory or bifocal phases, is not so innocent as it may seem. More than a hundred years ago, white abolitionist and supporter of women's rights

William Lloyd Garrison mounted an intriguing argument in his extemporaneous speech delivered at the Seneca Falls convention. He spoke of "intelligent wickedness, a design on the part of those who have the light to quench it, and to do the wrong to gratify their own propensities, and to further their own interests" (as quoted in Schneir, 1972, p. 87). Garrison believed that this tendency toward male monopolization (which I consider consistent with male scholarship) was fueled by pride and a desire for domination that makes men degrade women to make them "mere vassals." He concluded:

> Never can it be said that the victims are as much to be blamed as the victimizer; that the slaves are to be as much blamed as the slaveholders and slave-drivers; that the women who have no rights, are to be as much blamed as the men who have played the part of robbers and tyrants. We must deal with conscience.
>
> *(as quoted in Schneir, 1972, p. 88)*

My optimism is tempered both by faltering economies and lines drawn in the sand on several sides of the issue of feminist research. My hope is that any adversarial feelings will be replaced by cooperation and coalition-building—among the few characteristics consistently associated with women and feminine people in our literature. If that happens, I see the possibility of reconciling women's growing demands for equitable treatment with the needs of any organization in the postmodern era.

I acknowledge that even the best, most inclusive scientific research will not by itself save women's careers. Political and organizational leadership is required as well. Feminist and multifocal scholarship has suggested the necessity of a widespread sense of stewardship and clear vision of just what an egalitarian work life for women in public relations would look like. Through this analysis, we learned how professional groups such as PRSA and IABC, alarmed by the trend toward feminization of the field, commissioned major projects to study the status of women. Such joint commitments that could encompass professional societies, political groups, individual organizations, and their employees hold the greatest hope for changing the pattern of women's work life in public relations.

By adding a sixth phase to Tetreault's (1985) theory, we acknowledge that the burden falls on women to keep the home fires burning while they pursue their professional and academic goals. Doing research on the organizational context for excellence in public relations provides the opportunity to focus on positive change for the field. This kind of research will become increasingly critical as women crash through the glass ceiling and are promoted to positions beyond the technician's role, positions of greater and greater responsibility. As women ascend to the managerial and executive levels, they may find it increasingly difficult to integrate their work, personal, and community lives. We need research that recognizes and supports the whole person, the entire range of their responsibilities and life roles.

We need research today for the workplace of tomorrow, a workplace firmly situated in the knowledge-based economy and increasingly staffed by women in public relations. Public relations is all about relationships; we need to study new systems for the employer–employee relationship in this postmodern era.

Notes

1 For other approaches to feminist phase theory, see McIntosh (1983), Schuster and Van Dyne (1985), and Warren (1989).

2 For example, Lerner, 1990; McIntosh, 1983; Schuster and Van Dyne, 1985; Tetreault, 1985; Twombly, 1993; Warren, 1989.

3 Creedon (1991) did analyze a single important theoretical strain within the larger body of knowledge of the field. She found what she called a "suggestion" of gender bias in the roles research of Broom and Dozier, when contrasted with roles research undertaken by feminist scholars such as Piekos and Einsiedel (1989) and Ferguson (1987). The difference was that the former developed what she considered a ranking role structure and the latter, a linking role structure.

4 The proportion of female *students* is far greater than a simple majority. As early as 1990, Becker (1990) reported that about 80% of the public relations students in the approximately 200 U.S. universities offering communication majors were women.

5 A parallel example can be found in writing about homosexuality. Miller's (1995) survey of the last 125 years of gay and lesbian history established 1869 as the year the word "homosexual" was created and adopted by sexologists. This represented an effort to replace moral and religious attitudes condemning same-sex relationships with a more scientific and medical perspective. However, this new way of perceiving homosexuality still set it apart from the rest of society—discrediting those who lived gay or lesbian lives.

6 For a brief historical look at how U.S. researchers have explored differences between women and men, see Bem (1994).

7 For just a glimpse of the depth of research along these lines, see Bakan (1966), Jacklin and Maccoby (1975), Deaux (1976), S. Cox (1976), Bernard (1976), Spence and Helmreich (1980), Benderly (1987), and Wetherell (1989).

8 For solid discussions of the concept of "voice," see K. Foss and S. Foss (1989) and Wood and R. Cox (1993).

9 According to U.S. Bureau of Labor Statistics (as cited in Maryland Work-Life Alliance PowerPoint, n.d.), workers aged 45 to 64 represent the fastest-growing segment of the country's labor force.

10 Ivins (2002) and other politicians might add a fifth dimension: women's *political* lives. This despite Finch (1901), whom Ivins quoted as saying, "Women's participation in political life would involve the domestic calamity of a deserted home and the loss of the womanly qualities for which refined men adore women and marry them" (p. A25).

11 I am reminded of the children's book *The Giving Tree* (Silverstein, 1964), in which the mother ends up as nothing more than a stump for her son.

12 The Alliance is a coalition of public, private, and nonprofit organizations that educates employers about the importance of creating healthy environments that promote work–life balance.

13 These employer best-practices come for the MWLA "Workplace Excellence" program. See the website at www.worklifealliance.org.

14 I chose to begin this analysis with 1976 because that was the year I began my graduate education in public relations. Thus I am particularly familiar with the literature from that point forward.

15 During the 1980s, the *Public Relations Review* abstracted papers delivered at conferences of societies such as the International Communication Association and the Association

for Education in Journalism and Mass Communication. These brief research reports were included in my analysis, so in a sense the content of many convention papers was reflected there. Also, during the 1980s, the *PRR* published extended abstracts of many conference papers. These research-in-briefs were included in my analysis.

16 Twombly (1993) termed her feminist phase research on the literature of community colleges a "content analysis." My own study (and I would argue hers, as well) did not fit the traditional description of content analysis. Instead, I consider my research more of a "content inventory," along the lines of Broom et al. (1989).

17 If gender concerns were only marginal in a study, I did not attempt to categorize it in *any* of Tetreault's (1985) phases.

18 Portions of the analysis and discussion in this chapter developed from that paper.

19 Hon (1995) conducted 37 long interviews with female practitioners and three focus groups with several of these women to arrive at an understanding of how women experience the field. To be sure she was capturing the essence of their remarks, she sent a preliminary synthesis of results to six of the participants for their review and confirmation.

20 Solutions went well beyond women themselves or "blaming the victim" to transformation of society. This empowering aspect of the research; its combined methodology that gives participants voice and does not privilege the insights of the researcher over the researched; its valuation of the feminine; and, especially, the centrality of women's experiences place this article clearly in the feminist phase.

21 For more on feminism and double consciousness, a term more generally understood to characterize race relations, see Fetterley (1978).

Acknowledgments

This chapter appeared as a paper submitted to the *Journal of Public Relations Research*, August 2005. It was published in vol. 18, no. 3, of the *JPRR* in 2006 (pp. 115–140).

References

Allen, B. J. (1995). "Diversity" and organizational communication. *Journal of Applied Communication Research, 23,* 143–155.

Bakan, D. (1966). *Isolation and communion in western man: The duality of human existence.* Boston: Beacon Press.

Becker, L. B. (1990). Enrollments increase in 1989, but graduation rates drop. *Journalism Educator, 45*(3), 4–15.

Bem, S. L. (1994, 17 August). In a male-centered world, female differences are transformed into female disadvantages. *Chronicle of Higher Education,* pp. B1–B3.

Benderly, B. L. (1987). *The myth of two minds: What gender means and doesn't mean.* New York: Doubleday.

Bernard, J. (1976). Sex differences: An overview. In A. G. Kaplan & J. P. Bean (Eds.), *Beyond sex-role stereotypes: Readings toward a psychology of androgyny* (pp. 10–26). Boston: Little, Brown.

Broom, G. M. (1982). A comparison of sex roles in public relations. *Public Relations Review, 8*(3), 17–22.

Broom, G. M., & Dozier, D. M. (1985, August). Determinants and consequences of public relations roles. Paper presented to the Public Relations Division, Association for Education in Journalism and Mass Communication, Memphis, TN.

Broom, G. M., Cox, M. S., Krueger, E. A., & Liebler, C. M. (1989). The gap between professional and research agendas in public relations journals. *Public Relations Research Annual 1*, 141–154.

Bryant, G. (1984). *The working woman report: Succeeding in business in the 80's*. New York: Simon & Schuster.

Camden, C., & Witt, J. (1983). Manager communicative style and productivity: A study of female and male managers. *International Journal of Women's Studies, 6*(3), 258–269.

Caplan, P. J. (1985). Introduction to special issue on sex roles and sex differences and androgyny. *International Journal of Women's Studies, 8*(5), 437–440.

Carlson, R. (1985). Masculine/feminine: A personalogical perspective. *Journal of Personality, 53*(2), 384–399.

Cline, C. G., Toth, E. L., Turk, J. V., Walters, L. M., Johnson, N., & Smith, H. (1986). *The velvet ghetto: The impact of the increasing percentage of women in public relations and business communication*. San Francisco: IABC Foundation.

Cox, S. (1976). *Female psychology: The emerging self*. Chicago: Science Research Associates.

Cox, T. (1990). Problems with research by organizational scholars on issues of race and ethnicity. *The Journal of Applied Behavioral Science, 26*, 5–23.

Creedon, P. J. (1991). Public relations and "women's work": Toward a feminist analysis of public relations roles. *Public Relations Research Annual, 3*, 67–84.

Deaux, K. (1976). *The behavior of men and women*. Monterrey, CA: Brooks/Cole.

Dervin, B. (1987). The potential contribution of feminist scholarship to the field of communication. *Journal of Communication, 37*(4), 107–119.

Doonan, A. L. (1993). The role and status of women in higher education fund raising. Unpublished master's thesis, University of Maryland, College Park.

Dozier, D. M. (1987, May). Gender, environmental scanning, and participation in management decision-making. Paper presented to the Public Relations Interest Group, International Communication Association, Montreal.

Ferguson, M. A. (1987, May). Utility of roles research to corporate communications: Power, leadership and decision making. Paper presented to the International Communication Association, Montreal.

Fetterley, J. (1978). *The resisting reader: A feminist approach to American fiction*. Bloomington: Indiana University Press.

Foss, K. A., & Foss, S. K. (1989). Incorporating the feminist perspective in communication scholarship: A research commentary. In K. Carter & C. Spitzack (Eds.), *Doing research on women's communication: Perspectives on theory and method* (pp. 65–91). Norwood, NJ: Ablex.

Frieze, I. H., Parsons, J., Johnson, P. B., Ruble, D. N., & Zellman, G. L. (1978). *Women and sex roles*. New York: W.W. Norton.

Gould, S. J. (1981). *The mismeasure of man*. New York: W.W. Norton.

Gregg, N. (1987). Reflections on the feminist critique of objectivity. *Journal of Communication Inquiry, 1*(1), 8–18.

Grunig, L. A. (1986, October). Global analysis: Toward a general systems theory of public relations. Paper presented to the Sixth International Conference on Culture and Communication, Philadelphia.

Grunig, L. A. (1988). A research agenda for women in public relations. *Public Relations Review, 14*(3), 48–57.

Grunig, L. A. (1994, July). Requisite variety in public relations research. Paper presented to the International Public Relations Research Symposium, Bled, Slovenia.

Grunig, L. A. (1995, July). A feminist phase analysis of women in postmodern public relations. Paper presented to the International Public Relations Research Symposium, Bled, Slovenia.

Grunig, L. A. (2000). A feminist phase analysis of research on women in postmodern public relations. In D. Moss, D. Verčič, & G. Warnaby (Eds.), *Perspectives on public relations research* (pp. 89–120). London: Routledge.

Grunig, L. A., Grunig, J. E., & Dozier, D. M. (2002). *Excellent public relations and effective organizations: A study of communication management in three countries.* Mahwah, NJ: Lawrence Erlbaum Associates.

Harding, S. (1986). *The science question in feminism.* Ithaca, NY: Cornell University Press.

Hare-Mustin, R. T., & Maracek, J. (1988). The meaning of difference: Gender theory, postmodernism, and psychology. *American Psychologist, 43*(6), 455–464.

Herndon, S. L., & Kreps, G. L. (1993). *Qualitative research: Applications in organizational communication.* Cresskill, NJ: Hampton Press.

Hon, L. C. (1992). Toward a feminist theory of public relations. Unpublished doctoral dissertation, University of Maryland, College Park.

Hon, L. C. (1995). Toward a feminist theory of public relations. *Journal of Public Relations Research, 7*(1), 27–88.

Humphrey, K. S. (1990). Entrepreneurial women in public relations: Why open collars? Unpublished master's thesis, University of Maryland, College Park.

Ivins, M. (2002, May 11). Women's choice. *The Washington Post,* p. A25.

Jacklin, C. N., & Maccoby, E. E. (1975). Sex differences and their implications for management. In F. E. Gordon & M. H. Strober (Eds.), *Bringing women into management* (pp. 23–38). New York: McGraw-Hill.

Johnson, F. L. (1984). Positions for knowing about gender differences in social relationships. *Women's Studies in Communication, 7,* 77–82.

Jones, C. A. (1991). Obstacles to integrating scholarship on women into public relations education: Strategies for curriculum transformation. Unpublished master's thesis, University of Maryland, College Park.

Keller, E. F. (1985). *Reflections on gender and science.* New Haven, CT: Yale University Press.

Kucera, M. (1994). Doing it all: Why women public relations managers tend to fulfill both the managerial and technical roles. Unpublished master's thesis, University of Maryland, College Park.

Lerner, G. (1990). To think ourselves free. Review of *Transforming knowledge* by E. Minnich, *Women's Review of Books, 3,* 10–11.

Lowery, S. A., & DeFleur, M. L. (1995). *Milestones in mass communication research: Media effects* (3rd ed.). White Plains, NY: Longman.

McIntosh, P. (1983). Interactive phases of curricular re-vision: A feminist perspective. Working Paper Series No. 124. Wellesley, MA: Wellesley College Center for Research on Women.

Miller, N. (1995). *Out of the past: Gay and lesbian history from 1869 to the present.* New York: Vintage.

Minnich, E. K. (1990). *Transforming knowledge.* Philadelphia, PA: Temple University Press.

Moses, Y. T. (1989). *Black women in academe: Issues and strategies.* Project on the Status and Education of Women, Association of American Colleges, Washington, DC.

Nieves-Squires, S. (1991). *Hispanic women: Making their presence on campus less tenuous.* Project on the Status and Education of Women, Association of American Colleges, Washington, DC.

Nkomo, S. M. (1992). The emperor has no clothes: Rewriting "race in organizations." *Academy of Management Journal, 17,* 487–513.

Pagani-Tousignant, C. (2003, October). Building credibility, confidence and respect: The business rationale for work–life balance. Presentation to the Public Relations Society of American Annual Conference, New Orleans.

Pearce, W. B., & Freeman, S. (1988). On being sufficiently radical in gender research. *Women's Studies in Communication, 7*(3), 65–68.

Piekos, J. M., & Einsiedel, E. F. (1989, August). Gender and decision-making among Canadian public relations practitioners. Paper presented to the Association for Education in Journalism and Mass Communication, Washington, DC.

Pien, M. J. (1994). The use of coalitions in the practice of strategic public relations. Unpublished master's thesis, University of Maryland, College Park.

Rakow, L. F. (1986). Rethinking gender research in communication. *Journal of Communication, 36*(4), 11–26.

Rakow, L. F. (1987). Looking to the future: Five questions for gender research. *Women's Studies in Communication, 10,* 79–86.

Reskin, B. F. (1988). Bringing the men back in: Sex differentiation and the devaluation of women's work. *Gender & Society, 2*(1), 58–81.

Schneir, M. (1972). Declaration of sentiments and resolutions, Seneca Falls. In M. Schneir (Ed.), *Feminism: The essential historical writings* (pp. 76–82). New York: Vintage Books.

Schuster, M., & Van Dyne, S. (Eds.). (1985). *Women's place in the academy: Transforming the liberal arts curriculum.* Totowa, NJ: Rowman & Allanheld.

Silverstein, S. (1964). *The giving tree.* New York: Harper.

Spence, J. T., & Helmreich, R. L. (1980). Masculine instrumentality and feminine expressiveness: Their relationships with separate role attitudes and behaviors. *Psychology of Women Quarterly, 5*(2), 147–163.

Spitzack, C., & Carter, K. (1987). Women in communication studies: A typology for revision. *The Quarterly Journal of Speech, 73,* 401–423.

Tetreault, M. K. (1985). Feminist phase theory: An experience-derived evaluation model. *Journal of Higher Education, 56*(4), 363–384.

Tong, R. (1989). *Feminist thought: A comprehensive introduction.* Boulder, CO: Westview.

Toth, E. L. (1988). Making peace with gender issues in public relations. *Public Relations Review, 14*(3), 36–47.

Toth, E. L., & Cline, C. G. (Eds.). (1989). *Beyond the velvet ghetto.* San Francisco: IABC Research Foundation.

Twombly, S. B. (1993). What we know about women in community colleges: An examination of the literature using feminist phase theory. *Journal of Higher Education, 64*(2), 186–210.

Warren, K. (1989). Rewriting the future: The feminist challenge to malestream curriculum. *Feminist Teacher, 4,* 46–52.

Wetherell, B. L. (1989). The effect of gender, masculinity, and femininity on the practice of and preference for the models of public relations. Unpublished master's thesis, University of Maryland, College Park.

Wood, J. T., & Cox, R. (1993). Rethinking critical voice: Materiality and situated knowledges. *Western Journal of Communication, 57,* 278–287.

Work in the balance: Involving employees in development of work/life strategies brings benefits all around. (2001, April 23). *pr reporter*, p. 3.

Wright, D. K., Grunig, L. A., Springston, J. K., & Toth, E. L. (1991). *Under the glass ceiling: An analysis of gender issues in American public relations, 14*(2). New York: Foundation for Public Relations Research.

3

THE RELATIONSHIP BETWEEN PUBLIC RELATIONS AND MARKETING IN EXCELLENT ORGANIZATIONS

Evidence from the IABC Study

James E. Grunig and Larissa A. Grunig

Abstract

Our basic premise is that organizations are best served by the inherent diversity of perspectives provided by separate public relations and marketing functions. Theory developed in the IABC Excellence Project shows that public relations makes an organization more effective when it identifies strategic constituencies in the environment and then develops communication programs to build long-term, trusting relationships with them. Participation in strategic management provides the integrating link for public relations to enhance organizational effectiveness. To provide its unique contribution, however, public relations must be separate from other management functions. However, communication programs should be integrated or coordinated by a public relations department; and that department should have a matrix arrangement with other departments it serves. Therefore, we advocate integrated marketing communication of advertising and marketing public relations. We add that an IMC program should be coordinated through the broader public relations function. Data are presented from the Excellence Study confirming that public relations is most excellent when it is strategic and when marketing does not dominate public relations. However, public relations was equally excellent when housed in a single department or in specialized communication departments. Beyond structure, we add that marketing communication theories, if applied by an integrated department, differ in important ways from public relations theory and that discussion and research are needed to resolve these differences and to integrate the theories into a broader communication theory.

Key Words

Excellent public relations, integrated communication, integrated marketing communication, public relations and strategic management, structure of public relations and marketing departments

Introduction

The role of public relations in management and its value to an organization have been debated for at least 100 years. The debate has centered on the question of whether the role of public relations is to support marketing or whether it serves a broader social and political function. Tedlow (1979) studied the history of corporate public relations from 1900 to 1950 and concluded that the public relations function survived during that half century because it fulfilled the broader function:

> Public relations has promised two benefits to business: increased sales and protection from unpopularity which could lead to detrimental governmental or regulatory agency activity . . . It is not as a sales device, however, but as a method for protection against the political consequences of a hostile public opinion that corporate public relations has been most influential. If it had been restricted to sales promotion, public relations might have been absorbed by advertising departments and could have been dismissed as a footnote to business history. Instead, it grew into a tool for dealing with many publics, including residents of plant communities, employees, suppliers and dealers, and politicians as well as customers.
>
> *(Tedlow, 1979, pp. 193, 196)*

The debate has continued, however, and has become intense in recent years as both scholars and practitioners have debated the relationship of public relations to the concepts of integrated marketing communication (IMC) and integrated communication (IC). White and Mazur (1995) captured this debate when they described three possible "futures" for public relations:

> There are a number of possible futures for public relations. In the first scenario, it becomes largely a technical practice, using communication techniques to support marketing activities and is involved in work on product and corporate branding, corporate reputation, market penetration and development.
>
> In the second, public relations will increasingly become a social practice, helping organizations fit into their social environments, and working on relationships between groups to help bring about social and economic development, and to help in completing social tasks.

These futures are not mutually exclusive. Public relations is a strategic and enabling practice. To progress, it will need to mark out its agenda, and to invest in a programme of research and development to do this.

(White and Mazur, 1995, p. 266)

Both Tedlow's two historical paths for public relations and White and Mazur's three future scenarios center on the relationship between public relations and marketing: Is one a subset of the other, does one serve the other, or do the two provide different but equally important contributions to an effective organization? In this article, we address both the theoretical and empirical literature about this relationship. In doing so, we conclude with the overarching premise that *the organization is best served by the inherent diversity of perspectives provided by marketing and public relations when those functions remain distinct, coordinated yet not integrated.* To develop this premise, we begin with theoretical discussions of structural relationships between public relations and marketing.

Structural Relationships of Public Relations and Marketing

Kotler and Mindak (1978) were among the first to address the relationship between public relations and marketing when they outlined five alternative arrangements: (1) separate but equal functions (marketing and public relations have different functions, perspectives, and capabilities); (2) equal but overlapping functions (both are important and separate functions but they share some terrain, especially product publicity and customer relations; in addition, public relations serves as a "watchdog" on the social responsibility of marketing); (3) marketing as the dominant function (marketing manages the relationship with all publics in the same way as the relationship with customers—"megamarketing"); (4) public relations as the dominant function (if public relations builds relationships with all key publics of the organization, then programs to build relationships with customers—i.e., marketing—would be a subset of public relations); and (5) marketing and public relations as the same function (public relations and marketing converge in concepts and methodologies, and a single department manages the external affairs of the company).

Hallahan (1992) modified Kotler and Mindak's typology to include six arrangements:

(1) celibate (only one of the functions exists); (2) coexistent (the two functions operate independently); (3) combative (the two functions are at odds); (4) cooptive (one function usurps the other); (5) coordinated (the two functions are independent but work closely together); or (6) combined (the two functions operate within a single unit).

Public relations scholars and professionals have expressed fear of arrangements in which marketing dominates public relations or when the two are combined into a single unit—arrangements that Lauzen (1991, 1992) has called "marketing imperialism" and "encroachment" on public relations territory. Marketing professionals presumably would feel the same about public relations departments taking over the marketing function. In a book on hospital public relations, for example, Lewton (1991) described the problems of either a dominant or combined structure:

> Obviously, when the issue is one of merging both functions, and either public relations being "under marketing," or marketing being "under public relations," some concerns are inevitable, just as there would be concerns if a hospital were going to have the human resources department report to finance, or medical staff relations report to the legal department. In a public relations–marketing merger, the PR professionals wonder why their discipline is seen as a subset of marketing (which it isn't), and wonder what marketing number-crunchers know about media and stakeholder relations. They're concerned that other noncustomer audiences will be ignored. If marketing is placed under public relations, marketers wonder how a PR vice-president can make decisions on pricing or set up an effective sales rep program. They're concerned that their customers—who are their universe—will get lost in the midst of "all those audiences."
>
> *(Lewton, 1991, p. 51)*

In contrast to the frequent discussion in the theoretical literature about subservient relationships between public relations and marketing, Hunter (1997) found in a representative sample of 75 of the 300 largest U.S. corporations that public relations and marketing most commonly are separate but equal management partners. Of these corporations, 81% had separate public relations and marketing departments. In two-thirds of the cases the two departments were on the same level; and when one was above the other, public relations was as likely to be above marketing as below.

About a third of the public relations departments reported directly to the CEO and a third to a vice-president of corporate communication. The other third reported to other vice-presidents or lower managers. Few public relations departments reported to or were integrated into a marketing department in these companies. As might be expected, Hunter (1997) also found that marketing is more likely to be dominant in consumer product companies, for whom the consumer stakeholder is most important. Public relations, however, dominated in utilities, which are regulated and for which government and other stakeholders are crucial.

Hunter (1997) followed up his survey with qualitative interviews with public relations executives in six companies. In contrast to discussions in the literature of conflict between public relations and marketing, he found that these executives described their relationships with marketing as positive. Marketing and public relations departments cooperated as equal partners who respected the contributions of the other.

The situation that Hunter (1997) found in the United States suggests that we should examine not whether public relations and marketing should be integrated or merged but how they work together most fruitfully in successful, well-managed organizations. That question was a major one that we addressed in a 10-year study of excellence in public relations and communication management.

Principles from the Excellence Study

Together with four colleagues, we began a major research project in 1985 with financial support from the IABC (International Association of Business Communicators) Research Foundation. The project addressed two major research questions: (1) What values does public relations/communication management have for an organization? and (2) How should the public relations function be organized to contribute most to organizational effectiveness? The answer to the first research question provided an overarching theoretical principle that explained why the principles for organizing the public relations function make an organization more effective. One of these key principles defined the relationship of public relations to strategic management. Two others defined the relationship of public relations to marketing and other management functions. (The theoretical principles were developed in J. Grunig [1992]; some results were presented in Dozier, L. Grunig, and J. Grunig [1995]; and complete results were presented in L. Grunig, J. Grunig, and Dozier [2002]).

The Value of Public Relations

The literature on organizational effectiveness indicates, first, that organizations are effective when they attain their goals (L. Grunig, J. Grunig, & Ehling, 1992). However, it also suggests that these goals must be appropriate for the organization's internal and external environment—which consists of strategic constituencies (stakeholders or publics). If an organization chooses appropriate goals, strategic constituencies will support the organization and, in doing so, provide it with a competitive advantage (Verčič & J. Grunig, 1995). If it chooses inappropriate goals, the constituencies will organize and constrain the ability of the organization to achieve its mission. To be effective, therefore, organizations must build long-term relationships with the publics in their environment that have consequences on organizational decisions or upon whom those decisions have consequences.

Organizations plan public relations programs strategically when they identify strategic publics and use communication programs to build stable, open, and trusting *relationships* with them. Thus, the quality of these relationships is an important indicator of the long-term contribution that public relations makes to organizational effectiveness.

Strategic Management as the Key to Excellent Public Relations

Participation in strategic management provides the integrating link that makes it possible for the public relations function to contribute to achieving the goals of an organization. Excellent public relations departments contribute to decisions made by the dominant coalition that runs an organization by providing information to those senior managers about strategic publics. Organizations use strategic management to define their missions and make "relatively consequential decisions" (Mintzberg, 1994, p. 27), but they do so through an iterative process of interacting with their environments. Most theories of strategic management do not suggest a formal mechanism in the organization for interacting with the institutional, social, and political component of the environment and do not acknowledge the presence of public relations (see, e.g., Ring, 1989). To a public relations scholar, however, public relations departments provide the obvious mechanism for organizations to interact with strategic constituencies that make up their social and political environments (for additional conceptualizations of public relations and strategic management, see J. Grunig & Repper [1992], Verčič & J. Grunig [1995], J. Grunig [1996], and J. Grunig [1997]).

When public relations is part of the organization's strategic management function, public relations departments are likely to manage communication programs strategically. The senior public relations manager helps to identify the stakeholders of the organization by participating in central strategic management. He or she then develops programs at the functional level of the public relations department to build long-term relationships with these strategic publics. In this way, public relations communicates with the publics that are most likely to constrain or enhance the effectiveness of the organization.

The role of public relations in strategic management is most clear if we take a postmodern view of strategic management as a subjective process in which the participants from different management disciplines (such as marketing, finance, law, human resources, or public relations) assert their disciplinary identities (Knights and Morgan, 1991; Knights, 1992). A rational approach to strategic management would suggest that participants come together to find the best solution to problems they agree on. The subjective view, however, suggests that participants in strategic management from different disciplines recognize different problems as important as well as different solutions. Marketing would see the problem of selling products as most important, manufacturing the problem of producing products, human resources the problem of motivating employees, and finance the problem of acquiring resources. The value of public relations, therefore, is that it brings a different set of problems and possible solutions into the strategic-management arena. In particular, it brings the problems of stakeholder publics into decision-making—publics that make up the environment of the organization.

Public Relations and Other Management Functions

Among the principles of excellent public relations that increase organizational effectiveness, the research team proposed that integrating all communication functions through the public relations department enhances the ability of the communication function to participate in strategic management. With such integration, public relations departments are arranged into horizontal structures that reflect the strategic publics or stakeholders of the organizations. The managers of these subfunctions—such as employee relations, marketing communication, investor relations, or community relations—have a matrix relationship with both the public relations department and the functional department they serve (see also Tierney, 1993, pp. 217–221).

However, the decision of which publics are most strategic at a particular time is made by the senior public relations officer in collaboration with the CEO and other members of the organization's dominant coalition; and resources are moved from program to program depending on which publics are most strategic in different situations. With such integration, marketing communication reports to public relations but serves marketing, employee communication reports to public relations but serves human resources, and so forth.

Four principles of public relations excellence specify the relationship of public relations to strategic management and to other management functions such as marketing:

1. The public relations function should be located in the organizational structure so that it has ready access to the key decision-makers of the organization—the dominant coalition—and so that it can contribute to the strategic management processes of the organization.
2. All communication programs should be integrated into or coordinated by the public relations department.
3. Public relations should not be subordinated to other departments such as marketing, human resources, or finance.
4. Public relations departments should be structured horizontally to reflect strategic publics and so that it is possible to reassign people and resources to new programs as new strategic publics emerge and other publics cease to be strategic.

Integrating Communication: IMC or IC

In the United States and throughout the world, there has been an intense debate over whether public relations, advertising, and sales promotion should be integrated into a program called "integrated marketing communication." IMC consists of integrating what Harris (1991) called "marketing public relations" with advertising. In Harris' terms, "corporate public relations" remains a separate function and is not placed under the marketing function. This concept of integrated marketing communication fits the definition of the American Association of Advertising Agencies (AAAA):

> A concept of marketing communications planning that recognizes the added value of a comprehensive plan that evaluates the strategic role of a variety of disciplines—general advertising, direct response, sales promotion, and public relations—and combines these disciplines to provide clarity, consistency and maximum communication impact.
>
> *(as quoted in Duncan and Caywood, 1996, p. 18)*

One can hardly deny the merits of integrating all marketing communication functions (see, e.g., Hunt & J. Grunig, 1994, Chapter 19). However, the view of public relations held by most adherents of IMC is extremely narrow, as has been documented by several studies (e.g., Canonico, 1994; Hunter, 1997; Tierney, 1993; Tillery, 1995). Most adherents of IMC see public relations as a technical support function and not as a management function, consider public relations to be press agentry or product publicity alone, and deal solely with customer publics. In addition, most interest in IMC seems to have come from advertising professionals and agencies (Hunter, 1997; Tierney, 1993); and most studies that have shown support for IMC from the profession have been studies of marketing managers and have been sponsored by advertising associations (see Duncan and Caywood, 1996, pp. 19–20).

To overcome the objections to IMC from public relations scholars and professionals, adherents of the concept began to use the term "integrated communication" (IC) in place of IMC (Duncan, Caywood, & Newsom, 1993; Newsom & Carroll, 1992). Dropping the "M" from "IMC" was intended to make the concept more palatable to public relations as well as advertising and marketing professionals by expanding the definition to include stakeholders other than consumers.

Duncan and Caywood (1996) proposed seven stages through which communication programs can be integrated: awareness, image integration, functional integration, coordinated integration, consumer-based integration, stakeholder-based integration, and relationship management integration. Their last two stages closely resemble the integration of communication through the public relations function that we have proposed in this chapter. Indeed, Duncan and Caywood stated that public relations will come to the fore in the last two stages of integration, while pointing out the first five stages emphasize marketing communication and customer relations only:

> Although the full role of public relations may have seemingly been limited in the first five stages to the promotional aspects of marketing public relations, the sixth stage demands a fully integrated corporate communications

function. Communication at the corporate stage of integration must include employees, the media, community leaders, investors, vendors, suppliers, competitors, government at all stages, and so on.

(Duncan and Caywood, 1996, pp. 21–31)

Gronstedt (1996) proposed a similar "stakeholder relations model" that included 11 stakeholder groups, only one of which is consumers, and described several "receiving tools," "interactive tools," and "sending tools" that come from the toolbags of public relations, marketing, and advertising. Nevertheless, Gronstedt placed consumers at the center of his stakeholder diagram in the belief that the consumer always is the most strategic stakeholder.

We disagree with that fundamental premise. One can make an equally good case that employees or investors are the most strategic public. In reality, however, different publics are more or less strategic for different kinds of organizations; and which public is most strategic changes as situations change. For example, investors may be most strategic during a takeover attempt; employees may be most strategic following downsizing; and donors generally will be most strategic for nonprofit organizations.

The integration of communication functions that we propose, therefore, incorporates these higher levels of integration proposed by IMC theorists. The major difference is that we do not propose moving integration upward through the marketing communication function. Rather we propose beginning at the highest level of integration and then pulling marketing communication and communication programs for other stakeholders into the public relations function. Drobis (1997–98), then the CEO of Ketchum Public Relations Worldwide, took the same position when he declared that "integrated marketing communication is dead":

> It died because we never could decide if it was a tool to help sell advertising and public relations agency services or if it was a true, complete communications discipline. As a result, the term "integrated marketing communications" was frequently abbreviated to "integrated communications" and came to stand for many things, but nothing in particular. Admittedly, integrated marketing communications as it was originally conceived seemed to stand for the blending of multiple forms of marketing communications. Still, given its potential for greatness, the discipline withered under the chronic stress of being misunderstood by public relations professionals, many of whom consider the role of public relations in "integrated marketing communications" too narrow. Let's just call its cause of death "unknown."
>
> *(Drobis, 1997–98, p. 6)*

Drobis went on to say that "integrated communication" must go beyond marketing to encompass employee and labor relations, investor relations, government affairs, crisis and risk management, community affairs, customer service and just about any other facet of management where effective communications is a critical success factor.

(p. 7)

He concluded:

Public relations practitioners are in the best position to manage the integrated communications process because, unlike other communications disciplines, they are involved in every facet of the organization. It is their job to listen and respond to the full range of important stakeholders.

(p. 9)

In summary, the theoretical discussions of and research on the relationship between marketing and public relations suggest that few public relations and marketing functions actually have been merged into single departments and that the two separate functions generally work well together. They work together well because public relations departments possess the environmental scanning and communication expertise needed by marketing and other management functions. The discussion of IMC and IC then suggests that all communication functions should be integrated into or coordinated by the public relations department—that is, IC.

In practice, communication professionals who provide marketing communication skills (both advertising and marketing public relations) have different technical expertise than do other specialized public relations people (Spicer, 1991). Therefore, marketing communication programs often are housed in separate departments from other public relations functions even though they practice IMC—usually in business units rather than at headquarters (Hunter, 1997, Chapter 10). We propose for strategic reasons, however, that marketing communication report to or at least be coordinated by a corporate-level public relations department.

The IABC Excellence Study provided evidence both on the strategic role of public relations and its relationship to marketing—evidence to which we now turn.

Research Evidence from the Excellence Study

The Excellence research project consisted of two empirical stages. In the first stage, the research team administered three questionnaires to the head of public relations, the CEO, and an average of 14 employees in 323 organizations in the United States, Canada, and the United Kingdom. These organizations were chosen to include corporations, government agencies, nonprofit organizations, and associations; large and small organizations; and some organizations believed to be excellent and some less than excellent.

The Excellence Theory consisted of relationships among variables from such subtheories as public relations roles, participation in strategic management, and models of communication. The subtheories were operationalized into some 1,700 questions on the three questionnaires. We used factor analysis to reduce these variables to a single index after first combining a number of indicators of variables into indices. We then correlated the overall index of Excellence with related variables, such as the relationship between public relations and marketing. Finally, we used the index to identify 24 organizations with the highest and lowest scores on the overall Excellence factor and conducted qualitative research on these organizations to gain insight into how excellent public relations came about in different organizations as well as detail on the outcomes produced by Excellence.

The Value of Public Relations

The major premise of the Excellence Theory stated that communication has value to an organization because it helps to build good long-term relationships with strategic publics, so measures of the value of public relations were perhaps the most important variables to be included in the Excellence factor. We measured the value of communication through the method of compensating variation (Ehling, 1992), by which we asked the CEO to estimate the value of public relations in comparison with other management functions and to estimate the rate of return to communication. We also asked the top communicator to make similar estimates and to predict the estimates that the members of senior management who made up the dominant coalition of decisions makers in the organization would make on the same variables.

Both the CEOs and top communicators estimated the return to public relations highly—186% and 197%, respectively. The heads of public relations underestimated the CEO's estimate, however: 131%. On the question that asked the CEOs and public relations heads to compare the value of the public relations department with the typical organizational department, respondents were told that 100 was the value of a typical department. CEOs provided a mean score of 159, heads of public relations a mean of 189. Again, the PR heads underestimated the value that the CEO would assign to the department: 138.

In the qualitative portion of the study, we asked CEOs to explain why they assigned the value they did to their public relations departments. Their explanations provided further evidence that our theory of the contribution of public relations to organizational effectiveness was accurate (L. Grunig, Dozier, & J. Grunig, 1994). The support came more in the form of their explanations of the value of public relations, however, than from estimates of monetary value. As we had theorized, CEOs and public relations managers said they believed that credible, positive relationships serve as a buffer between the organization and its key constituencies in times of conflict and crisis.

At least one top communicator was reluctant to link dollar figures to public relations efforts because of fear that the numbers would seem almost unbelievably high. When participants in the qualitative research did attempt to talk about the value of public relations in dollar amounts, the numbers actually were high. Some estimated that they had saved their organization millions of dollars in fending off lawsuits. One CEO acknowledged that his entire association had been saved by the successful handling of a crisis.

Contribution to Strategic Management

Our research about the value of public relations was most useful when we could correlate estimated values with the characteristics of excellent public relations, such as involvement in strategic management and the relationship between public relations and marketing. For strategic management, we asked CEOs and heads of public relations units to describe the extent to which public relations contributes to four strategic functions in their organizations: strategic planning, response to major social issues, major initiatives such as acquisitions or new products and programs, and routine operations such as employee communication or media relations.

For the overall sample, we found that public relations units most often contribute to routine operations and in response to major social issues. They are less likely to participate in major initiatives and, especially, in strategic planning. We also asked what public relations units do to contribute to strategic management when they are involved in the process. The responses showed that communication units that participate in strategic planning most often do so through informal approaches, contacts with influential people outside the organization, and judgment based on experience. The typical public relations department less often conducts research or uses other formal approaches to gathering information for strategic planning—an indication that many communication units are not qualified to make a full contribution to strategic planning. However, this picture changed dramatically when we looked at the departments that were most valued by their CEOs and that conform most to our criteria for excellence.

Strategic Management as Seen by CEOs

To develop a relatively simple picture of how CEOs view excellent public relations, we placed organizations into three categories based on responses to a questionnaire item that asked respondents to compare the value of public relations with the value of other management functions. Most (212) of the responses fell into the category between 100 and 200, which is labeled medium value in Table 3.1. Thirty-eight CEOs rated public relations in the low category (below 100), and 34 rated it in the high category (above 200).

Table 3.1 shows that participation of public relations in these strategic organizational functions significantly and strongly distinguished the levels of value CEOs assigned to public relations. Likewise, Table 3.1 shows that the CEOs of highly

TABLE 3.1 Comparison of Means for Contributions to Strategic Management by Public Relations Departments Valued Differently by CEOs

Variable	Low Value (n=38)	Medium Value (n=212)	High Value (n=34)	F
Contribution to organizational functions				
Strategic planning.	6.56	8.89	13.04	21.96★★
Response to major social issues.	8.78	11.95	14.27	22.57★★
Major initiatives.	8.24	10.90	14.20	30.06★★
Routine operations.	10.09	12.71	15.17	26.98★★
Contribution to strategic management (if any)				
Regular research activities.	5.05	8.29	11.07	15.86★★
Research for specific questions.	6.76	9.56	11.88	15.74★★
Other formal approaches.	6.11	9.12	11.72	18.22★★
Informal approaches.	7.74	10.54	14.21	33.18★★
Contacts with knowledgeable people outside organization.	8.88	11.32	15.55	32.52★★
Judgment based on experience.	8.89	11.38	14.45	19.37★★
Other variables				
Percentage return on public relations.	126%	178%	265%	9.36★★ 14.83★★[1]

Notes:
★ $p < .05$.
★★ $p < .01$.

[1] Calculated after scores were transformed to a square root to reduce skew.

Except for the percentages, the means in this table came from an open-end, "fractionation scale." With this scale, respondents provided a score from zero to as high as they wanted to go. They also were told that 100 is a typical response on all of the items in the questionnaire as a reference point. To reduce skew, a square-root transformation was performed. Thus, in this table a mean of 10—the square root of 100—represents this reference point.

valued departments assigned a return on investment in public relations about twice as high as for the weakly valued departments.

Factor Analysis and Canonical Correlation of Characteristics of Public Relations and Value of Communication

The first column of Table 3.2 shows the results of the factor analysis that identified 20 key characteristics of excellent public relations departments and the organizational context that were measured in the questionnaires completed by CEOs, heads of public relations, and employees. A reliability analysis verified that all of these characteristics made up a single index of Excellence in public relations (Cronbach's alpha was .85).

In this chapter, we have conceptualized only the strategic management variables in Table 3.2. Detailed conceptualizations of the other variables can be found in J. Grunig (1992) and Dozier, L. Grunig, and J. Grunig (1995). All of these variables are included in Table 3.2, however, so that the contribution of strategic management to the perceived value of public relations can be compared with the other public relations variables.

TABLE 3.2 Factor Analysis to Produce Index of Excellence and Canonical Correlation of Variables Measuring Value of Public Relations with Other Excellence Variables

Variable	Factor Score	Canonical Variate Score
Characteristics of public relations and organization (Variable group 1)		
CEO variables		
PR in strategic planning.	.28	.64
Importance of communication with external groups.	.34	.47
Preference for two-way asymmetrical model.	.39	.51
Preference for two-way symmetrical model.	.33	.42
Preference for managerial role.	.36	.58
Preference for senior adviser role.	.35	.56
Public relations head variables		
PR in strategic planning.	.56	.64
Estimate of preference for the two-way asymmetrical model by the dominant coalition	.48	.34
Estimate of preference for the two-way symmetrical model by the dominant coalition.	.55	.44
PR head in manager role.	.56	.38
PR head in senior adviser role.	.49	.26
Knowledge of two-way asymmetrical model.	.64	.43
Knowledge of two-way symmetrical model.	.67	.39
Knowledge of managerial role.	.72	.45
Estimate of support for women in organization.	.50	.43
Participative organizational culture.	.24	.11
Value of public relations (Variable group 2)		
CEO variables		
Support for PR by dominant coalition.	.41	.37
Value of PR department.	.32	.38
Public relations head variables		
Perceived support for PR by dominant coalition.	.57	.41
Estimated value dominant coalition would assign to PR.	.57	.23
Canonical correlation		**.70

Notes:
* $p < .05$.
** $p < .01$.

After constructing this scale of Excellence, we used canonical correlation to separate the characteristics of public relations from the values assigned to public relations and to show the strength of the relationship between the two sets of variables. Canonical correlation works much like factor analysis, but the technique makes it possible to determine if two groups of variables correlate with each other simultaneously—in this case, Excellence of public relations and value of public relations. Canonical correlation produces "canonical variates" that are much like factors except that the variates separate the blocks of variables and the procedure computes an overall canonical correlation between the blocks. The correlations of each variable with the underlying variate also indicate the strength of the relationship of each variable with the underlying variate.

The second column of Table 3.2 shows that canonical correlation essentially reproduced the Excellence factor. All but one of the variables have high correlations with the underlying variate: Participative organizational culture has a positive but low correlation. The canonical correlation between the two sets of variables is high, supporting the theoretical soundness of the Excellence Theory. In addition, the second column of Table 3.2 shows that involvement of public relations in strategic planning and the CEOs' preference that the senior public relations person be a manager or senior adviser increased the perceived value of public relations most. As we theorized, CEOs estimated higher values for public relations when it fulfills a strategic managerial role.

Relative Support for Public Relations and Marketing

In the questionnaire completed by the senior public relations officer, a series of three questions asked whether the organization had separate communication units for "marketing-related public relations" and another for "public affairs"—essentially the distinction that Harris (1991) and others have made between "marketing public relations" and "corporate public relations." A second question asked which unit had the larger budget. We then asked, "Regardless of whether you have separate units, which function—public affairs or marketing-related public relations—receives more support from senior administrators—the dominant coalition?"

This third question was most useful in analyzing the relationship between the support for marketing and public affairs communication programs and overall public relations Excellence. Table 3.3 shows the mean score for the overall index of Excellence and each Excellence variable when support for marketing communication was higher, when support for public affairs was higher, and when the support was "approximately equal." On the overall index, Excellence was below average when marketing received greater support, average when public affairs received greater support, and above average when the two received approximately equal support. The differences were statistically significant.

Table 3.3 shows essentially the same pattern for most of the individual Excellence variables, although some of the differences were not significant. In some

TABLE 3.3 Comparison of Means on 20 Excellence Variables and Overall Index of Excellence by PR Heads' Perceived Support for Public Relations and Marketing by Dominant Coalition

	Support is greater for			
	Marketing (n = 75)	PR (n = 104)	Equal (n = 137)	F
	(Z scores)			
Characteristics of public relations and organization				
CEO variables				
PR in strategic planning.	−.16	.03	.14	2.49★
Importance of communication with external groups.	−.19	.12	.09	2.54★
Preference for two-way asymmetrical model.	−.29	.05	.21	6.62★★★
Preference for two-way symmetrical model.	−.32	.13	.11	4.68★★★
Preference for managerial role.	.01	.09	.07	0.14
Preference for senior adviser role.	−.15	.16	.09	2.18
Public relations head variables				
PR in strategic planning.	−.17	−.07	.13	2.89★★
Estimate of preference for the two-way asymmetrical model by the dominant coalition.	−.05	−.05	.08	0.44
Estimate of preference for the two-way symmetrical model by the dominant coalition.	−.17	.00	.11	2.31★
PR head in manager role.	−.11	−.02	.09	1.13
PR head in senior adviser role.	−.10	−.03	.04	0.51
Knowledge of two-way asymmetrical model.	−.15	−.04	.07	1.28
Knowledge of two-way symmetrical model.	−.15	.02	.04	1.12
Knowledge of managerial role.	−.06	−.09	.02	0.33
Estimate of support for women in organization.	−.31	.11	.05	5.47★★★
Participative organizational culture.	.25	−.11	−.04	3.76★★
Value of public relations				
CEO variables				
Support for PR by dominant coalition.	−.19	.21	.00	3.63★★
Value of PR department.	−.15	.19	−.03	2.27★
Public relations head variables				
Perceived support for PR by dominant coalition.	−.31	.08	.07	4.98★★★
Estimated value dominant coalition would assign to PR.	−.12	.06	−.04	0.78
Overall Excellence Index	−.22	.05	.12	3.62★★

Notes:
★*p* < .10.
★★*p* < .05.
★★★*p* < .01.

cases, though, the mean for the variables was highest either when public affairs received greater support or when the support was even. Almost always, the mean was lower when marketing communication received greater support. The most important lack of difference in means indicated that public relations was about equally likely to perform a managerial or senior adviser role with all three levels of support, and CEOs were equally likely to prefer such a managerial role. Levels of knowledge to perform a two-way symmetrical or asymmetrical model of public relations and the managerial role also were not significantly different.

However, CEOs valued and supported public relations significantly less when marketing communication received greater support and when the PR head estimated less support from the dominant coalition. Most importantly, CEOs were significantly less likely to see public relations as a strategic management function and as a two-way function when marketing communication received greater support from the dominant coalition. The same was true when the top com- municator said he or she participated in strategic planning and when he or she estimated that the dominant coalition would prefer the two-way symmetrical model. Interestingly, the PR heads estimated that women received significantly less support in organizations where marketing communication dominated. In contrast to the pattern of Table 3.3, however, organizations that emphasized marketing communication over public affairs were most likely to have participative organizational cultures, in contrast to authoritarian cultures.

Overall, then, Table 3.3 supports that idea that public relations is most likely to be excellent when marketing communication does not dominate the communi- cation function. Public relations has its greatest value when that function and the marketing function are treated as equal partners in management.

Organization of the Communication Function

The initial Excellence Theory specified that organizations should integrate or coordinate their communication activities through a central public relations func- tion rather than having independent units for such communication programs as marketing communication, employee communication, investor relations, or media relations—either as stand-alone units or units that are subordinated to other functions such as marketing, human resources, or finance. Independent units challenge strategic public relations because it is difficult to shift resources from one set of stakeholder publics to another when those publics become more or less strategic to organizational interests.

Some of the organizations we studied had a single public relations department, some had one or more specialized departments, and some had public relations programs administered by non-public relations departments. The latter were most likely to be programs for consumers (marketing), employees (human resources), or investors (finance). However, even these latter programs were relatively rare.

Most public relations functions were organized either through a central public relations department or one or more specialized departments (see Table 3.4).

Table 3.4 compares the means on the overall index of Excellence for these three departmental arrangements. Excellence was slightly above average for centralized departments, about average for specialized departments, and below average for programs in non-PR departments. The differences were not significant, however. Although Table 3.4 shows that the non-PR departments have the lowest maximum and minimum scores, the standard deviations for all three groups are close to the standard deviation of 1.0 that characterizes z-scores.

In short, the departmental arrangement seems to make little difference, although these organizations rarely subordinated public relations to other functions. Central public relations departments were no higher in Excellence than a series of specialized units, although our data could not show what if any coordination occurred among the specialized units. What seemed to matter most was the support given to a broad public relations function by the dominant coalition and the world view of the dominant coalition that public relations is a strategic management function rather than merely a supporting function for other units such as marketing.

Qualitative Results

When we followed up the quantitative survey and data analysis with long interviews of the heads of public relations and the CEOs of the most-excellent organizations in the sample, we found further evidence that public relations is valued most when it operates as a strategic management function, as a two-way symmetrical model, and as an equal partner with marketing and other management function.

When asked why they assigned high values to the contribution of public relations, CEOs of several of the top-ranked organizations said they especially valued the contributions of public relations in dealing with activist groups. One CEO, for example, explained his top communicator's influence within the organization as a result of his training all members of the management staff in what he, the CEO, called "symmetrical negotiations or communication." That training

TABLE 3.4 Comparison of Means on Overall Excellence by Type of Communication Department

Department type	Number	Mean	Standard Deviation (Z-Scores)	Minimum	Maximum
Central PR	146	.06	.86	−1.93	3.05
Specialized PR	149	.01	.93	−1.98	3.55
Non-PR	26	−.16	1.14	−2.40	2.79

Notes: F = 0.64, not significant.

has resulted in an approach to communication that the CEO considered "uniform" and described as "an open, discussed decision that we will engage in discussions no matter how frustrating, no matter how unnerving, no matter how ignorant they [the activist publics] are." He told us that although some other senior executives in his industry may not value this kind of sophisticated public relations, many do. Their understanding of two-way communication, in particular, has served them well. Through this and numerous other, equally compelling, interviews, we determined that two-way symmetrical public relations, touted in the scholarly literature as the normative approach to excellence, seems to be emerging in the actual practice of the field as well.

We also found evidence that public relations makes its greatest contribution when it is aligned with the strategic management of the organization. The vice-president of public affairs in one of the top-ranked companies explained the relationship between public affairs and strategic planning as follows:

> Most people perceive strategic planning over here at this end of the corporation and if you get through R&D, marketing and manufacturing and all these things somewhere at the other end, you have someone worrying about public affairs and public relations. My answer is that they have a linear view of a corporation. If you view a corporation as being a [cyclical] work process . . . then you take that linear view of the corporation and bend it around into a circle. Then it's funny, what comes together in the circle—strategic planning and public affairs.

This astute professional argued that everything in a company has to do with relations with the outside world. He also explained public affairs as more of a two-way than a transmittal process. Thus, in his opinion, "It's perfectly logical for the public relations function to be directly tied to the strategic function."

If public relations is to participate in the strategic planning process of the organization, then what must be its position relative to marketing? According to several of the executives we interviewed in both public relations and in top management *per se*, that relationship should be characterized as "peer professional." That is, public relations practitioners must be on a par (in terms of expertise, brains, respect, and salary) with their counterparts in marketing—as in law, science, lobbying, and so forth. At times, of course, the functions actually may operate in opposition.

One public relations manager in a gas and electric company we studied pointed out that although public relations and marketing do many similar things, marketing has an easier time demonstrating its impact. As a result, the potential for subjugation exists. So far, public relations in that utility has been able to maintain its critical role in the arena of customer service because utilities increasingly are adopting a demand-side philosophy. She called this "de-marketing," or trying to give customers what they want while pushing for energy conservation.

Our interviews of CEOs with excellent public relations departments showed that top management is better prepared to make informed decisions when it relies on the distinct perspectives of both marketing and public relations. The CEOs told us they value public relations most for the broad view of the environment—both internal and external—that it provides. We came to understand that the environment of any organization and even its inner workings truly are enacted. "Enacted" means that the organization or its surroundings will not be perceived as the same by different people in the same organization. So, top management's exposure to a *variety* of perceptions becomes critically important.

Thus public relations counsel is not the only wisdom CEOs hear—and rightly so. They listen, as well, to financial people, to legal staffs, and to marketing experts. To some of the people we interviewed, the advice coming from the communication department balances counsel emanating from other quarters. As one top communicator said: "You're going to find people in the organization—some of them at pretty senior levels—who are going to say, 'Don't talk; don't say a word. We might be sued or we're going to damage our market.'" He saw his role as countering that closed attitude. However, he reminded us that communicators must be at a level of responsibility and respect to guarantee that their opinion carries equal weight. And, sometimes that counsel is most credible when it emanates from an outside firm rather than a staffer. As one agency head described his value to a client:

> I believe he trusts my opinion and judgement; and he knows above all that I won't bullshit him, that I'll tell him what the truth is . . . I still maintain that the PR guy has got to bring to the table the outside perspective that is by definition lacking by those inside the organization. Otherwise, the outside perspective is not going to be at the table when decisions are made.

In a comment typical of the two dozen CEOs we interviewed at length, one top manager explained: "Those of us who think lawyer-like, those of us who think CEO-like, those of us who think technical-like don't always take the big picture. And that's what the public relations/communication expert's forte is: to take that big picture, to place it in the instant context, and to make sure that the system responds to what the real issues are."

This quote is a plain-language, real-world version of the more theoretical argument proposed by social psychologist Weick (1979). His notion of *requisite variety* holds that there must be as much diversity inside the organization as outside for the organization to build effective relationships with all of its strategic publics—both internal and external. More specifically, Weick maintained that what he called the "enactment pool" or the perspectives of those (such as public relations professionals or marketers) who do the enacting should be matched to the degree of variation present in the marketplace. Enacting the environment takes place at the boundary between the organization and the groups that matter to it—groups we call "strategic publics." Public relations professionals are boundary spanners. We assume the primary responsibility for defining, characterizing, and then responding to those stakeholders that have the potential to most help or hinder our organization.

From Structure to Theory: Different Approaches of Public Relations and Marketing

The Excellence Study, therefore, seems to provide compelling evidence in support of separate marketing and public relations functions and of integrating communication programs—not just marketing communication programs—through the public relations department or by coordinating a set of specialized public relations departments. One major hurdle remains, however, before communication programs can be fully integrated: Public relations theorists and marketing communication theorists—especially advertising scholars—conceptualize communication in very different ways. Many integrated communication programs, however, apply marketing communication theory rather than public relations theory to communication management and in ways that we believe do not result in effective communication.

Although we prefer our conceptual approach to that of an advertising or marketing approach, we recognize the value of different approaches and conceptual world views. Therefore, in concluding this chapter, we describe differences between the two types of theory that require discussion and debate to find the contributions that each approach can make to a comprehensive theory of public relations and to resolve conceptual differences between the approaches.

We identify, therefore, these characteristics of marketing communication theory that differ from our public relations approach:

1. *The recurring ideas that all publics can be treated as though they are consumers, that consumers are the only publics that matter, and that there is no difference between markets and publics.* Markets essentially consist of individuals making individual decisions. Publics are collectivities—groups—that try to change organizational behaviors and the societal or governmental structures that make up the social-political environment of organizations. Thus marketing strategies aimed at individuals, such as the social marketing campaign of the U. S. Partnership for a Drug Free America, have little effect when a problem such as drug use results from the structure of society (see Wallack et al., 1993). Likewise, marketing concepts are of little use in dealing with activist groups, which affected nearly every organization in the sample for the Excellence Study.

2. *A tendency to overgeneralize the importance of marketing or of communication,* with statements such as "everything is marketing and marketing is everything" or "all communication is marketing and all marketing is communication" (Schultz et al., 1993, p. 45). Philosophers of science say that if something is

everything, one cannot distinguish it from anything else and, therefore, it also is nothing. We believe there is more to marketing than communication and to communication than marketing.

3. *The application of the concept of exchange to all relationships.* Economic relationships, such as those important in marketing, usually may involve an exchange; but one needs to build social and personal relationships on the expectation that reciprocity may not occur. For example, Fisher and Brown (1988) proposed what we consider to be one better principle of relationship building: Be unconditionally constructive, even if the other side does not reciprocate. Huang (1997) also has developed a typology of relationships with publics that include such concepts as trust and mutuality of control.

4. *"Speaking with one voice" as an advantage touted for integrating the communication functions of the organization.* The concept also goes by the terms "orchestration," "consistent voice," and "seamless communication" (Duncan and Everett, 1993). Newsom and Carroll (1992) decried what they considered the "Tower of Babel" that results from people in public relations and marketing communicating with different voices. Moriarty (1993) called for a "synergy of persuasive messages." We question, however, whether these catchy phrases mean that dialogue, interaction, learning, and innovation—the essence of what we call two-way symmetrical communication—are to be discouraged. We believe all members of organizations should be encouraged to speak *and listen* to many members of publics and markets in many voices so that they get new ideas and innovate. The organization may gain an advantage in speaking with one voice, but it suffers the disadvantage of listening with one ear.

5. *Defining two-way communication as a response to a message rather than a reciprocal and continuous process of listening and dialogue* (e.g., Schultz et al., 1993, p. 123). In our strategic theory, public relations is an ongoing process built into the organizational structure in which the ideas of publics are brought into the decision-making processes of management and in which affecting the behavior of management is just as important as affecting the behavior of publics.

6. *Overemphasis on the behavior of publics and underemphasis on the behavior of management.* It is much easier to control one's own behavior than that of others. Thus, the purpose of public relations is to contribute to organizational decision-making so that the organization behaves in ways that publics are willing to support rather than in ways that publics oppose with their own behaviors.

7. *An emphasis on symbols and their effects on the cognitions and attitudes of publics rather than on the behavioral relationship of organizations and publics* (see, J. Grunig, 1993a, 1993b). Marketing communication concepts such as identity, image, brand, and reputation (e.g., Rebel, 1997; Van Riel, 1995) suggest that the right message can implant the corporate "identity" into the public's "image" and, by implication, that one can manage reputation by managing the

production and distribution of symbols. In our view, the reputation of a corporation consists of the behaviors of the corporation that publics recall cognitively. The value of a brand lies not just in the recognition of a name but in the trust people have in a company and its products. Thus, we believe the most effective way to manage a reputation or brand image is by using two-way symmetrical communication to help manage the organizational behaviors that produce a bad reputation and to develop a trusting relationship with both consumer markets and publics. To a great extent, these marketing concepts have been derived from personality theories whereas our concepts come from theories of participatory democracy. A Danish handbook on public relations explained the difference this way:

> Parallel with the fact that modern marketing sees the organisation as a personality, we see the business as a *citizen* with what that implies of duties (in the form of responsibility for and *adaptation* to the whole) and rights (in the form of a right to *argument* [sic] for and pursue one's objectives).
> *(Blach and Hojberg, 1989, cited in Biker and Hovgaard, 1994)*

Conclusion

We began with the premise that organizations are best served by the inherent diversity of perspectives provided by the marketing and public relations disciplines. The data presented from the IABC study have confirmed that premise: Public relations is most excellent when it exists as a separate strategic management function from marketing. We concluded, however, by pointing out that marketing *communication* theories when applied in an integrated communication department differ in important ways from our public relations theories. The discipline of communication management, like organizations, should benefit from the diversity of these perspectives. Much discussion and research are needed, however, to resolve the differences and integrate the most useful concepts from each perspective.

Acknowledgments

This chapter was originally published in the special issue of the *Journal of Marketing Communications*, 4(3) (1998), 141–162, "The Strategic Role of Corporate and Marketing Communications," Guest Editors, Danny Moss and Gary Warnaby, The Manchester Metropolitan University, Manchester, United Kingdom.

References

Biker, B. D., & Hovgaard, V. (1994). Rational relations: The rationality of organizations in a communication-theoretical perspective. *International Public Relations Review, 17*(1), 16–26.

Blach, T., & Højberg, J. (1989). *PR-Håndbog i information og public relations.* Copenhagen: Borgen.

Canonico, G. C. (1994). Integrated marketing communications: Its role in public relations education. Unpublished undergraduate honors thesis, Syracuse University, Syracuse, New York.

Dozier, D. M. with Grunig, L. A., & Grunig, J. E. (1995). *Manager's guide to excellence in public relations and communication management.* Mahwah, NJ: Lawrence Erlbaum Associates.

Drobis, D. R. (1997–98). Integrated marketing communications redefined. *Journal of Integrated Communications, 8,* 6–10.

Duncan, T., & Caywood, C. (1996). The concept, process, and evolution of integrated marketing communication. In E. Thorson, & J. Moore (Eds.), *Integrated communication: Synergy of persuasive voices* (pp. 13–34). Mahwah, NJ: Lawrence Erlbaum Associates,

Duncan, T., & Everett, S. (1993). Client perceptions of integrated marketing communications. *Journal of Advertising Research, 33*(3), 30–39.

Duncan, T., Caywood, C., & Newsom, D. (1993, December). Preparing advertising and public relations students for the communications industry in the 21st century. Report of the Task Force on Integrated Communications.

Ehling, W. P. (1992). Estimating the value of public relations and communication to an organization. In J. E. Grunig (Ed.), *Excellence in public relations and communication management* (pp. 617–638). Hillsdale, NJ: Lawrence Erlbaum Associates.

Fisher, R., & Brown, S. (1988). *Getting together: Building a relationship that gets to yes.* Boston: Houghton Mifflin.

Gronstedt, A. (1996). Integrating marketing communication and public relations: A stakeholder relations model. In E. Thorson, & J. Moore (Eds.), *Integrated communication: Synergy of persuasive voices* (pp. 287–304). Mahwah, NJ: Lawrence Erlbaum Associates.

Grunig, J. E. (Ed.). (1992). *Excellence in public relations and communication management.* Hillsdale, NJ: Lawrence Erlbaum Associates.

Grunig, J. E. (1993a). On the effects of marketing, media relations, and public relations: Images, agendas, and relationships. In W. Armbrecht, H. Avenarius, & U. Zabel (Eds.), *Image und PR* (pp. 263–295). Opladen, Germany: Westdeutscher Verlag.

Grunig, J. E. (1993b). Image and substance: From symbolic to behavioral relationships. *Public Relations Review, 91*(2), 121–139.

Grunig, J. E. (1996). Public relations in strategic management and strategic management of public relations: theory and evidence from the IABC Excellence Project. Paper presented to the Conference on Strategic Planning in Public Relations, Department of Communication, United Arab Emirates University, 17–18 December.

Grunig, J. E. (1997). Public relations management in government and business. In J. L. Garnett, & A. Kouzmin (Eds.), *Handbook of administrative communication* (pp. 241–283). New York: Marcel Dekker.

Grunig, J. E., & Repper, F. C. (1992). Strategic management, publics, and issues. In J. E. Grunig (Ed.), *Excellence in public relations and communication management* (pp. 117–158). Hillsdale, NJ: Lawrence Erlbaum Associates.

Grunig, L. A., Dozier, P. M., & Grunig, J. E. (1994) *IABC Excellence in public relations and communication management, Phase 2: Qualitative study, initial data analysis cases of excellence.* San Francisco: IABC Research Foundation.

Grunig, L. A., Grunig, J. E., & Dozier, D. M. (2002). *Excellent public relations and effective organizations: A study of communication management in three countries.* Mahwah, NJ: Lawrence Erlbaum Associates.

Grunig, L. A., Grunig, J. E., & Ehling W. P. (1992). What is an effective organization? In J. E. Grunig (Ed.), *Excellence in public relations and communication management* (pp. 65–90). Hillsdale, NJ: Lawrence Erlbaum Associates.

Hallahan, K. (1992, August). A typology of organizational relationships between public relations and marketing. Paper presented to the Association for Education in Journalism and Mass Communication, Montreal.

Harris, T. L. (1991). *The marketer's guide to public relations.* New York: Wiley.

Huang, Y. H. (1997). Public relations strategies, relational outcomes, and conflict management strategies. Unpublished doctoral dissertation, University of Maryland, College Park, MD.

Hunt, T., & Grunig, J. E. (1994). *Public relations techniques.* Fort Worth, TX: Harcourt Brace.

Hunter, T. (1997). The relationship of public relations and marketing against the background of integrated communications: A theoretical analysis and empirical study at US-American corporations. Unpublished master's thesis, University of Salzburg, Salzburg, Austria.

Knights, D. (1992). Changing spaces: The disruptive impact of a new epistemological location for the study of management. *Academy of Management Review, 17,* 514–536.

Knights, D., & Morgan, G. (1991). Corporate strategy, organizations, and subjectivity: A critique. *Organisation Studies, 12,* 251–273.

Kotler, P., & Mindak, W. (1978). Marketing and public relations: Should they be partners or rivals? *Journal of Marketing, 42*(10), 13–20.

Lauzen, M. M. (1991). Imperialism and encroachment in public relations. *Public Relations Review, 17*(3), 245–256.

Lauzen, M. M. (1992). Public relations roles, intraorganizational power, and encroachment. *Journal of Public Relations Research, 4,* 61–80.

Lewton, K. L. (1991). *Public relations in health care: A guide for professionals.* Chicago: American Hospital Publishing.

Mintzberg, H. (1994). *The rise and fall of strategic planning.* New York: Free Press.

Moriarty, S. E. (1993). The circle of synergy: Theoretical perspectives and an evolving IMC research agenda. In E. Thorson & J. Moore (Eds.), *Integrated communication: Synergy of persuasive voices* (pp. 333–354). Mahwah, NJ: Lawrence Erlbaum Associates.

Newsom, D. A., & Carroll, B. J. (1992, August). The Tower of Babel: A descriptive report on attitudes toward the idea of integrated communication programs. Paper presented to the Association for Education in Journalism and Mass Communication, Montreal.

Rebel, H. (1997). Towards a metaphorical theory of public relations. In D. Moss, T. MacManus, & D. Verčič (Eds.), *Public relations research: An international perspective* (pp. 199–224). London: International Thomson Business Press.

Ring, P. S. (1989). The environment and strategic management. In J. Rabin, G. J. Miller, & W. B. Hildreth (Eds.), *Handbook of strategic management* (pp. ix–xxi). New York: Marcel Dekker.

Schultz, D. E., Tannenbaum, S. I., & Lauterborn, R. E. (1993). *Integrated marketing communications.* Chicago: NTC Business Books.

Spicer, C. H. (1991). Communication functions performed by public relations and marketing practitioners. *Public Relations Review, 17*(3), 293–306.

Tedlow, R. S. (1979). *Keeping the corporate image: Public relations and business, 1900–1950.* Greenwich, CT: JAI Press.

Tierney, J. P. (1993). The role of public relations in integrated marketing communications: A preliminary study. Unpublished master's degree thesis, University of Maryland, College Park, MD.

Tillery, R. (1995, April). The organization of the public relations function: A literature review from 1991–1993. Paper presented to the Mid-Atlantic Graduate Communications Conference, University of Maryland, College Park, MD.

Van Riel, C. B. M. (1995). *Principles of corporate communication*. London: Prentice-Hall.

Verčič, D., & Grunig, J. E. (1995, July). The origins of public relations theory in economics and strategic management. Paper presented to the Second International Public Relations Research Symposium, Bled, Slovenia.

Wallack, L., Dorfman, L., Jernigan, D., & Themba, M. (1993). *Media advocacy and public health*. Newbury Park, CA: Sage.

Weick, K. E. (1979). *The social psychology of organizing* (2nd ed.). Reading, MA: Addison-Wesley.

White, J., & Mazur, L. (1995). *Strategic communications management: Making public relations work*. Wokingham: Addison-Wesley.

4

REFURNISHING THE GRUNIG EDIFICE

Strategic Public Relations Management, Strategic Communication and Organizational Leadership

Nigel M. de Bussy

Abstract

This chapter discusses the formidable challenge identified by James E. Grunig in 2006 of institutionalizing strategic public relations as a bridging rather than a buffering activity, so that strategic public relations management becomes standard in most organizations and most people think of public relations that way. The concept of strategic public relations management is contrasted with strategic communication, stakeholder management and corporate social responsibility. The chapter concludes that strategic public relations management (when properly understood) is the responsibility of organizational leaders at all levels and from a variety of disciplines – not just public relations specialists alone.

Key Words

bridging, buffering, organizational leadership, public relations, strategic communication, strategic public relations management

Introduction

James E. Grunig published a major retrospective paper entitled 'Furnishing the edifice: Ongoing research on public relations as a strategic management function' (Grunig, 2006). The article staunchly defended the Excellence Theory – the 'edifice' of the paper's title – against the attacks of critics (e.g., Curtin & Gaither, 2005; Holtzhausen & Voto, 2002). Grunig described the Excellence edifice as a general theory about the strategic management role of public relations (Grunig, 2006). Using this metaphorical representation, Grunig compared a theoretical framework with a plan for a new building. Every time the same plan is used, it can be improved upon and the building can be furnished in different ways. Grunig described how he and his collaborators have continually furnished the theoretical edifice of strategic public relations management over a 40-year period, by refining and extending the basic structure. New 'rooms' have been added steadily, i.e., concepts and tools that public relations professionals can use in their strategic management roles, and the work is ongoing (Grunig, 2006). Finally, Grunig (2006) identified what he saw as the next major challenge for researchers working in this tradition: how to institutionalize public relations as a bridging rather than a buffering activity, so that strategic public relations management becomes standard in most organizations and most people think of public relations that way.

This chapter reflects on the formidable challenge of institutionalizing strategic public relations management. In so doing, it draws on an earlier work of J. Grunig, his 1993 article 'Image and substance: From symbolic to behavioral relationships'. The chapter contends that the terms 'strategic public relations management' and 'strategic communication' are far from synonymous, and that confusion between the two concepts is one of the major barriers to meeting the challenge of institutionalization. In the spirit of proposing new furnishings for the basic edifice, this chapter takes a fresh approach to the 'dominant coalition' debate (Berger, 2005; Dozier, Grunig, & Grunig, 1995). Arguably the key to institutionalizing strategic public relations management (in the sense of the term referred to here) does *not* lie in the position of the top communicator or of the public relations department in the organizational hierarchy. Rather, the most important factor is the orientation of organizational leaders at all levels towards both 'strategic' and 'moral' stakeholders (Frooman, 1999), i.e., not only those who can affect the achievement of the organization's objectives (strategic stakeholders) but also those *affected by* the organization (moral stakeholders). Other authors refer to these two stakeholder categories as 'influencers' and 'claimants' respectively (e.g., Kaler, 2002; Mitchell, Agle, & Wood, 1997). This chapter will explore the somewhat paradoxical notion that public relations does not have a monopoly on 'strategic public relations management'.

The chapter proceeds as follows. First, the concept of strategic public relations management is explored. Next, the implications of the term 'strategic communication' are discussed; its meaning is contrasted with that of strategic public relations management. Then, parallels are drawn between the notions of strategic public relations management, stakeholder orientation and corporate social responsibility. This is followed by some observations on the barriers to the practice of strategic public relations management *by public relations specialists* at the top level of organizations. Finally, the case for understanding 'strategic public relations management' as a general attribute of best practice organizational leadership is developed.

The Nature of Strategic Public Relations Management

J. Grunig regards the development of the general theory of strategic public relations management associated with his name – the Excellence Theory – as serendipitous (Grunig, 2006). Four key elements which Grunig had been working on, in some cases since the 1960s – the situational theory of publics, organizational theory, the symmetrical model of public relations, and evaluation research – came together as a general theory during the course of the Excellence Project, a $400,000 research effort commissioned by the International Association of Business Communicators in 1985 (Grunig, 2006). Using the typology developed in the context of stakeholder theory (Donaldson & Preston, 1995), it can be seen that the Excellence Theory has instrumental, descriptive and normative aspects. It is instrumental because of the claim that if organizations practise the generic principles of excellent public relations, they will be more effective in achieving their overall goals. This is usually measured by Excellence scholars in terms of return on investment in strategic public relations management (Grunig, 2006). The Excellence Theory is descriptive because it claims to describe aspects of reality, i.e., the generic Excellence principles are statements about how at least some organizations actually behave. This proposition has been empirically supported by a number of scholars (e.g., Yun, 2006). Above all else, Excellence is a normative theory that makes claims about how public relations *should* be practised. It is a best practice rather than a best fit or contingency theory. Proponents of the Excellence Theory have specifically claimed it is applicable in diverse cultural settings (e.g., Lim, Goh, & Sriramesh, 2005; Rhee, 2002). However, this proposition has been strongly rejected by postmodern critics of the Excellence Theory (Bardhan, 2003; Holtzhausen, Petersen, & Tindall, 2003).

Grunig (2006) makes a clear distinction between evaluating public relations at the program level versus its contribution to overall organizational effectiveness. The Excellence Study was specifically designed to investigate the latter, i.e., the contribution of strategic public relations management to the achievement of organizational objectives. From the perspective of many practitioners or business school academics, this research question has almost 'taken-for-granted' legitimacy (Suchman, 1995). Postmodern and critical scholars, however, have a different worldview (Grunig & White, 1992), conceptualizing public relations in terms of organizational activism which resists dominant power, desires change and has an implicit political motivation (Holtzhausen & Voto, 2002; L'Etang, 2005). Such theorists urge 'postmodern' public relations practitioners to contest organizational objectives in preference to helping uncritically to achieve them. Grunig's riposte to this line of argument is that public relations cannot fulfil the organizational activist role unless it is empowered through possessing influence in the decision-making process (Grunig, 2006). Grunig's explanation of how strategic public relations management creates value for organizations is that it helps to satisfy stakeholder goals as well as those of the organization. If this is not done, it is likely stakeholders will oppose the organization in ways that add to the risks and costs of doing business (Grunig, 2006). Hence, strategic public relations management (in the sense of the term used in this discussion) should actively take stakeholder perspectives into account when formulating organizational objectives and policy. To the extent that this happens in practice, calls for organizational activism appear somewhat superfluous (Holtzhausen & Voto, 2002). In a similar vein, Steyn has explored the contribution of public relations to organizational strategy in a series of papers (e.g., Steyn, 2007; Steyn & Niemann, 2010). Steyn's major contribution is a focus on 'enterprise strategy': the broadest, overarching level of strategy which addresses the relationship of an organization with society. Steyn proposes that enterprise strategy (also known by a variety of other names including 'societal role strategy' and 'bridging strategy') is the most appropriate level for the strategic contribution of public relations (Steyn & Niemann, 2010).

Berger (2005), a critical theorist, raised a number of objections to the assumptions of the Excellence Theory about the role of public relations within the dominant coalition. In particular, he pointed out that dominant coalition decisions influenced by strategic public relations may subsequently be overturned or modified as a result of alternative power dynamics within the organization. Another possibility is that public relations professionals may simply succumb to the pressure for organizational compliance (Berger, 2005). Leaving aside the implicit assumptions of this critical narrative regarding the inherent malfeasance of corporate leaders, the debate raises another possibility. Rather than focus on the representation, power and behaviour of public relations specialists within the dominant coalition, the values of strategic public relations management could be internalized by other (often more powerful) organizational leaders. This scenario will be explored in greater depth later in the chapter.

Grunig (2006) makes his perspective on the values of strategic public relations management abundantly clear. The appropriate strategic imperative is to cultivate high-quality, long-term relationships with publics or stakeholders who are affected by organizational actions or make demands on the organization in relation to issues of importance to them. The term 'cultivation' is referred to by Grunig (2006) as the potential heir to the symmetrical model, the cause of so much angst in the public relations literature (e.g., Holtzhausen et al., 2003; McKie & Munshi, 2007). Grunig (2006) draws a sharp distinction between buffering and bridging activities. Regrettably, public relations is best known for the former. Buffering refers to the use of communication to insulate the organization from its stakeholders, in order to maintain the status quo. Bridging, in contrast, implies building linkages with stakeholders and a willingness to be genuinely responsive to their needs and expectations. The notion of bridging is equivalent to Grunig's theoretical edifice of public relations as a strategic management function (Grunig, 2006). The next section contrasts this conceptualization of strategic public relations management with the notion of strategic communication.

Strategic Communication: Its Uses and Abuses

In the inaugural issue of the *International Journal of Strategic Communication*, Hallahan, Holtzhausen, van Ruler, Verčič, and Sriramesh (2007, p. 3) defined strategic communication as 'the purposeful use of communication by an organization to fulfill its mission'. The authors elaborated on this basic definition by stating that strategic communication refers to self-presentation and promotion by organizations through the intentional activities of leaders, employees, and communication practitioners. Explicitly, strategic communication is said to be practised not only by public relations specialists but also by marketers and a range of other managers. While Hallahan et al. (2007) acknowledged that building relationships or networks could play a role in the strategic process, it seems clear the authors intended to downplay the importance of engaging with stakeholders and publics. Indeed, later in the article, Hallahan et al. implied that public relations scholars who emphasize relationships and relational outcomes had lost sight of the primary focus of their discipline. Clearly this criticism would apply not only to Ledingham and Bruning (2000), the authors cited by Hallahan et al. (2007), but also to Grunig (e.g., Grunig, 2006; Grunig, Grunig, & Dozier, 2006) and others who define public relations in terms of relationships (e.g., Hutton, 1999).

Certainly Hallahan et al. (2007) were correct to state that knowledge of communication science is essential to understanding the processes involved in relationship building, although the same could be said for various psychological theories. However, they go on to claim that mutually satisfying relationships (with publics or stakeholders) are necessary but insufficient for organizations to achieve strategically important goals, and that the focus of theory and research should be on how communication contributes to an organization's purpose for being (p. 10). From a strategic public relations perspective, this statement of priorities is precisely the wrong way round. The primary significance of communication in this context is that it can help build mutually satisfying relationships; it is those relationships which contribute to the organization's purpose for being – not the communication directly. Moreover, long-term supportive relationships can be built only when organizations also behave in ways considered acceptable by their stakeholders. Hence, it is critically important for public relations to contribute to what Steyn calls enterprise strategy (Steyn, 2007; Steyn & Niemann, 2010). An undue focus on persuasive communication as proposed by Hallahan et al. (2007) would miss this point entirely.

The term strategic communication is used not only in civilian organizations but also by the military (Murphy, 2008) and in the context of public diplomacy (Nye, 2004). According to the U.S. Department of Defense, the primary supporting capabilities of strategic communication are 'public affairs, aspects of Information Operations (principally psychological operations), military diplomacy, defense support to public diplomacy, and visual information' (Murphy, 2008, p. 1). Nye (2004) described strategic communication as a dimension of public diplomacy involving the development of a set of simple themes, in a similar vein to typical advertising or political campaigns. These themes can be promoted in a campaign using symbolic events and communications (Nye, 2004). These definitions appear to be consistent with Hallahan et al.'s (2007) view that 'persuasion is the essence of strategic communication' (p. 24). In 2012, the Public Relations Society of America unveiled yet another new definition of the discipline: 'public relations is a strategic communication process that builds mutually beneficial relationships between organizations and their publics' (Sebastian, 2012). The new definition begs the question as to whether 'strategic communication' – persuasive communication often utilizing simple themes and symbolic events – is really the most effective way for organizations to build mutually beneficial relationships with their publics or stakeholders. Dialogic communication based on intense listening, a willingness to change one's own position, and genuinely turning towards the partner in dialogue would seem a far more promising long-term approach (de Bussy, 2010).

Almost two decades ago, J. Grunig (1993) published a seminal paper exploring these themes. Grunig argued at the time that public relations was undergoing a paradigm struggle 'between practitioners who use only superficial symbolic activities – the quest for positive images – and those who build substantive behavioral relationships between organizations and publics' (p. 121). Grunig (1993) went on to make clear his view that symbolic communication used in isolation does not make organizations more effective. However, he was equally clear that both symbolic and behavioural relationships are integral to the theory and practice of public relations, arguing the two are 'intertwined like the strands of a rope' (p. 136). In the course of explicating what is meant by 'behavioral relationships', Grunig (1993) listed seven key dimensions of relationship quality: reciprocity, trust, credibility, mutual legitimacy, openness, mutual satisfaction, and mutual understanding (p. 135). Symbolic relationships, Grunig argued, are important at the micro-level of public relations programs. However, at the macro-level of organizational effectiveness the critical factor is the quality of the organization's relationships with its publics or stakeholders. The seven dimensions of relationship quality listed above, which can be readily measured, are integral to the achievement of organizational goals. Nearly 20 years later, it seems the paradigm struggle is far from over.

The concept of strategic public relations management, in the sense of the term used by Grunig (2006), has now been explicated and compared with the notion of strategic communication (Hallahan et al., 2007), which often involves attempts at persuasion based on symbolism and the dissemination of strategic messages. Both are integral to public relations, yet strategic communication remains the 'strand of the rope' most readily identified with the discipline by outsiders and many practitioners. Even when the dominant coalition accepts strategic advice from public relations, they still usually demand 'deliverables' that require technical communication skills (Berger, 2005). The strategic communication and relationship cultivation dimensions of public relations can be complementary, but only if primacy is given to relationships. If organizations do not listen and respond to their stakeholders, attempts at persuasion may well constitute ultimately counter-productive buffering activities. Confusing strategic communication with the broader task of strategic public relations management represents a significant barrier to the institutionalization of the latter as standard organizational practice. The next section discusses the parallels between strategic public relations management and the concepts of stakeholder engagement and corporate social responsibility, the latter largely developed by authors who would never identify themselves as public relations theorists and who generally ignore relevant public relations literature. This section begins to address the paradoxical question raised in the chapter introduction: does public relations have a monopoly on 'strategic public relations management'?

Strategic Public Relations Management, Stakeholder Engagement and Corporate Social Responsibility

As discussed in the previous sections, Grunig regards strategic public relations management as involving the cultivation of high-quality, long-term relationships with publics or stakeholders who are affected by organizational actions or make demands on the organization in relation to issues of importance to them (Grunig, 2006). This conceptualization of strategic public relations management is at the heart of the theoretical edifice which represents Grunig's crowning achievement. Yet these ideas are not unique to the field of public relations. In the same year that Grunig and Hunt (1984) published *Managing Public Relations*, which explicated the two-way symmetrical model integral to Grunig's theoretical project, R. Edward Freeman produced the highly influential book *Strategic Management: A Stakeholder Approach* (1984). By 2007, 179 articles directly addressing Freeman's work had appeared in the 11 leading academic journals in the fields of management and business ethics (Laplume, Sonpar, & Litz, 2008). In 2010, Freeman and collaborators published a 'state-of-the-art' review of stakeholder theory after a quarter of a century of development (Freeman, Harrison, Wicks, Parmar, & de Colle, 2010; Parmar, Freeman, Harrison, Wicks, Purnell, & de Colle, 2010). Stakeholder theorists from the management discipline often frame their propositions in terms of business enterprises, rather than organizations in general. Freeman and colleagues see stakeholder theory as relevant to problems of value creation and trade, as well as the ethics of capitalism (Parmar et al., 2010). They argue stakeholder theory can help shape management thinking about these two broad problems. Crucially, stakeholder theory is said to propose as a unit of analysis 'the relationships between a business and the groups and individuals who can affect or are affected by it . . . from a stakeholder perspective, business can be understood as a set of relationships among groups that have a stake in the activities that make up the business' (p. 405). Hence, it is apparent that the language of stakeholder theory bears a striking resemblance to that of strategic public relations management.

Yet public relations scholars naïvely searching for references to their discipline in the voluminous stakeholder literature will be sorely disappointed. Sadly, the public relations edifice is entirely ignored by leading stakeholder theorists in the management field. The legions of MBA students produced by business schools who go on to run important organizations may well be familiar with the notion of stakeholder management, yet their curriculum will generally have provided no reference whatsoever to strategic public relations management. The recent state-of-the-art review by Freeman and colleagues discussed the implications of stakeholder theory for a variety of disciplines including strategic management, accounting, marketing and finance (Parmar et al., 2010). Yet of the management function with the most relevance to the application of stakeholder theory in practice – public relations – not a mention. In the 43-page paper summarizing the views of Freeman and colleagues on the state of the art of their favourite theory, the word 'communications' is used just once (aside from in the reference list) in the context of a brief mention of a marketing article. The word 'dialogue' also appears only once; not in connection with dialogic communication with stakeholders but with reference to dialogue about the theory itself (Parmar et al., 2010). While Hallahan et al. (2007) overstated the importance of strategic or persuasive communication at the expense of cultivating relationships with publics, stakeholder theorists in the management discipline have contrived to jettison communication almost entirely from their conceptualizations. To draw on Grunig's (1993) analogy, they are working with only one strand of the rope. The Grunig edifice, together with the concept of dialogue, has much to offer stakeholder theory. However, it seems unlikely a concept labelled as 'strategic public relations management' would carry much weight among the ranks of the Academy of Management. This is largely because of the association of public relations with the most negative usages of the term strategic communication, and a sheer lack of familiarity with the relational perspectives developed in the public relations field.

During the 1980s and 1990s, corporate social responsibility (CSR) was typically conceptualized in terms of corporate social performance (CSP) encompassing the notions of social issues in business and corporate responsiveness to those issues (Carroll, 1979; McWilliams & Siegel, 2001). By the turn of the century, however, stakeholder theory had become the dominant paradigm in CSR scholarship (McWilliams & Siegel, 2001). CSR is today frequently defined in stakeholder terms (Dahlsrud, 2008). Ironically, the leading proponents of stakeholder theory now seek to distance themselves from CSR. Freeman and colleagues criticize CSR on the grounds that it involves a separation of business and societal interests as well as business and ethics; they claim that by adding social responsibilities to existing financial ones, CSR exacerbates the problem of capitalism and ethics (Parmar et al., 2010). For example, the large banks and other institutions at the heart of the Global Financial Crisis of 2008 typically had CSR policies and programs in place, but they did not see ethics as connected to their everyday work of value creation – as a result, they ended up destroying value for the entire economy (Parmar et al., 2010). The criticisms of Freeman and colleagues (Parmar et al., 2010) are especially pertinent in light of the trend over the past decade towards a 'strategic' approach to CSR. For example, McWilliams and Siegel (2001) argued that the ideal level of CSR can be determined by cost benefit analysis. To maximize profit, businesses should offer 'precisely' the level of CSR at which increased revenue (from increased demand) equals the cost of the CSR program (p. 125). This highly instrumental perspective is an invitation to stakeholder cynicism. In contrast, Basu and Palazzo (2008) have proposed taking an intrinsic rather than extrinsic approach. Instead of focusing on external environmental pressures as the driver of CSR, they advocate studying internal institutional determinants such as managerial sensemaking (how an organization makes sense of its world). In this way, the degree to which CSR is authentically embedded in an organization's identity, communication and behaviour could be evaluated (Basu & Palazzo, 2008).

The basic approach Basu and Palazzo advocate has an affinity with the concept of stakeholder orientation (de Bussy, 2010). Both refer to fundamental attributes of the managerial mindset and do not assume a separation of business and ethics. Similarly, Grunig's conceptualization of strategic public relations management is fundamentally a theory about the psyche of organizational leaders (Grunig, 2006). Undoubtedly, the selection of a bridging versus a buffering approach will at times be a matter of contingency. Not every stakeholder is necessarily legitimate and therefore deserving of open engagement (de Bussy, 2008). Nevertheless, the general disposition of organizational leaders towards bridging rather than buffering, dialogue rather than persuasion, is a function of their psychological and managerial orientation. Strategic public relations management (Grunig, 2006) and stakeholder theory (Freeman, 1984; Freeman et al., 2010) are both normative philosophies of management with inextricable instrumental overtones, i.e., both exhort managers to 'do the right thing' and suggest that the consequences will be mutually beneficial for organizations and publics or stakeholders alike. Paradoxically, however, 'doing the right thing' *only* in order to gain a selfish advantage is likely to be counterproductive. Perceived motivations are important (Sjovall & Talk, 2004). Stakeholders and publics may detect and punish organizations they suspect of insincerity. This is the inherent danger of 'strategic CSR' and putting strategic communication (defined primarily in terms of persuasion and symbolism) ahead of relationships. The next section offers some observations on the barriers to the practice of strategic public relations management *by public relations specialists* at the top level of organizations.

Strategic Public Relations Management in the Dominant Coalition

One of the key findings of the Excellence Study concerned the importance of the position of public relations within the organizational hierarchy (Dozier et al.,

1995). The theory holds that public relations is unlikely to be excellent unless the dominant coalition is supportive and the 'top communicator' is both a member of the dominant coalition and has the knowledge to practise public relations strategically (Dozier et al., 1995). Public relations must enjoy autonomy and should not be subordinate to other management functions such as marketing or human resources (Dozier et al., 1995). However, even if all these conditions are met, there are still remaining barriers to the practice of strategic public relations management by *public relations practitioners* at the top level of organizations. Two studies on the perceptions of senior organizational leaders, one conducted in the UK and one in Australia, highlight the issues (Benn, Todd, & Pendleton, 2010; Murray & White, 2005). Based on interviews on corporate reputation with 14 CEOs of large British organizations, Murray and White (2005) found that the more visible the public relations person is in the communication process, the more likely are receivers to perceive the message as 'spin'. In a study on CSR involving interviews with nine senior Australian organizational leaders, Benn et al. (2010) report the same finding. Respondents in their study actively avoided mentioning the role of public relations professionals in CSR activities, even with respect to CSR communication. Benn et al. (2010) inferred from this that 'to advocate the overt use of public relations would result in CSR activities being perceived as spin rather than as something that was deeply embedded within the organization' (pp. 418/419). The comment of one respondent, a CEO in the resources industry, was particularly illuminating. According to Benn et al. (2010, p. 417), 'Despite listing activities which would be broadly recognized as public relations, he did not specify it as public relations work and concluded with references to authenticity and walking the talk.' Benn et al. concluded that one obstacle to a greater strategic role for public relations at the top level relates to the 'public relations industry's own public relations' (p. 417).

The studies by Murray and White (2005) and Benn et al. (2010) both found varied expectations on the part of senior managers with regard to the role of public relations. Admittedly, the sample sizes in both studies were small. Nevertheless, two decades on from the commencement of the Excellence Study, at least some organizational leaders still view the role of public relations as limited to external media communication (Benn et al., 2010). When pressed, many CEO respondents in the British study said public relations provides media relations services (Murray & White, 2005). However, terminology appears to be an issue in Britain as the majority of respondents differentiated between public relations and 'corporate communications' (Murray & White, 2005). More profoundly, in their descriptions of the role of public relations or corporate communications, the CEO participants effectively indicated that communication professionals do not have a significant impact on policy. The respondents said that public relations, by itself, cannot create reputation because reputations are gained by consistently delivering on promises. Public relations can only 'enhance what is already there'. The role of public relations is to get credit for the good things the organization is doing (Murray & White, 2005, p. 350). The CEOs saw *themselves* and their fellow board members as the ultimate stewards of corporate reputation. Public relations provides advice and oversees communication activities (Murray & White, 2005). There are two major implications of this discussion. Strategic public relations management (the 'edifice') is inevitably the responsibility of leaders at all levels in the organization, not just public relations specialists. Whenever an organizational promise is made and kept (or not as the case may be), stakeholder relationships are affected. Even if no-one considered public relations a pejorative term, and public relations enjoyed unfettered influence in the dominant coalition, that reality would remain unchanged. Second, the policy setting and communication aspects of strategic public relations management, the organization's behavioural and symbolic relationships (Grunig, 1993), are indeed inextricably linked. However, the policy setting (whoever is responsible for it) must always come first. Actions will always speak louder than words. So long as public relations continues to be seen as first and foremost a communication function, outsiders (including most organizational leaders) will assume that it does not have much potential to contribute to 'enterprise strategy' (Steyn & Niemann, 2010). And even if communicators are allowed to contribute, the results may well be perceived as 'spin' regardless of their inherent merits. Yet the management approach most closely aligned with strategic public relations – stakeholder theory – appears blind to the crucial contribution of communication (especially dialogic communication) to the cultivation of relationships. Stakeholder theorists have not (yet) developed a comprehensive framework for managing relationships and are unaware of the ready-made model offered by public relations (Freeman et al., 2010; Grunig, 2006). The final section of this chapter provides some concluding remarks about strategic public relations management as a general attribute of best practice organizational leadership.

Strategic Public Relations Management as a General Attribute of Organizational Leadership

This chapter has explored the concept of strategic public relations management, understood in terms of the theoretical framework of the Excellence Study which Grunig (2006) refers to as the 'edifice'. Although behavioural and symbolic relationships are indeed intertwined like strands of a rope (Grunig, 1993), there are inherent dangers in over-emphasizing strategic communication as a paradigm for understanding the field of public relations (Hallahan et al., 2007). Strategic public relations management and strategic communication are by no means equivalent concepts. In the field of management, stakeholder theory has emerged over much the same timeframe as strategic public relations management. However, the principles of stakeholder management have considerably greater representation than the theoretical edifice of public relations in the mainstream management literature. Thus, stakeholder theory is more likely to influence at least those organizational leaders who have undertaken an MBA. The apparent failure of stakeholder theorists to appreciate the significance of communication to organizational/stakeholder relationships is a notable weakness of their work. Both strategic public relations management and stakeholder theory are normative theories with instrumental implications. Both must be aware of the need for authenticity, as illustrated by the inherent dangers of adopting a 'strategic CSR' approach. Strategic public relations is not – and cannot be even in principle – solely a task for public relations specialists. Organizational relationships with publics and stakeholders are the responsibility of leaders at all levels, no matter what their professional affiliation.

If public relations itself has a public relations problem which constrains its ability to contribute strategically at the highest organizational levels (Benn et al., 2010), one potential solution is to inculcate the values of strategic public relations among specialists in other fields who are already – or potentially could become – organizational leaders. Stakeholder theory is a valuable contribution in this regard but, as discussed above, it is currently incomplete both as a theory which explains the nature of organizational relationships with stakeholders and as a roadmap for management practice. The 'missing link' is communication, specifically dialogic communication which is, in spirit, not dissimilar to Grunig's concept of symmetrical public relations (e.g., Grunig et al., 2006). Today's publics and stakeholders are often well aware of the existence of strategic communication programs. Overt attempts at persuasion are frequently counterproductive and perceived as 'spin'. The challenge facing proponents of strategic public relations management is not necessarily how to gain personal membership of the dominant coalition, but how to spread the *ideas* of bridging, relationship cultivation, and dialogic communication amongst those with power and influence in organizations. Public relations specialists will always be needed to create and implement communication programmes. However, the fundamental orientation underpinning a genuine commitment to bridging and dialogue is not the exclusive terrain of public relations. Indeed, labelling this orientation as public relations may be part of the problem. The fundamental principles and values of strategic public relations management – the Grunig edifice – should be standard operating practice for all organizational leaders, not only public relations managers. If progress could be made in this direction, the potential contribution to societal welfare is immense. However, to paraphrase Grunig (2006, p. 172), whether most people will ever think of *public relations* 'in that way', is another (ultimately less important) question altogether.

References

Bardhan, N. (2003). Rupturing public relations metanarratives: The example of India. *Journal of Public Relations Research, 15*(3), 225–248.

Basu, K., & Palazzo, G. (2008). Corporate social responsibility: A process model of sensemaking. *Academy of Management Review, 33*(1), 122–136.

Benn, S., Todd, L., & Pendleton, J. (2010). Public relations leadership in corporate social responsibility. *Journal of Business Ethics, 96*(3), 403–423.

Berger, B. K. (2005). Power over, power with, and power to relations: Critical reflections on public relations, the dominant coalition, and activism. *Journal of Public Relations Research, 17*(1), 5–28.

Carroll, A. B. (1979). A three-dimensional conceptual model of corporate social performance. *Academy of Management Review, 4*(4), 497–505.

Curtin, P. A., & Gaither, T. K. (2005). Privileging indentity, difference, and power: The circuit of culture as a basis for public relations theory. *Journal of Public Relations Research, 17*(2), 91–115.

Dahlsrud, A. (2008). How corporate social responsibility is defined: An analysis of 37 definitions. *Corporate Social Responsibility and Environmental Management, 15*(1), 1–13.

de Bussy, N. M. (2008). Applying stakeholder thinking to public relations: An integrated approach to identifying relationships that matter. In B. van Ruler, D. Verčič, & A. T. Verčič (Eds.), *Public relations metrics* (pp. 282–300). New York: Routledge.

de Bussy, N. M. (2010). Dialogue as a basis for stakeholder engagement: Defining and measuring the core competencies. In R. L. Heath (Ed.), *The Sage handbook of public relations* (2nd ed., pp. 127–144). Thousand Oaks, CA: Sage.

Donaldson, T., & Preston, L. E. (1995). The stakeholder theory of the corporation: Concepts, evidence, and implications. *Academy of Management Review, 20*(1), 65–91.

Dozier, D. M., Grunig, J. E., & Grunig, L. A. (1995). *Manager's guide to excellence in public relations and communication management.* Mahwah, NJ: Lawrence Erlbaum Associates.

Freeman, R. E. (1984). *Strategic management: A stakeholder approach.* Boston: Pitman.

Freeman, R. E., Harrison, J. S., Wicks, A. C., Parmar, B. L., & de Colle, S. (2010). *Stakeholder theory: The state of the art.* Cambridge: Cambridge University Press.

Frooman, J. (1999). Stakeholder influence strategies. *Academy of Management Review, 24*(2), 191–205.

Grunig, J. E. (1993). Image and substance: From symbolic to behavioral relationships. *Public Relations Review, 19*(2), 121–139.

Grunig, J. E. (2006). Furnishing the edifice: Ongoing research on public relations as a strategic management function. *Journal of Public Relations Research, 18*(2), 151–176.

Grunig, J. E., & Hunt, T. (1984). *Managing public relations.* New York: Holt, Rinehart & Winston.

Grunig, J. E., & White, J. (1992). The effect of worldviews on public relations theory and practice. In J. E. Grunig (Ed.), *Excellence in public relations and communication management* (pp. 31–64). Hillsdale, NJ: Lawrence Erlbaum Associates.

Grunig, J. E., Grunig, L. A., & Dozier, D. M. (2006). The Excellence theory. In C. H. Botan & V. Hazleton (Eds.), *Public relations theory II* (pp. 19–54). Mahwah, NJ: Lawrence Erlbaum Associates.

Hallahan, K., Holtzhausen, D. R., van Ruler, B., Verčič, D., & Sriramesh, K. (2007). Defining strategic communication. *International Journal of Strategic Communication, 1*(1), 3–35.

Holtzhausen, D. R., & Voto, R. (2002). Resistance from the margins: The postmodern public relations practitioner as organizational activist. *Journal of Public Relations Research, 14*(1), 57–84.

Holtzhausen, D. R., Petersen, B. K., & Tindall, N. T. J. (2003). Exploding the myth of the symmetrical/asymmetrical dichotomy: Public relations models in the new South Africa. *Journal of Public Relations Research, 15*(4), 305–341.

Hutton, J. G. (1999). The definition, dimensions and domain of public relations. *Public Relations Review, 25*(2), 199–214.

Kaler, J. (2002). Morality and strategy in stakeholder identification. *Journal of Business Ethics, 39*(1/2), 91–99.

Laplume, A. O., Sonpar, K., & Litz, R. A. (2008). Stakeholder theory: Reviewing a theory that moves us. *Journal of Management, 34*(6), 1152–1189.

Ledingham, J. A., & Bruning, S. D. (Eds.). (2000). *Public relations as relationship management: A relational approach to the study and practice of public relations.* Mahwah, NJ: Lawrence Erlbaum Associates.

L'Etang, J. (2005). Critical public relations: Some reflections. *Public Relations Review, 31*(4), 521–526.

Lim, S., Goh, J., & Sriramesh, K. (2005). Applicability of the generic principles of excellent public relations in a different cultural context: The case study of Singapore. *Journal of Public Relations Research, 17*(4), 315–340.

McKie, D., & Munshi, D. (2007). *Reconfiguring public relations: Ecology, equity and enterprise.* London: Routledge.

McWilliams, A., & Siegel, D. (2001). Corporate social responsibility: A theory of the firm perspective. *Academy of Management Review, 26*(1), 117–127.

Mitchell, R. K., Agle, B. R., & Wood, D. J. (1997). Toward a theory of stakeholder identification and salience: Defining the principle of who and what really counts. *Academy of Management Review, 22*(4), 853–886.

Murphy, D. M. (2008). The trouble with strategic communication(s). Center for Strategic Leadership, U.S. Army War College: Issue Paper, 2-08. Retrieved from: http://www. dtic.mil/cgi-bin/GetTRDoc?Location=U2&doc=GetTRDoc.pdf&AD=ADA477745.

Murray, K., & White, J. (2005). CEOs' views on reputation management. *Journal of Communication Management, 9*(4), 348–358.

Nye, J. S. (2004). *Soft power: The means to success in world politics.* New York: Public Affairs.

Parmar, B., Freeman, R. E., Harrison, J. S., Wicks, A. C., Purnell, L., & de Colle, S. (2010). Stakeholder theory: The state of the art. *The Academy of Management Annals, 4*(1), 403–445.

Rhee, Y. (2002). Global public relations: A cross-cultural study of the Excellence theory in South Korea. *Journal of Public Relations Research, 14*(3), 159–184.

Sebastian, M. (2012, 2 March). PRSA announces the final definition of 'public relations'. Retrieved from: www.ragan.com.

Sjovall, A. M., & Talk, A. C. (2004). From actions to impressions: Cognitive attribution theory and the formation of corporate reputation. *Corporate Reputation Review, 7*(3), 269–281.

Steyn, B. (2007). Contribution of public relations to organizational strategy formulation. In E. L. Toth (Ed.), *The future of excellence in public relations and communication management* (pp. 137–172). Mahwah, NJ: Lawrence Erlbaum Associates.

Steyn, B., & Niemann, L. (2010). Enterprise strategy: A concept that explicates corporate communication's strategic contribution at the macro-organisational level. *Journal of Communication Management, 14*(2), 106–126.

Suchman, M. C. (1995). Managing legitimacy: Strategic and institutional approaches. *Academy of Management Review, 20*(3), 571–610.

Yun, S-H. (2006). Toward public relations theory-based study of public diplomacy: Testing the applicability of the Excellence study. *Journal of Public Relations Research, 18*(4), 287–312.

5

SYMMETRY, SOCIAL MEDIA, AND THE ENDURING IMPERATIVE OF TWO-WAY COMMUNICATION

Sandra Duhé and Donald K. Wright

Abstract

James E. Grunig's contributions of the four models of public relations practice predated the emergence of social media platforms by nearly three decades, yet his concept of symmetrical communication remains both relevant and timely in a rapidly expanding online environment. In this chapter, we trace how his work has influenced current scholarship in social media, discuss ties between symmetry and the evolving concept of interactivity, offer insights into how social media have impacted the practice of public relations, and provide examples of how a strategic mindset (or lack thereof) affects the outcomes of social media use.

Key Words

public relations, social media, symmetrical communication

Introduction

When James E. Grunig—hereafter referred to as Grunig—first examined public relations behavior in terms of one-way and two-way communication, email was in the infancy of its development (Grunig, 1976). His initial research into what would become four resilient models of public relations practice predated release of the World Wide Web by nearly 20 years and the emergence of social networking technologies by nearly 30 years (Zakon, 2011). Numerous scholars, practitioners, and technophiles have proclaimed the revolutionary impact of emerging media on the communication process. While writing this chapter, we pondered whether new media have actually *changed* public relations *per se* or instead continue to provide new channels that allow, and perhaps even compel, organizations to be more *symmetrical* in their communication with publics. We believe the latter is a more accurate description of emerging media impacts on public relations and a testament to the enduring relevance of the two-way symmetrical model.

In this chapter, we begin by describing Grunig's concept of symmetry and his views on how new media are affecting the field of public relations. We then trace how Grunig's contributions (and that of his co-researchers) have been incorporated in new media research over time and draw ties between symmetrical communication and the evolving concept of interactivity in online environments. Although we assert emerging media have not changed the relationship-building objectives of public relations, we do recognize and delineate social media impacts on how organizations communicate with their publics and what these impacts imply for the practice of public relations. We conclude with several examples of organizational successes and failures in social media to illustrate these points.

Grunig's Concept of Symmetry

In Grunig's (2001) view, symmetry implies a give-and-take communication *process*, rather than an outcome, that involves listening, negotiation, argumentation, dialogue, understanding, and relationship building. Although conflicts between organizations and their publics may be resolved through symmetrical communication, it is likewise possible that conflicts are merely reduced, and the parties involved agree to disagree on particular issues. Both organizations and their publics defend and attempt to enhance their self-interests, which are ever-present in the communication process. A balancing of these interests is the goal of symmetrical communication. In response to critics of Grunig and Grunig's (1992) assertion that the two-way symmetrical model of public relations is the most effective and ethical approach to the practice, Grunig (2001) was clear in distinguishing how symmetry differs from pure accommodation:

> I have never defined the symmetrical model as the accommodation of a public's interests at the expense of the organization's self-interest. In fact, the concept of symmetry directly implies a balance of the organization's and the public's interests. Total accommodation of the public's interests would be as asymmetrical as unbridled advocacy of the organization's interests.
>
> *(p. 15)*

The ability to practice symmetrical communication is hampered when organizations have no interest in establishing a dialogue with groups they consider to be offensive, foolish, or otherwise off-putting. Grunig (2001) noted, however, that, through dialogue, organizations "have improved their relationship with groups they previously considered morally repugnant" (p. 15) and warned that organizations, whether corporate or activist, "far too often believe . . . that the organizations' stances are morally superior" (p. 15). Such preconceived notions limit opportunities for organizational learning from publics and often underlie fears related to social media use. Grunig (2001) added that although it may be unethical for an organization to succumb to the wishes of a repugnant group, it is not unethical to have a dialogue with their representatives. Grunig (2006) also stressed that organizations willing to practice two-way symmetrical communication via traditional or emerging media would elevate their ethical standards and that the public relations function should serve as the ethical manager for the organization. Motion (2001) regarded the potential for organizations to attract "unintended" publics online as an avenue to "create new communication opportunities" (p. 223). Social media certainly offer these opportunities.

Grunig's Views on Social Media

Grunig (2009) described new digital media as having the potential of being yet another passing public relations fad (similar to branding, IMC, ROI, and CSR), depending on whether public relations is viewed as a messaging or a strategic management function. If practitioners view public relations as the publicity arm of an organization reliant on the mass distribution of one-way, persuasive messages aimed at fulfilling only the organization's interests, then the inherent two-way characteristic of social media undoubtedly presents a paradigmatic shift in how they practice public relations. Practitioners (and/or their managers) adhering to "a traditional paradigm of public relations that views public relations as a messaging, publicity, informational, and media relations function" (p. 4) tend also to have an "illusion of control" in regard to messaging that the interactive, unpredictable nature of social media obviously upsets. Practitioners with this worldview of public relations (and skill sets limited to media production and publicity) are more likely to use social media as just another one-way, message-posting channel.

For practitioners who view public relations as a strategic management function grounded in two-way, mutually beneficial dialogue, however, social media do not present a revolutionary shift in public relations approach as much as they provide an increasingly sophisticated, interactive supplement for relationship building. Grunig (2009) argued that new media facilitate application of, rather than change, global generic principles of public relations including (1) access of the chief communication officer to the dominant coalition; (2) integration/coordination of all public relations functions within an organization; (3) separation of public relations as its own management function; (4) leadership of the function by a strategic manager instead of a technician; (5) involvement in strategic decision-making; (6) two-way and symmetrical communication; (7) diversity; and (8) ethics. He further suggested that digital media can be helpful in overcoming some of the contextual challenges (e.g., social/culture, political, economic) that make application of the generic principles difficult in some countries. "If the social media are used to their full potential," he stated, "I believe they will inexorably make public relations practice more global, strategic, two-way and interactive, symmetrical or dialogical, and socially responsible" (p. 1). Grunig's research in two-way communication has informed numerous public relations studies of new media.

In recent years, Grunig's contributions to the social media dialogue have come not from the scholarly literature but from comments he has posted on blogs. For example, Falconi (2008) reported on a lively interchange where Grunig made the following comments:

- I have long had an interest in the potential of cyber media (including discussion groups, listservs, web pages, blogs, and the new social media) for use in public relations.
- I continue to believe the cyber media have great potential for research and listening, but I also see great potential for dialog, or two-way symmetrical communication. My reading of blogs by public relations professionals also suggests that most of them see this same potential.
- I believe the new media are perfect for practicing the two-way symmetrical model. I think it would be difficult to practice any of the other models effectively with the new media. Unfortunately, I'm afraid a lot of public relations practitioners try to practice these other models with cyber media.
- Historically, whenever a new medium is invented, people use it in the same way that they used the existing media. So, for example, when television was invented journalists tended to use it like radio by simply televising someone reading the news rather than using pictures.
- With today's new cyber media, public relations practitioners first used it like they used publications—as a means of dumping information on the public (following either the press agentry or public information model). With the advent of Web 2.0, however, practitioners seem to be adopting a dialogical model by listening to publics, discussing problems and issues with them, and interpreting their organization's actions and behaviors to publics.
- Using the press agentry or public information models, therefore, is a complete waste of the potential of the new media.

Grunig's Influence on New Media Research

New media research has been reported in public relations journals over the course of three decades, with topics ranging from early 1980s' predictions of how the Internet would revolutionize public relations practice; to theoretical frameworks of dialogic communication in the late 1990s; to more contemporary accounts of perceptions, applications, and concerns regarding the global expansion of social media (Duhé, 2012). Despite which medium was considered "new" at the time of publication, many of these roughly 150 studies incorporated time-tested principles, theories, and models offered by Grunig, his colleagues, and his students. An interesting measure of the growth and development of new media in public relations research is the reality that nearly 30 percent of the papers presented at the 15th Annual International Public Relations Research Conference in 2012 focused on some aspect of social and other emerging media. We discuss a few of those studies here to convey the enduring imperative of two-way communication and the lasting relevance of Grunig's contributions over time and across media.

One of the earliest new media studies to draw on Grunig's two-way communication models was Harris, Garramone, Pizante, and Komiya's (1985) examination of how computers could provide an ongoing flow of information between politicians and their constituents. The authors found that elected officials with outgoing personal communication styles were more likely to adopt the then-new technology. In 1998, Kent and Taylor proposed a theory-based framework for facilitating dialogic communication between organizations and their publics online. Specifically, they offered five website design principles (dialogic loop, useful information, generation of return visits, ease of interface/navigation, and conservation of visitors) that still today are pervasively cited in the literature and have been effectively applied to emerging media including wikis (Hickerson & Thompson, 2009), Facebook (Bortree & Seltzer, 2009), Twitter (Rybalko & Seltzer, 2010), and blogs (Merritt, Lawson, Mackey, & Waters, 2012). Kent and Taylor (1998) explained that understanding of dialogic communication is a prerequisite for understanding symmetrical communication. That is, dialogic communication provides a "type of relational interaction" (p. 323) that complements the two-way symmetrical communication process discussed by Grunig and Grunig (1992).

Another early attempt to examine the Grunig two-way models in the context of new media involved a survey of senior-level corporate public relations officers (Wright, 1998). This article pointed out the Internet's potential to enhance two-way communication in both external and internal settings. Additional work by this author (Wright, 2004) confirmed and supported Grunig's theorizing about the importance of two-way communication.

McKeown and Plowman (1999) applied Grunig's (1982) situational theory of publics to study how U.S. presidential candidates used the Web for the first time in 1996 to communicate with voters. They observed use of the two-way asymmetrical model to attract donations and volunteers but found campaigns lacking in two-way symmetrical communication. Jo and Kim (2003) were among the first to recognize a tie between website interactivity (e.g., feedback and choice features) and relationship building. Using an experimental design and Hon and Grunig's (1999) relationship attributes, the researchers discovered that the presence of interactive features on websites made a significant contribution to the quality of organization–public relationships. They noted, however, that "public relations practitioners do not fully use the Internet to enhance interactions between organizations and their publics" (2003, p. 217)—a theme that resonates throughout the course of new media research in public relations journals. In 2004, Naudé,

Froneman, and Atwood likewise studied the relationship between website interactivity (defined as the presence of playfulness, choice, connectedness, information collection, and reciprocal communication elements) and symmetrical communication. In their review of South African NGO websites, they, too, found interactivity lacking but concluded that each of the four models of public relations (Grunig & Grunig, 1992) could be practiced online.

Symmetrical communication is not always the most appropriate choice for organizations, however. In 2006, Reber, Gower, and Robinson analyzed how celebrities facing litigation used websites for disseminating messages. They concluded that the two-way asymmetrical model (Grunig & Grunig, 1992) has potential for application in the increasing use of personal websites in litigation public relations. Although asymmetry provides more monologue than dialogue, the authors explained that an imbalanced approach to two-way communication provides the messaging control frequently sought in legal matters. Conversely, Kang and Norton (2006) argued that two-way symmetrical communication was essential for top U.S. universities to meet their relationship-building goals with strategic publics, but found these highly regarded institutions of higher learning were not "fully embracing the strength of their Web sites . . . in their relational communication capabilities" (p. 428).

Chen (2007) used Hon and Grunig's (1999) relationship attributes to explore journalist perceptions of candidate websites in the 2004 Taiwan presidential election. She suggested that although the medium has the potential to enhance organizational relationships with journalists, websites alone are not a sufficient means of doing so. Searson and Johnson (2010) applied principles of two-way symmetrical communication to Latin American government websites and suggested that websites could be classified based on the level of sophistication of interactive features they employ. For example, a low level of interactive sophistication would include provision of an organization's virtual and physical contact information whereas a high level of interactive sophistication would include blogs, forums, and surveys. Moving beyond websites, Waters and Jamal (2011) observed consistent use of one-way communication models on Twitter, despite the social network site's inherent capability for two-way communication and its potential for interactive relationship building online. Interactivity is of ongoing interest in new media literature and has clear ties to symmetrical communication.

Symmetry and Interactivity

The emerging concept of virtual interactivity and Grunig and Grunig's (1992) description of symmetrical communication have been occasionally linked in public relations journal articles, and we believe this connection warrants more attention. Research findings repeatedly reveal a lack of interactivity in online environs, regardless of how interactivity is defined. Interactivity, much like corporate social responsibility, is a multi-faceted concept, and its operationalization and measurement are of interdisciplinary interest (Duhé, 2012). However, a present lack of consistency in the definition of interactivity poses a challenge to public relations researchers who are eager to more specifically describe how interactivity in new media settings contributes to mutually beneficial relationship building. Here, we highlight communication scholarship about interactivity that draws on Grunig's research in the hope that further discussion of the link between symmetry and interactivity will aid in establishing a theoretical framework for interactivity as it relates to public relations online. We agree with Motion's (2001) assertion that "the concept of interactivity is fundamental to understanding electronic communication" (p. 223).

Downes and McMillan (2000) traced the concept of interactivity in communication over time, finding literature addressing interaction in human communication, interaction between humans and computers, and interaction in computer-mediated communication. McMillan (1999) captured the essence of interactivity online when she described it as part of "an information-rich environment in which the individual can not only respond to the site creator but can also become an active communicator" (p. 388). This definition aligns well with the give-and-take nature of Grunig's (2001) explanation of symmetry in communication, which readily translates to social media settings. McMillan (1999) further highlighted the connection between public relations goals and the extent to which organizations engage in dialogic communication with their audiences, stating: "If their goal is publicity or propaganda, there may be little reason to use an interactive medium" (p. 389).

As Grunig (2009) noted, much of the brouhaha surrounding the global expansion of social media comes from practitioners (and other observers) who see public relations as a message delivery/publicity function rather than as an interctive, strategic management function. In its most effective form of practice, public relations involves an *ongoing* negotiation of positions, policies, and expectations between organizations and their publics—a journey more than a destination. Symmetrical communication is, by its nature, interactive communication. Social media, however, have made the process more visible, and the stakes a bit higher, given the unpredictable dynamic of human communication added to the possibility of interactions going viral (Coombs, 2012; Scott, 2010).

Grunig's two-way theories also have impacted the literature of public relations ethics. Noted public relations ethics scholar Shannon Bowen (2004) has suggested Grunig's two-way symmetrical model is congruent with a deontological ethical perspective that is grounded in the "moral duty to do what is right based on universal norms of obligation" (p. 70). Hon (2006) agreed. All of this is consistent with Pearson's (1989) suggestions that organizations have moral duties to engage in dialogue with their strategic publics.

Undoubtedly, some sense of control is lost as public relations evolves from a one-to-many model to a more socially distributed form of practice that involves multiple participants seamlessly shifting between roles of sender and receiver (Downes & McMillan, 2000; Smith, 2010). After finding a positive correlation between Hon and Grunig's (1999) relationship outcomes (trust, satisfaction, commitment, and control mutuality) and relational maintenance strategies (conversational voice and relational commitment), Kelleher (2009) added evidence to the idea of a distributed model of public relations, "one in which key outcomes of public relations are fostered by a wide range of people communicating interactively while representing an organization" (p. 172). He likewise distinguished functional interactivity, which focuses on design features similar to those proposed by Kent and Taylor (1998), from contingency interactivity, which focuses on how message content depends on previous message exchanges. In other words, contingency interactivity indicates that as the communication process becomes more iterative and reciprocal, exchanges become more interactive, and more positive relational outcomes are expected.

We would be remiss if this chapter filled with praise for Grunig's two-way symmetrical model of communication did not include thoughts from some who have questioned whether this model is realistic. Roper (2005), for example, claimed most organizational relationships are asymmetrical because one organization usually has the upper hand in terms of resources. And as Hon (2006) pointed out, "This power differential allows organizations to choose a strategy of responding to activist concerns by providing small concessions that deflect criticism" (p. 55).

Referring to the models of public relations, Downes and McMillan (2000) suggested that the "study of interactivity needs to move beyond how organizations define their communication goals to how communication participants perceive the goals of those with whom they communicate" (p. 172). Interactivity, then, is a means for mutual understanding, the primary goal of symmetrical communication. Relationships must first be established, however, for online exchanges to be meaningful, and increasingly these relationships are "complex, interdependent, and typically global" (Motion, 2001, p. 225).

McMillan (2002) used the four models of public relations as the basis for proposing a four-part model of cyber-interactivity. The model was structured according to two dimensions: direction of communication (one-way or two-way, drawn from Grunig & Grunig, 1989) and level of receiver control (low or high, drawn from Bordewijk & van Kaam, 1986). McMillan (2002) classified the online intersection of these dimensions as follows:

1. *Monologue* (analogous to the press agentry/publicity model):
    - one-way direction of communication;
    - low level of receiver control;
    - senders create and distribute content to attract, promote, persuade;
    - characteristic of most corporate websites.

2. *Feedback* (analogous to the public information model):
    - one-way direction of communication;

- high level of receiver control (in that feedback is permitted);
- no guarantee that sender will respond to feedback received;
- characteristic of sites with feedback tools (e.g., email links).

3. *Responsive dialogue* (analogous to the two-way asymmetrical model):
   - two-way direction of communication;
   - low level of receiver control;
   - sender still has primary control over the communication process;
   - characteristic of sites dedicated to customer/volunteer support.

4. *Mutual discourse* (analogous to the two-way symmetrical model):
   - two-way direction of communication;
   - high level of receiver control;
   - sender/receiver roles are interchangeable; each becomes a participant;
   - characteristic of social media.

McMillan's (2002) model serves as an intriguing lens for researching online communication interactivity in terms of not only direction, but also control—key variables in the oft-termed "revolutionary" impact social media are having on the practice of public relations. She acknowledged that each of the four types of communication presented in the model (monologue, feedback, responsive dialogue, and mutual dialogue) has an appropriate place in online environments, similar to Naudé, Froneman, and Atwood's (2004) suggestion that each of the models of public relations can be enacted online. McMillan (2002) additionally recognized that mutual discourse presents the greatest level of threat to an organization: "In these unfettered environments that allow a free-flow of two-way communication, all visitors to the website have the potential to participate in the website as both senders and receivers" (p. 285).

Through a series of interviews with "ordinary" users of communication technology, Quiring (2009) identified five dimensions of interactivity: social, individual, technological, image, and content. Whereas only a few of his interviewees related the idea of interactivity to technology, image, or content, an overwhelming number of his respondents associated interactivity with social and individual purposes. That is, interactivity was most often associated with what users could "accomplish by using media in terms of self-development, social influence and social relationships" (p. 914). This finding complements Wright and Hinson's (2010) observation that "new communications media now represent one of the world's major sources of social interaction as people share stories and experience with each other" (p. 4). Social media are increasingly interactive, driven by user-generated content, and used to meet a variety of communication goals, including storytelling, collaboration, thought leadership, empowerment, and dissent. As such, they have notable implications for the practice of public relations.

Social Media Impacts on the Practice of Public Relations

Definitions of social media are plentiful, and their application and technical capabilities continue to evolve. Since their paper in 2006 (Wright and Hinson, 2006), Wright and Hinson (2011) have reported findings from longitudinal data regarding how public relations practitioners worldwide perceive, use, and evaluate the effectiveness of social media use in the workplace. They summarized the description of social media as venues delivering "web-based information created by people with the intention of facilitating communication" (Wright & Hinson, 2010, p. 4). In their most recent study, Wright and Hinson (2012) found social networks such as Facebook were the emerging media used the most in public relations practice, followed by micro-blogs such as Twitter and video-sharing sites such as YouTube.

A review of three decades of new media research in public relations journals, anecdotal evidence, and insights provided by the Arthur W. Page Society's report, *The Authentic Enterprise* (2007), reveals several major themes in how social media are affecting the practice of public relations:

- *Challenges for a technical model of the practice.* Communication trends over time, including those related to corporate social responsibility, websites, and transparency, have increased public expectation of information access and flow, and each, in its own way, has pushed organizations (not all willingly) toward two-way communication with publics. For those practitioners, industry observers, and executives who view public relations primarily as a strategic management function grounded in public relationships, social media are yet another venue to conduct those practices, albeit with their own set of challenges. For those who more narrowly define the practice as the technical functions of media production and publicity, however, social media are having a more profound effect. Practitioners with this worldview will either continue to use social media in a one-way manner and/or make highly visible mistakes in transitioning to two-way communication methods in ways that are counterproductive to organizations, publics, and the profession.

- *Erosion in perceptions of control.* Just as communication trends have moved organizations toward two-way communication, so, too, have they continued to dilute the ability of organizations to control messaging about their operations. Increasingly, the "one-to-many" models of public relations are giving way to more symmetrical, interactive, socially distributed methods of co-creating brands, experiences, opinions, and products. Social media are keenly designed to facilitate this collaborative process, but occasionally have unpredictable and disproportionate effects. Concerns regarding issues of risk, ethics, law, and privacy have led many organizations to develop social media policies in an attempt to place some bounds on employee use of social media.

Control in the form of gatekeeping has diminished as well. No longer are traditional media the sole mass distribution source of information. Social media allow public relations practitioners to become active participants in public forums, but fellow users are increasingly wise to those who would attempt to deceive or mask their identity as paid advocates for an organization. A widening spread of citizen journalism, with varying degrees of quality, objectivity, and accuracy, offers opportunities for practitioners to be directly involved in public discussions but requires transparency and authenticity for information to be regarded as credible.

- *Demand for strategic managers with interdisciplinary knowledge.* Mutual understanding requires interdisciplinary understanding. There are myriad technical, social/cultural, psychological, legal, political, and economic considerations involved in building relationships through mediated channels. Interactivity, engagement, and measurement are of burgeoning and multidisciplinary interest. Social media provide a viable source of organizational learning. Although their management is frequently housed in public relations, effective use of social media requires collaboration and some level of consistency within organizations. Public relations practitioners who proactively build relationships with legal, human resources, marketing, and information technology experts—and apply what they learn to social media use—can more readily tie their work to strategic imperatives and provide a business case for more open, symmetrical communication with publics. Internal communication becomes more important so that employees can be better informed representatives of an organization both online and offline. The expansion and potential influence of participants in the public relations process make strategic communication all the more essential and the work of the public relations practitioner "at once more interesting, valuable and challenging than the work we have been asked to do in the past" (Arthur W. Page Society, 2007, p. 17). Social media and a growing expectation for symmetrical communication provide public relations professionals with "the opportunity to take on a larger role within the enterprise and to provide greater value to it and its growing network of constituencies . . . or risk being marginalized" (p. 10). We suspect social media, and whatever other two-way communication trends are yet to come, will further broaden the divide between public relations technicians and public relations managers, with the strategic contributions of the latter enhancing the professionalism of the field.

Social Media Case Study Highlights

As mentioned several times in this chapter, a frequent criticism of much of the use of social media in public relations practice is the concern too many practitioners only use these new media to disseminate information and do not capitalize upon the potential social media offers for effective two-way communication.

In many ways this criticism suggests there is a considerable disconnect between what is really happening in social media and what public relations scholars say is happening. As evidence of this, we note the following highly successful public relations campaigns that employed strategic communication thinking with the effective use of social media to enhance two-way communication in both asymmetric and symmetric categories.

- The "Army Strong" campaign of the US Army (working with Weber Shandwick) that included the first official soldier blog for sharing unfiltered views of military life. This blog now receives more than a million visits each year.
- Volkswagen's work on a new media campaign in association with the MWW Group that made the VW GTI the world's first car launched exclusively on a mobile device. The campaign involved no paid advertising. There were 1.5 million downloads of the mobile telephone app. That led to an 80 percent jump in test drives of the vehicle.
- The Coca-Cola Company's Expedition 206 Campaign that effectively used social media platforms Facebook, YouTube, Twitter, and Flickr to follow three young people on a mission to make people happy in the 206 countries and territories where Coca-Cola is sold.
- Plus, Newell Rubbermaid's efforts with its Sharpie brand on Facebook (currently 1.5 million fans); Burger King's order-taking chicken; Procter & Gamble's Old Spice guy; Kohl's giving $10 million to schools via Facebook; the Facebook event unveiling the 2011 Ford Explorer; and Domino's Pizza's use of Facebook to revamp its brand image.

While praising the effective use of the social media campaigns listed above, we would be remiss if we failed to mention some of the many situations where social media have been used ineffectively. These include, but certainly are not limited to: BP's response to the Gulf of Mexico oil spill; Denny's accidentally pointing customers to a Taiwanese boy's abandoned Twitter account on the back of its menus; Nestlé's fight with Greenpeace; the misuse of Twitter by basketball star LeBron James in his attempts to capitalize on speculation that he might switch teams from Cleveland to Miami; Price Chopper, a grocery store chain, complaining to a customer's boss after the customer criticized the chain on Twitter; and Mercedes criticized for requiring users to "like" the brand on Facebook before they could learn about a soon-to-be-launched Twitter ad campaign. In many instances, social media missteps can be attributed to a lack of understanding (or even blatant disregard) of the overarching strategic imperatives of an organization and/or a misguided attempt to control the flow of information when a crisis erupts.

Conclusion

The impact of Grunig's pioneering research into the directional nature of public relations behavior, communication symmetry, and the four models of public relations practice is pervasively evident in more than three decades of public relations scholarship. Evident, too, are scholarly challenges to Grunig's ideas alongside his lively, highly specific responses to critics. Such is the way of scholarship. From a definitional standpoint, good theory is supposed to stand the test of time, yet it is still impressive when it does. Despite vast and continuing advancements in communication technology, Grunig's concept of symmetry remains relevant regardless of the channels used by organizations to establish and maintain relationships with their publics. Each of the public relations models can be applied online, and the fit between symmetrical communication and the evolving concept of interactivity is a natural one that we believe calls for further attention and development.

Grunig's career-long focus on the managerial aspects of public relations practice has increasing importance in social media environments. The controlling, persuasive, and sometimes manipulative motives of one-way communication are quickly identified and frequently rebuked by publics who expect to be not only recipients, but also active participants in message and brand formation. These interactive venues require public relations practitioners to be risk managers, organizational strategists, crisis responders, and intelligence gatherers in addition to their roles as advocates. Thus, organizations of all types will continue to need communication managers (rather than technicians) who understand contemporary communication environments, hold a worldview of public relations that is based on relationships (rather than publicity), and have the interdisciplinary knowledge to effectively serve in the higher ranks of organizations—just as Grunig predicted.

References

Arthur W. Page Society. (2007). The authentic enterprise. Retrieved from: http://www.awpagesociety.com/images/uploads/2007AuthenticEnterprise.pdf.

Bordewijk, J. L., & van Kaam, B. (1986). Towards a new classification of tele-information services. *InterMedia, 14*(1), 16–21.

Bortree, D. S., & Seltzer, T. (2009). Dialogic strategies and outcomes: An analysis of environmental advocacy groups' Facebook profiles. *Public Relations Review, 35*(3), 317–319.

Bowen, S. A. (2004). Expansion of ethics as the tenth generic principle of public relations excellence: A Kantian theory and model for managing ethical issues. *Journal of Public Relations Research, 16*(1), 65–92.

Chen, Y-N. K. (2007). A study of journalists' perception of candidates' websites and their relationships with the campaign organization in Taiwan's 2004 presidential election. *Public Relations Review, 33*(1), 103–105.

Coombs, W. T. (2012). The emergence of the paracrisis: Definition and implication for crisis management. In S. Duhé (Ed.), *New media and public relations* (2nd ed., pp. 267–276). New York: Peter Lang.

Downes, E. J., & McMillan, S. J. (2000). Defining interactivity: A qualitative identification of key dimensions. *New Media & Society, 2*(2), 157–179.

Duhé, S. (2012). A thematic analysis of 30 years of public relations literature addressing the potential and pitfalls of new media. In S. Duhé (Ed.), *New media and public relations* (2nd ed., pp. xiii–xxvi). New York: Peter Lang.

Falconi, T. M. (2008). Engaging (and grilling) the social side of James Grunig. Retrieved from: http://www.prconversations.com/index.php/2008/10/engaging-and-grilling-the-social-side-of-james-grunig/.

Grunig, J. E. (1976). Organizations and public relations: Testing a communication theory. *Journalism Monographs*, No. 46.

Grunig, J. E. (1982). The message–attitude–behavior relationship: Communication behavior of organizations. *Communication Research, 9*, 163–200.

Grunig, J. E. (2001). Two-way symmetrical public relations: Past, present, and future. In R. L. Heath (Ed.), *Handbook of public relations* (pp. 11–30). Thousand Oaks, CA: Sage.

Grunig, J. E. (2006). Research in public relations: Current status and new directions. *Anàlisi: Quaderns de Comunicació I Cultura (Spain), 34*, 49–65.

Grunig, J. E. (2009). Paradigms of global public relations in an age of digitalization. *PRism, 6*(2). Retrieved from: http://www.prismjournal.org/.

Grunig, J. E., & Grunig, L. A. (1989). Toward a theory of the public relations behavior of organizations: Review of a program of research. *Public Relations Research Annual, 1*, 27–63.

Grunig, J. E., & Grunig, L. A. (1992). Models of public relations and communication. In J. E. Grunig (Ed.), *Excellence in public relations and communication management* (pp. 285–325). Hillsdale, NJ: Lawrence Erlbaum Associates.

Harris, A., Garramone, G., Pizante, G., & Komiya, M. (1985). Computers in constituent communications. *Public Relations Review, 11*(3), 34–39.

Hickerson, C. A., & Thompson, S. R. (2009). Dialogue through wikis: A pilot exploration of dialogic public relations and wiki websites. *PRism, 6*(1). Retrieved from: http://www.prismjournal.org.

Hon, L. (2006). Negotiating relationships with activist publics. In K. Fitzpatrick & C. Bronstein (Eds.), *Ethics in public relations: Responsible advocacy* (pp. 53–69). Thousand Oaks, CA: Sage.

Hon, L., & Grunig, J. E. (1999). *Guidelines for measuring relationships in public relations.* Gainesville, FL: The Institute for Public Relations.

Jo, S., & Kim, Y. (2003). The effect of Web characteristics on relationship building. *Journal of Public Relations Research, 15*(3), 199–223.

Kang, S., & Norton, H. E. (2006). Colleges and universities' use of the World Wide Web: A public relations tool for the digital age. *Public Relations Review, 32*(4), 426–428.

Kelleher, T. (2009). Conversational voice, communicated commitment, and public relations outcomes in interactive online communication. *Journal of Communication, 59*, 172–188.

Kent, M. L., & Taylor, M. (1998). Building dialogic relationships through the World Wide Web. *Public Relations Review, 24*(3), 321–334.

McKeown, C. A., & Plowman, K. D. (1999). Reaching publics on the Web during the 1996 presidential campaign. *Journal of Public Relations Research, 11*(4), 321–347.

McMillan, S. J. (1999). Health communication and the Internet: Relations between interactive characteristics of the medium and site creators, content, and purpose. *New Media & Society, 11*(4), 375–390.

McMillan, S. J. (2002). A four-part model of cyber-interactivity: Some cyber-places are more interactive than others. *New Media & Society, 4*(2), 271–291.

Merritt, S., Lawson, L., Mackey, D., & Waters, R. D. (2012). If you blog it, they will come: Examining the role of dialogue and connectivity in the nonprofit blogosphere. In S. Duhé (Ed.), *New media and public relations* (2nd ed.). New York: Peter Lang.

Motion, J. (2001). Electronic relationships: Interactivity, Internet branding and the public sphere. *Journal of Communication Management, 5*(3), 217–230.

Naudé, A. M. E., Froneman, J. D., & Atwood, R. A. (2004). The use of the Internet by ten South African non-governmental organizations: A public relations perspective. *Public Relations Review, 30*(1), 87–94.

Pearson, R. (1989). Beyond ethical relativism in public relations: Coorientation, rules and the idea of communication symmetry. *Public Relations Research Annual, 1,* 27–63.

Quiring, O. (2009). What do users associate with interactivity? A qualitative study on user schemata. *New Media & Society, 11*(6), 899–920.

Reber, B. H., Gower, K. K., & Robinson, J. A. (2006). The Internet and litigation public relations. *Journal of Public Relations Research, 18*(1), 23–44.

Roper, J. (2005). Symmetrical communication: Excellent public relations or a strategy for hegemony? *Journal of Public Relations Research, 17*(1), 69–86.

Rybalko, S., & Seltzer, T. (2010). Dialogic communication in 140 characters or less: How Fortune 500 companies engage stakeholders using Twitter. *Public Relations Review, 36*(4), 336–341.

Searson, E. M., & Johnson, M. A. (2010). Transparency laws and interactive public relations: An analysis of Latin American government web sites. *Public Relations Review, 36*(2), 120–126.

Scott, D. M. (2010). *The new rules of marketing and PR.* Hoboken, NJ: John Wiley & Sons.

Smith, B. G. (2010). Socially distributing public relations: Twitter, Haiti, and interactivity in social media. *Public Relations Review, 36*(4), 329–335.

Waters, R. D., & Jamal, J. Y. (2011). Tweet, tweet, tweet: A content analysis of nonprofit organizations' Twitter updates. *Public Relations Review, 37*(3), 321–324.

Wright, D. K. (1998). *Corporate communications policy concerning the Internet: A survey of the nation's senior level, corporate public relations officers.* Gainesville, FL: The Institute for Public Relations.

Wright, D. K. (2004, March). Towards a receiver-focused model of the communication process. Paper presented at the International Public Relations Research Conference, South Miami, Florida.

Wright, D. K., & Hinson, M. D. (2006, March). Weblogs and employee communication: Ethical questions for corporate public relations. Paper presented at the International Public Relations Research Conference, Coral Gables, Florida.

Wright, D. K., & Hinson, M. D. (2010, Summer). How new communications media are being used in public relations: A longitudinal analysis. *Public Relations Journal, 4*(3). Retrieved from: http://www.prsa.org/Intelligence/PRJournal/.

Wright, D. K., & Hinson, M. D. (2011, Summer). A three-year longitudinal analysis of social and emerging media use in public relations practice. *Public Relations Journal, 5*(3). Retrieved from: http://www.prsa.org/Intelligence/PRJournal/.

Wright, D. K., & Hinson, M. D. (2012, Fall). Examining how social and emerging media have been used in public relations between 2006 and 2012: A longitudinal analysis. *Public Relations Journal, 6*(4), 1–40. Retrieved from http://www.prsa.org/Intelligence/PRJournal/Documents/2012WrightHinson.pdf.

Zakon, R. H. (2011). Hobbes' Internet timeline 10.2. Retrieved from: http://www.zakon.org/robert/internet/timeline/.

6

ALIGNING PUBLIC RELATIONS WITH THE DEMANDS OF GLOBALIZATION

Conceptual Foundations for a Theory of Global Public Relations

Krishnamurthy Sriramesh, Yunna Rhee, and Minjung Sung

Abstract

The current era of globalization has increased the significance of public relations, especially at the cross-national and cross-cultural levels. This chapter reviews the impact of globalization on public relations practice and scholarship and how current public relations scholarship has attempted to prepare the industry for a global practice. The generic principles and socio-cultural variables that should be taken into consideration while applying the principles are presented here. The chapter also discusses the studies based on these two streams of thought and how those studies have helped reduce the level of ethnocentricity in the body of knowledge of public relations. Looking to the future, the chapter contends that many more empirical studies from around the world are needed to confirm the theorizing that has evolved from the Excellence Project.

Key Words

environmental variables, ethnocentricity, Excellence Project, generic principles, global public relations, globalization, public relations

Public Relations in a Globalizing World

Globalization has become the buzzword of the 21st century. Concomitantly, the term *global public relations* has also become an oft-used phrase, especially in the past decade. Beyond terminology, globalization has certainly influenced public relations practice and scholarship significantly. Given this relationship between globalization and public relations, it is appropriate to ask whether globalization is new. If one were to observe current discussions about globalization closely, one is left with the impression that globalization is a 21st-century phenomenon previously unknown to the human race. The literature cautions us from making such erroneous assumptions reminding us that globalization has been present in human history. Frank (1998) made the interesting assertion that between 1400 and 1800 some Asian economies mirrored dominant Atlantic and European economies that also resulted in trade with these economies. In particular, Frank mentions India and China as matching Atlantic and European economies not only in population size but also economic output—not unlike what one sees in the current era of globalization. Bordo, Cavalho, and Meissner (2010) identified the period between 1880 and 1913 as the first era of globalization and saw parallels in many aspects of globalization from that era to the current one. Debeljak (2009) identified two eras of globalization that preceded the current one: the *imperial* 16th century and the *colonial* 19th century. The current era of globalization has been dominated by *corporate* activities and consequences.

These activities and consequences have created a spurt in demand for public relations activities at the global level from all three types of organizations: corporations, non-profits, and governments. However, with new opportunities come new challenges as well, which begs the question: Is the public relations field adequately equipped to respond to the challenges of communicating with culturally diverse audiences—a hallmark of globalization? Although public relations has been practiced in various forms around the world since pre-biblical times, in the 20th century, public relations largely developed as a Western practice influenced by the US, the UK, and a few Western democracies. The relatively young scholarly body of knowledge of public relations, with its roots in the mid-1970s, also had developed rather ethnocentrically (Sriramesh, 2002). This ethnocentricity has largely restricted the utility of public relations practice and scholarship in a globalizing world, even though in the past decade there has been an increased awareness of the impact of cross-cultural differences on public relations (Sriramesh, 2010).

One would have to contend that the strong foundations to reduce this ethnocentricity were laid by the first multinational research study in this field that was headed by J. Grunig (1992). Funded by the International Association of Business Communicators (IABC) in 1984, this study, popularly known as the *Excellence Project* (J. Grunig, 1992; Dozier, L. Grunig, & J. Grunig, 1995; L. Grunig, J. Grunig, & Dozier, 2002) provided the conceptual elements and empirical evidence from three Anglo-Saxon countries. The resulting conceptualization has helped spawn a body of knowledge of global public relations that can make public relations practice and the body of knowledge more multi-cultural and thereby less ethnocentric.

When planning public relations programs in multiple countries, does one set up programs unique to each country, replicate the same program in multiple countries, or do something in between? The generic principles of public relations, an outcome of the Excellence Project, provide a set of principles that can form the foundation for a strategically managed public relations program in multiple countries. The Excellence Project also offered the *environmental variables* that should help to tailor the generic principles to local socio-cultural conditions in a country. The rest of this chapter discusses these two elements that are cogent to our discussion of globalization and public relations. In doing so, we will also review studies conducted in several parts of the world to assess the validity and reliability of the generic principles and the utility of culture, broadly defined, to public relations. Readers will note that several other chapters in this volume also address different aspects of these two streams of conceptualization.

Generic Principles of Public Relations

Based on the 14 "characteristics for excellent public relations" that developed from the Excellence Project, Verčič, J. Grunig and L. Grunig (1996) identified ten, what they termed "generic principles" that could be helpful to organizations practicing global public relations. These principles, the authors contended, could be applied in different nations and cultures after "localizing" them to the specific socio-cultural environment present in those nations. This section briefly describes the ten principles and then reviews studies that have relied on the principles to help build a body of knowledge of global public relations. The ten generic principles are:

1. *Involvement of public relations in strategic management.* An organization that practices excellent public relations develops programs that help it to communicate effectively with its stakeholders. The rationale behind this principle is that involvement by public relations departments improves communication efficacy by providing the organization input from stakeholders, thereby helping align organizational activities with the expectations of stakeholders.

2. *Empowerment of public relations in the dominant coalition or a direct reporting relationship to senior management.* The dominant coalitions (DC) of organizations consist of "the group of individuals within an organization with the power to affect the structure of the organization, define its mission, and set its course through strategic choices the coalition makes" (Dozier, J. Grunig, & L. Grunig, 1995, p. 15). When an organization empowers the senior public relations manager either by including such a person in the coalition or by providing access to the DC through a direct reporting relationship, the deliberations of these senior managers will benefit from the information about stakeholders that the public relations manager can bring to organizational policy-making. Such policies, it is presumed, are going to be more congruent with the expectations and values of organizational stakeholders, thereby improving the relationships between these entities and the organization.

3. *Integrated public relations function.* Organizations that practice excellent public relations tend to integrate all communication functions under a single

department or, at the very least, provide a mechanism that coordinates the communication activities of the various departments. Such integration of communication functions helps the organization communicate with a uniform voice, thereby improving impact, ensures better use of available resources, and facilitates the development of effective programs that are better aligned to the changing landscape of strategic publics.

4. *Public relations as a management function separate from other functions.* It is not uncommon for organizations to place public relations in departments such as marketing or advertising. Such practices usually relegate public relations to a supporting, technical role, thereby not harnessing the strategic potential of public relations. Because public relations reflects the "voices" of multiple stakeholders in the organization's decision-making deliberations, subjugating it to a restricted function such as product advertising or marketing, would adversely impact on organizational decision-making and make such policies less holistic.

5. *Public relations unit headed by a manager rather than a technician.* While not understating the critical work that communication technicians perform, excellent public relations departments should be led by a senior communication manager as he/she has the level of education, professionalism, and knowledge level to strategically manage public relations programs for the department. If such a senior manager is not present in the public relations department, it is unlikely that public relations programs will be aligned with the strategic goals of an organization, with the expectations and values of stakeholders of the organization, and help develop relationships with stakeholders. In order for public relations to contribute to organizational effectiveness, it is critical that managers who have the knowledge and experience in strategic communication management lead the department.

6. *Two-way symmetrical model of public relations.* One of the key characteristics of excellent public relations is that it practices the two-way symmetrical model or the mixed-motive model[1] more often than other models.[2] When the two-way symmetrical model is practiced, the organization aims to seek mutual understanding between itself and its strategic publics rather than pushing and promoting only the organization's positions or messages. Use of social scientific research for better understanding of stakeholders differentiates the two-way models from the one-way public relations models. In addition, the two-way symmetrical model employs not only the traditional mass media, but also resorts to interpersonal communication methods in interacting with the stakeholders. The expected outcome of the two-way symmetrical model is the development of positive relationships with stakeholders, which may provide much-needed support for the organization in future crisis and conflict situations. The two-way symmetrical model provides the foundations for public relations to expand its boundaries as a relationship management function and harness the true potential of strategic public relations.

7. *A symmetrical system of internal communication.* Organizations practicing excellent public relations are also more likely to have a symmetrical system of internal communication, where employees are given autonomy and allowed to participate in decision-making processes. In other words, an organization's symmetrical internal communication practice complements its external communication practice. In organizations practicing excellent public relations, employees are treated as one of the most important stakeholders who can greatly affect the development and management of positive relationships with external stakeholders by becoming organizational ambassadors.

8. *Knowledge potential for managerial role and symmetrical public relations.* In the Excellence study, the quantitative research results indicated that the knowledge potential was one of the strongest predictors of public relations excellence. That is, when a public relations department is staffed by practitioners who have been educated in strategic public relations and have been actively involved in professional pursuits, that organization is more likely to practice excellent public relations. In particular, practitioners who are trained to enact managerial roles in public relations and are knowledgeable in symmetrical models of public relations contribute to public relations excellence. These practitioners also tend to actively participate in professional associations and are regularly exposed to professional literature.

9. *Diversity embodied in all roles.* According to the principle of requisite variety, effective organizations have as much diversity inside the organization as in the environment. When a public relations department embraces a diverse workforce—men and women practitioners who have different cultural, racial, and ethnic backgrounds—it can better understand the divergent perspectives, values, and expectations of organizational stakeholders. In such a diverse department, the internal culture would be more agile and flexible to accommodate the two-way symmetrical communication model, which leads to excellence in public relations.

10. *Organizational context for excellence.* As will be explained in the next section, the Excellence Study also identified several contextual variables that influence public relations excellence. An organization's participative internal culture facilitates public relations excellence. This is in line with the finding that the symmetrical internal communication system is linked to public relations excellence. An organization with a participative culture empowers its own employees and has the highest potential of empowering its stakeholders by listening to their opinions and allowing their input to influence organizational decision making. Another condition that contributes to public relations excellence is the existence of activist pressures. Organizations that have experienced activist pressure better understand the importance of two-way communication and are more likely to practice excellent public relations.

The members of the Excellence Project conceptualized that excellent public relations can contribute to organizational effectiveness. By strategically managing communication programs, public relations can help the organization meet its goals such as increasing understanding, changing attitudes or behavior, or building and fostering mutually beneficial relationships with stakeholders. By managing potential conflicts proactively, public relations can help reduce the costs of litigation, pressure, and regulation. In addition, L. Grunig, J. Grunig, and Verčič (1998) also posited that excellent public relations could increase job satisfaction among employees by using symmetrical communication. Verčič et al. (1996) contended that these principles are indeed normative, but it is possible to practice the generic principles of excellent public relations in diverse cultural contexts around the world after localizing them.

Over the years, the generic principles have been applied by studies from many parts of the world to examine and describe a nation's public relations practice (Grunig et al., 1998; Huang, 1997; Kaur, 1997; Lim, Goh, & Sriramesh, 2005; Ni, 2008; Rhee, 2002; van Gorp & Pauwels, 2007; Watsona & Sallot, 2001; Wu & Taylor, 2003; Yeo & Sriramesh, 2009; Yun, 2007). Kaur (1997) studied the impact of privatization on public relations in Malaysia and found the generic principles of excellence could be applied to that setting. The competitive economic environment and growing pressure from strategic publics resulted in the increasing use of symmetrical communication by practitioners there, and the importance of knowledge of the managerial role was raised. J. Grunig, L. Grunig, and Verčič (1998) extended the Excellence Study by replicating it in Slovenian organizations. They explored how the change in Slovenia's political system from communism to democracy and its economic change to privatization of business organizations affected public relations practice there. They found that the generic principles of Excellence had been practiced in Slovenia. Huang (1997) explored the applicability of Excellence principles in Taiwanese practice within the conflict resolution context. In a later study on Taiwanese public relations practitioners, Wu and Taylor (2003) used the generic principles as a conceptual background for evaluation of the current status and future directions for public relations. A study of South Korean public relations practice was conducted by Rhee (2002), in which she found that the Excellence principles indeed explained Korean public relations practice and the association between the cultural variables and public relations Excellence variables.

Watsona and Sallot (2001) surveyed 151 corporate Japanese PR professionals in their study in which they adopted the generic principles and found that Japanese organizations' public relations practice resembled Western models. In her study of Chinese public relations, Ni (2008) tested the Excellence principles with specific focus on employee communication and employee–organization relationships. She posited that integrating employee communication into managerial practice is a key factor that should be considered for Chinese organizations to practice excellent public relations. Belgian scholars, van Gorp and Pauwels (2007) examined the extent to which the Excellence principles were adopted in their country's public relations practice. They found that almost half of the organizations have an integrated communication department, and when a practitioner was oriented more toward marketing and sales, they were more likely to have a seat on the executive committee. Similar to the results of the Excellence Project, women practitioners were enacting more of a 'communication technician' role which, in the authors' opinion, reflected the relatively low regard for public relations.

Lim, Goh, and Sriramesh (2005) applied four generic principles in their study of strategic public relations management in Singapore. Based on a quantitative survey and qualitative interviews, they found that the generic principles related to strategic public relations management were applicable to organizations in Singapore. Yeo and Sriramesh (2009) collected data from both in-depth interviews and self-reported logs of daily activities that showed that although top communicators in Singapore enjoy strategic reporting and unhindered access to senior management, paradoxically, senior management had mixed worldviews of the importance of public relations to their organization. Further, Singapore's top in-house practitioners lacked the strategic knowledge to enact the managerial role as they were too focused on technical work. The authors offered recommendations on how the level of public relations professionalism can be raised in Singapore and proposed that practitioners striving to fully equip themselves with the relevant academic knowledge of what makes communication excellent would be a good starting point. Instead of examining a specific nation's public relations practice, Yun (2007) adopted a sampling strategy of cultural grouping (individualist vs. collectivist) and tested the individual generic principles on those groups. He found that, except for the symmetric internal communication principle, other generic principles were found to have universal factor structure.

The sparse, yet growing, literature on the generic principles suggests that the Excellence Project has provided a foundation for a more systematic analysis of public relations around the world. The generic principles also help us critically think about how public relations is currently practiced and aspire to different or better forms of practice. It would not be an exaggeration to say that these principles have contributed to the advancement of the public relations discipline on the international scale. However, it is also undeniable that the application of the generic principles concept to global public relations may run the risk of being ethnocentric, as these concepts are developed based on a project conducted in Anglo-Saxon countries (Sriramesh, 2002). The specific environmental variables discussed in the next section help apply these principles in diverse cultural settings and make it possible for these principles to become more culturally relativistic.

Application of the Principles to Specific Cultural Environments

The generic principles reviewed above can only be deemed "generic" if they are applicable across a range of cultures. However, such application will have to take into account local socio-cultural conditions. Several studies (J. Grunig & L. Grunig, 2001; L. Grunig, J. Grunig, & Verčič, 1998; Sriramesh & Verčič, 2001, 2009a; Verčič et al., 1996; Wakefield, 1997) have reiterated that five specific variables should be considered when the generic principles are applied globally. These variables are: (1) culture including language; (2) the political and economic system; (3) the media system; (4) the level of activism; and (5) the level of development. Sriramesh and Verčič (2003) regarded a country's political system, the level of (economic) development, and the level of activism as elements of infrastructure and re-classified these variables into three factors: a country's infrastructure, media environment, and social culture. Subsequently, however, Sriramesh and Verčič (2009a) reverted to the five-variable model. This section will review these variables and some of the studies that have provided empirical evidence on the relationship between these variables and public relations.

Culture

Anthropologists have offered hundreds of definitions for the term "culture" (Sriramesh, 2009). Hofstede, one of the first to empirically study cultural dimensions in relation to organizations, defined culture as "the collective programming of the mind which distinguishes the members of one human group from another" (1984, p. 21). The author noted that culture has a great impact on the way people communicate. Gudykunst (1998) asserted that for improved communication, understanding cultural differences is essential.

Hofstede (1984, 1998) identified five dimensions of culture based on his data from managers in over 50 countries: (1) power distance; (2) collectivism/ individualism; (3) femininity/masculinity; (4) uncertainty avoidance; and (5) long-term/short-term orientation. Although these dimensions have proved very useful in linking culture with organizational processes, it is important to recognize that they do not constitute all aspects of culture, only those that Hofstede was able to discern from his data. *Power distance* is the extent to which social stratification confers unequal power to members of different strata. The less powerful members of organizations or societies often are at the receiving end of this inequality in power. *Collectivism* is the degree to which individuals of a culture value the individual over the collectivity. People in collective cultures identify themselves with the group, displaying high loyalty to the collective, whereas cultures with strong individualism encourage competition and value personal achievement. *Masculinity* refers to the distribution of roles based on sexes, with societies assigning gender-based roles to the two sexes. Women are often perceived as caring and nurturing and therefore are assigned to such roles in organizations or hospitality and service industries, whereas men are perceived as being more aggressive and often linked to more corporate activities. *Uncertainty avoidance* indicates a society's tolerance for ambiguity. It denotes the extent to which members of a society feel uncomfortable in unstructured situations. In organizational contexts, automation, rules and rituals, high levels of formalization, etc. are used as tactics to cope with ambiguity. The fifth dimension, *long-term or short-term orientation*, is based on Confucian dynamism. Long-term orientation is associated with values such as thrift and perseverance, whereas short-term orientation is associated with respect for tradition and a strong concern for establishing the truth.

There are other dimensions of culture that are useful for our purposes apart from those offered by Hofstede. Hall (1976) classified cultures according to high context and low context. In high-context cultures, tradition and history frame the world, and members of these cultures prefer brief and indirect communication. They are reluctant to disclose inside operations and therefore organizational contexts, information tends to be abstract and indirect without details. Asian countries tend to be high-context cultures, while most Western countries belong to low-context cultures, where clear and direct communication is preferred. There are correlations between some of Hofstede's dimensions and the level of context with more individualistic countries tending also to favor lower-context idiosyncracies.

In the field of public relations, many researchers have examined the influence of culture on public relations, contending that culture plays a key role in the practice of public relations. Based on his ethnographic study in India, Sriramesh (1992) argued that societal culture highly influenced how public relations was practiced; the societal culture with class orientation and high power distance directly affected the management philosophy of organizations, and in turn, managers who were elitist power holders made most decisions. In that situation, public relations is primarily employed as a technical function as part of press agentry. Sriramesh and White (1992) maintained that the generic principles would be more conducive in countries with collectivist cultures, low power distance, low uncertainty avoidance, and feminine cultures. From a similar perspective, Sriramesh, Kim and Takasaki (1999) analyzed public relations in three Asian cultures: India, Japan, and South Korea. In an attempt to link the models of public relations and culture, the authors found that the press agentry/publicity model and the personal influence model were frequently adopted among these three countries. They argued that the findings resulted from the countries' cultural elements, such as collectivism, high context, and high power distance.

Sharpe (1992) and Epley (1992) maintained that researchers and practitioners of public relations need to be knowledgeable of the cultural implications because different cultures view the practice and management of public relations in different ways. According to Ihator (2000), international public relations practitioners need to recognize and be sensitive about the differences in local cultures and business practices, because the communication style varies in different cultures. That is, recognition of one's own culture and acceptance of other cultures are the best approach to the global audience.

Several researchers regard Confucianism as a critical cultural factor that influences how public relations is practiced in some of the countries in Asia. Kim

(2003) identified four Confucian principles that influence the Korean public relations practice: (1) indirect communication; (2) the family chief orientation; (3) the Confucian worldview; and (4) face saving. An interesting study compared the public relations practices of domestic and multinational Korean companies in relation to culture and found that the two types of companies varied their public relations to cater to the cultural characteristics of their audiences. The concept of *guanxi* has been linked with public relations by several scholars from Asia (Aw, Tan, & Tan, 2002; Huang, 2001; Hung, 2003; Kipnis, 1997; Tan, 2000). All of these studies emphasized the use of *guanxi* for public relations as a replica of the personal influence model (Sriramesh, 1992) where public relations practitioners build personal relationships with strategic individuals (such as journalists or government officials) and in a *quid pro quo* manner do favors for them to get publicity-oriented or other favors in return.

According to Huang (2000), Confucian culture leads to a unique cultural characteristic, *gao guanxi* that is nothing but the use of the personal influence model. As one of the few scholars who assessed all five of Hofstede's dimensions in a single study, Rhee (2002) maintained that Confucianism and collectivism are positively correlated with the level of public relations excellence in Korea, noting: "[A]lthough conceptually affiliated with high power distance, . . . Confucianism may not be detrimental to achieving excellence in public relations" (p. 185). Her reasoning was because Confucianism valued such things as harmony and family values, these contributed to linking this philosophy with public relations.

Sriramesh (1996) found that personal influence and power distance had a significant influence on public relations activities in India. Similarly, Bardhan (2003) pointed out that personal contact and cultivation of interpersonal relationships play a critical role in media relations in the country as well. Based on her examination of a case of a multinational corporation in Korea, Sung (2006) pointed out that the company adopted several public relations strategies to emphasize its commitment to the Korean market and local employees in order to overcome Korea's "in-group culture," which stems from collectivism. This cultural characteristic often results in strong cohesive power among those who belong to a group, while excluding out-group people. Therefore, multinational corporations often develop programs that involve Korean organizations in order to show in-group membership.

Media Systems

Media and public relations have a critical relationship; media relations is a major part of public relations practices because the mass media have the power to influence an organization's activities. A large portion of media content comes from public relations sources. Furthermore, the mass media play a critical role in the process of image shaping of organizations and nations (Sriramesh & Verčič, 2009b).

Ever since Siebert, Peterson, and Schramm (1956) offered their seminal conceptualization of different media systems around the world, scores of scholars have contributed to the development of normative theories of the mass media (see Sriramesh & Verčič, 2009b, for a review of studies and the link between mass media and public relations). Hachten (1992) identified five types of media systems across the world: (1) the authoritarian system; (2) the Western system; (3) the communist system; (4) the revolutionary system; and (5) the developmental system. In an authoritarian media system, he maintained, the media work for those in power. The Western system, which is represented by American and the Western European media, is associated with freedom of the press. In a communist system, the Communist Party or the government owns and controls the media to manage the people. A revolutionary system is often illegal or subversive and consists of underground media produced outside the country. This system is designed to depose the government. The developmental media system is a variation of the authoritarian system and found in developing countries where the state controls the media. Information is used for national development, and individual rights are overlooked.

Hiebert (1992) argued for a new model of media system analysis for multinational public relations. He argued that old ways of theorizing the media system are outmoded because political ideologies that were based on such systems as the Soviet system no longer exist. He suggested new theories based on pragmatic considerations for communication effectiveness. Sriramesh and Verčič (2009b) offered three factors – (1) media *control*, (2) media *diffusion*, and (3) media *access* – that help the public relations practitioners understand the global media environment so that they can employ the appropriate communication channels. Since public relations practitioners constantly use the media in communicating messages to publics, who controls the media and their content is critical; pressure on editorial freedom influences the free flow of information in the particular society. Media diffusion, or "the extent to which the media permeate a given society" (p. 78) is significant in that public relations professionals try to place information in a certain medium in order to reach a targeted audience. Finally, understanding the extent to which the media are accessible to individuals or groups in a society allows public relations practitioners to understand the public opinion and gauge activism.

Meanwhile, the development of media technology and the media environment, especially the emergence of social media, is expected to influence how public relations is practiced globally as well. Wakefield (2011) argued that social media would provide individuals with the means to influence the behaviors of organizations across borders, which may result in more accountable and responsible communication.

Level of Development

Although the term "level of development" can have several meanings, today, development refers to the state where everyone in a country has equal opportunities to improve the quality of his/her life. After examining development initiatives run by the government in the Middle East, Latin America, and Sub-Saharan Africa, Al-Enad (1990) maintained that public relations was part of development communication to liberate and organize publics. In the Middle East, public relations is called "general relations" because authorities are sensitive to the concept of public opinion. Moreover, propaganda may play an important role in developing countries by maintaining the equilibrium of the social system, although it may be unethical in nature.

On the other hand, Kruckeberg (1995–1996) refuted Al-Enad's relativistic proposition and argued that two-way symmetrical communication was most likely to develop in Middle East culture. According to him, in every country or culture, two-way symmetrical public relations exists, regardless of situations and environments. Furthermore, he argued that public relations professionals should play the role of interpreters, ethicists, and social policy-makers of their organizations, which will be challenged in the "global village" (p. 37) where the values and belief systems across the globe will confront one another. Verčič et al. (1996) maintained that generic principles should be applied slowly and gradually with changes in the societal culture and the political-economic system in countries with a low level of development. They suggested that the variable of development might take in other variables. In particular, a country's level of economic development has an impact on how public relations is performed. For example, illiteracy and the lack of sufficient communication infrastructure are obstacles in conducting an information campaign (Sriramesh & Verčič, 2009a).

Political and Economic Systems

Often closely related to each other, political and economic systems influence the practice of public relations. Sriramesh and Verčič (2001) argued for the importance of comparative research on the relations between political ideologies and public relations because a country's political environment determines the nature of public relations. They maintained that the Western definition of public relations was based on a democratic political structure. Therefore, the practice of public relations can vary all over the world. However, Verčič et al. (1996) found that generic principles still could be applied and adjusted if strategic research was well conducted. From case studies of public relations in different social, political, and economic contexts, Culbertson, Jeffers, Stone, and Terrell (1993) suggested that social, political, and economic variables were closely related and influenced public relations practices. Kaur (1997) examined the contribution of privatization and sophistication of public relations management in Malaysia and concluded that the extent of privatization influenced strategic management of public relations. Singh (2000) also found the impact of changes in economic systems on the public relations practice in India. Several studies that examined Eastern European countries such as Germany, Romania, and Slovenia demonstrated that the development of public relations is greatly influenced by the country's political and economic environment (Bentele & Peter, 1996; Turk, 1996; Verčič et al., 1996).

Level of Activism

Although only a limited amount of public relations research has been done on activism at the global level, activism has great implications for public relations. Public relations researchers examined activist groups or organizations and concluded that these groups were strategic publics that constrained an organization's autonomy to achieve its goals and mission (J. Grunig, 1989, 2000; J. Grunig & L. Grunig, 1997).

J. Grunig and Jaatinen (1998) examined the types of activism related to political systems and differentiated the activist power based on the activists' relationship with the government. In a pluralist system, several activist groups compete with one another to influence policy-making, whereas the government organizes or helps generate activists to dominate the political system in a corporatist system. Kovacs (2001) examined the strategies and impact of activist groups with regard to policy-making and programming of British broadcasting, and maintained that pressure groups built strategic relationships to impact their targets. Therefore, public relations should be engaged in, and facilitate public debate in, civil society and build relationships.

According to Kim and Sriramesh (2009), those who practice public relations globally need to be aware of the level of activism in different societies because socio-cultural environmental factors influence the frequency and nature of collective behaviors in a particular society. The authors identified two dimensions of activism: the intensity of action, and the diversity of issues in a given society. The intensity of activism is influenced by various environmental factors such as politics, economic development, culture, and media. The breadth of activism also reflects the diversity of socio-cultural variations in the society. Furthermore, it depends on how the media report confrontations and collective actions within that particular country.

Conclusion

As the first multinational empirical study of its kind, the Excellence Project certainly has laid the conceptual foundations for a solid theory of global public relations. The generic principles and cultural variables that help us apply these principles at the global level appear to be very logical and sound. However, much of that theorizing is based on empirical data from Anglo-Saxon cultures. Although several studies from Asia and a few other parts of the world have addressed different aspects of these concepts, these studies are few and far between. If public relations practice and scholarship are to evolve from the current ethnocentricity, there is a dire need for greater numbers of studies from different socio-cultural environments that not only describe how public relations is currently being practiced in those cultures but more importantly, why such a practice exists and what purposes it serves. Unless we have empirical data from a variety of socio-cultural environments, existing public relations theorizing at the global level will remain conceptual and not empirical. Looking to the future, one hopes that within the next decade there will be enough empirical data from diverse environments for the field to claim a truly global theory of public relations. Young scholars and current graduate students will be the key drivers of this development in the body of knowledge.

Notes

1 J. Grunig and L. Grunig (1992) proposed that in actual public relations practice, Excellent public relations deviates from pure symmetrical public relations and can be described as a combination of the two-way asymmetrical and symmetrical models: mixed motive—public relations. It is a concept from the game theory that Murphy (1991) introduced to public relations theory. It refers to the phenomenon of the public relations people being motivated by both their loyalty to and by the publics affected by the behavior of the organization that employs them.
2 Other public relations models include press agentry, public information, and two-way asymmetrical models. The model of press agentry describes propagandistic public relations that seeks media attention in almost any way possible. Practitioners of this model use a one-way, source-to-receiver communication model. The public information model is a truth-oriented approach to public relations. The practitioners strive to provide accurate information to the public, but they do not disclose unfavorable information voluntarily. The two-way asymmetrical model is characterized by unbalanced, one-sided communication. The practitioners of this model use social science theory and the research of attitudes and behaviors to persuade the public to accept the organization's point of view or to behave as the organization wants (J. Grunig & Hunt, 1984).

References

Al-Enad, A. (1990). Public relations' roles in developing countries. *Public Relations Quarterly*, *35*(1), 24–26.

Aw, A., Tan, S. K., & Tan, R. (2002). *Guanxi* and public relations: An exploratory qualitative study of the public relations–*Guanxi* phenomenon in Singapore firms. Paper presented to the Public Relations Division at the 52nd annual conference of the International Communication Association, Seoul, Korea, July.

Bardhan, N. (2003). Rupturing public relations metanarratives: The example of India. *Journal of Public Relations Research, 15*(3), 225–248.

Bentele, G., & Peter, G-M. (1996). Public relations in the German Democratic Republic and the new federal German states. In H. M. Culbertson & N. Chen (Eds.), *International public relations: A comparative analysis* (pp. 349–367). Mahwah, NJ: Lawrence Erlbaum Associates.

Bordo, M. D., Cavallo, A. F., & Meissner, C. M. (2010). Sudden stops: Determinants and output effects in the first era of globalization, 1880–1913. *Journal of Development Economics, 91*(2), pp. 227–241.

Culbertson, H. M., Jeffers, D. W., Stone, D. B., & Terrell, M. (1993). *Social, political, and economic contexts in public relations: Theory and cases.* Hillsdale, NJ: Lawrence Erlbaum Associates.

Debeljak, A. (2009). In praise of hybridity: Globalization and the modern Western paradigm. Paper presented at the 15th International Public Relations Symposium, Lake Bled, Slovenia, July.

Dozier, D., Grunig, L. A., & Grunig, J. E. (1995). *Manager's guide to excellence in public relations and communication management.* Mahwah, NJ: Lawrence Erlbaum Associates.

Epley, J. (1992). Public relations in the global village: An American perspective. *Public Relations Review, 18*(2), 109–116.

Frank, A. G. (1998). *ReOrient: Global economy in the Asian age.* Berkeley: University of California Press.

Grunig, J. E. (1989). Toward a theory of the public relations behavior of organizations: Review of a program of research. *Journal of Public Relations Research, 1*(1), 27–63.

Grunig, J. E. (1992). *Excellence in public relations and communication management.* Hillsdale, NJ: Lawrence Erlbaum.

Grunig, J. E. (2000). Collectivism, collaboration, and societal corporatism as core professional values in public relations. *Journal of Public Relations Research, 12*(1), 23–48.

Grunig, J. E., & Grunig, L. A. (1992). Models of public relations and communication. In J. E. Grunig (Ed.), *Excellence in public relations and communication management* (pp. 285–326). Hillsdale, NJ: Lawrence Erlbaum Associates.

Grunig, J. E., & Grunig, L. A. (1997). Review of a program of research on activism: Incidence in four countries, activist publics, strategies of activist groups, and organizational response to activism. Paper presented at the Public Relations Research Symposium, Lake Bled, Slovenia.

Grunig, J. E., & Grunig, L. A. (2001). Auditing a global or multi-organizational public relations function. *Jim and Lauri Grunig's research: A supplement of pr reporter, 14,* 4 pp.

Grunig, J. E., & Hunt, T. (1984). *Managing public relations.* New York: Holt, Rinehart & Winston.

Grunig, J. E., & Jaatinen, M. (1998). Strategic, symmetrical public relations in government: From pluralism to societal corporatism. *Journal of Communication Management, 3*(3), 218–234.

Grunig, L. A., Grunig, J. E., & Dozier, D. M. (2002). *Excellent public relations and effective organizations: A study of communication management in three countries.* Mahwah, NJ: Lawrence Erlbaum Associates.

Grunig, J. E., Grunig, L. A., & Verčič, D. (1998). Are the IABC's excellence principles generic?: Comparing Slovenia and the United States, the United Kingdom, and Canada. *Journal of Communication Management, 2*(4), 335–356.

Gudykunst, W. B. (1998). *Bridging differences: Effective intergroup communication* (3rd ed.). Thousand Oaks, CA: Sage.

Hachten, W. A. (1992). *The world news prism: Changing media of international communication* (3rd ed.). Ames, IA: Iowa State University Press.

Hall, E. T. (1976). *Beyond culture.* Garden City, NY: Anchor Press/Doubleday.

Hiebert, R. E. (1992). Global public relations in a post-communist world: A new model. *Public Relations Review, 18*(2), 117–126.

Hofstede, G. (1984). *Culture's consequences: International differences in work-related values* (abridged ed.). Newbury Park, CA: Sage.

Hofstede, G. (1998). Think locally, act globally: Cultural constraints in personnel management. *Management International Review, 38* (special issue), 7–26.

Huang, Y. (1997). Public relations strategies, relational outcomes, and conflict management. Unpublished doctoral dissertation, University of Maryland, College Park.

Huang, Y. (2000). The personal influence model and *Gao Guanxi* in Taiwan Chinese public relations. *Public Relations Review, 26*(2), 219–236.

Huang, Y. (2001). Values of public relations: Effects on organization–public relationships mediating conflict resolution. *Journal of Public Relations Research, 13*(4), 265–301.

Hung, C. J. F. (2003). Culture, relationship cultivation, and relationship outcomes: A qualitative evaluation on multinational companies' relationship management in China. Paper presented to the Public Relations Division at the 53rd annual conference of International Communication Association, San Diego, May.

Ihator, A. (2000). Understanding the cultural patterns of the world: An imperative in implementing strategic international PR programs. *Public Relations Quarterly, 45*(4), 38–44.

Kaur, K. (1997). The impact of privatization on public relations and the role of public relations management in the privatization process: A qualitative analysis of the Malaysian case. Unpublished doctoral dissertation, University of Maryland, College Park.

Kim, J-N., & Sriramesh, K. (2009). A descriptive model of activism in global public relations research and practice. In K. Sriramesh, & D. Verčič (Eds.), *The global public relations handbook* (rev. ed.). New York: Routledge.

Kim, Y. (2003). Professionalism and diversification: The evolution of public relations in South Korea. In K. Sriramesh & D. Verčič (Eds.), *The global public relations handbook: Theory, research, and practice* (pp. 106–120). Mahwah, NJ: Lawrence Erlbaum Associates.

Kipnis, A. (1997). *Producing Guanxi: Sentiment, self, and subculture in a North China village.* Durham, NC: Duke University Press.

Kovacs, R. (2001). Relationship building as integral to British activism: Its impact on accountability in broadcasting. *Public Relations Review, 27*(4), 321–336.

Kruckeberg, D. (1995–1996, Winter). The challenge for public relations in the era of globalization. *Public Relations Quarterly, 40*(4), 36–39.

Lim, S., Goh, J., & Sriramesh, K. (2005). Applicability of the generic principles of Excellent public relations in a different cultural context: The case study of Singapore. *Journal of Public Relations Research, 17*(4), 315–340.

Murphy, P. (1991). The limits of symmetry: A game theory approach to symmetric and asymmetric public relations. In J. Grunig & L. Grunig (Eds.), *Public relations annual* (pp. 115–132). Hillsdale, NJ: Lawrence Erlbaum Associates.

Ni, C. (2008). Internal/employee communication and organizational effectiveness: A study of Chinese corporations in transition. *Journal of Contemporary China, 17*(54), 167–189.

Rhee, Y. (2002). Global public relations: A cross-cultural study of the Excellence Theory in South Korea. *Journal of Public Relations Research 14*(3), 159–184.

Sharpe, M. L. (1992). The impact of social and cultural conditioning on global public relations. *Public Relations Review, 18*(2), 103–107.

Siebert, F. S., Peterson, T., & Schramm, W. (1956). *Four theories of the press.* Urbana: University of Illinois Press.

Singh, R. (2000). Public relations in contemporary India: Current demands and strategy. *Public Relations Review, 26*(3), 295–313.

Sriramesh, K. (1992). Societal culture and public relations: Ethnographic evidence from India. *Public Relations Review, 18*(2), 201–211.

Sriramesh, K. (1996). Power distance and public relations: An ethnographic study of Southern Indian organizations. In H. M. Culbertson & N. Chen (Eds.), *International public relations: A comparative analysis* (pp. 171–190). Mahwah, NJ: Lawrence Erlbaum Associates.

Sriramesh, K. (2002). The dire need for multiculturalism in public relations education: An Asian perspective. *Journal of Communication Management, 7*(1), 54–77.

Sriramesh, K. (2009). Culture and public relations. In K. Sriramesh & D. Verčič (Eds.), *The global public relations handbook* (rev. ed.). New York: Routledge.

Sriramesh, K. (2010). Globalization and public relations: Opportunities for growth and reformulation. In R. L. Heath (Ed.), *Handbook of public relations* (2nd ed.). Thousand Oaks, CA: Sage.

Sriramesh, K., & Verčič, D. (2001). International public relations: A framework for future research. *Journal of Communication Management, 6*(2), 103–117.

Sriramesh, K., & Verčič, D. (2003). *The global public relations handbook: Theory, research, and practice.* Mahwah, NJ: Lawrence Erlbaum Associates.

Sriramesh, K., & Verčič, D. (2009a). A theoretical framework for global public relations research and practice. In K. Sriramesh & D. Verčič (Eds.), *The global public relations handbook: Theory, research, and practice.* Mahwah, NJ: Lawrence Erlbaum Associates.

Sriramesh, K., & Verčič, D. (2009b). Mass media and public relations. In K. Sriramesh & D. Verčič (Eds.), *The global public relations handbook: Theory, research, and practice.* Mahwah, NJ: Lawrence Erlbaum Associates.

Sriramesh, K., & White, J. (1992). Societal culture and public relations. In J. E. Grunig (Ed.), *Excellence in public relations and communication management* (pp. 597–616). Hillsdale, NJ: Lawrence Erlbaum Associates.

Sriramesh, K., Kim, Y., & Takasaki, M. (1999). Public relations in three Asian cultures: An analysis. *Journal of Public Relations Research, 11*(4), 271–292.

Sung, M. (2006). Global public relations in South Korea: A case study of a multinational corporation. In M. G. Parkinson & D. Ekachai (Eds.), *International and intercultural public relations: A campaign case approach* (pp. 187–203). Boston: Allyn and Bacon.

Tan, S. L. (2000). *Guanxi and public relations in Singapore: An exploratory study.* Master's thesis, Nanyang Technological University, Singapore.

Turk, J. V. (1996). Romania: From publicitate past to public relations future. In H. M. Culbertson & N. Chen (Eds.), *International public relations: A comparative analysis* (pp. 341–347). Mahwah, NJ: Lawrence Erlbaum Associates.

Van Gorp, B., & Pauwels, L. (2007). Positioning and role of public relations in large Belgian organizations. *Public Relations Review 33*(3), 301–305.

Verčič, D., Grunig, J. E., & Grunig, L. A. (1996). Global and specific principles of public relations: Evidence from Slovenia. In H. Culbertson & N. Chen (Eds.), *International public relations: A comparative analysis* (pp. 31–65). Mahwah, NJ: Lawrence Erlbaum Associates.

Wakefield, R. (1997). *International public relations: A theoretical approach to Excellence based on a worldwide Delphi study.* Unpublished doctoral dissertation, University of Maryland, College Park.

Wakefield, R. (2011). Critiquing the generic/specific public relations theory: The need to close the transnational knowledge gap. In N. Bardhan & C. K. Weaver (Eds.), *Public relations in global cultural contexts: Multi-paradigmatic perspectives* (pp. 167–190). New York: Routledge.

Watsona, D., & Sallot, Lynn. (2001). Public relations practice in Japan: An exploratory study. *Public Relations Review, 27*(4), 389–402.

Wu, M., & Taylor, M. (2003). Public relations in Taiwan: Roles, professionalism, and relationship to marketing. *Public Relations Review, 29*(4), 473–483.

Yeo, S. L., & Sriramesh, K. (2009). Adding value to organizations: An examination of the role of senior public relations practitioners in Singapore. *Public Relations Review, 35*(4), 422–425.

Yun, S. (2007). Exploring the embassy sampling strategy for large-scale cross-national study in replicating the normative theory of global public relations. *Public Relations Review, 33*(2), 224–226.

7

CONCEPTUALIZING PUBLICS AND CONSTRUCTING PUBLIC RELATIONS THEORY

The Situational Theory of Problem Solving and Its New Research

Jeong-Nam Kim and Lan Ni

Abstract

The situational theory of problem solving (STOPS) has evolved from its parent theory, the situational theory of publics (STP), constructed by James Grunig. The situational theory of problem solving extends the theoretical utilities and power of the situational theory of publics as it inherits STP's theoretical assumptions such as communication as a purposive, coping tool for problematic life situations. This chapter first briefly reviews the common theoretical elements between the STP and STOPS, then introduces the new theoretical features of STOPS, followed by highlights in new public relations research originating from the STOPS. Finally, it discusses several new developmental research agendas triggered by the STOPS.

Key words

boundary spanning, communicative action, cybercoping, hot issue, megaphoning, publics, public segmentation, referent criterion, scouting, situational theory of problem solving, situational theory of publics

Introduction

The situational theory of publics (STP) has provided the basis for public relations by defining and identifying one of the two key terms in public relations: "publics." James Grunig first constructed the theory of decision–making and information behaviors (in "The Role of Information in Economic Decision Making," 1966) and then went on to propose several more theories that have contributed greatly to public relations literature. In this brief chapter we review the new situational theory that originated from his situational theory of publics. The main aim of the chapter is to discuss the applicability and utility of the new situational theory in constructing other theoretical concepts and models and to outline several new research territories emerging from the situational theory of problem solving. Although the outlined research directions are not meant to be exhaustive, we hope that this chapter will act as a catalyst for researchers to continue what Grunig started in the 1960s and to develop more applications of theoretical constructs in that direction.

Situational Theory of Publics and Situational Theory of Problem Solving

In this section, we first illustrate the differences between the situational theory of publics (STP) and the situational theory of problem solving (STOPS) (Figure 7.1). We will then introduce the major premises and variables of the STOPS and highlight the connections between the two theories. There are four major differences between the STP and the STOPS. First, the situational theory of publics adopted a narrower conceptualization of active communication behaviors. It used only information acquisition, which included information seeking and attending, to describe an active public. However, members of an actively communicating public typically engage not only in active information seeking but also in active information sharing and selecting. In problem solving, selecting certain information over other information and sharing information deemed to be important with others facilitate problem solving because such information behaviors can reproduce or reinforce similar problem perceptions among people and better mobilize necessary attention to and resources for dealing with the problem (Chwe, 2001; Gamson, 1992). The STOPS, therefore, includes a broader definition of publics' communication behaviors.

Second, an earlier version of the situational theory of publics included the concept of a referent criterion. This concept was later dropped because it failed to predict information seeking and attending (Grunig, 1997). However, according to several researchers, the referent criterion was found to have conceptual and practical benefits in explaining and classifying the behaviors of publics (e.g., Kim, Ni, & Sha, 2008). Therefore, the utility of this concept has been reconsidered and redefined and reinstated in the situational theory of problem solving.

Third, in its original formulation, the theory of publics only considered perceptual variables as causal antecedents to communication behavior. The situational theory of problem solving has tested and supported a more immediate antecedent variable to communicative action, i.e., a motivational variable (Kruglanski, 1996). In doing so, motivational components have been separated out in the definition and measurement of problem recognition (i.e., the phrase "stop to think about the problem," which has been used to measure problem recognition).

Finally, recognized as a public relations theory, the situational theory of publics has often been considered useful only for public relations practices. However, the situational theory of problem solving recognized the origin of STP from a theory

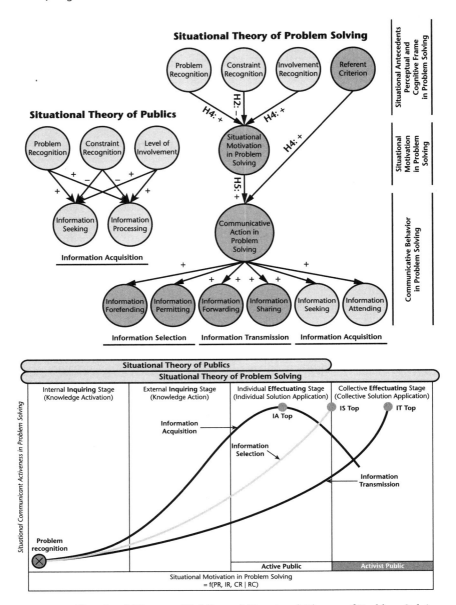

FIGURE 7.1 Situational Theory of Publics and Situational Theory of Problem Solving

of decision-making and information use and expanded the applicability and utility of the STP. By broadening the definition and scope of the dependent variable of the STP from information acquiring to multivariate concepts of communicative action—information acquiring, sharing, and selecting—the theory of problem solving has become a more general theory of communication and problem solving.

In this section, we will discuss the development of the situational theory of publics into the situational theory of problem solving. The STOPS incorporates a new concept, *communicative action in problem solving* (CAPS), as its dependent variable (Kim, Grunig, & Ni, 2010). CAPS is introduced as a more generalized concept for active communication behaviors. It consists of four subvariables— *information forwarding, sharing, forefending,* and *permitting*—in addition to the two dependent variables of the theory of publics, *information seeking* and *information attending* (originally termed *information processing*). Active communication behaviors could mean more than active consumption (seeking or attending) of information related to a problematic situation. According to CAPS, situation-specific communication behaviors span active selection and transmission of information regarding problematic situations. In this vein, as CAPS incorporates proactive and reactive information transmission and selection, it increases the conceptual power and validity of the situational theory.

In addition, to explain communicative action, STOPS refines the independent variables of the situational theory of publics: *problem recognition, constraint recognition, involvement recognition,* and *referent criterion*. Notably, problem recognition and referent criterion have been redefined, and involvement has been renamed. The situational theory of publics defines problem recognition as occurring when "people detect that something should be done about a situation and stop to think about what to do" (Grunig, 1997, p. 10). In contrast, the new theory conceptualizes problem recognition as "a perceptual state one experiences after the failure of preconscious problem solving" (Kim & Grunig, 2011, p. 12). Problem recognition is now conceptualized as detection of a perceptual-cognitive problem. It is defined as "one's perception that something is missing and that there is no immediately applicable solution to it" (Kim & Grunig, 2011). In addition, by separating the "stop to think" about a problematic situation from the previous definition of problem recognition, the current theory now includes a situation-specific motivation. Situational theorists note that a person may detect a problem but may not stop what he or she is doing to do something about it. The state of "stop to think about what to do" conceptually falls into a motivational dimension rather than a perceptual dimension. The new motivational variable mediates the effects of antecedent perceptual variables on communicative behaviors.

The STOPS also redefines the referent criterion as "any knowledge or subjective judgmental system that influences the way in which one approaches problem solving," which includes "decisional guidelines or decision rules perceived as relevant to a given problem" (Kim & Grunig, 2011, p. 15). Unlike the referent criterion that was conceptualized in the previous theory of publics, a referent criterion can now be imported from prior problematic situations or can be one *improvised* at an early phase of a new problem-solving situation.

New Public Relations Concepts Crafted Using the Situational Theory of Problem Solving

The theory of problem solving has helped generate several new concepts and extend its utilities beyond public relations in areas where the concept of "publics" is necessary. In this section, we briefly review the research based on CAPS and STOPS. Four areas are identified: (1) refined typology of publics; (2) new method of public segmentation; (3) redefined communication objectives; and (4) new contexts of public research such as hot-issue publics and public diplomacy, internal relations, and health communication.

Lan Ni and Jeong-Nam Kim (2009) have proposed a new taxonomy of publics by further breaking down active and aware publics in controversial, prolonged issues. In our taxonomy (see Figure 7.2), active and aware publics are classified into eight subpublics based on three properties: (1) the history of problem solving; (2) the extent of activeness in problem solving; and (3) the openness to approaches in problem solving. The theoretical utility and validity of this public typology are well demonstrated when we apply the taxonomy to various social, political, and economic issues that are controversial and common in most societies. For example, the new typology of subpublics would find its application in identifying publics regarding environmental issues such as global warming and political controversies such as abortion or gay-lesbian marriages.

Notably, the typology has conceptual ties with the situational theory of problem solving in that each subpublic is uniquely identified with its information selectivity, information transmission, and information acquisition. Aware publics and active publics possess different characteristics in terms of their communicative behaviors. Some could be fresher (vs. chronic) in their problem perceptions and motivation. Some would be more proactive and motivated in thinking about and dealing with the problem/issue situation. Also, some of the aware and active publics would be more closed-minded in their thinking about the situation and the solution. The differences in the characteristics between aware or active publics produce different issue-dynamics and institution–public interactions. Thus, classifying and under-standing of the subpublics within prolonged, controversial issues will be useful for public relations practitioners and academic researchers who are interested in public opinions and issue-related interactions of individuals with other social members.

Another important application of the STOPS is public segmentation. In the STP tradition, public segmentation was mainly performed through the Canonical Correlations method. In a recent article in *PRism,* Kim (2011b) introduced and demonstrated the "summation method" of public segmentation using three predictor variables: (1) problem recognition; (2) involvement recognition; and (3) constraint recognition. The intuitive conceptualization and computational ease of the summation method have made it a useful supplement to the existing Canonical Correlations method.

The situational theory of problem solving consists of four different types of vari-ables: (1) perceptual; (2) cognitive frame; (3) motivational; and (4) communicative

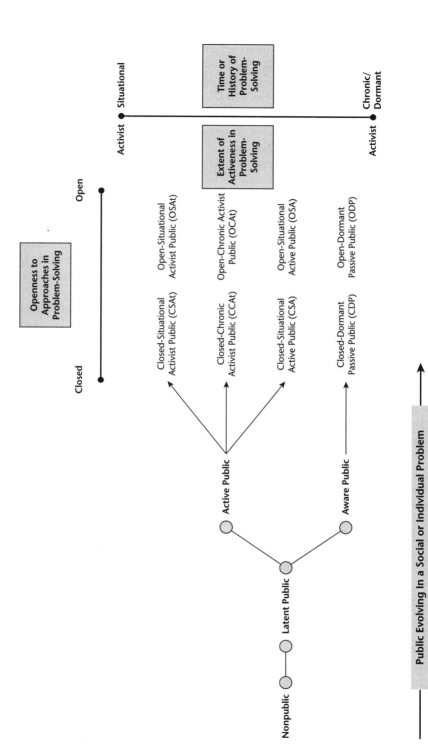

FIGURE 7.2 Illustration of Publics Evolving from Three Key Problem-solving Characteristics

behaviors. These variables are used for distinct communication objectives. Traditionally, most communication objectives from message senders (an organization) have focused on influencing message recipients (members of publics) so as to increase knowledge, favorable attitude, and desired behaviors of these target publics. This approach is useful in achieving normative goals in a society, such as in health education or risk communication, yet the associated communication is often one-way, with a top-down flow of influence, or at times for the asymmetrical purpose of serving the interests of message senders. One key challenge in this approach is its effectiveness or feasibility. As is known by many health campaigners and risk communicators, the effect size of such one-way, unilateral, persuasion-based approaches is in general disappointingly small. Alternatively, the situational variables of problem perception (being aware of the risks) and perceived constraints, and information forwarding and sharing information behaviors about the problem (risks) can be more realistic and feasible communicative objectives (see Kim & Ni, 2013, for a full review of setting communication objectives corresponding to public segmentation).

In communication situations related to health risks, the alternative communication objectives can be used to track the changes in the situational variables among the members of publics. In particular, based on the purpose of health interventions, objectives can be set to increase the sense of seriousness and connection to the health risks (increasing problem recognition) and lift the barriers for members of publics to do something about the problem (decreasing constraint recognition). The effectiveness of the proposed communication program or policy intervention can be measured by the changes of perception, which would lead to an increase in one's motivation in dealing with the given problem, and this in turn will lead to voluntary communicative actions such as information seeking and information forwarding/sharing by the members of publics.

The theoretical variables of the STOPS can therefore provide nonfinancial indicators for the effectiveness of public relations programs/interventions. For example, assessed before and after programs and policy interventions in controversial issues, the problem recognition, involvement recognition, constraint recognition, situational motivation, and information forwarding (i.e., the variables from STOPS) of active publics could be used to judge the success of such interventions.

The situational theory of problem solving recently also found application in socio-political hot issues to further the understanding of "hot-issue publics" (Aldoory & J. Grunig, 2012; J. Grunig, 1997). In a recent study, STOPS was applied to a national hot issue in Korea (the issue of the import of beef from the US), which had drawn massive media coverage over a six-month period. The study replicated the original STOPS model and further investigated the effects of cross-situational variables such as SES, demographics on situational perceptions and communicative behaviors (Kim, Ni, Kim, & Kim, 2012).

The dependent variable of the STOPS (i.e., the CAPS model) was applied to build a theoretical account of how it works and what to do regarding individual communicative behaviors and perceptions about foreign countries—sociological public diplomacy (research on "soft power," see *International Journal of Intercultural Communication* (Kim, 2012), and a book chapter on foreign publics' consumption of cultural products). In these studies and a theoretical essay, CAPS/STOPS helped highlight the presence and paths of individual and collective information behaviors regarding foreign cultural products and their influence on foreign publics' perception of goodwill (soft power) toward the country of origin of the cultural products.

The theoretical variables and premises included in the STOPS and CAPS lead to the development of new theoretical concepts related to communicative behaviors by internal publics (e.g., employees) such as *megaphoning, scouting,* and *microboundary spanning* (Kim, 2011a; Kim & Rhee, 2011). Internal publics such as employees or university students who have relational interactions with their host organizations tend to engage in information behaviors regarding their work and organization-related information in both online and offline communicative networks. For example, employees with poor (good) relationships engage in more negative (positive) information forwarding and sharing against (for) their business or organization and further look for opportunities to penalize (reward) their host organization during organizational turbulence (e.g., a crisis)—*megaphoning.* Employees with good quality relationships volunteer to identify strategic information, such as new trends, ideas for business innovations (strategic opportunities), and potential risks and problems (strategic threats), and circulate it within the organization—*scouting.* Interestingly, individual employees and their routine communicative behaviors play the role of "boundary spanning" between the organization and its various social, institutional constituencies as they seek, attend, forward, share, forefend, and permit information related to their daily interests and operational routines in both task and societal environments. Such information behaviors by employees increase organizational effectiveness and adaptation in a competitive, uncertain organizational environment and are critical to the success and failure of the organization—*microboundary spanning.*

In addition, the two theories have been applied to health and risk communication contexts (health donations such as organs and blood). In a recent study, STOPS was replicated in the issue of the shortage of organ donations to test the predictive power of situational variables in the behavioral intentions to be a registered health donor. More interestingly, the same study introduced the new concept of the problem chain-recognition effect. The *problem chain-recognition effect* refers to the increased likelihood of recognizing similar types of problems/issues as one becomes active in an anchoring problem/issue. As individuals become communicatively active about a problem, they tend to obtain and exchange more information on the problem and are thus more likely to find related problems—a *chain recognition* of related or similar types of problems/issues. This recognition then increases chances of the realization of the embeddedness of the given problem (e.g., finding a cure for spinal muscular atrophy using stem cell research) within a larger problem network (e.g., federal regulation of stem cell research in general), and has notable implications regarding cultivating and transferring problem recognition of more salient issues, such as shortage of registered organ donors, to less-salient issues such as shortage of minority bone marrow donors. It can also be applied to increasing problem chain recognition in other types of social problems such as environmental concerns (e.g., from local air quality to a global climate change issue), and may increase voluntary problem-solving behaviors (e.g., recycling intentions).

Another health communication research derived from STOPS and CAPS is *cybercoping* among networked publics, and collective effectuating of individual health problems. In this study, the CAPS variables—information forwarding and information seeking—define cybercoping through online media (e.g., blogging) and information behaviors through online relational networks as means of fostering better health-problem solving—a mere communication effect. Studies conducted with patients with chronic illnesses such as HIV, cancer, lupus, and depression found coping effects through active information behaviors, and further explain boundary conditions of effective cybercoping (Kim & Vibber, 2012).

Finally, in 2012, a special issue of the *International Journal of Strategic Communication* was devoted to the strategic values of communicative actions of publics and stake-holders. This special issue focuses on two key phenomena in strategic communi-cation: quality and types of relationships with strategic constituencies and their communicative actions set off from the relational history. The special issue captures and illustrates the fact that quality and types of relational history provide a contextual background that triggers and magnifies desirable (undesirable) communicative action for (against) organizations/institutions such as positive (negative) information forwarding and sharing about organization-related problems/issues. This special issue started with a theoretical frame based on CAPS and STOPS to explain the role and values of relationships that trigger positive and negative communicative actions among members of strategic publics. Following this theoretical introduc-tion, a series of detailed research programs have been presented in the subfields of strategic communication management, such as public relations, consumer research, marketing communication, internal communication, tourism management, and public diplomacy.

Overall, CAPS and STOPS have directly and indirectly generated research programs on publics' communicative behaviors in different types of life situations and contexts. They explain the communication processes of members of publics. Furthermore, these theories help develop communication management programs to intervene in individual, institutional, and social problems, such as increased exposure to risks and increased conflict and animosity among social actors, to enhance problem-solving efforts through the tools of public segmentation, setting alternative communication objectives, and diagnosing key challenges to employee communication that pose strategic threats to organizational effectiveness.

Emerging Research from the Situational Theory of Problem Solving

The situational theory of problem solving has a general premise: the more one commits to problem solving, the more the person becomes acquisitive, selective, and transmissive of information pertaining to the problem. The theory attends to the communication aspects of human behaviors and related interactional dynamics. For that reason, it claims its theoretical stakes in many individual and social phenomena related to human communication.

In megaphoning and scouting, for instance, STOPS and CAPS provide conceptual building blocks to build other theoretical models and new concepts by utilizing the information behaviors in three domains (selectivity, transmission, and acquisition). In addition, the situational variables of problem recognition, involvement recognition, and constraint recognition help predict when individuals with a controversial social issue would engage in computer-mediated communication, e.g., flaming behaviors. Using the theoretical formulation on communicative action of a motivated problem solver, interesting new concepts and research applications have been developed in a relatively short period of time. In this concluding section, we outline and propose several emerging research agendas utilizing the situational theory of problem solving.

Measurement, Evaluation, and Strategizing Using Causes of Situation-Specific Perception

How to measure and evaluate public relations at both the functional level and the program level are key challenges that face public relations practitioners. At the program level, the situational theory of problem solving provides useful nonfinancial metrics in both types of public relations situations: public-initiated problem (PPR) and organization-initiated (OPR; Kim & Ni, 2013). The effectiveness of interventions in "de-creating" a public about an issue can best be measured and traced through the observed levels of problem and involvement recognition of the given issue among the members of active and aware publics. In this vein, their situational motivation and information seeking, forwarding, and forefending (permitting) may also indicate the progress of problem solving and issue resolution for both organizations and publics. Likewise, the effectiveness of organizational policy and communication programs can be tracked by the changes in levels of problem and involvement recognition and constraint recognition. The particular benefit of tracking situational perceptual variables lies in the ability to identify and monitor the causes of publics' constraint recognition and to judge the effectiveness of interventions as organizations change (i.e., remove perceived barriers). Practical guidelines could be of importance to practitioners if they were to learn to use the situational theory in measuring and evaluating communication interventions and programs and to develop communication strategies via the conceptual meanings of situational variable and their interrelationships (e.g., how situational perception increases or decreases motivation and information behaviors related to problems).

The Publics and Their Communicative Actions in Environmental Issues

In recent years, the government and the scientific community alike have recognized climate change as a priority and have actively set out to engage and educate publics about it in an effort to increase the problem recognition and inculcate a sense of risk about climate change and environmental challenges. Several notable behavioral change theories such as the Theory of Planned Behaviors or persuasive theories have been recommended and sought for the task of public engagement. The situational theory and the theoretical understanding about publics and their perception, cognition, motivation, and communication that it generates are significant in the areas of environmental communication and public policy-making. Public segmentation by Ni and Kim (2009) can help communicators and policy-makers understand behavioral characteristics of strategic aware and active publics on environmental issues. It is also interesting to look at the problem chain-recognition effect to elicit lay citizens' situational motivation in environmental problems and in turn their communicative action and behavioral intentions of following expert-recommended actions of preserving the environment.

Information Behaviors and Communicating Risks and Health Problems

The situational theory of problem solving presents a unique niche of health and risk communication research. Health and risk communication research programs typically use theories of social influence, are campaign-focused, and aim at behavioral changes. Historically, the situational theory (both the theory of publics and the theory of problem solving) has chosen a different path by selecting its dependent variables as communicative behaviors instead of actual "behaviors" related to the problem. As has been discussed at length in earlier reviews (J. Grunig, 1989, 1997), it is more reliable and valid to predict communicative action instead of the direction or valence of one's position (attitude) or behavior (behavioral intention). Kim, Shen, and Morgan (2011) have already shown how the STOPS can be applied in health communication research. While the STOPS avoids over-claiming its utility for all types of health communication situations, there are abundant areas of application if we consider "health risks" to be "life problems" in essence that all individuals encounter and become motivated to deal with constantly. Thus, the understanding that the situational theory offers on individuals' perception, cognitive frame, motivation, and voluntary information behaviors provides useful theoretical and intervention-development tools for health and risk communicators. For example, STOPS has been applied in research on health information behaviors and their consequences on psychological and physical coping among patients with chronic health problems such as depression, cancer, HIV, and lupus (Kim & Lee, in press). The findings indicate the existence and effects of collective effectuating of individual health problems and generate implications for health policy and digitalized community-building among chronic patients.

Information Behaviors of Lay Publics and Experts on Scientific Advancement and Controversies

One function of STOPS is to describe a problem solver's perceptive, cognitive, and communicative patterns. One promising area of applying the theory is the differences and similarities in perceptive, cognitive, and communicative characteristics of experts and scientists and lay, ordinary individuals. Based on the understanding from the proposed research, science education and research training for researchers and students could identify common pitfalls in conducting academic investigation (e.g., self-fulfilling information forefending). Another promising research program is to apply the situational theory of problem solving in identifying nonexpert, strategic publics in the areas of issues related to science and technological controversies. Though lay citizens lack knowledge and understanding of scientific and technical details, they are beneficiaries or risk bearers of new technological or scientific advancement (e.g., GMO, NANO technologies), therefore expert groups and policy-makers cannot ignore these citizens' interests and motivated (communicative) behaviors related to the science/technological issues. Publics should then need to be identified and understood better for more effective policy-making and mutual understanding related to technology and scientific advancement. Little research has been published in the areas of science communication and public (mis)understanding of science. Thus, the payoffs in conducting research using theoretical predictions provided by the situational theory seem to be huge.

The Public Segmentation and Communication Objectives in Two Types of PR Situations

Kim and Ni (2013) proposed two common public relations situations: *Public-initiated PR (PPR) problems* and *Organization-initiated PR (OPR) problems*. PPR problems are triggered by a public's problem recognition and the goal of the organization is to *de-create* publics or decrease their situational perception, negative cognitive frame, motivation, and communicative actions through cooperative and co-facilitative efforts for the public's problem solving. OPR problems begin with an organization's problem recognition. As an organization faces a problem that prohibits or hinders the accomplishment of its mission, it tries to create aware and active publics about the challenge and attempts to increase situational perception, motivation, and communicative actions and to install a new cognitive frame related to the challenge. These two PR situations help map various PR campaigns in a rather simple classificatory system and assist with the development of communication and intervention strategies. Further, if these are combined with the newly crafted public typology (e.g., Ni & Kim, 2009) and public segmentation method (i.e., summation procedure; Kim, 2011b), there are additional strategic and tactical guidelines that public relations practitioners may use in practice. Such prescriptive research is in demand and the situational variables could provide an inventory of nonfinancial communication objectives.

Digitalized, Networked Publics, Their Information Behaviors, and Social Consequences

As many social institutions and individuals migrate their activities to the computer-mediated, digitalized, networked community, many new phenomena have arisen. Digital publics are a new social phenomenon that has resulted from the emergence of mobile communication technologies. Increasingly the dense communicative network infrastructure enables individuals to communicate with ease, causing institutions to face new interaction patterns and social communicative norms. One emerging research in this transition is to catalogue the similarities and dissimilarities of online and offline publics, their behavioral characteristics, the causes and consequences of such public behaviors, and the impacts at the individual, group, and societal levels. Potential areas for research include online publics and issue creation, patterns of collectivity formation (coalition building), empowering and bargaining strategies of digital publics, the communicative tactics of digital publics such as flaming, public norms within an issue, tracking of issue volatility and chronicity for the controversial issues, and group polarization between publics and counterpublics related to digital, network-based interaction. Research is necessary to identify positive consequences of digitalization and networking communication technologies: in problematic collective effectuating—group polarity, multifarious and glocalized issues and conflicts, as well as in promising collective effectuating—coping with individual challenges through public formation about the problem by marginalized and isolated members of publics.

Megaphoning of Strategic Publics and Its Impacts on Strategic Management Process

The newly constructed concepts of positive and negative megaphoning, scouting, and microboundary spanning (Kim & Rhee, 2011) were first used in the employee or internal publics. As a natural progression for good concepts, researchers have started thinking whether these concepts could explain communicative behaviors other than employee publics. In the special issue of the *International Journal of*

Strategic Communication, negative megaphoning by consumers was studied in the online setting (Bach & Kim, 2012). For the tourism industry, positive mega-phoning by tourists and its causal model were tested (Choi & Cai, 2012). In addition, the value of a good-quality relationship between a municipal government and its citizens was tested to assess how far citizens would tolerate lowering the quality of their residential life and engage in less negative megaphoning for civic issues (Lovari, Martino, & J. Kim, 2012). In a case study, employees with a good relationship with their management and company showed less negative mega-phoning and helped the organization overcome the crisis situation (Mazzei, Kim, & Dell'Oro, 2012).

The concept of megaphoning is of more particular interest because of the changing communication environment caused by the use of Twitter, SNS, and other online, mobile, computer-mediated communication settings. Investigation of which other factors motivate members of various strategic publics to engage in information behaviors is another newly emerging area of inquiry. In the above-mentioned studies, the communication approach (i.e., symmetrical communica-tion), situational perception, and relational quality were identified as causes and mediators of megaphoning. However, the non–situational and personal motivators (e.g., feeling of agency or social recognition) that may influence megaphoning remain unexplored.

Information Behaviors of Publics and Reputation, Branding, and Identity Building

As members of various types of stakeholders and publics are motivated and engage in active communication behaviors, they can make cognitive footprints for other individuals. In essence, active publics are producers of information sought by others through information forefending. The information produced is circulated by the producers within and beyond their social, personal networks. Furthermore, in the digitalized era the information produced by active publics is likely to be in digital format, and once created is almost impossible to remove. This presents an important challenge to organizations and institutions who want to cultivate a good reputation, brand, and identity. If negative information is produced and digitalized, such information can easily be retrieved by other motivated communicators (problem solvers) who enter the situation. For example, very often customers perform a Google search and read other users' reviews in the process of making a decision to buy. The challenges to corporate or institutional reputation are not the negative messages themselves but the producers of those messages. It is important to build a theoretical understanding of who engages in positive and negative information behaviors and produces and circulate information in and around organizations, and how and why they do so. More research on information behaviors and its role in reputation management or branding is necessary. The focus of reputation and branding research has been more on the cognitive process of evaluative information (attitude formation) but in the digitalized, networked society it has shifted to the communicative process of production, selection, and circulation of evaluative information. The situational theory of problem solving and communicative action in problem solving are significant in providing theoretical accounts for the processes of reputation formation and branding.

Diasporas, Their Motivated Communication, and Public Diplomacy

Traditional public diplomacy has been targeted toward spreading positive messages to foreign publics with strategic importance. This old paradigm may not disappear in the new century, yet governmental control regarding the content and amount of information circulated among members of foreign publics has dwindled considerably. As communication and physical transportation become cheaper, easier, and more frequent, first-hand experiences and witness accounts of a given country are becoming more common, interpersonal, and horizontal (vs. secondhand, mass-mediated, and vertical) communication—we are in the era of "sociological public diplomacy" (Yun & Kim, 2008; Yun & Vibber, 2012). In sociological public diplomacy, people-to-people interactions are more important in determining the favorability and intensity of developing goodwill among foreign publics. Additionally, self-selected topics and agenda are key in the discussion of a country that is of interest to foreign publics. This is how diasporas and residents and tourists would select and share information about a given country. Microdiplomacy by migrants and diasporas are very important areas to research, and the situational theory of problem solving provides a descriptive model of when and why micro-diplomats are motivated to generate and circulate information to others.

Conclusion

This chapter has reviewed the origins of the situational theory of problem solving from the situational theory of publics. Few public relations theories existed when young James Grunig started his scholarly career in the 1960s. Theorizing in the field of public relations flourished mostly after Grunig formally used the situational theory of publics to define "publics," a then primitive concept (vs. scientific concept) lacking conceptual explication and method of identification. The situational theory of publics and the situational theory of problem solving are humbly put at the bottom of public relations scholarship, perhaps to be forgotten as too old or an under-claimed theory than its deemed power. It might be correct to state that the situational theory is rarely up front in recent research, as our public relations community has diligently constructed new theories and procedures to improve public relations practice and enhanced its contribution to its hosting organization and society. Yet, no skyscrapers can be constructed without a foundation stone, a stable and robust base. The base itself may be rarely attended to as the building goes up and wide, but just as public relations research and practice cannot be what they are today without two of their most passionate scholars, James and Larissa Grunig, the scholarly edifice of the Grunigs would not have flourished without the situational theory of publics.

Situational theorists like us consider the power and applicability of the situational theory to go beyond the field of public relations. As we make the situational theory of problem solving a more general theory applicable to various problematic situations that humans encounter and experience, we envision the new situational theory will help construct new concepts and theories in various fields where people's problem-solving efforts occur and where communicative actions become necessary.

It is rare for a theory to continue and evolve over a half-century period. The situational theory of publics is an exemplary manifestation of Jim Grunig's scholarly excellence and shows that a good theory never stagnates and that theorists in different generations continue to co-construct the theory. In the future, we hope researchers in communication and public relations will generate more solutions in the above-mentioned communication problems and trigger more interest among researchers and practitioners who deal with diverse communication problems with various publics. In that way, the Grunigs' legacy will continue to flourish and deliver value to other communication fields and to people in need of a good theory to understand and overcome problematic life situations better.

References

Aldoory, L., & Grunig, J. E. (2012). The rise and fall of hot-issue publics: Relationships that develop from media coverage of events and crises. *International Journal of Strategic Communication, 6,* 93–108.

Bach, S. B., & Kim, S. (2012). Online consumer complaint behaviors: The dynamics of service failures, consumers' word of mouth, and organization–consumer relationships. *International Journal of Strategic Communication, 6,* 59–76.

Choi, S-H., & Cai, L. A. (2012). Destination loyalty and communication: A relationship-based tourist behavioral model. *International Journal of Strategic Communication, 6,* 45–58.

Chwe, M. S-Y. (2001). *Rational ritual: Culture, coordination, and common knowledge.* Princeton, NJ: Princeton University Press.

Gamson, W. A. (1992). The social psychology of collective action. In A. D. Morris & C. Mueller (Eds.), *Frontiers of social movement theories* (pp. 53–76). New Haven, CT: Yale University Press.

Grunig, J. E. (1966). The role of information in economic decision making. *Journalism Monographs,* No. 3.

Grunig, J. E. (1989). Publics, audiences and market segments: Models of receivers of campaign messages. In C. T. Salmon (Ed.), *Information campaigns: Managing the process of social change* (pp. 197–226). Newbury Park, CA: Sage.

Grunig, J. E. (1997). A situational theory of publics: Conceptual history, recent challenges and new research. In D. Moss, T. MacManus, & D. Verčič (Eds.), *Public relations research: An international perspective* (pp. 3–46). London: ITB Press.

Kim, J-N. (2011a). Understanding strategic value of good employee relationships and employee communicative actions: For better corporate branding and reputation management. *Insight Train, 1*(1), 52–69.

Kim, J-N. (2011b). Public segmentation using situational theory of problem solving: Illustrating summation method and testing segmented public profiles. *PRism, 8*(2), Retrieved from: http://www.journal.org/homepage.html.

Kim, J.-N. (2012). Special issue: Strategic values of relationships and the communicative actions of strategic publics. *International Journal of Strategic Communication, 6*(1), 1–12.

Kim, J-N., & Grunig, J. E. (2011). Problem solving and communicative action: A situational theory of problem solving. *Journal of Communication, 61*, 120–149.

Kim, J-N., & Lee, S. (in press). Communication and cyberspacing: Coping with chronic illness through communicative action in online support networks. *Journal of Health Communication.*

Kim, J-N., & Ni, L. (2013). Integrating formative and evaluative research in two types of public relations problems: A review of research programs within the strategic management approach. *Journal of Public Relations Research, 25*, 1–29.

Kim, J-N., & Rhee, Y. (2011). Strategic thinking about employee communication behavior (ECB) in public relations: Testing the models of megaphoning and scouting effects in Korea. *Journal of Public Relations Research, 23*, 243–268.

Kim, J-N., & Vibber, K. (2012). Networked sociability and cybercoping: The effects of enabled personal networks and enhanced health outcomes among chronic health problem solvers. In S. Duhé (Ed.), *New media and public relations* (2nd ed.) (pp. 218–229). New York: Peter Lang.

Kim, J-N., Grunig, J. E., & Ni, L. (2010). Reconceptualizing the communicative action of publics: Acquisition, selection, and transmission of information in problematic situations. *International Journal of Strategic Communication, 4*(2), 126–154.

Kim, J-N., Ni, L., & Sha, B-L. (2008). Breaking down the stakeholder environment: A review of approaches to the segmentation of publics. *Journalism & Mass Communication Quarterly, 85*(4), 751–768.

Kim, J-N., Shen, H., & Morgan, S. (2011). Information behaviors and problem chain recognition effect: Applying situational theory of problem solving in organ donation issues. *Health Communication, 26*, 171–184.

Kim, J-N., Ni, L., Kim, S-H., & Kim, J. R. (2012). What makes people hot: Applying the situational theory of problem solving to hot-issue publics. *Journal of Public Relations Research, 24*, 144–164.

Kruglanski, A. W. (1996). Motivated social cognition: Principles of the interface. In E. T. Higgins & A. W. Kruglanski (Eds.), *Social psychology: Handbook of basic principles* (pp. 493–520). New York: Guilford.

Lovari, A., Martino, V., & Kim, J.-N. (2012). Citizens' relationship with a municipality and their communicative behaviors in negative civic issues. *International Journal of Strategic Communication, 6*, 17–30.

Mazzei, A., Kim, J-N., & Dell'Oro, C. (2012). Strategic value of employee relationships and communicative actions: Overcoming corporate crisis with quality internal communication. *International Journal of Strategic Communication, 6*, 31–44.

Ni, L., & Kim, J-N. (2009). Classifying publics: Communication behaviors and problem-solving characteristics in controversial issues. *International Journal of Strategic Communication, 3*(4), 1–25.

Yun, S-H., & Kim, J-N. (2008). Soft power: From ethnic attraction to national attraction in sociological globalism. *International Journal of Intercultural Relations, 32*(6), 565–577.

Yun, S-H., & Vibber, K. (2012). The strategic values and communicative actions of Chinese students for sociological Korean public diplomacy. *International Journal of Strategic Communication, 6*, 77–92.

8

MEASURING THE EDIFICE

Public Relations Measurement and Evaluation Practices Over the Course of 40 Years

Fraser Likely and Tom Watson

Abstract

Public relations measurement and evaluation practices have been major subjects for practitioner and academician research from the late 1970s onwards. This chapter will commence with a brief survey of the historical evolution of the research into these practices. Then, we will discuss James E. Grunig's enduring contribution to their theorization, particularly with financial and non-financial indicators of public relations value. Next, we will consider the current debate on financial indicators, focusing on Return on Investment and alternative methods of financial valuation. Finally, we will look to the future at the measurement and evaluation practices that will attract academic and practitioner research interest.

Key Words

evaluation, financial value, measurement, return on investment

Measurement and Evaluation in Historical Perspective

Early Seedlings of Research

As recently as 2008, an international Delphi study of academics, practitioners and professional association leaders found that the top three research topics for public relations were all connected with measurement, expressions of value and the contribution of public relations to the organization:

1. public relations' role in contributing to strategic decision-making, strategy development and realisation and organisational functioning;

2. the value that public relations creates for organisations through building social capital; managing key relationships and realising organisational advantage;
3. the measurement and evaluation of public relations both offline and online.

(Watson, 2008, p. 111)

These are not new of course, since the history of practices of measurement of the output and outcomes of public relations activity can be traced back to the late 18th century and was evident in the United States and Germany in the following century (Lamme & Russell, 2010; Watson 2012a). At the beginning of the 20th century, Cutlip (1994) identified early monitoring practices in Boston while public relations pioneers such as Edward L. Bernays and Arthur W. Page extensively used opinion research for the monitoring of public opinion and the shaping of communication strategies (Ewen, 1996; Griese 2001). By mid-century, and aided by the operations of press clippings agencies in many countries, many public relations practitioners were monitoring media coverage and undertaking simple measurement of volume (typically column inches) and judgements on its tonality (Plackard & Blackmon, 1947; J. L'Etang, pers. comm. January 10, 2011).

Watson (2012a) has observed that the late 1960s and the 1970s were a period when books and articles addressing public relations evaluation started to appear. These were written by both academics and by practitioners. In 1969, Robinson's *Public Relations and Survey Research* was published. Pavlik says that '[Robinson] predicted that PR evaluation would move away from seat-of-the-pants approaches and toward "scientific derived knowledge"' (1987, p. 66). Robinson confidently stated that practitioners would no longer rely on anecdotal, subjective measures of success; they 'would begin to use more systematic measures of success, primarily social science methods such as survey research' (Pavlik, 1987).

Later Flowering of Research

While there was a trickling stream of publications from both academics and practitioners in the early 1970s, the prime catalyst was a conference held in 1977 at the University of Maryland, chaired by James E. Grunig, in partnership with AT&T. This was followed by the first scholarly special issue, 'Measuring the Effectiveness of Public Relations', in *Public Relations Review*'s Winter 1977 edition, featuring papers from the conference.

In the decade or so that followed the Maryland/AT&T event, there was a flowering of research in the field. Watson (2012a) notes that US journals featured articles and research from Broom (Broom & Dozier, 1983), Dozier (Broom & Dozier, 1983; Dozier, 1984, 1985) and J. Grunig (1979, 1983; Grunig & Hickson, 1976). Cline (1984) produced an annotated bibliography of evaluation and measurement in public relations and organizational communication conducted between 1974 and 1984. Books, chapters and articles, by both academicians and practitioners, were written on such subjects as methodological techniques, evaluation of public relations programmes (such as employee, community relations or marketing communication programmes), evaluation of communication campaigns, measurement of communication channels, measurement of communication products and measuring return on public relations investment (for examples of practitioners, see Graves, 1975; Jacobson, 1982; Sinickas, 1983; Strenski, 1980; Worcester, 1983; for academics, see, for example, Lerbinger, 1978; McElreath, 1975, 1980, 1981; Wright, 1979). Measurement and evaluation consultancies, either as independent firms or as arms of public relations agencies, were growing in number. Booth (1986) portrayed the pioneering work of such public relations researchers as Lloyd Kirban of Burson Marsteller (Kirban, 1983), Michael Rowan (Strategic Information Research Corporation of Hill & Knowlton), Sharyn Mallamad (Needham Porter Novelli), Lisa Richter (Opinion Research of Fleishman-Hilliard) and Frank Walton (Research & Forecasts of Ruder, Finn & Rotman). In particular, Walter Lindenmann of Ketchum (Lindenmann 1979, 1980) was very prolific and helped drive the subject higher up the practitioner agenda.

The public relations service business of media analysis, which had started growing in the mid-1960s (Weiner, 2011, pers. comm.), started to expand with Katie Delahaye Paine announcing her first publicity measurement system in 1987 and establishing the Delahaye measurement business soon after. Pessolano (1985) wrote one of the first articles on the use of the then new desktop computer for analyzing media coverage. In the late 1980s, public relations measurement and evaluation were still largely in the domain of clippings counts, with limited, simple media analysis mainly related to volume and tonality of coverage, much as it has been since the 1930s (Watson, 2012a).

In 1990, there was another major publication event when *Public Relations Review* had another special edition on evaluation, 'Using Research to Plan and Evaluate Public Relations' (Summer 1990). It demonstrated that measurement and evaluation were consistently part of academic and professional discourse. All the authors emphasized the need for public relations to be researched, planned and evaluated – using robust social science techniques. This attitude was particularly fostered by Broom and Dozier's seminal publication, *Using Research in Public Relations* (1990).

This flowering continued through the 1990s, with regular appearances of measurement and evaluation research in academic journals and association and trade magazines. J. Grunig cites 1996 as a pivotal year, an 'explosion of interest' (Grunig, 2008) that lasted throughout the next decade. The summit meeting of academics and practitioners in October 1996, to discuss standards for measuring public relations effectiveness, ultimately fostered the 1997 founding of the US Commission on Measurement and Evaluation, under the umbrella of the Institute for Public Relations. J. Grunig influenced the change in name from the US Commission to just the Commission by sponsoring the first 'international' member (Fraser Likely) in 2001. Today, both the Commission and the trade body, the Association of Measurement and Evaluation of Communication (AMEC) are international, though only the Commission has a unique membership comprised of both academics and practitioners.

By 2000, there was enough interest in measurement and evaluation to have specialized newsletters and magazines devoted to the subject, such as PR Publishing's *Jim and Lauri Grunig's Research* (a supplement in *PR Reporter*) and Melcrum Publishing's *Total Communication Measurement*. By 2012, the public relations measurement and evaluation literature had grown by leaps and bounds, populated with trade associations briefs, White Papers from commissions, books, articles, blogs and websites devoted to the subject.

Towards Excellence

James E. Grunig and the Excellence Study

The date of 1977 and the journal special issue were not the beginning of J. Grunig's engagement with the theory and practice of measurement and evaluation but they indicate when scholarly and industry joint discourse on these topics became public. Joint discourse became a notable feature in J. Grunig's measurement and evaluation research efforts, from this AT&T conference to the IABC Research Foundation-funded Excellence Study to his founding status as a member of the Institute for Public Relation's Commission on Measurement and Evaluation. In the years between 1977 and 2012, J. Grunig played an important role in bridging the gap between academic research and practitioner research on measurement and evaluation and helping practitioners apply theory to their measurement practice (for a recent example, see Paine, 2007).

In the 1980s, J. Grunig commenced work on the IABC research project that was to lead to the Excellence Study (J. Grunig, 1992; Grunig, Grunig, & Dozier, 2002). This evolved from the AT&T research as J. Grunig explains:

> [M]y Maryland colleague, Mark McElreath (now at Towson University), had alerted me to this difference between evaluating public relations programs and evaluating the overall contribution of the public relations function to organizational effectiveness. Thus, the Excellence Study offered the possibility of constructing a grand theory of the value of public relations.
> *(Grunig, 2006a, p. 158)*

The AT&T work J. Grunig addressed was at the programme level, rather than at the level of the public relations department or that of the organization. It was undertaken under a broad mandate, to 'develop measures for and means of evaluating the effectiveness of public relations' for AT&T Corporation (Grunig, 2006a, p. 8). The results of the study (see also Tirone, 1977, for the Bell System case) were applied to evaluate a wide range of public relations activity, at the levels of communication product production and dissemination, communication channels and messages and communication campaigns and programmes. J. Grunig wrote that the research had been an important step on the path to the development of theories of public relations and strategic management: 'Public relations could not have a role in strategic management function unless its practitioners had a way to measure effectiveness' and added with considerable irony that 'the public relations trade press today continues to debate how to evaluate public relations—a problem that I think we solved in the late 1970s with the AT&T research' (2006a, p. 157).

The IABC study was concerned with explaining the value of public relations, which went beyond basic methods of media analysis or programme evaluation. J. Grunig realized that although programme evaluation was important for formative and summative purposes, 'it did not show the overall value of the public relations function to the organization' (Grunig, 2006a, p. 158). This type of observation, however, has not deterred a generation of practitioners from being constantly engaged in a fruitless search for either a single method to evaluate all public relations activity (the so-called 'silver bullet') or to demonstrate that financial value can be divined from the measurement of public relations outputs such as media coverage (Gregory & Watson, 2008).

In the 1980s, J. Grunig had researched the notions of financial results arising from public relations activity while preparing the Excellence Study. In his 2006 article he discusses the concept, but before this is considered, the outcomes of his earlier research in the 1980s are worthy of reflection, as they show the difference so often found between practitioners' perception of client or employers' needs for data and the actual views of those people:

> Although we concluded that it is difficult to place a monetary value on relationships with publics, in order to measure ROI exactly, our interviews with CEOs and senior public relations officers revealed numerous examples of how good relationships had reduced the costs of litigation, regulation, legislation, and negative publicity caused by poor relationships; reduced the risk of making decisions that affect different stakeholders; or increased revenue by providing products and services needed by stakeholders. Those examples provided powerful evidence of the value of good relationships with strategic publics.
>
> *(Grunig, 2006a, p. 159)*

So relationships with strategic publics could offer tangible and intangible value that aided the operations of organizations, through retention of the 'licence to operate', cost reduction and improved revenue. These were not the classic financial ROI but they were evidence of public relations creating and maintaining different types of value. As J. Grunig notes earlier in the same section of the paper, 'Much of this effort (to determine a positive financial return) has been devoted to research at the program level' (p. 159) and this has had a minimizing effect upon acceptance of public relations as a strategic activity: 'For the most part, I believe these explanations of ROI rationalize the enduring belief among practitioners and their clients that traditional publicity-oriented public relations creates value though a change in one of these cognitive concepts' (p. 159). In other words, the pursuit of ROI by so many in the public relations field (including the consultancy and the media analysis service sectors) continues to pigeonhole public relations as the 'symbolic, interpretive paradigm' that focuses on publicity messaging (Grunig, 2009, p. 9).

From strictly a measurement and evaluation perspective, the Excellence Study contributed two significant findings. First, it described a typology for measurement, consisting of five levels where public relations could add value (Grunig et al., 2002, p. 91). They were, in ascending value: (1) individual message or publication level (which could also include communication products and communication channels); (2) programme (or campaign) level; (3) function (or department) level; (4) organizational (or enterprise) level; and (5) societal level. As indicated, much of the literature, in particular the practitioner literature, on public relations measurement and evaluation prior to the release of the third book in the Excellence Study series, was confined to the first two levels of analysis. In fact, it could be said that there was a good degree of confusion between these two levels, between the terms that signify results at each level: output, outtake, and outcome.

Second, it separated the idea of financial value from that of the non-financial value of public relations' effectiveness. While the authors stated that they 'reject any simplistic notion that the only relevant contribution public relations makes is a monetary one—direct to the bottom line' (Grunig et al., 2002, p. 97), they did develop and apply the financial construct of compensating variation to a determination of financial value of public relations programmes with various stakeholders. They also suggested that 'one way to estimate the total value of public relations is to determine the ways in which the function benefits an organization or society and then develop non-financial indicators of these benefits' (p. 101). These non-financial indicators were concerned with the results of stakeholder relationships. Subsequent research on financial indicators primarily, if not exclusively, by practitioners, which we shall shortly see, became engaged with: (1) the continuing knotty debate over concepts of Return on Investment; and (2) the two parallel but separate streams of discussion that have bedevilled relations practice: the continued emphasis on publicity-oriented messaging – the 'symbolic, interpretive paradigm' (Grunig, 2009, p. 9) – which stands well away from the 'behavioural, strategic management paradigm' (p. 9) that is at the heart of the Excellence Study and its subsequent developments.

Interestingly enough, the greatest uptake since the Excellence Study has been with the concept of financial indicators, not with the concepts of levels (typologies) of public relations' effectiveness measurement or non-financial indicators. A number of typologies have been developed, including by Likely (2000), Macnamara (1999) and the International Association for the Measurement and Evaluation of Communications (AMEC, 2011). On the other hand, very little research has been conducted on non-financial indicators. The most relevant example of the interest in financial indicators is the debate over the application of the Return on Investment (ROI) metric, which was identified by J. Grunig in the mid-1980s, and still resonates today. This debate will form much of the discussion in the remainder of this chapter, as it illustrates a current trend and future directions of development in measurement and evaluation.

The Search for Financial Metrics

Evolution of Return on Investment Usage

'Return on Investment' (ROI) is frequently defined in management and market-ing literature as a measure of financial effectiveness concerned with returns on capital employed in (profit-making) business activities (Best, 2009; Drury, 2007; Moutinho & Southern, 2010). It is expressed as a ratio of income or earnings divided by the costs that had been applied to generate the income or earnings. In formal public relations nomenclature, the *Dictionary of Public Relations Measurement and Research* defines ROI as 'an outcome variable that equates profit from investment' but does not attempt to classify a 'public relations ROI', other than as a 'dependent variable' (Stacks, 2006, p. 24). In public relations practitioner language, ROI is applied in a much looser form to indicate the results of activity. In 2004, a report by the (then) Institute of Public Relations in the UK defined ROI as 'a ratio of how much profit or cost saving is realised from an activity, as against its actual cost, which is often expressed as a percentage' (Institute of Public Relations & Communication Directors Forum, 2004, p. 15). The report, however, added that, 'in reality few PR programmes can be measured in such a way because of the problems involved in putting a realistic and credible financial value to the results achieved. As a result, the term PR ROI is often used very loosely' (p. 15).

The term has been used in public relations discourse for more than 40 years. The British public relations writer and educator Sam Black commented that it was 'fashionable' to measure ROI in business, 'but in the field of public relations it has little significance' (1971, p. 100). Merims (1972), a practitioner with Motorola, proposed an ROI model in the *Harvard Business Review* that surely gave the concept a fillip in North America. There has been regular interest in the concept over the years by practitioners (for example, Lee, 2002; Marken, 1988; Sierra, 2003; Sinickas, 2003; Williams, 1992; Wood, 2004). The concept of ROI has also been given expression as market mix modelling, a financial indicator promoted by some consultancies in the past decade (Likely, Rockland, & Weiner, 2006).

Watson's (2005) study of more than 200 articles on measurement and evaluation found that the term was not widely used or recognized in academic discourse. Gaunt and Wright (2004), however, found that 88% of a sample of international public relations practitioners were interested in an ROI tool and 65% considered that ROI could be applied to judgements on public relations effectiveness. Gregory and Watson (2008) also noted that use of the term ROI was extant in practice and called for greater academic engagement with practice issues such as the use of business language, including ROI, and communication scorecards.

Outside North America and Europe, Australian studies (Simmons & Watson, 2006; Watson & Simmons, 2004) found that ROI was not used as terminology but business indicators such as sales, turnover and savings were used by 44% of respondents to a national survey. Xavier, Patel, Johnston, Watson, and Simmons (2005) identified that activity outcomes such as increases in share price or changes in government policy were used by 29.66% of award-winning case studies. In the Asia-Pacific region, Macnamara (1999) advocated the use of the language of accountability embodied in concepts such as management-by-objectives, total quality management and quality assurance to position public relations as a contributor to strategic decision-making. Macnamara later identified that 'public relations and corporate communication practitioners are under pressure to evaluate their work, particularly in terms of outcomes and Return on Investment' (2007, p. 1), which indicated the increasing application of business nomenclature, as he had earlier forecast.

Professional literature and practitioner discourse, such as discussions and presentations at the European Summits on Measurement and the IPR Measurement Summits in the United States, however, clearly show that ROI is a term widely used, if not tightly defined. The 2004 study by the (then) Institute of Public Relations in the UK found that 34% of respondents considered public relations budgets in term of ROI and 60% used a notion of ROI to measure public relations activity in some way. It summarized the responses as, 'some inclination towards seeking a form of ROI that could be applied universally' (IPR/CDF, 2004, p. 6).

Recently, Watson and Zerfass (2011) researched understanding of ROI in both the UK (Watson, 2011; a pilot study) and across Europe in the annual European Communications Monitor survey (Zerfass, Verhoeven, Tench, Moreno, & Verčič, 2011). They posed two questions

Q1: Do you regularly use the term 'ROI' or 'Return on Investment' when planning and evaluating communication activities?

Q2: Would you agree or disagree with (seven) statements? [Four of them were consistent with the standard economic definition of ROI.]

Based on 2,209 valid responses, the headline result for the usage of the term 'ROI' or 'Return on Investment' when planning and evaluating communication activities was a 1.1% separation between those who responded Yes (47.6%) and No (46.5%) with 5.9% giving a 'Don't know the term' response. There were also workplace, regional and hierarchic differences across the continent. The same question analysed by the types of organization at which respondents are employed, however, gave a wider indication of ROI usage according to workplace, with those in consultancies and agencies most supportive (59.3%) and practitioners in governmental organizations least supportive (28.2%) and only marginally less than non-profit organizations (32.5%). The usage of ROI in European regions was closely clustered for both Yes and No with the Yes headed by Southern Europe at 50.4% and separated by only 4.4% from the lowest response in Western Europe (45.7%). As regards hierarchy, Chief Communication Officers (or equivalent title) and Agency CEOs showed 53.7% support for usage whereas middle and junior-level staff (team members) were more reluctant at 34.5%.

The second question on ROI explored practitioner perceptions of ROI, especially the linkage between the profit-to-costs ratio which is expressed in business literature (and in some public relations literature, notably IPR/CDF, 2004), and communication outcomes or the achievement of communication objectives. Seven propositions were presented and distributed. Broadly, there was a continued expression by this large group of communicators that ROI and communication could be linked, but in two separated modes.

The most positive response was that 'ROI can be expressed in achievement of communication objectives' (83.1%), followed by the financially linked indicator, 'ROI requires financial assessments of the resources needed for communication' (72.5%) and then 'ROI can demonstrate the non-financial value of communication' (70.5%). The next three propositions dealt with communication's contribution to organizational strategy, a standardized financial valuation of communications results, and the ratio of financial profit arising from communication set against its costs. They all gained more than 50% support from this large, multinational sample of communicators. Only one, 'ROI has to be defined in monetary terms' gained less than 50% support.

Descriptions of ROI Fall into Two Categories

The propositions can thus be placed into two separate and apparently conflicting categories: the financial and non-financial. The 'financial' category proposes that ROI is shaped by financial assessment of resources and a standardized financial evaluation of results which results in a ratio of profit and costs arising from communication activity. Added together, these have a mean of 61.1%. The 'non-financial' are composed of ROI as an expression of achievement of objectives, the creation of non-financial value and contribution to formation of organizational strategy. These average 72.1%.

The 'financial' version is closer to the classic ratio which has challenged practitioners for the past 40 years as it has not been possible to obtain the data to demonstrate financial results, other than in highly specialized disaggregated cases where the sole method of publicity was PR (probably media relations) and the objective was for a specific sales or financial result. While practitioners appear to know that ROI is a widely accepted financial indicator based on so-called 'hard data' and does not account for intangibles, they press on with a belief that a solution will come but agreed measures have not emerged.

The 'non-financial' group of propositions is similar to the 'outflow' concepts first proposed by the Swedish Public Relations Association (SPRA, 1996) and theoretically underpinned by Zerfass (2008). It also links with models of communication management used by many central European corporations which have integrated business and communication strategies, using tools such as communication scorecards (Zerfass, 2008). It is relevant that German communicators were the third lowest users of ROI (34.1%; 12th ranked) as a term because more differentiated forms of planning and measurement have been discussed in this professional community for many years (Zerfass, 2010). Among that nation's examples are Deutsche Telekom, Audi and Henkel which have integrated models of monitoring and management. For them, brand value, reputation and value creation linked to corporate objectives and non-financial key performance indicators are more important than achievement of a profit-to-cost ratio.

Overall, responses to the transnational survey indicate that European public relations practitioners conceive of ROI in a more non-financial frame, thus opposing the established understanding of the concept in business administration and management science. Watson and Zerfass (2011) considered that a 'quasi-ROI', focused on non-financial objectives and outcomes appears to be well supported already by European practitioners and can be fostered by methods that help practitioners to manage and advance future activities such as models of communication management, including communication scorecards and value link models.

These integrate public relations and corporate communications within the whole business planning and monitoring process (the German 'communication controlling' model; cf. Zerfass, 2010) rather than being treated as a promotional add-on or a functional activity. However, the complexity of communication processes and their role in business interactions mean it is not possible to calculate Return on Investment in financial terms. Consequently, they concluded that public relations practitioners should refrain from using the term in order to keep their vocabulary compatible with the overall management world.

James E. Grunig on ROI

Subsequent to the publication of this research, two European researchers engaged in an email dialogue with J. Grunig that was published online by the Institute for Public Relations (IPR Research Conversations, October 2011). The main elements were as follows:

> *James E. Grunig*: I'm very interested in looking at the value of public relations in terms of nonfinancial indicators or as intangible assets. Essentially, I argue that the value of public relations can be found in the relationships it cultivates with publics/stakeholders. Relationships are intangible assets, but they can be measured. In addition, it is possible to conceptualize the

financial returns to relationships; they reduce costs, reduce risk, and increase revenue. However, it is difficult, if not impossible, to measure, or attribute these financial costs to specific relationships. They are long-term, lumpy, and often keep things from happening. Thus, we should measure relationships but explain their value conceptually to understand (but not measure) the ROI of public relations.

Tom Watson and Ansgar Zerfass: We agree with all of your statement, with one exception. We are rigorous about the problems of applying ROI out of its business context, as PR's use (or abuse) of ROI does it no good with decision-making managers who have an accounting or financial management background. Research has found these views in central Europe amongst business managers in charge of 'controlling' (similar to audit) and it is beginning to be identified in the UK. These high-level managers simply don't recognize ROI in the form that it is presented to them by PR staff or consultants with 'PR metrics' or in the concept of ROI outside strictly financial parameters. Hence, we are encouraging PR folks to find their own language which is more accurate, such as value creation or value links, etc. The 'Outflow' concept which came from Sweden in 1996 is more pertinent than ROI.

James E. Grunig: No disagreement here. I talk more about the value of public relations than about ROI. As I said, you can explain the value of relationships; but you really can't measure a financial return to compare with the money invested in it. I tend to use the term ROI because PR people want to hear it used. I will now cease and desist from using it.

Tom Watson and Ansgar Zerfass: Glad to hear we are on the same track . . . this is really a big discussion over here and we feel that a sound position will be supported by those communication officers (often with a managerial background) who are now in charge, while some suppliers still have to do their homework. Understanding that cultivating relationships, listening and issues management is more important than talking and image building is of course difficult and it will take continuous efforts to explain.

The importance of this particular debate is that (1) it offers a clear rejection of the ROI terminology by J. Grunig: 'I will now cease and desist from using it'; (2) it brings the 'communication controlling' model from central Europe into the international arena; and (3) it is counter to the prevailing industry desire to re-define ROI in a public relations context.

The Barcelona Principles Propagate Practitioner Interest in Financial Metrics

In 2010, the second European Summit on Measurement in Barcelona, which is the annual gathering of the International Association for the Measurement and Evaluation of Communication (AMEC) and thus of the public relations measurement service sector, adopted a statement of seven principles about measurement of public relations and corporate communication activity. Called the Barcelona Declaration of Measurement Principles (AMEC, 2010), it was a normative statement that laid emphasis on the measurability of communication activity and specifically rejected Advertising Value Equivalence (AVE) as a valuation of public relations activity. Of the seven principles, three link with the social science emphasis of Excellence Theory, namely: (1) the importance of goal setting and measurement; (2) measuring the effect on outcomes is preferable to measuring media results; and (3) the effect on business results can and should be measured where possible.

These 'Barcelona Principles' were quickly adopted by public relations professional and industry bodies in the UK, North America and globally (Watson, 2012b). They are a baseline which the public relations organizations are using to encourage higher standards in research, planning and measurement. However, this statement – especially the third principle of measuring effects on business results – has led to a revival of industry attempts to define a public relations ROI (PR ROI). At its 2011 Summit in Lisbon, one outcome was that over 80% of delegates identified the need to define PR ROI as the main industry research need. This led to the formation of a task force in North America, led by the Council for Public Relations Firms, and involving members of AMEC and the Public Relations Society of America (PRSA). By late 2011, it had produced a draft report on ROI, entitled *Money Matters*, which was circulated for comment. Its emphasis was almost wholly on economic outcomes of public relations activity and largely ignored situations in which monetary value creation is either not relevant or only a minor part of objectives and strategies. This stance was a throwback to the critique of placing financial valuation on relationships that had been explored in the 1980s by the team preparing the Excellence Study and referred to earlier (Grunig, 2006a). At the time of writing (April 2012), the final version of the report had not been published.

Consideration of Other Financial Metrics Besides ROI

In 2012, Canadian practitioner Fraser Likely proposed the use of two other financial metrics and suggested a set of principles for their, as well as that of ROI, appropriate and accurate application (Likely, 2012). Organizations have three drivers for financial performance: (1) increased revenue; (2) decreased costs or expenditure; and (3) cost avoidance through reduced operational and regulatory risks. Likely acknowledges that public relations practitioners 'have long sought to demonstrate how [their] work contributes to these three drivers' (p. 2). Likely argued that if public relations practitioners were to employ the financial indicator ROI, they should do so in the same way that financial managers and accountants do. They should not try to redefine the term or to use it other than how it was intended. ROI is a financial metric that includes net returns and gross investments applied at the level, and only at the level, of the organization itself. Thus, the term ROI cannot be used as a financial measure for a communication channel (for example, Twitter or YouTube), a communication campaign (for example, marketing communication or employee engagement) or a communication function (for example, Investor Relations or Public Relations Department). In addition to ROI, he identified two other financial metrics that may be more appropriate: Benefit-Cost Ratio (BCR) and Cost-Effectiveness Analysis (CEA). He argues that BCR and CEA are 'more applicable and perhaps more useful than the utilization of a ROI measure' (p. 2).

The BCR metric and the ROI metric are similar in methodology, but the former is used to predict benefits or returns while the latter applies to actual benefits or returns. BCR is best used to assess a proposal or to choose between several alternative ones, to build a business case (Schmidt, 2009). Though it was not labelled as BCR, the most extensive discussion of the use of BCR in PR/C has been by William Ehling (1992). The term he used was *compensating variation*, the same term employed throughout the Excellence Study. Compensating variation is a form of BCR, not ROI. Since then, both academics and practitioners have employed modifications of compensating variation and thus BCR (Shaffer, 2004; Sinickas, 2003, 2004, 2009; Smith, 2008; Weiner, Arnorsdottir, Lang, & Smith, 2010). Yet again, a CEA metric is different from the ROI metric (Levin & McEwan, 2001). CEA compares the relative costs and the outcomes (effects) of two or more courses of action or activities, but it does not assign a monetary value (financial return) to the measure of effect. Like the ROI metric and unlike the BCR metric, CEA applies actual, realized investments or costs. Unlike the ROI metric but like the BCR metric, it applies intangible benefits as effectiveness measures. In public relations, effectiveness may be such measures as channel reach, accuracy of media reporting, length of time on a site, or number of re-tweets (Paine, 2011). Likely states that in a public relations department, BCR and CEA financial metrics have the possibility of greater utility in providing valuable financial measures for the many categories of investments than does the utilization of a ROI measure. These two are underused currently (Likely, 2012, p. 19). He also argued that most of what public relations consultants and practitioners now call ROI measurement, including that of marketing mix modelling or similar approaches using multivariable statistical methods, are not true ROI metrics since they do not include time-delayed net returns as well as all-in gross investments – at the level of the organization (p. 14).

Conclusion

The debate over valid methods of measurement and evaluation of public relations has a considerable history. It is characterized by the repetition of themes – such as the desire for a single method of measurement (the so-called 'silver bullet'), the search for valid financial metrics of value created by public relations, and the adoption of business language to demonstrate alignment with management and the organization – that have kept public relations away from the strategic perspective and focused on the narrower measurement of programmes. As Gregory and Watson commented:

> The measurement of reputation and the desire of some practitioners to imply an ROI for public relations activity have increased the drive towards the use of business language and ironically, a single-method evaluation, in distinction to business itself, which is looking for a multiplicity of evaluative methods.
>
> *(2008, p. 340)*

However, more recent development such as Communication Controlling, communication scorecards and alternative metrics such as Benefit-Cost Ratio (BCR) and Cost-Effectiveness Analysis (CEA) bring public relations strategy and its planning, measurement and evaluation back to the tenets of Excellence Theory. They show that the Excellence Theory, despite accelerated time pressures upon public relations practice and the uncertain impacts of social media and the Internet, has an enduring validity and relevance to public relations practices, especially measurement and evaluation.

In particular, the Excellence Study introduced five levels of analysis for measuring public relations value. Over the past 40 years, the first two levels, those of products/channels/messages and of programmes/campaigns, have received a considerable amount of research from academicians and practitioners. We believe the problems have been solved at both levels. Regarding the first level, we think that the current movement to 'standardize' (Geddes, 2011; Stacks & Michaelson, 2011) measurement methodologies will erase any confusion with the measurement of communication channels and message dissemination, be they traditional or social media-mediated channels. At the second level, we agree with J. Grunig's (2006a) observation regarding programmes and campaigns. Campaign outcome measurement can be standardized, given the knowledge we now have. We also agree that the financial metric ROI is not appropriate in the measurement of communication campaign effects. The programme/campaign measurement wheel need not be reinvented every decade. That is why we find AMEC's Validated Metrics approach to be lacking the foundation of years and years of programme/campaign measurement knowledge.

On the other hand, the three higher levels – function, organization and societal – have not received the attention they require. This involves measurement of the public relations department's participation in the strategic management of the organization, measurement of relationships and the intangible assets, and perhaps tangible assets, created by those relationships that the organization has with its publics and stakeholders and measurement of the social responsibility that organizations have to the welfare of society (Grunig, 2008). There is not the same depth of knowledge available that is offered by the first two levels of analysis. We consider that these three levels should be the target for academic and practitioner measurement research efforts over the next decade.

Encouraging efforts have been made. At the level of the function, as noted in the online dialogue between J. Grunig, Watson and Zerfass (IPR, 2011), 'Communication Controlling' or communication performance management has evolved in Germany and Austria since the middle of the first decade. This is a total approach to communication planning and management that aligns corporate and organizational strategy with communication strategy in such a manner as to place communication as a core activity. It is, thus, closely aligned with Excellence Theory because corporate communications directors and the communication strategy are at the heart of the organization and not a secondary or tertiary level function, distant from the dominant coalition. Communication Controlling formulates and demonstrates the contribution of value to the organization by corporate communication and public relations activity: It has 'the purpose of enhancing and demonstrating what communications contribute to corporate value creation [and] makes the alignment of communications activities with the corporate strategy a key deliverable' (DPRG/ICV, 2011, p. 11). It is thus measurable at all stages of communication activity, using a four-stage value link approach that comprises Input–Output–Outcome–Outflow (p. 13). At the levels of the organization and society, some work has been done on intangible assets or non-financial indicators. Phillips (2005) has conducted extensive research on these areas. J. Grunig took on the task on behalf of the IPR's Commission on Public Relations Measurement and Evaluation. This should be a priority area for measurement research in the coming decade.

While we understand the desire to find a single financial bullet whereby the public relation service sector could measure 'public relations', we hope that practitioners will not continue to pursue the unattainable goal of a PR ROI. We suggest that the alternatives of BCR and CEA proposed by Likely (2012) be studied further and that, with an understanding that the ROI metric only can be measured at the level of the organization, research be conducted on other financial indicators for measuring intangible assets.

Public relations measurement and evaluation will continue to be important practice issues in the next ten years. The developments we have discussed above have real potential to meet the challenges that Gregory and Watson (2008) identified. If public relations measurement and evaluation is like a game of basketball, we need a strong team of practitioners and academics working in the same direction, with the same understanding, with the same goals. One player's high-scoring game is not enough for the team to win (Grunig, 2006b). J. Grunig worked with both academics and practitioners on measurement and evaluation research. We strongly believe that for public relations measurement to advance, both in scholarship and in practice, then additional events, commissions, task forces and paper and book opportunities that mix academics and practitioners together are a must.

References

AMEC International Association for the Measurement and Evaluation of Communications, (2010). *Barcelona Declaration of Measurement Principles*. London: AMEC. Available at: http://amecorg.com/wp-content/uploads/2011/08/Barcelona_Principles_for_PR_Measurement.pdf.

AMEC International Association for the Measurement and Evaluation of Communications. (2011). *AMEC valid metrics*. London: AMEC. Available at: http://amecorg.com/2011/10/amec-valid-metrics/.

Best, R. J. (2009). *Market-based management: Strategies for growing customer value and profitability* (5th ed.). Upper Saddle River, NJ: Pearson Prentice Hall.

Black, S. (1971). *The role of public relations in management*. London: Pitman.

Booth, A. L. (1986). Strength in numbers. *Public Relations Journal*, September.

Broom, G. M., & Dozier, D. M. (1983). An overview: Evaluation research in public relations. *Public Relations Quarterly, 28,* 5–8.

Broom, G. M., & Dozier, D. M. (1990). *Using research in public relations*. Englewood Cliffs, NJ: Prentice Hall.

Cline, C. G. (1984). *Evaluation and measurement in public relations and organizational communication: A literature review*. San Francisco: IABC Foundation.

Cutlip, S. M. (1994). *The unseen power: Public relations, a history*. Hillsdale, NJ: Lawrence Erlbaum Associates.

Deutsche Public Relations Gesellschaft & Internationaler Controller Verein (DPRG/ICV), (2011). *Position paper: Communication controlling*. Berlin: DPRG.

Dozier, D. M. (1984). Program evaluation and the roles of practitioners. *Public Relations Review, 10*(2), 13–21.

Dozier, D. M. (1985). Planning and evaluation in public relations practice. *Public Relations Review, 11,* Summer.

Drury, C. (2007). *Management and cost accounting* (7th ed.). London: Cengage.

Ehling, W.P. (1992). Estimating the value of public relations and communication to an organization. In J. E. Grunig (Ed.), *Excellence in public relations and communication management*. Hillsdale, NJ: Lawrence Erlbaum Associates.

Ewen, S. (1996). *PR! A social history of spin*. New York: Basic Books.

Gaunt, R., & Wright, D. K. (2004). Examining international differences in communications measurement: Benchpoint global measurement study 2004. Paper presented at the PR Measurement Summit, September 21–24, Durham, NJ.

Geddes, D. (2011). *Framework, standards, and metrics: PR research priorities, part 2*. Institute for Public Relations Research Conversations blog, November 1, 2011. Retrieved from: http://www.instituteforpr.org/2011/11/framework-standards-and-metrics-pr-research-priorities-part-2/ (accessed 7 April, 2012).

Graves, J. J. (1975). The job isn't done until you evaluate the impact. *Public Relations Journal*, September, 32.

Gregory, A., & Watson, T. (2008). Defining the gap between research and practice in public relations programme evaluation – towards a new research agenda. *Journal of Marketing Communications, 14*(5), 337–350.

Griese, N. L. (2001). *Arthur W. Page: Publisher, public relations pioneer, patriot.* Atlanta, GA: Anvil Publishers.

Grunig, J. E. (1979). The status of public relations research. *Public Relations Quarterly, 20,* 5–8.

Grunig, J. E. (1983). Basic research provides knowledge that makes evaluation possible. *Public Relations Quarterly, 28*(3), 28–32.

Grunig. J. E. (Ed.). (1992). *Excellence in public relations and communication management.* Hillsdale, NJ: Lawrence Erlbaum Associates.

Grunig, J. E. (2006a). Furnishing the edifice: Ongoing research on public relations as a strategic management function. *Journal of Public Relations Research, 18*(2), 151–176.

Grunig, J. E. (2006b). After 50 years: The value and values of public relations. 45th Annual Distinguished Lecture of the Institute for Public Relations, Yale Club, New York, November 9.

Grunig, J. E. (2008). Conceptualizing quantitative research in public relations. In B. van Ruler, A. Tkalac Verčič, & D. Verčič (Eds.), *Public relations metrics: Research and evaluation.* New York: Routledge.

Grunig, J. E. (2009). Paradigms of global public relations in an age of digitalization. *Prism 6*(2). Retrieved from: http://www.instituteforpr.org/2011/10/a-dialog-on-roi/ (accessed 2 April 2012).

Grunig, J. E., Grunig, L. A., & Dozier, D. M. (2002). *Excellent public relations and effective organizations: A study of communication management in three countries.* Mahwah, NJ: Lawrence Erlbaum Associates.

Grunig, J. E., & Hickson, R. H. (1976). An evaluation of academic research in public relations. *Public Relations Review, 2,* 31–43.

Institute of Public Relations & Communication Directors' Forum (IPR/CDF) (2004). *Best practice in the measurement and reporting of public relations and ROI.* London: Institute of Public Relations. Available at: http://www.cipr.co.uk/content/policyresources/cipr-research-and-reports.

Institute for Public Relations (2011). A dialogue on ROI. *Research Conversations.* Gainesville, FL: IPR. Available at: http://www.instituteforpr.org/2011/10/a-dialog-on-roi/.

Jacobson, H. (1982). Guidelines for evaluating public relations program. *Public Relations Quarterly,* Summer, 7–10.

Kirban, L. (1983). Showing what we do makes a difference. *Public Relations Quarterly, 28*(3), 22–28.

Lamme, M. O., & Russell, K. M. (2010). Removing the spin: Towards a new theory of public relations history. *Journalism & Communication Monographs, 11*(4), 281–362.

Lee, T. J. (2002). Calculating ROI for communication. *Strategic Communication Management, 6*(6), 11.

Lerbinger, O. (1978). Corporate use of research in public relations. *Public Relations Review,* Winter, 11–19.

Levin, H. M., & McEwan, P. J. (2001). *Cost-effectiveness analysis: Methods and applications.* Thousand Oaks, CA: Sage Publications.

Likely, D. F. (2000). Communication and public relations: Made to measure. *Strategic Communication Management, 4*(1). Retrieved from: http://www.instituteforpr.org/wp-content/uploads/2006_SCM_Likely.pdf (accessed 6 April 2012).

Likely, D. F. (2012). Principles for the use of return on investment (ROI); Benefit-cost ration (BCR); And cost-effectiveness analysis (CEA) financial metrics in a public relations/communication (PR/C) department. Paper presented at 15th International Public Relations Research Conference, 8–10 March, Miami, FL.

Likely, D. F., Rockland, D., & Weiner, M. (2006). *Perspectives on ROI of media relations publicity efforts.* Gainesville, FL: Institute for Public Relations. Retrieved from: http://www.instituteforpr.org/topics/media-relations-publicity-efforts/.

Lindenmann, W. K. (1979). The missing link in public relations research. *Public Relations Review, 5*(1), 26–36.

Lindenmann, W. K. (1980). Hunches no longer suffice. *Public Relations Journal,* June, 10.

Lindenmann, W. K. (2005). Putting PR measurement and evaluation into historical perspective. Gainesville, FL: Institute for Public Relations. Retrieved from: http://www.instituteforpr.org/wp-content/uploads/PR_History2005.pdf (accessed April 7, 2012).

Macnamara, J. R. (1999). Research in public relations: A review of the use of evaluation and formative research. *Asia Pacific Public Relations Journal, 1*(2), 107–134.

Macnamara, J. R. (2007). *Return on investment (ROI) of PR and corporate communication.* Sydney: Mass Communication Group.

Marken, G. A. (1988). Public relations and sales: There must be a measurable relation. *Business Marketing,* April, 94–97.

McElreath, M. P. (1975). Public relations evaluative research: A summary statement. *Public Relations Review,* Winter, 129–136.

McElreath, M. P. (1980). *Priority research questions for public relations for the 1980s.* New York: Foundation for Public Relations Research and Education.

McElreath, M. P. (1981). *Systematic public relations: A workbook on how to measure the effectiveness of public relations.* Lexington, MA: Ginn Publishing.

Merims, A. (1972). Marketing's stepchild: Product publicity. *Harvard Business Review,* November/December, 107–113.

Moutinho, L., & Southern, G. (2010). *Strategic marketing management.* Andover: Cengage.

Paine, K. D. (2007). *Measuring public relationships: The data-driven communicator's guide to success.* Berlin, NH: KD Paine & Partners.

Paine, K. D. (2011). *Measure what matters: Online tools for understanding customers, social media, engagement and key relationships.* Hoboken, NJ: John Wiley & Sons.

Pavlik, J. (1987). *Public relations: What research tells us.* Newbury Park, CA: Sage.

Pessolano, F. J. (1985). Analyzing media coverage by computer. *Bank Marketing,* April, 38–43.

Phillips, D. (2005). Towards relationship management. Paper presented at the Alan Rawel CIPR Academic Conference, Chartered Institute of Public Relations, London.

Plackard, D. H., & Blackmon, C. (1947). *Blueprint for public relations.* New York: McGraw-Hill.

Robinson, E. J. (1969). *Public relations and survey research.* New York: Appleton-Century-Crofts.

Schmidt, M. J. (2009). *Business case essentials: A guide to structure and content.* Boston: Solution Matrix Ltd.

Shaffer, J. (2004). Four steps to demonstrating communication ROI. *Communication World On-Line,* November.

Sierra, L. (2003). Sierra's theory of communicativity: Calculating the value of organizational communication through cost, effort and perception. *Communication World,* June/July, 38–41.

Simmons, P., & Watson, T. (2006). Public relations evaluation in Australia: Practices and attitudes across sectors and employment status. *Asia Pacific Public Relations Journal,* (2). Retrieved from: http://www.deakin.edu.au/artsed/apprj/vol6no2.php#8.

Sinickas, A. (1983). Are you ready for a communication audit? *Communication World*, October. Retrieved from: http://www.sinicom.com/homepages/pubs.htm.

Sinickas, A. (2003). Focus on behaviour change to prove ROI. *Strategic Communication Management*, 7(6), 12–13.

Sinickas, A. (2004). Top tip: Calculating ROI. *Internal Communication Measurement Manual*, 138–141. Available at: http://www.sinicom.com/Sub%20Pages/pubs/articles/article 130.pdf.

Sinickas, A. (2009). Measure your ROI – fast. *The Ragan Report*, February.

Smith, B. G. (2008). *Representing PR in the marketing mix: A study on public relations variables in marketing mix modeling.* Institute for Public Relations. Retrieved from: http://www.instituteforpr.org/topics/pr-marketing-mix/ (accessed 9 April 2012).

SPRA (Swedish Public Relations Association) (1996). *Return on communications.* Stockholm: Swedish Public Relation Association (Svenska Informationsforening).

Stacks, D. W. (Ed.). (2006). *Dictionary of public relations measurement and research.* Gainesville, FL: Institute for Public Relations, 26. Retrieved from: http://www.instituteforpr.org/wp-content/uploads/PRMR_Dictionary.pdf.

Stacks, D. W., & Michaelson, D. (2011). Standardization in public relations measurement and evaluation. *Public Relations Journal, 5*(2). Retrieved from: http://www.prsa.org/SearchResults/download/6D050201/0/Standardization_in_Public_Relations_Measurement_an (accessed 7 April 2012).

Strenski, J. B. (1980). Measuring public relations results. *Public Relations Quarterly, 25*(2), 11–13.

Tirone, J. F. (1977). Measuring the Bell System's public relations. *Public Relations Review, 3*(4), 21–38.

Watson, T. (2005). ROI or evidence-based PR: The language of public relations evaluation. *Prism, 3*(1). Retrieved from; http://www.prismjournal.org/fileadmin/Praxis/Files/Journal_Files/Issue3/Watson.pdf (accessed 30 March 2012).

Watson, T. (2008). Public relations research priorities: A Delphi study. *Journal of Communication Management, 12*(2), 104–123.

Watson, T. (2011). An initial investigation on the use of 'Return on Investment' in public relations practice. *Public Relations Review, 37*, 314–317.

Watson, T. (2012a). The evolution of public relations measurement and evaluation. *Public Relations Review*, doi:10.1016/j.pubrev.2011.12.1018 (In press).

Watson, T. (2012b). Advertising value equivalence – PR's illegitimate offspring. Paper presented at 15th International Public Relations Research Conference, 8–10 March, Miami, FL.

Watson, T., & Noble P. (2007). *Evaluating public relations* (2nd ed.). London: Kogan Page.

Watson, T., & Simmons, P. (2004). Public relations evaluation: Survey of Australian practitioners. Paper presented to the Australian and New Zealand Communication Association Conference, July 7–9, Sydney, Australia.

Watson, T., & Zerfass, A. (2011). Return on investment in public relations: A critique of concepts used by practitioners from communication and management sciences perspectives. *PRism 8*(1). Retrieved from: http://www.prismjournal.org/fileadmin/8_1/Watson_Zerfass.pdf (accessed 30 March 2012).

Weiner, M., Arnorsdottir, L., Lang, R., & Smith, B. G. (2010). *Isolating the effects of media-based public relations on sales: Optimization through marketing mix modeling.* Gainesville, FL: Institute for Public Relations. Retrieved from: http://www.instituteforpr.org/topics/media-based-pr-_on_sales (accessed 30 March 2012).

Williams, L. W. (1992). Calculating your return on investment: Measuring the impact of your PR programs on the bottom-line. Workshop at the Institute for International Research Conference, Toronto, Canada, January.

Woods, J. A. (2004). Communications ROI. *Communications World, 21*(1), 28–31.

Worcester, R. M. (1983). The role in research in evaluating public relations programs. *IPRA Review*, November, 16–19.

Wright, D. K. (1979). Some ways to measure public relations. *Public Relations Journal*, July, 19–22.

Xavier, R., Patel, A., Johnston, K., Watson, T., & Simmons, P. (2005). Using evaluation techniques and performance claims to demonstrate public relations impact: An Australian perspective. *Public Relations Review, 31*(3), 417–424.

Zerfass, A. (2008). The corporate communication scorecard. In B. van Ruler, A. Tkalac Verčič, & D. Verčič (Eds.), *Public relations metrics: Research and evaluation* (pp. 139–153). London: Routledge.

Zerfass, A. (2010). Assuring rationality and transparency in corporate communications. Theoretical foundations and empirical findings on communication controlling and communication performance management. In M. D. Dodd, & K. Yamamura (Eds.), *Ethical issues for public relations practice in a multicultural world, 13th International Public Relations Research Conference* (pp. 947–966). Gainesville, FL: Institute for Public Relations.

Zerfass, A., Verhoeven, P., Tench, R., Moreno, A., & Verčič, D. (2011). *European Communication Monitor 2011: Empirical insights into strategic communication in Europe. Results of an empirical survey in 43 countries.* Brussels: EACD, EUPRERA.

9

STRATEGIC COMMUNICATION AND CONFLICT RESOLUTION

Contributions to Institutionalization in Public Relations

Kenneth D. Plowman and Robert I. Wakefield

Abstract

The convergence of strategic communication, conflict resolution and institutionalization has its roots in the tutelage of the authors of this chapter by their respective dissertations' mentor, James E. Grunig. It begins with a summary of literature from other domains and from public relations, strategic communication, and conflict resolution. It provides a brief discussion of a study conducted last year by the authors and one of their graduate students at Brigham Young University, Alex Curry. It then explores the relationship between the three concepts and provides suggestions for making strategic public relations more enduring in organizations, regardless of who is supervising the program.

Key Words

conflict resolution, institutionalization, strategic communication, two–way models of communication

Introduction

The convergence of strategic communication, conflict resolution and institutionalization has its roots in the tutelage of the authors of this chapter by their dissertation mentor, James E. Grunig. The term *strategic management* in organizational public relations was the precursor to *strategic communication* (Grunig & Repper, 1992) where strategic management in the field was defined essentially as goal–setting, environmental scanning of potential issues, and the building of long-term relationships with key publics or stakeholders.

In 2011, Plowman investigated the evolving nature of strategic communication planning in the field of public relations based in part on Hallahan, Holthausen, Van Ruler, Verčič, and Sriramesh's definition of strategic communication as "the purposeful use of communication by an organization to fulfill its mission" (2007, p. 3). The legitimacy of the term *strategic communication* was further established in 2012 with the adoption of a new definition of public relations by the Public Relations Society of America: "Public relations is a strategic communication process that builds mutually beneficial relationships between organizations and their publics."

In Plowman's (2011) study it was evident that leadership of the U.S. military in Iraq was using conflict resolution techniques to carry out strategic communication as well as sustaining those plans amid the relatively rapid turnover of public relations or public affairs personnel—the institutionalization of strategic public relations across changing personnel in organizations. So, as strategic communication focuses an organization on planning with goals, attendant measurable objectives, and evaluation criteria, conflict resolution provides expertise for public relations professionals to carry out the plan. Institutionalization then renews the structure of the planning and sustains it as the organization evolves and personnel change over time.

J. Grunig (2006) was one of the first scholars to introduce the need for institutionalizing the public relations function in organizations. Institutionalization is a term from business management and other domains which is defined as the infusion of underlying, sustainable, "rule-like" values and procedures into an organization regardless of particular circumstances affecting the entity or of the individual personalities and philosophies of its main executives (Zucker, 1977).

Grunig believed that for public relations professionals to gain respect and maximum impact within their organizations, public relations needs to be institutionalized. He wrote that "a major task remains . . . in institutionalizing strategic public relations as actual practice in most organizations" (2006, p. 171). His assumption was that current organizational communication efforts too often are not based on enduring standards of effectiveness but on arbitrary or traditional presumptions of executives who are in charge at any given time. When one regime leaves a certain organization and is replaced by another, whether it be senior heads of public relations or chief executives, within a relatively short time the communication program looks entirely different than it did before the transition. This seems to happen particularly in smaller corporations and not-for-profit entities (Wakefield, Plowman, & Curry, in press). Sometimes the changes that occur in these transitions lead to needed improvements, but more often they simply reflect what the new managers think public relations should entail, whether or not that is based on proven standards of effectiveness.

A necessary part of this debate on institutionalization is addressed to public relations—to its role, if any, in fostering institutionalization for the organizations it serves. The question is relevant because Grunig seemed to accept both sides of the debate. While he observed a strong need for greater institutionalization of public relations, he also saw public relations as a function that should help guide institutions toward strategic change. Grunig is not alone in this thinking. Yi (2005), for example, argued that strategic public relations can help entities identify relationships in their environment and continually adjust to changes in those relationships. Grunig took this concept one step further; he proclaimed that in facilitating organizational adaptation, public relations practitioners could help legitimize their own function. Understanding this, scholars have been attempting to establish a body of knowledge about the fundamental principles needed to effectively practice strategic communication and to make it more valuable and respected.

This chapter, then, continues conversations between the authors and Grunig about strategic communication, conflict resolution, and institutionalization. It begins with a summary of literature from other domains and from public relations, strategic communication, and conflict resolution. It provides a brief discussion of a study conducted last year by the authors and one of their graduate students at Brigham Young University, Alex Curry (Wakefield, Plowman, & Curry, in press). That study looked at organizations where executive transitions had occurred and determined whether the public relations programs remained intact or changed as a result of the transition. When changes took place, were they positive, harmful, or neutral for the entities involved? The chapter then explores the relationship between strategic communication, conflict resolution, and institutionalization, and provides suggestions for making strategic public relations more enduring in organizations, regardless of who is supervising the program.

Strategic Communication and Planning

Argenti, Howell and Beck (2005) defined *strategic communication* "as communication aligned with the company's overall strategy, to enhance its strategic positioning." Also writing about strategic communication, Botan (2006) identified differences among the terms grand strategy, strategy, and tactics. He defined strategic communication as planned communication that begins and ends with publics. He differentiated grand strategy as strategy involving policy, alliances, values, and goals (minus the tactics), while strategy is more the planning, maneuvering of ideas, argument, and persuasion. He defined the tactical level as the actual operational doing and practices. He also said that every tactical communication is judged on the relationship surrounding that communication, because the relationship of the parties involved in the communication is the basis for belief in that communication.

Ideally, strategic communication occurs at the leadership levels of an organization and is then carried out at the tactical levels. It educates and informs publics—but the most effective communication changes behavior. Strategic communication sets measureable communication goals and considers the long-term effects on key publics or strategic stakeholders while constantly scanning the organizational environment for issues that might affect the organization (Grunig & White, 1992).

In the seminal article on strategic communication in the inaugural issue of the *International Journal of Strategic Communication*, Hallahan et al. (2007) covered the origins of strategic communication from several fields. They defined communication as "the constitutive activity of management" (p. 27). They cited Mintzberg's (1990) discussions about environmental scanning of stakeholders, issues management, and the integration of communication. They also addressed the term strategic, citing its origins in warfare. Mintzberg (1994) defined strategy as a plan for a future course of action and further explained it as a pattern of or consistency in behavior over time. This consistency is usually a combination of deliberate and emergent strategies. Deliberate strategies are realized while emergent strategies are realized but not expressly intended. Such strategies incorporate the concept of stakeholder relationships from Botan (2006), Hallahan et al. (2007), Hon and Grunig (1999), and Ledingham and Bruning (2000).

Steyn (2007) differentiated communication management and strategic communication. She said that public relations helps an organization adapt to its stakeholder environment in serving both the organization and the public interest. By acting socially responsible and building mutually beneficial relationships, an organization gains trust and builds a good reputation with its stakeholders. Steyn then operationalized communication strategy as *deliberate*, combining several elements of planning. These processes draw a map of stakeholders, think through the consequences of organizational goals on those stakeholders, and address those consequences by deciding what should be communicated and what should be achieved by this communication.

Strategic Communication and Conflict Resolution

Admiral James G. Stavridis spoke about strategic communication as follows:

> Effective communication requires leaders of an organization to take an early and persistent role in deciding how ideas and decisions are shaped and delivered. Certainly in the national security context, a leader can improve the effects of operational and policy planning by ensuring communications implications of that planning are considered as early as possible in the process. If planning is done in that fashion, then it is likely that the communications associated with it will indeed be strategic in its effects.
>
> *(Stavridis, 2007, p. 4)*

This quote adds to planning and leadership aspects of strategic communication and negotiates how these ideas are delivered. Argenti (2005), Plowman (1995, 1998), and many others have argued for public relations having a seat at the management decision table so that the ideas discussed above have a better chance to make it into strategic communication plans. However, Putnam (1994, 2004, 2009, 2010) argued for the transformation of the process; strategic communication needs to resolve real problems so that there is not just conflict solution but conflict resolution so that problems remain permanently solved. Indeed, J. Grunig explained symmetrical public relations as "the use of bargaining, negotiating and strategies of conflict resolution to bring about symbiotic changes in the ideas, attitudes, and behaviors of both the organization and its publics" (1989, p. 29).

As stated, conflict resolution and negotiation have been topics for discussion in public relations since 1989, when J. Grunig linked the concepts to the two-way models of public relations. Murphy (1991) then proposed game theory, attaching terms like win/win to the symmetrical model and win/lose to the asymmetrical model and using the term mixed motives to describe a combination of both. Plowman (1995) developed a number of negotiation strategies that fit into a mixed motive model that encompassed the entire spectrum between the two-way asymmetrical and the two-way symmetrical models. It included strategies of contention, avoidance, accommodation, compromise, cooperation, unconditionally constructive, win/win or no deal, and principled. In 2001, Plowman, Briggs, and Huang added the term mediated or cultural. Then in 2007, Plowman tested those strategies in a case study. Although contention was used the most, it was usually in conjunction with the principled strategy. Mediation, however, was determined to be the most productive technique in resolving conflict. Also in 2007, Plowman added perseverance, a tenth strategy.

Related studies in public relations and conflict resolution have included the contingency model of conflict (Cancel, Cameron, Sallot, & Mitrook, 1997). That study initially developed 87 specific tactics to utilize in conflict resolution. This stream of research led to many other studies (Shin, Jin, Cheng, & Cameron, 2003) and is similar to contingency theory, where use of any given tactic depends on the situation.

In 2010, Christen and Lovaas developed what they called a dual-continuum approach to conflict management in public relations, extending the work of Cameron and his associates. This approach is similar to mixed motives and looks at the advocacy or contention of Plowman (2007) and accommodation or cooperation (Plowman, 2007) to examine these strategies in a non-linear fashion. Christen and Lovaas maintained that real-world disputes are far more complex than a single continuum can represent, and that in a cooperative win/win situation (Plowman, 1996; Thomas, 1976) where contention and cooperation overlap, there cannot be a single continuum. They said, "Any situation that involves separate, simultaneous movement toward or away from [either contention or cooperation] . . . can create an untenable paradox." As conflict resolution and public relations become more developed, more complexity is added to strategies and tactics.

Complexity also is a major factor in multi-party negotiations, which could be a next step in public relations research to incorporate strategic communication and institutionalization. For example, Plowman (2004) investigated the hot waste issue in Utah and found that contention was the most used strategy, but was most often combined with the principled strategy. If those strategies were not successful, then role players turned to avoidance. During the third round of negotiation, role players started using cooperation and compromise. This created a less confrontational atmosphere and the role players were more inclined to discuss alternatives. The most useful strategy in resolving the hot waste issue, however, was mediation.

Most research in conflict resolution has involved just two-party disputes, but in reality and especially for public relations, often more than one stakeholder is involved. Lawrence Susskind, from the Harvard Program on Negotiation, addressed public relations and conflict resolution in public disputes in 1996 (Susskind & Field, 1996). His book described public relations using terms that essentially equate to one-way and asymmetrical models, and then used a version of Fisher, Ury, and Patton's (1991) mutual gains approach to resolve public disputes in a symmetrical manner. However, more work needs to be done in multiparty disputes, and now public relations is beginning to address such negotiations.

This chapter, then, claims that strategic communication and conflict resolution play strong roles in creating strategic plans, and that the management process of communication (Hallahan et al., 2007) leads to action plans, goals and objectives, stakeholders or key publics, communication tactics, and measurable outcomes. But where does institutionalization fit into the puzzle? This is discussed below.

Theoretical Basis for Institutionalization

The idea of institutionalization has been studied for several decades. Meyer and Rowan (1977) defined it as the construct "by which social processes, obligations, or actualities come to take on a rule-like status in social thought and action" (p. 341). Scott (1987) added that through institutionalization, "individuals come to accept a shared definition of social reality—a conception whose validity is seen as independent of the actor's own views or actions but . . . as defining the 'way things are' and/or the 'way things are to be done'" (p. 496). Fleck (2007) noted that enduring fundamentals are important not just for individual organizations but also for industries and even societies.

Selznick (1957), an early institutionalization theorist, viewed it as a "process . . . that happens to the organization over time" (p. 16) through the decisions and activities that sustain widely accepted values and norms. A U.S. Agency for International Development report likewise referred to institutionalization as "an ongoing process in which a set of activities, structures, and values becomes an integral and sustainable part of an organization" (USAID, 2000, p. 1). Sandhu (2008) added that institutionalization occurs when these values and activities are maintained from generation to generation.

Eisenstadt (1964) explained that these institutionalized norms are "oriented to the solution of certain problems inherent in a major area of social life" (p. 235). If that is true, that institutionalization helps solve problems, this would imply a need for adaptation. At the same time, however, the principles of institutionalization provide "relative permanence" to structures, boundaries, and philosophies (Zucker, 1977).

Leadership plays an important role in institutionalization. Fleck (2007) explained:

> The key tasks of leaders include the definition of institutional mission and role; the institutional embodiment of purpose; the defense of institutional integrity; and the ordering of internal conflict. It is up to leadership to not only to create but to preserve [these] values.
>
> *(p. 68)*

Organizations or industries that institutionalize within these widely accepted constructs help themselves to generate success and respect. Scott (1987) explained that organizations "conform to a set of institutionalized beliefs because they . . . are rewarded for doing so through increased legitimacy, resources, and survival capabilities" (p. 498). Fleck (2007) noted the importance of industries in this institutionalization processes because when an entire industry has legitimacy, it helps strengthen the environment of good will toward organizations within the industry.

Zucker (1977) suggested three variables that affect how much institutionalization will occur in a given entity or industry. The first is the degree to which knowledge of expected behaviors is transmitted to successive actors within the institution. For example, a mission statement works only if it is continually reinforced. The second variable is the extent to which the behaviors are sustained once the knowledge has been transmitted. The final criterion is the degree to which attempts to change traditions are resisted. Zucker explained, "Acts high on institutionalization will be resistant to attempts to change them through personal influence because they are seen as . . . imposed on the setting" from new and often distrusted people, such as a new executive (p. 730).

Zucker's (1977) final point is what generates criticism toward institutionalization. Because of its innate resistance to change, some scholars see institutionalization as overly inflexible. Oliver (1992) wrote that institutionalization possesses "inertial qualities" that "constrain fundamental design change" (p. 566). Tushman and Romanelli (1985) argued that institutionalization harbors unproductive "conformity generating processes" (p. 193).

Despite the problems that can arise from too much rigidity, Eisenstadt (1964) explained how institutionalization can be an adaptive, positive process, even in the context of natural and constant change:

> The very attempt to institutionalize any such system creates in its wake the possibility for change. These are possibilities not only for general, unspecified change but for more specific changes, which develop not randomly but in

relatively specific directions, to a large extent set by the very process of institutionalization.

(p. 236)

If change amidst stability seems contradictory, scholars have explained how it is possible. Selznick (1957) perceived that organizations can be adaptive if they are institutionalized around values rather than technical processes. "To institutionalize," he explained, "is to *infuse with value* beyond the technical requirements of the task at hand" (p. 17). Scott (1987) added that with bureaucratized processes, quick adaptation is difficult; but when stability comes from enduring values and culture, adaptation is possible because it comes from shared culture rather than imposed processes. "When beliefs are widely shared and categories and procedures are taken for granted, it is less essential that they be formally encoded in organizational structures" (p. 507).

To this point, then, the chapter has looked at institutionalization as a requirement for enduring legitimacy, coupled with an ability to adapt to needed changes through shared value systems. Institutionalization can be sustained in organizations, industries, and entire societies. Stability is not inherently a static phenomenon, however; various factors can lead to necessary and even desired changes. Therefore, a critical decision in institutionalization is to strike a proper balance between stability and change (Selznick, 1996). From here on, the chapter explores how this relates to strategic communication.

Institutionalization and Public Relations

Until now, "very little attention has been paid to institutionalisation as a relevant . . . perspective for public relations" (Jensen, 2008, p. 113). Scholars have only in the past half-decade or so advocated the need to institutionalize public relations principles and practices. For example, J. Grunig (2007) asserted, "The practice of public relations is in dire need of conceptualization (of theoretical thinking) about what public relations is, what its value is to organizations and society, and what its core values should be" (p. 1). He also was one of the first to argue for "institutionalizing strategic public relations as actual practice" (Grunig, 2006, p. 171). Arnold (1995) and Macnamara (2006) have issued similar calls, and Nielsen (2006) observed: "The standing and reputation of our own profession could benefit from a coming together around a shared set of values that speak about what we believe our responsibilities are and what we hold as important about what we do" (p. 1).

To a limited extent, these encouragements toward more institutionalization are starting to be answered. In 2008, the European Public Relations Education and Research Association (EUPRERA) emphasized institutionalization at its annual conference. More recently, a special issue of the *Journal of Strategic Communication* looked at the subject. Zerfass (2009), the editor of that edition, acknowledged that he gained "inspiration" for the topic from an earlier version of this chapter presented by Wakefield (2008) at the International Public Relations Research and Education Conference in Miami.

In another article about institutionalization in public relations, Yi (2005) wrote:

> Many public relations scholars have called for the institutionalization of . . . the public relations profession itself. L. Grunig, J. Grunig, and Dozier (2002) suggested that "public relations could provide an institutionalized mechanism within organizations for empowering otherwise powerless publics and for incorporating considerations of ethics and social responsibility into management decision processes."
>
> *(p. 326)*

Institutionalization is sought for various functions within public relations as well as for the industry. Sandhu (2008) noted a 10-year study by Rao and Kumar (1999) that showed a 40% increase in investor relations departments in Fortune 500 firms. Sandhu then suggested possible reasons for what may be the beginnings of institutionalization of this specialized sub-function of public relations:

> Two main reasons for the increase are mounting external pressure of the newly established stockholder activism as well as increasing demands of financial analysts. It would be worthwhile to expand this model of analysis towards the establishment of new branches of public relations, e.g. social media and online public relations or diversity or heritage PR.
>
> *(Sandhu, 2008, p. 130)*

Distinctions such as these carry more weight when related to the arguments that institutionalization is important for industries and functions within industries well. As Scott (1987) said, a given industry gains legitimacy when it is institutionalized because people outside that industry can then clearly understand its core principles and functions as well as its value to the greater society.

The public relations field today not only seems short on legitimacy but it often faces downright disparagement (Burger, 2007). Several scholars have reflected that institutionalization would make public relations more legitimized and more adaptable to change if it were centered on overall strategic values. Macnamara (2006), however, contended that if any institutionalization has occurred in the field, it has gone in the wrong direction, emphasizing tactical procedures over the strategic. He said, "Public relations [has] continued down its practical path . . . based on outdated assumptions about the effects of communication" (p. 6). This practical path, he added, begins with university public relations curriculum, where students learn "how to write news releases, brochures, advertisements and scripts, work with producers and designers to arrange events – but with little or no understanding of what effects if any their work might produce within the groups that they target" (p. 9). This technical focus hardly seems to be rectified by the more recent obsession towards creating blogs, tweets, and viral videos. When the institutionalization of strategic values of environmental scanning, issues anticipation, relationship building, and reputation management occurs (Grunig, 2007; Macnamara, 2006), public relations can then accomplish what it was intended to do: help entities maintain enduring legitimacy within their respective environments. But to enact these strategic processes, the industry must have its own enduring legitimacy.

Sandhu (2008) suggested factors that could institutionalize and legitimize public relations. The first factor consists of regulations that necessitate public relations expertise, such as reporting requirements of the Securities and Exchange Commission. The second stems from demands of stakeholders. J. Grunig (2007) stated that the key reason for public relations is to build relationships with these publics. The final factor is that organizations tend to watch each other, as Sandhu explained, and therefore they may incorporate communication programs into their system partly because similar entities have done the same thing.

Sandhu (2008) also outlined factors of institutionalization that occur inside an organization. One is the access a function has to the top decision-making executives, and Sandhu argued that continual access would be one indicator of the institutionalization of public relations. Another factor is independence, or the autonomy of an organizational unit to function without undue constraints. Sandhu stated that "many organizations have overt or hidden 'turf wars' between various communication functions." For example, "The PR function can be a subsidiary of the marketing department, on the same level or above the marketing department. The higher the independence of the organizational function, the higher its institutionalization within the organization" (p. 135).

Exploration of Institutionalization in Public Relations

Recently, the authors and one of their graduate students conducted a multiple-case study of six organizations to determine the nature and extent of institutionalization in their public relations programs (Wakefield, Plowman, & Curry, in press). The study included two transnational corporations, a small university, a political office in the Western United States, and two military units headquartered in Iraq. Data was gathered through emails and personal interviews with heads of public relations in these entities. The authors also examined relevant internal emails, organizational and industry newsletters, communication plans, PowerPoint presentations, and other documents. Direct or participant observation also was incorporated into four of the organizations.

Although the full-scale results of the study will not be detailed in this chapter (they can be found in Wakefield, Plowman, & Curry, in press), the overall conclusions are certainly relevant here. Institutionalization would suggest that there should be some common inception of basic principles and procedures wherever a given function is practiced and regardless of who may be in charge of the given organizational units. For example, when attorneys or accountants enter any organization where their function is practiced, they likely would recognize a certain stability surrounding the basic principles, standards, and even regulations comprising the function, no matter whose name was attached to the function's directorship or to senior management of the organization.

The authors' analysis showed some support for institutionalization. However, it also found that strategic communication does not have nearly the same levels of institutionalization within organizations as do other professions. Observation of the military units and one of the large corporations indicated that institutionalization *can* occur through a strategic mission and ongoing commitment to genuine relationship building and that such institutionalization can be a positive force for organizations. For example, while institutionalization rendered the military units too rigid in certain instances, in an environment where rules and loyalty can mean the difference between life and death, even that rigidity has a place. The establishment of traditional norms and behaviors also enhanced the larger corporation's ability to fully understand its stakeholder environment and to adjust to its ever-changing mandates.

By contrast, the smaller and more entrepreneurial corporation, the university and the political entity indicated that attempts to institutionalize communications still seem subject to the whims and often misguided understanding of public relations by organizational leaders. Even many years of quality communications can be quickly overturned by leaders of organizations who do not understand its fundamental purposes. With capricious reductions of staff or elimination of vital activities, organizations become vulnerable to future problems or even major crises.

Too often, senior executives do not seem to foresee or even care about liabilities created in their own entities when public relations programs are devalued. Coombs and Holladay (2009) offered a stark example of this in their discussion of comments issued by Dawn Fenton, a consultant on corporate social responsibility (CSR). Fenton has said that communication practitioners should be kept as far away as possible from CSR programs—that, in the words of Coombs and Holladay, other, supposedly more enlightened managers "should do the serious planning and policy making for CSR. Public relations should be brought in at the end simply to help communicate the CSR messages to external constituents" (p. 97). However, as Coombs and Holladay noted:

> From this perspective communication practice is not a strategic management function. Rather, it is simply a tactic or tool used to communicate decisions made by others. This demonstrates a complete lack of regard for the knowledge and skills public relations could contribute to CSR research, policy formulation, and implementation. [Such] views devalue strategic communication.
>
> *(2009, pp. 97–98)*

Contributions of Strategic Communication and Conflict Resolution to Institutionalization in PR

So, which factors are most likely to lead to institutionalization? One is the leadership provided by public relations practitioners and the legitimacy and adaptability of strategic communication plans that endure over time and through various changes in an organization. Strategic communication programs constantly scan the environment to ensure long-term issues are addressed with key publics. Conflict resolution skills also can be critical to correlate the institutionalization of larger organizations with that of strategic communication. Conflict resolution skills add to the leadership abilities of practitioners, especially the ability to deal with multiple publics on complex issues.

Another is sheer size and complexity of an organization. Larger organizations tend to be more bureaucratic, with more ingrained structure, policies, and traditions than those in most of the smaller entities. As a result of this, even when changes occur in public relations leadership, there may be few changes in the function. By contrast, smaller corporations can be much more entrepreneurial in nature and therefore less prone to have established the more traditional public relations efforts. In such cases it becomes easier for organizational leaders to use turnover of senior public relations officers as an excuse to disband the strategic aspects of the function in favor of publicity or promotion alone.

The way the organization operates within its environment should also be a factor, as Sandhu (2008) suggested in his study. For the military units in the authors' study, it was extremely important for everyone to be on the same page, as it were, to maximize the self-preservation of all soldiers. For the large firm, the tight competition and traditions of the industry helped foster continuity. The environment also was mentioned in the political office, with an electorate that had expectations regardless of who was in office at a given time. In all of these cases, it seemed that strategic outcomes were seen as more important than any specific tactics. However, individual whims and philosophies of the organizational leaders still carried too much weight in most of the organizations studied.

As for the public relations field as a whole, it may be growing in legitimacy because of the increasingly dynamic environment that affects organizations. And yet it seems that the field still has far to go before being permeated by institutionalization of values and standards. In smaller organizations, particularly those that are more closely affected by turnover in leadership and personnel, institutionalization may be even less promising. It also has been difficult so far to see correlations between institutionalization and the ability of public relations officers to serve as change agents in organizations.

References

Argenti, P. A. (2005). *Corporate communication.* Chicago: Irwin Professional.

Argenti, P. A., Howell, R. A., & Beck, K. A. (2005). The strategic communication imperative. *MIT Sloan Management Review, 46*(3), 83–89.

Arnold, J. (1995). IMC: Much ado about little. *The Public Relations Strategist, 1*(4), 29–33.

Botan, C. H. (2006). Grand strategy, strategy and tactics in public relations. In C. H. Botan, & V. Hazleton (Eds.), *Public relations theory II* (pp. 223–248). Mahwah, NJ: Lawrence Erlbaum Associates.

Burger, C. (2007). Through the years. *The Public Relations Strategist, 13*(4), 18–23.

Cancel, A. E., Cameron, G. T., Sallot, L. M., & Mitrook, M. A. (1997). It depends: A contingency theory of accommodation in public relations. *Journal of Public Relations Research, 9*, 33.

Christen, C. T., & Lovaas, S. (2010). The dual-continuum approach: An extension of the contingency theory of conflict management. Paper presented at the annual meeting of the Association for Education in Journalism and Mass Communication, Denver, CO, August.

Coombs, W. T., & Holladay, S. J. (2009). Comparing apology to equivalent crisis response strategies: Clarifying apology's role and value in crisis communication. *Public Relations Review, 34*, 252–257.

Eisenstadt, S. N. (1964). Institutionalization and change. *American Sociological Review, 29*(2), 235–247.

Fisher, R., Ury, W., & Patton, B. (1991). *Getting to yes: Negotiating agreement without giving in* (2nd ed.). New York: Penguin Books.

Fleck, D. (2007). Institutionalization and organizational long-term success. *Brazilian Administration Review, 4*(2), 64–80.

Grunig, J. E. (1989). Symmetrical presuppositions as a framework for public relations theory. In C. H. Botan & V. Hazleton, Jr. (Eds.), *Public relations theory* (pp. 17–44). Hillsdale, NJ: Lawrence Erlbaum Associates.

Grunig, J. E. (2006). Furnishing the edifice: Ongoing research on public relations as a strategic management function. *Journal of Public Relations Research, 18*(2), 151–176.

Grunig, J. E. (2007). After 50 years: The value and values of public relations. Annual distinguished lecture, the Institute for Public Relations. Retrieved from: http://www.instituteforpr.org/edu_info/values_after_50_years/ (accessed Sept. 25, 2007).

Grunig, J. E., & Repper, F. C. (1992). Strategic management, publics, and issues. In J. E. Grunig (Ed.), *Excellence in public relations and communication management* (pp. 91–108). Hillsdale, NJ: Lawrence Erlbaum Associates.

Grunig, J. E., & White, J. (1992). The effect of worldviews on public relations theory and practice. In J. E. Grunig (Ed.), *Excellence in public relations and communication management* (pp. 31–64). Hillsdale, NJ: Lawrence Erlbaum Associates.

Grunig, L. A., Grunig, J. E., & Dozier, D. M. (2002). *Excellent public relations and effective organizations: A study of communication management in three countries.* Mahwah, NJ: Lawrence Erlbaum Associates.

Hallahan, K., Holthausen, D., Van Ruler, B., Verčič, D., & Sriramesh, K. (2007). Defining strategic communication. *International Journal of Strategic Communication, 1*(1), 3–35.

Hon, L. C., & Grunig, J. E. (1999). *Guidelines for measuring relationships in public relations.* Gainesville, FL: The Institute for Public Relations, Commission on PR Measurement and Evaluation.

Jensen, I. (2008). Institutionalization—The social reality of corporate communication. In E. Invernizzi, T. M. Falconi, & S. Romenti (Eds.), *Institutionalising PR and corporate communication: Proceedings of the EUPRERA 2008 Milan Congress* (Vol. 1, pp. 100–119). Milan: Pearson.

Ledingham, J. A., & Bruning, S. D. (2000). *Public relations as relationship management.* Mahwah, NJ: Lawrence Erlbaum Associates.

Macnamara, J. (2006). The fork in the road of media communication practice and theory. Paper presented at the 4th Annual Summit on Measurement, Portsmouth, NH, 29 Sept.

Meyer, J., & Rowan, B. (1977). Institutionalized organizations: Formal structure as myth and ceremony. *American Journal of Sociology, 83*(2), 340–363.

Mintzberg, H. (1990). The design school: Reconsidering the basic premises of strategic management. *Strategic Management Journal, 11,* 171–195.

Mintzberg, H. (1994). *The rise and fall of strategic planning.* New York: The Free Press.

Murphy, P. (1991). The limits of symmetry: A game theory approach to symmetric and asymmetric public relations. *Public Relations Research Annual, 3,* 115–131.

Nielsen, B. (2006). The singular character of public relations in a global economy. Annual distinguished lecture of the Institute for Public Relations, London, October 11.

Oliver, C. (1992). The antecedents of deinstitionalization. *Organization Studies, 13*(4), 563–588.

Plowman, K. D. (1995). Congruence between public relations and conflict resolution: Negotiational power in the organization. Unpublished doctoral dissertation, University of Maryland, College Park.

Plowman, K. D. (1996). Negotiation and two-way models of public relations. Paper presented at the Public Relations Division, Annual Conference of Association for Education in Journalism and Mass Communication. Anaheim, California.

Plowman, K. D. (1998). Power in conflict for public relations. *Journal of Public Relations Research, 10*(4), 237–262.

Plowman, K. D. (2004). Multiparty conflict and public relations. In *Proceedings of 7th International Public Relations Research Conference* (pp. 44–45). Miami, FL.

Plowman, K. D. (2007). Public relations, conflict resolution, and mediation. In E. L. Toth (Ed.), *The future of excellence in public relations and communication management: Challenges to the next generation* (pp. 85–102). Mahwah, NJ: Lawrence Erlbaum Associates.

Plowman, K. D. (2011). Strategic communication planning: A multiple case study from Iraq and Kuwait. In *Proceedings of the 14th International Public Relations Research Conference* (pp. 689–706), Miami, FL.

Plowman, K. D., Briggs, W. G., & Huang, Y. H. (2001). Public relations and conflict resolution. In R. L. Heath (Ed.). *Handbook of public relations* (pp. 301–310). Thousand Oaks, CA: Sage Publications.

Putnam, L. L. (1994). Challenging the assumptions of traditional approaches to negotiation. *Negotiation Journal, 10,* 337–346.

Putnam, L. L. (2004). Transformations and critical moments in negotiation. *Negotiation Journal, 20,* 275–295.

Putnam, L. L. (2009). Exploring the role of communication in transforming conflict situations: A social construction view. In G. J. Galanes & W. Leeds-Hurwitz (Eds.), *Socially constructing communication* (pp. 189–209). Creskill, NJ: Hampton Press.

Putnam, L. L. (2010). Negotiation and discourse analysis. *Negotiation Journal, 26,* 145–154.

Rao, H., & Kumar S. (1999). Institutional sources of boundary-spanning structures: The establishment of investor relations departments in the Fortune 500 industrials. *Organization Science, 10*(1), 27–42.

Sandhu, S. (2008). Institutionalization of public relations? Indicators and implications from the perspective of organizational institutionalism. In E. Invernizzi, T. M. Falconi, & S. Romenti (Eds.), *Institutionalising PR and corporate communication: Proceedings of the EUPRERA 2008 Milan Congress* (Vol. 1, pp. 120–144). Milan: Pearson.

Scott, W. R. (1987). The adolescence of institutional theory. *Administrative Science Quarterly, 32*(4), 493–511.

Selznick, P. (1957). *Leadership in administration.* New York: Harper & Row.

Selznick, P. (1996). Institutionalism "old" and "new." *Administrative Science Quarterly, 32*(4), 493–511.

Shin, J-H., Lin, Y., Cheng, I-H., & Cameron, G. T. (2003). Exploring the contingency of conflict management in organization–public conflicts. Unpublished paper presented at the Public Relations Division of the National Communication Association, Miami Beach, FL.

Stavridis, J. G. (2007). Strategic communication and national security. *Joint Forces Quarterly, 46*(3), 4–7.

Steyn, B. (2007). Contribution of public relations to organizational strategy formulation. In E. L. Toth (Ed.), *The future of excellence in public relations and communication management* (pp. 137–172). Mahwah, NJ: Lawrence Erlbaum Associates.

Susskind, L., & Field, P. (1996*). Dealing with an angry public: The mutual gains approach to resolving disputes.* New York: The Free Press.

Thomas, K. (1976). Conflict and conflict management. In M. Dunnette (Ed.), *Handbook of industrial and organizational psychology.* Chicago, IL: Rand-McNally.

Tushman, M. L., & Romanelli, E. (1985). Organizational revolution: A metamorphosis model of convergence and reorientation. In L. L. Cummings & B. M. Staw (Eds.), *Research in organizational behavior* (pp. 171–222). Greenwich, CT: JAI Press.

USAID (2000). Project. Retrieved from: http://www.qaproject.org/methods/resinst.html.

Wakefield, R. I. (2008). Institutionalizing public relations: Progress or pipe dream? Presentation at 11th Annual International Public Relations Research Conference, March 6–9, Miami, FL.

Wakefield, R. I., Plowman, K. D., & Curry, A. (in press). Institutionalizing public relations: An international multiple-case study. *Journal of Public Relations Research.*

Yi, H. (2005). The role of communication management in the institutionalization of corporate citizenship: Relational convergence of corporate social responsibility and stakeholder management. Unpublished master's paper, University of Maryland, College Park.

Zerfass, A. (2009). Editor's introduction: Institutionalizing strategic communication: Theoretical analysis and empirical evidence. *International Journal of Strategic Communication, 3*(2), 69–71.

Zucker, L. G. (1977). The role of institutionalization in cultural persistence. *American Sociological Review, 42*(5), 726–743.

10

POWER AND INFLUENCE
IN PUBLIC RELATIONS

Bruce K. Berger and Bryan H. Reber

Abstract

This chapter reviews the current landscape of power and influence studies and looks ahead to an uncertain future. We divide the literature into four somewhat overlapping and arbitrary categories: the managerial, rhetorical/discourse, and the sociological, and critical perspectives. We summarize research in each area and then assess the value of such studies. We close by highlighting some game-changing research that seems required to advance our theorizing of power in, around, and through public relations.

Key words

critical theory work, discourse, dominant coalition, influence, power, public relations, strategic power relations

Introduction

Power and influence are in the DNA of public relations, but they have remained largely invisible in literature in the field until recently. The Grunigs and their colleagues addressed the importance of power in public relations through their managerial approach and their emphasis on negotiated relationships and outcomes. Only in the past decade, however, have a growing number of power and influence studies, essays, and theoretical perspectives emerged to compete for our attention and endorsement (e.g., Berger 2005, 2007; Berger & Reber, 2006; Courtright & Smudde, 2007; Curtin & Gaither, 2007; Diga & Kelleher, 2009; Edwards, 2006, 2009; Heath, Motion, & Leitch, 2010; Holtzhausen, 2000; Holtzhausen & Voto, 2002; Ihlen, van Ruler, & Fredriksson, 2009; L'Etang & Pieczka, 2006; Motion

& Weaver, 2005; O'Neil 2003, 2004; Porter & Sallot, 2005; Porter, Sweetser Trammel, Chung, & Kim, 2007; Reber & Berger, 2006; Roper, 2005; Smudde & Courtright, 2010).

The Current Landscape

The Managerial Perspective: Structures, Functions and Roles

Excellence Theory, Empowerment and Managerial Roles

If public relations theorizing is an ongoing conversation about the nature of practice (Berger & Reber, 2006), then one of the earliest voices about power in public relations belongs to those who developed and tested the Excellence Theory (e.g., Dozier, Grunig, & Grunig, 1995; J. E. Grunig, 1992; J. E. Grunig, & Hunt, 1984; Grunig, Grunig, & Dozier, 2002). In this "managerial perspective," the public relations function manages strategic communications to help organizations achieve particular goals with various publics, solve problems, and capitalize on opportunities. The level of focus is organization–public relationships, the avowed goal of which is to achieve "win–win" relationships.

Power comes into play because organizational governance and decision-making grow out of conflict and struggle among competing actors and interests inside organizations (Mintzberg, 1983; Pfeffer, 1981, 1992). These struggles produce organizational politics, and much of the conflict is aimed at gaining membership in, or influencing those members in the *dominant coalition*—typically a group of high-level executives who make the important strategic choices, allocate resources, and shape organizational values and ideologies (J. E. Grunig, 1992). What this means for public relations is that the practice is what it is in any organization "because the people who have power in an organization choose that behavior" (J. E. Grunig, 1992, p. 23).

Practitioners have long decried their relative lack of power in strategic decision-making. They know that power and influence are crucial to getting things done, so they need a seat at the table when important decisions are made. "Only as part of the dominant coalition could public relations professionals be influential enough to shape the organization's ideology" (L. A. Grunig, 1992, p. 491). However, practitioners are often absent during these strategic moments. The Grunigs and their colleagues acknowledged the importance of structural and cultural forms of power. They explored the dominant coalition and related issues of power-control, empowerment, and the managerial role, and they identified some cultural factors that influence empowerment and excellence in practice. These include a supportive organizational context; the support of top management; and equal opportunities for women and men of diverse ethnic, cultural, and racial back-grounds to lead the function and carry out its roles.

Perceptions of roles by practitioners and organizational executives are a central power issue, and research has differentiated the technical versus managerial roles (Broom & Dozier, 1986; Dozier, 1992; Dozier & Broom, 1995). As technicians, practitioners carry out production activities (e.g., writing, design, and distribution activities) but are not engaged in policy decision-making. As managers, practitioners possess similar skills but also have research, problem-solving, and strategic-thinking capabilities, and are accountable for results. Dozier and Broom (1995) claimed that "knowledge to enact the manager role was the single most powerful correlate of excellence in public relations and communication management" (p. 4). Professionals who possess such managerial skills, sufficient experience, and a managerial perspective are therefore more likely to ascend to the dominant coalition (J. E. Grunig, 1992; L. A. Grunig et al., 2002).

The Excellence Theory emphasizes a relational orientation characterized by dialogue, compromise, and shared power. However, it acknowledges primacy of the dominant coalition and emphasizes the importance of an empowered public relations function that participates in strategic decision-making arenas so that the practice can help organizations solve problems, become more socially responsible, and acquire and maintain social legitimacy. It argues that professionals are more likely to be empowered if they possess managerial skills and a managerial world-view and subsequently enact the managerial role.

Power Relations and Influence Tactics and Strategies

These insights and concepts stimulated other scholars to explore power in and around the practice through this managerial perspective. Spicer (1997), for example, argued that a political system metaphor is the best way to understand relationships between public relations power and organizational power. In his view, practitioners must become more politically astute to increase their influence in the organization's political infrastructure. Building on role theory, Lauzen (1992) claimed the most senior leader in the function must enact the managerial role and "believe public relations is a powerful organizational function" (p. 77).

In a series of projects, Berger and Reber (Berger & Reber, 2006; Reber & Berger, 2006; Berger, 2007) dove more deeply into power relations in practice. They confirmed that most practitioners define practice as a strategic management function, and then they explored a nest of underlying power issues. These included influence tactics and strategies used to shape decisions, constraints on practice, and various forms of advocacy, dissent, and activism that practitioners might use to help their organizations "do the right thing." They discovered a variety of influence resources—individual, structural, relational, informational, and systemic resources—that can be developed and used in decision-making arenas to attempt to alter the structures and practices that govern organizational decisions and the practice itself. They concluded that practitioners must engage in strategic power relations to compete with other individuals and groups, all of whom use similar influence resources to affect decision-making.

O'Neil (2003, 2004) also investigated sources of influence among corporate practitioners. She found that executives' perceptions of the value of practitioners, along with enactment of the managerial role, reporting relationships, and years of experience contributed to organizational influence. Emerging research in the functional perspective focuses on practitioner power associated with expertise in use of new tools and technologies. Diga and Kelleher (2009) found that practitioners who use social network sites more often believe that doing so increases their personal prestige and expert and structural power. Porter and Sallot (2005) produced similar findings: practitioners believe their web skills provide greater influence in decision-making and help them move up in the organization. Porter, Sweetser Trammell, Chung, and Kim (2007) found that practitioners who blog regularly believe their personal prestige and expertise are enhanced. These self-reported perceptions are intriguing, though they do not provide evidence of actual change in power relationships inside organizations.

Rhetorical/Discourse Perspectives

Rhetorical and discursive theorists represent another set of voices in the conversation about power in public relations. They contend that practitioners and organizations create and use discourse strategically to influence truth, knowledge, and meaning in the larger social system. A discourse refers to a text or a set of statements, and "public relations is a discursive process concerned with influencing the concepts and systems of thought that shape how we think about and understand the world" (Motion & Leitch, 2009, p. 93). Rhetorical models analyze the role of persuasion in the development and use of power, and the focus in this line of scholarship is on discourse–organization–society relationships.

One of the few books devoted to power in public relations, edited by Jeffrey L. Courtright and Peter M. Smudde (2007), follows this rhetorical approach to analyze power. Viewed as both a process and outcome, power "constructs, regulates and perpetuates itself through symbols and the individuals that use them" (p. 4). Ten diverse power-in-practice case studies in the book range from rhetorical analysis of an active public's opposition to a corporate decision to change a philanthropic program, to analysis of the power of strategic discourse between a financial institution and regulators to stave off a crisis. These case studies help build an argument that power is inherent in public relations, and it is "obtained, used and misused to create and recreate worldviews for good or ill" (p. 3).

Public relations professionals exercise their power by producing and distributing symbols, creating and sharing organizational narratives, and "managing" issues. Through these actions and their use of communication skills, practitioners help their organizations construct identity and obtain prominence and reputation with publics. Courtright and Smudde believe that power can be positive for practitioners who can "empower people with humanistic attitudes, motives, and symbols of authority to act for the good of society" (p. 269). This humanistic use of power will lead practitioners to "ethically inspire cooperation between an organization and its publics" (p. 269).

Discourse also creates meaning and contributes to public relations power in global settings. Cultural meaning develops through discourse, and culture is at the center of public relations practice, which is grounded in power (Curtin & Gaither, 2007). Practitioners and their organizations are always in some relative position of power, because power makes no sense otherwise (p. 257). Public relations enacts its power through the creation of dominant discourses and the production and distribution of public relations materials. The creation of meaning is a contested process among producers and consumers who hold differing positions of power. Power is located in these relationships, and it plays an important role in creating discourses to shape perceptions and affect actions.

Heath, Motion, and Leitch (2010) also emphasize discourse as power, which they define as "a collective, relational resource co-defined and enacted through discourse-generated vocabularies" (p. 192). Power is reflected in how people think about reality, how they perceive themselves and others, and in societal and relational thoughts and considerations. This line of thinking suggests that leaders will make more reflective choices when they understand that power is rooted in discourse.

Leitch and Motion (2010) define public relations practitioners as "discourse technologists." Through rhetoric, organizations and publics compete to create meaning, which leads to development of power relationships. As "discourse technologists," public relations professionals attempt to create and shape discourses to affect thinking, perceptions, and behaviors by delegitimizing unfavorable meanings, creating new ones, or supporting existing favorable meanings. In this view, publics may hold a series or variety of views, and organization–public relationships are developed through a series of "power plays" (p. 109). Organizations create and distribute "bodies of text" that, over time, contribute to the construction of social reality. Ongoing attempts to create meaning through texts and channels have the ultimate goal of enacting power.

Sociological Perspectives

Substantial work has occurred to promote sociological theory as an alternate perspective through which to study and better understand public relations. A pre-conference workshop at the 56th annual International Communication Association meetings in Dresden, Germany in 2006; a special issue of *Public Relations Review* (2007), devoted to sociological theory in public relations; and a substantive collection of essays (Ihlen, van Ruler, & Fredriksson, 2009) are evidence of the movement within public relations scholarship to provide a voice for sociological theorists. Rooted in works by Bourdieu, Foucault, Giddens, Goffman, Habermas,

Luhmann, and Weber, among others, these approaches focus on the legitimacy of public relations practice at the societal level. Ihlen and van Ruler (2007) argue that the core question "for every PR researcher is how public relations works, what it does in, to and for organizations, publics, or in the public arena, e.g., society at large" (p. 248).

As noted earlier, most public relations theories and studies come from a structural or managerial perspective. One might say that the foundation of public relations scholarship is seen in these structural/managerial traditions. From those perspectives, the focus of public relations is on how the organization can interact with its publics; the practice is engaged in strategic development of communications to move organizational objectives forward. A power differential may well play a role from a managerial perspective, but that role does not necessarily take into account societal needs.

This void is filled when employing the sociological tradition of scholarship. Focus moves from a more micro perspective (i.e., organizations and their publics) to a more macro perspective (i.e., organizations and their relationships in broader society). The organization–public relationship may play a subordinate role. For example, the work of Bourdieu provides a conflict perspective that sees social actors competing to establish themselves through the use of material or symbolic capital. Public relations can assist social actors in their competition for power and influence (Ihlen, 2009). Sociological theories examine how power relationships develop, how legitimacy is gained and nurtured, and how meaning is socially constructed.

Bourdieu employs an "inherently relational view of the world [that] incorporates agency, structure, networks and discourse as mutually influential factors that shape overall power dynamics in society" (Edwards, 2006, p. 229). Bourdieu says meaning is constructed through use of symbolic power, which is especially relevant for communication professionals who create symbols. It is generated by dominant groups who may be "misrepresenting their interests to the public, thereby normalizing social structures and habitus that support their position" (Edwards, 2006, p. 230). Edwards suggests that public relations practitioners represent already powerful players, so the power playing field is decidedly uneven and this asymmetry may lead to questions of role legitimacy. Should organizations be able to subvert societal will? Does disparity inherently lead to an organization needing to prove its legitimacy?

Waeraas (2009) makes a case for Weber's processes of legitimacy and legitimation as a way to understand the relationship between conflict and public relations decisions. Legitimacy, according to Waeraas, occurs when organizations are unable to impose their will on consumers, regulators, community members, and so forth. Compliance to the will of the organization by publics is voluntary, and Weber defines this as "legitimacy." Organizations have legitimacy only as long as publics believe it is okay for the organization to exist. Legitimacy is socially constructed through organizational myths and charismatic leadership, according to Waeraas. Public relations, then, is instrumental in helping organizations acquire, cultivate, and maintain legitimacy.

The value and justification of viewing power in public relations through social theory are addressed in the final chapter of Ihlen, van Ruler and Fredriksson (2009). Here, Ihlen and Verhoeven (2009) draw five conclusions from the rich essays in this edited volume. First, public relations is a social activity in its own right. Second, public relations should be studied in a larger social context, and the book provides substantial support in this regard. Third, the central concepts in public relations scholarship relate to trust, legitimacy, understanding, and reflection. Fourth, relevant social issues highlighted in sociological approaches are power, behavior, and language. Finally, social theories provoke important and intriguing questions.

We couldn't agree more, especially with the latter point. Enriching and broadening public relations through social theories raises such crucial questions as: What does it mean to serve public interests? Can an organization not communicate? Where, or what is the point at which social actors and publics truly engage and work together; is that even possible? What other organizational practices or functions, beyond public relations, can organizations develop and use to acquire legitimacy in a dynamic world (Ihlen & Verhoeven, 2009)?

Critical Perspectives

In a reflective essay, L'Etang (2005) defined critical theory work in public relations as an interdisciplinary approach that challenges taken-for-granted assumptions in the field, critiques professional practices, and seeks to "transform those social, political and economic structures which limit human potential" (p. 521). Critical theorists, a fourth set of voices, seek to increase awareness of these structures and to transform lives by emancipating people from whatever circumstances and structures enslave them (Horkheimer & Adorno, 1982). In this view, power is located in the heart of public relations practices because "all thought is fundamentally mediated by power relations that are socially and historically constructed" (Kincheloe & McClaren, 1994, p. 139).

Critical studies often focus on issues of power and explain how large social actors use and misuse power to maintain an unjust status quo or to acquire more power and resources. We are not sure how many people have been liberated through the work of critical public relations theorists, or even how many people read critical works, but we believe critical scholarship is vital: it elevates the concepts of power, truth, and legitimacy and thereby may force the profession to be more reflective about its purposes and actual practices. Critical theorists push us to explain how and why the current situations and systems came into being, how they work and are maintained, who does and does not benefit from them, and what needs to be done to rectify the corresponding imbalances or inequities. Such reflection may lead us to confront issues of gender, race, class, and the processes of domination, hegemony, and marginalization in practice.

Critical theorists believe that PR practices and approaches help organizations to compete and to dominate—to influence and shape perceptions, attitudes, and beliefs; to promote preferred positions in discourse in public policy, political and economic realms; and to create "truths" that help achieve desired outcomes. Indeed, public relations is a growing social practice that is powering and empowered by globalization processes and new technologies. Its increasing deployment and adaptation fuel its own recognition and legitimacy as a profession. In helping social actors to gain power, public relations also helps the practice grow more powerful. Is it possible there might soon be a World Public Relations Corporation that is a major global actor in its own right, one that controls and distributes PR power and specialists to the highest bidders?

A Discursive Turn

Discourse analysis is also a predominant critical approach. As noted earlier, PR practitioners can be seen as "discourse technologists who play a central role in the maintenance and transformation of discourse" (Motion & Leitch, 1996, p. 298). The practice is thus part of a symbolic system where meaning, legitimacy, and truth, and the power to construct and shape them, are contested by multiple actors. Researchers investigate how practitioners create and deploy "discursive strategies to advance the hegemonic power of particular groups and to examine how these groups attempt to gain public consent to pursue their organizational mission" (Motion & Weaver, 2005, p. 50). In short, public relations is an approach in the struggle for and negotiation of power (Motion & Weaver, 2005).

Moreover, organizations produce and disseminate "bodies of texts" to multiple publics over time to construct meaning, which is an ongoing practice and which is the objective of power. This aligns with Bordieu's perspective, which sees social actors competing in power struggles to establish themselves in fields through the use of capital and symbolic resources (Ihlen, 2009). Edwards (2009) explored how the PR function in a national UK railroad company used social, economic, and cultural capital to create and maintain symbolic power and concluded that virtually every PR practice is linked to a struggle for symbolic power.

Challenging Managerial Assumptions

Critical theorists also challenge widely held assumptions in the managerial paradigm. Roper (2005), for example, analyzed the assumption that two-way symmetrical communication is ethical, concluding that it is a cloak for reinforcing hegemony. Through brief case analysis of Shell, the World Bank, and the World Trade Organization, she argued that while these organizations ostensibly negotiate policies with particular interest groups, their own interests are often given preference and emphasis. Any compromises are likely to favor corporations in the long term rather than issues groups. Indeed, negotiations among parties may be "just enough to quiet public criticism, allowing a business as usual strategy to remain in force" (p. 83).

Berger (2005) examined another widely held managerial assumption—the power of a dominant coalition. He discovered a matrix of constraints on public relations amid a chaotic and political world of management practice that render it difficult for practitioners to get things done and do the "right things" in organizations even when they want to. These impediments include the presence of not one but multiple power coalitions at different levels, shifting coalition venues and roles, multiple checkpoints on public relations power through review processes, and substantial pressures for organizational compliance. He argued that practitioners ought to use resistance activities to push back such constraints.

Holtzhausen (2000) and Holtzhausen and Voto (2002) focused on resistance in the form of internal activism at the individual practitioner level. Public relations practice is about "change or resistance to change" (Holtzhausen, 2000, p. 110), and ethical PR requires practitioners to become activists who represent the voices of employees and external publics, challenge unjust organizational actions, and create opportunities for debate and dissent. They warn practitioners against being co-opted by the dominant coalition or other power structures in organizations. They contend that professionals, even without authoritative or structural power, can exert influence by developing strong relationships, using expertise, gaining access to powerful individuals, and relying on their personal inner power. By taking on the role of organizational activists, practitioners may help emancipate organizations and the profession and institutionalize ethics into practice.

Into the Future

We began this chapter by noting a decade-long surge in studies that focus on power and influence in public relations. Now, we must ask: "So what?" Has anything changed as a result of this growing chorus of voices in the power and influence conversation? Has anyone paid attention to the conversation, apart from participants and like-minded colleagues? Isn't the managerial perspective still the dominant paradigm? Practitioners certainly believe so (Berger & Reber, 2006), and the "modern" definition of public relations unveiled in March 2012 by the Public Relations Society of America (www.prsa.org) clearly reinforces a functional and managerial perspective: "Public relations is a strategic communication process that builds mutually beneficial relationships between organizations and their publics." In our view, this "reality" underscores the need for even more discussions of power from diverse perspectives, and we respond to the "so what" question by sketching out some of the contributions that power theorists have made in the past decade. We then propose several research challenges for the future to help illuminate power and influence and push them to the foreground of thinking.

One contribution of this line of scholarship is expansion and enrichment of the vocabulary of power that was articulated in the Excellence Study, i.e., the dominant coalition, empowerment of diverse professionals, and the importance of the managerial role in engaging in power relations in organizations. Rhetorical and critical theorists, for example, employ and analyze such terms as discourse, domination, emancipation, hegemony, and ideology as they examine forms of political, economic, and cultural power. Social theories offer rich concepts such as symbolic capital, legitimacy, reflection, and linkages among truth, knowledge, and power, among others.

This expanded vocabulary creates a dynamic and alternative landscape of practice in which social actors, large and small, struggle to do far more than create "win–win" relationships with their publics or audiences. Social actors in a much larger though less visible sense struggle to continuously produce, shape, and promote preferred truths and meanings in order to acquire and maintain legitimacy, even as they achieve their particular goals to ensure their economic, political, and social success. Isn't this use of power and influence, which inevitably creates "win–lose" scenarios, a viable presentation of practice today? Why is it so difficult for so many of us to call things by their right names, or to describe things as they are? Don't knowledge and learning begin with accurate identification of the issue or issues?

Few dispute that public relations professionals play a central role in this ongoing symbolic competition that features the creation, production, distribution, management, and evaluation of words, symbols, images, sounds, events, and behaviors. Why public relations at all, if not to present an individual or organization in some manner that favorably differentiates the individual/organization from others through communication and interaction intended to achieve some goal? Since it is impossible to personally know all individuals and organizations, how will we come to learn about the individual/organization, or to form attitudes and perceptions about it, if not through the production and distribution of discourses in a hyper-communication world marked by increasingly short attention spans and yet wider and wider global exposure?

Indeed, this symbolic competition, these ongoing collisions of power and influence attempts by social actors, appears to be intensifying, given the dizzying revolution in communication technologies, the insistent press of globalization, and the rapid spread of new social formations and groups that enter the competition to advance their own issues and ideas. So how can we speak of public relations without acknowledging its power and influence DNA? One of the central contributions of these recent studies of power is just that effect: they "pull" power abruptly into the foreground of thinking and theorizing. So in these and other ways, the modest but growing number of power studies is important. They explicitly acknowledge the realities within the world of public relations and advocacy. We suspect, however, that more of the same, whether in critical, rhetorical, or managerial studies, will not be enough to change very much, or to advance practice, theorizing, or understanding. To do that requires research projects of a somewhat different scale or kind, so we close this chapter by sketching out some research topics for the perspectives we have reviewed.

Needed: More Explanatory Power for "Power"

Critical, rhetorical, and sociological studies in public relations are often theory-rich and data-poor. A growing chorus of voices in the past decade has clamored for more attention to power and influence in practice. Our theories, after all, are discourses, too, which compete for attention, seek supporters, and search for advocates. However, we need more data. We need more studies about power and influence that test, describe, clarify, and reveal to what extent and how the proposed theories work—that provide some explanatory power. We have some examples to build on, including case studies of Roule, the UK railroad entity (Edwards, 2009); the Life Sciences Network (Motion & Weaver, 2005); and the 10 diverse cases in Courtright and Smudde (2007). We also have qualitative studies of the dominant coalition (Berger, 2005) and professional activism (Holtzhausen, 2000), and quantitative studies of practitioner dissent and resistance tactics (Berger & Reber, 2006), among others.

To move forward with power and influence theorizing, however, we believe rich ethnographies like Burawoy's (1979) in-depth sociological study of Chicago industrial workers and the manufacturing of consent among them are needed to explore topics like hegemony and discourse production inside organizations. Discourse lends itself to analysis, and we can continue to deconstruct and analyze discourses after the fact. To provide more evidence and explanatory power, however, researchers must get inside discourse production to learn how they are crafted, who participates, how decisions are taken, what intentions guide actions, and how discourses traverse a dynamic life of their own.

Sociological theories provoke thinking and questioning about public relations (Ihlen & Verhoeven, 2009), and we believe such questions can be fruitfully applied to the managerial perspective as well. Many studies have been carried out to support the managerial perspective, e.g., measurement of dimensions of organization–public relationships and functional roles. However, we know far less about the sociology of relationship building and serving public interests. Depth interviews and large-scale surveys might be employed to answer questions in this realm. How is it possible, for example, for organizations to successfully serve public interests when some of those publics inevitably hold competing interests (Leitch & Motion, 2010)? Moreover, what exactly are "mutually beneficial relationships?" What is their look and feel? What is their life cycle? Can researchers document and illuminate the nature and construction of these relationships? Moreover, how do practitioners, as members of the dominant coalition or not, convince organizational leaders to intentionally pursue mutually beneficial relationship building? What influence tactics and strategies do they use to convince others of the rightfulness of this course of action?

Further, where or at what point can large social actors and publics actually work together? How many large social actors willingly engage in person(s) with such groups? Roper (2005) argued that true compromises are virtually impossible to achieve—that compromises often favor large actors in the long term and likely dilute the future negotiation power of groups. The managerial and functional perspective on power could benefit from depth qualitative studies that examine these and related questions about how specific "win–win" and "mutually beneficial" relationships are developed and maintained.

A Closer Look at the Profession and Systemic Power

We also believe it is important to examine two crucial structures in the field—the professional associations and the education systems that increasingly appear to shape the profession in the United States. L'Etang (2005) noted the absence of "class" studies in the field and suggested that an examination of practitioners was a good starting point. Speaking just of the United States in this regard, our knowledge of the overall composition of the profession is quite limited and likely misleading. For example, the largest professional association (PRSA) claims about 23,000 members, for which some demographic data are available. However, various estimates of the overall number of professionals in the field range from 250,000 to 350,000 individuals, and we know little about this larger group (the *90%*).

What we know about the profession is usually a reflection of what we know about the 23,000 members (the *10%*). These demographics likely overstate or understate the actual demographics of race, gender, organizational type, salary information, and other professional factors. One might argue, for example, that the 10% represent a "super class" of "moneyed" professionals and strategic influencers. After all, there are some barriers to joining this class. PRSA membership dues are about $400 annually, and conference fees and expenses can easily exceed $2,500. It's no surprise, then, that many PRSA members are corporate and agency employees, based in larger cities, with the financial wherewithal to fund participation. Surely it is more difficult for professionals working in nonprofits and small agencies or businesses to afford such memberships. Now, we are not claiming the 10% are a super class of professionals, nor that such a class even exists, but a comprehensive study of the composition of practitioners across the field—their educations, incomes, backgrounds, and other demographics—is long overdue. In helping large social actors to gain or maintain power, the power of the profession also grows, and we need to better understand who we are and who we serve and represent.

Similarly, close examination of the education systems and related structures that produce a growing number of young professionals would be valuable. Through certification procedures, education commissions, student professional associations, and growing interlocks between educational and professional leaders in association activities, education programs appear increasingly tied to PRSA. A comprehensive study of such interlocking relationships and university curricula, course contents, and teacher qualifications, along with student associations, internships, and related activities, would provide insights into the formation and ideologies of the next generation of leaders in the field.

Visible or not, power is ever present in, around, and through public relations practice. Ignoring this reality does not make power disappear. Power shapes what practitioners do, how they are perceived, and what public relations is and might be in organizations. Practitioners are touched by strategic power relations from the moment they enter practice and are slotted into an existing hierarchy and assigned a boss, a job description, and a set of objectives. As they grow into their professional roles, they engage in power relations inside their organizations through interactions with the dominant coalition and other structural forms of power, and in their relationships with others as they go about the production and management of diverse communication products and services. Externally, practitioners represent their organizations in competitive public arenas or more private channels through discourses and the use of symbolic capital and resources to achieve particular organizational goals. Strategic relations of power produce competition inside and outside the organization, and this competition in turn reproduces and redistributes power in those strategic relationships. Public relations is a social activity in its own right. Increasingly, the practice is a power system in its own right, too.

References

Berger, B. K. (2005). Power over, power with, and power to relations: Critical reflections on public relations, the dominant coalition, and activism. *Journal of Public Relations Research, 17*(1), 5–27.

Berger, B. K. (2007). Public relations and organizational power. In E. L. Toth (Ed.), *The future of excellence in public relations and communication management* (pp. 221–234). Mahwah, NJ: Lawrence Erlbaum Associates.

Berger, B. K., & Reber, B. H. (2006). *Gaining influence in public relations: The role of resistance in practice*. Mahwah, NJ: Lawrence Erlbaum Associates.

Broom, G. M., & Dozier, D. M. (1986). Advancement for public relations role models. *Public Relations Review, 12*(1), 37–56.

Burawoy, M. (1979). *Manufacturing consent: Changes in the labor process under monopoly capitalism*. Chicago: University of Chicago Press.

Courtright, J. L., & Smudde, P. M. (Eds.). (2007). *Power and public relations*. Cresskill, NJ: Hampton Press.

Curtin, P. A., & Gaither, T. K. (2007). *International public relations: Negotiating culture, identity and power*. Thousand Oaks, CA: Sage.

Diga, M., & Kelleher, T. (2009). Social media use, perceptions of decision-making power, and public relations roles. *Public Relations Review, 35,* 440–442.

Dozier, D. M. (1992). The organizational roles of communication and public relations practitioners. In J. E. Grunig (Ed.), *Excellence in public relations and communication management* (pp. 327–355). Hillsdale, NJ: Lawrence Erlbaum Associates.

Dozier, D. M., & Broom, G. M. (1995). Evolution of the manager role in public relations practice. *Journal of Public Relations Research, 7*(1), 3–26.

Dozier, D. M., Grunig, L. A., & Grunig, J. E. (1995). *Manager's guide to excellence in public relations and communication management*. Hillsdale, NJ: Lawrence Erlbaum Associates.

Edwards, L. (2006). Rethinking power in public relations. *Public Relations Review, 32*(3), 229–231.

Edwards, L. (2009). Symbolic power and public relations practice: Locating individual practitioners in their social context. *Journal of Public Relations Research, 21*(3), 251–272.

Grunig, J. E. (Ed.). (1992). *Excellence in public relations and communications management.* Hillsdale, NJ: Lawrence Erlbaum Associates.

Grunig, J. E., & Hunt, T. (1984). *Managing public relations.* New York: Holt, Rinehart & Winston.

Grunig, L. A. (1992). Power in the public relations department. In J. E. Grunig (Ed.), *Excellence in public relations and communications management* (pp. 483–501). Hillsdale, NJ: Lawrence Erlbaum Associates.

Grunig, L. A., Grunig, J. E., & Dozier, D. M. (2002). *Excellent public relations and effective organizations.* Mahwah, NJ: Lawrence Erlbaum Associates.

Heath, R. L., Motion, J., & Leitch, S. (2010). Power and public relations. In R. L. Heath (Ed.), *The Sage handbook of public relations* (2nd ed., pp. 191–204). Thousand Oaks, CA: Sage.

Holtzhausen, D. R. (2000). Postmodern values in public relations. *Journal of Public Relations Research, 12,* 93–114.

Holtzhausen, D. R., & Voto, R. (2002). Resistance from the margins: The postmodern public relations practitioner as organizational activist. *Journal of Public Relations Research, 14*(1), 57–84.

Horkheimer, M., & Adorno, T. W. (1982). *Dialectic of enlightenment.* New York: Continuum.

Ihlen, Ø. (2009). On Bourdieu: Public relations in field struggles. In Ø. Ihlen, B. van Ruler, & M. Fredriksson (Eds.), *Public relations and social theory: Key figures and concepts* (pp. 62–82). New York: Routledge.

Ihlen, Ø., & van Ruler, B. (2007). How public relations works: Theoretical roots and public relations perspectives. *Public Relations Review, 33,* 243–248.

Ihlen, Ø., van Ruler, B., & Fredriksson, M. (Eds.). (2009). *Public relations and social theory: Key figures and concepts.* New York: Routledge.

Ihlen, Ø., & Verhoeven, P. (2009). Conclusions on the domain, context, concepts, issues and empirical avenues of public relations. In Ø. Ihlen, B. van Ruler, & M. Fredriksson (Eds.), *Public relations and social theory: Key figures and concepts* (pp. 323–340). New York: Routledge.

Kincheloe, J. L., & McClaren, R. (1994). Rethinking critical theory and qualitative research. In N. Denzin & Y. Lincoln (Eds.), *Handbook of qualitative research* (pp. 138–157). London: Sage.

Lauzen, M. M. (1992). Public relations roles, intraorganizational power, and encroachment. *Journal of Public Relations Research, 4*(2), 61–80.

Leitch, S., & Motion, J. (2010). Publics and public relations: Effecting change. In R. L. Heath (Ed.), *The Sage handbook of public relations* (2nd ed., pp. 99–110). Thousand Oaks, CA: Sage.

L'Etang, J. (2005). Critical public relations: Some reflections. *Public Relations Review, 31,* 521–526.

L'Etang, J., & Pieczka, M. (Eds.). (2006). *Public relations: Critical debates and contemporary practice.* Mahwah, NJ: Lawrence Erlbaum.

Mintzberg, H. (1983). *Power in and around organizations.* Englewood Cliffs, NJ: Prentice-Hall.

Motion, J., & Leitch, S. (1996). A discursive perspective from New Zealand: Another world view. *Public Relations Review, 22*(3), 297–309.

Motion, J., & Leitch. (2009). On Foucault: A toolbox for public relations. In Ø. Ihlen, B. van Ruler, & M. Fredriksson (Eds.), *Public relations and social theory: Key figures and concepts* (pp. 83–102). New York: Routledge.

Motion, J., & Weaver, C. K. (2005). A discourse perspective for critical public relations research: Life sciences network and the battle for truth. *Journal of Public Relations Research*, *17*(1), 49–68.

O'Neil, J. (2003). An investigation of the sources of influence of corporate public relations practitioners. *Public Relations Review, 29*(2), 159–169.

O'Neil, J. (2004, Spring). Effects of gender and power on PR managers' upward influence. *Journal of Managerial Issues, 16*(1), 127–144.

Pfeffer, J. (1981). *Power in organizations.* Marshfield, MA: Pitman.

Pfeffer, J. (1992). *Managing with power: Politics and influence in organizations.* Cambridge, MA: Harvard Business School Press.

Porter, L. V., & Sallot, L. M. (2005). Web power: A survey of practitioners' World Wide Web use and their perceptions of its effects on their decision-making power. *Public Relations Review, 31*, 111–119.

Porter, L. V., Sweetser Trammell, K. D., Chung, D., & Kim, E. (2007). Blog power: Examining the effects of practitioner blog use on power in public relations. *Public Relations Review, 33*, 92–95.

Reber, B. H., & Berger, B. K. (2006). Finding influence: Examining the role of influence in public relations practice. *Journal of Communication Management, 10*(3), 235–249.

Roper, K. (2005). Symmetrical communication: Excellent public relations or a strategy for hegemony? *Journal of Public Relations Research, 17*(1), 69–86.

Smudde, P. M., & Courtright, J. L. (2010). Public relations and power. In R. L. Heath (Ed.), *The Sage handbook of public relations* (2nd ed., pp. 177–189). Thousand Oaks, CA: Sage.

Spicer, C. (1997). *Organizational public relations: A political perspective.* Mahwah, NJ: Lawrence Erlbaum Associates.

Waeraas, A. (2009). On Weber: Legitimacy and legitimation in public relations. In Ø. Ihlen, B. van Ruler, & M. Fredriksson (Eds.), *Public relations and social theory: Key figures and concepts* (pp. 301–322). New York: Routledge.

11

A PHILOSOPHY OF REFLECTIVE ETHICAL SYMMETRY

Comprehensive Historical and Future Moral Approaches in the Excellence Theory

Shannon A. Bowen and Tiffany Derville Gallicano

> The reward of doing one duty is the power to do another.
> *Rabbi Ben Azai (in Goodman, 1997)*

Abstract

Ethics is considered both an inherent feature of symmetry and a stand–alone principle of excellence. The ethics within the Excellence Theory was built upon by Bowen, who constructed Kantian ethical models supporting the Excellence Theory for both normative and positive use, examined the degree to which ethics is an essential part of each principle of excellence, studied the contributions of public relations ethics in the dominant coalition, and examined the moral nature of public relations in society. In this chapter, we discuss the role of trust and corporate social responsibility (CSR) in creating excellence, introducing additional consequentialist paradigms (act utilitarianism and rule utilitarianism) of ethics combined with deontology in a model we call reflective ethical symmetry. For the future implications of the theory, we examine the application of ethics among Millennial-generation practitioners as studied by Curtin, Gallicano, and Matthews.

Key Words

corporate social responsibility, ethics, Excellence Theory, reflective ethical symmetry, utilitarian theory

Introduction

Consider the role of ethics in public relations. Ethics affects decisions throughout the strategic management process, such as what research to conduct, what method to use, what questions to ask, and how to analyze the resulting data. Using that data and analyses to construct a strategy has myriad ethical components. Determining what facts are relevant to an issue also has an ethical component, as does seeking feedback from publics connected to the issue. The word choices in how we frame messages clearly involve ethical decisions, and the technical skills involved in designing public relations messages also necessitate decisions of priority, framing, and agenda. Evaluating the effectiveness of a public relations campaign sometimes requires candid honesty, as well. Whether they are undertaken consciously or not, ethical decisions are intertwined throughout the entirety of the public relations process. The Excellence Theory assumes that ethics is a part of each step of this process and that every principle of Excellence is imbued with ethics. This chapter examines the perspective in more detail, shows the growth and evolution of ethics and the Excellence Theory, and offers an analysis of the growing importance of ethics and corporate social responsibility brought about by demands for accountability, in addition to greater transparency and interactivity through social media.

The Excellence Theory examined the question of how public relations contributes at a maximal level to organizational effectiveness. Organizational effectiveness depends upon relationships between the organization and its publics: consumers, government regulators, communities, and so on. Public relations creates relational bonds between these groups; it allows us to build trust, to organize communication efforts, to share and create knowledge, to resolve conflict, and to thrive. J. E. Grunig often said that he saw ethics as an integral part of this process and as inherent in symmetry rather than a stand-alone component but shifted that perspective later. Perhaps in part due to many of the infamous scandals of the 1990s, ethics was added as a stand-alone principle of excellence in 1996— making ethics no longer simply inherent in the Excellence Theory but an obligatory consideration of excellence (Verčič, L. A. Grunig, & J. E. Grunig, 1996).

The "extent of ethics" chapter (Bowen, 2007) examined the degree to which ethics is an essential part of each principle of excellence. The following chapter (Bowen, 2010a) examined the philosophical nature of ethics in public relations itself, as it contributes to the public good in a democratic information society. The present chapter builds upon that framework by discussing the role of ethics and corporate social responsibility (or social responsibility) in creating excellence, introducing additional paradigms from moral philosophy in a model we call *reflective ethical symmetry*. Finally, we review the application of ethics in the Excellence Theory among the future of the field (Millennial-generation practitioners) as an indicator of how the Excellence Theory will carry forward into the future.

Relationship Ethics in Action: Trust

Ferguson (1984) was among the first to argue for a relationship basis for the public relations function. In the decades since the Excellence Study, and largely because of the Excellence Study, public relations has been redefined largely as relationship management, which is included here as the foundational aspect of our approach, as it appears to be the dominant theory of the field. The research by the Excellence team and their students led to the development of relationship variables (J. E. Grunig & Huang, 2000)—the basic components of the relationships that public relations seeks to build and maintain. Relationship maintenance strategies result in the building of relationship outcomes: control mutuality, commitment, satisfaction, and trust.

Although the prominence of relationship outcomes from the publics' perspectives depends on the context (e.g., Hon & Brunner, 2002; Ki & Hon, 2007), we argue that trust is the most pervasive and important factor, akin to the "backbone" of the relationship. Control mutuality, satisfaction, and commitment depend on trust (see Gallicano & Heisler, 2011; Jo, Hon, & Brunner, 2004). The other relationship outcomes are undermined if at least some degree of trust is not present; therefore, trust is the foundational element that must be present.

How can public relations build trust between an organization and its publics? It can create relationships, build them, and enhance them by helping the organization to act in a consistently ethical manner. Incorporating the views of various publics gained through two-way symmetrical dialogue (J. E. Grunig, 1989) helps the public relations professional advise the dominant coalition (Bowen, 2009) toward strategic management and planning that includes or respects the views and needs of publics. J. E. Grunig and Repper (1992) wrote:

> We define strategic symmetrically rather than asymmetrically. We believe that it is in the strategic interests of organizations to change their behavior when they provoke opposition from the environment as well as to try to change the behavior of environmental stakeholders.
>
> *(p. 123)*

By incorporating the values and desires of publics into the strategic management of the organization, the organization becomes more knowable to external publics.

Being able to know and understand the organization allows publics to build expectations of it. When the organization meets those expectations, trust begins to form. When the organization acts with ethical responsibility on a *consistent* basis, it increases its knowability and the expectations of publics are met, thereby building trust between organizations and publics. By the public relations function including ethical decision-making in strategic management, trust is created and built, and the organization and function become more excellent than they had been.

The question of building trust to create and sustain relationships with publics is then one of ethical consistency (Bowen, 2010a). Consistency, ethical analyses, and decision-making result in an organization being authentic, or genuinely being internally as it wants to appear to external publics (Arthur W. Page Society, 2007). Bowen (2010a) argued that consistency as a rational, philosophical approach builds trust because "If a public knows what to expect of an organization because it has been consistently rational in the past, it tends to trust the organization to continue being rational and fair in the relationship" (p. 580).

As early as 1983, Ryan and Martinson (1983) called on the public relations counsel to be the conscience of the corporation by helping it engage in ethical decision-making. The justification for public relations to be an ethical conscience was also linked to public interest (Ryan & Martinson, 1985), civil society (Taylor, 2010), systems theory and autonomy (Bowen, 2008b), professionalism (Wright, 1989), moral philosophy (Bowen, 2008a), and corporate social responsibility (Heath & Li, 2010). Clearly, there is a body of scholarly research and argument to support the idea of public relations acting as the ethical conscience within an organization.

The Excellence Theory concept of building relationships that help an organization to be excellent by creating trust between organization and publics is based on consistency. The public relations officer must be granted membership of the dominant coalition (Berger, 2005; Berger & Reber, 2006) to advise on ethics with autonomy, as a true part of the dominant coalition (Bowen, 2006, 2009), fully participating in decision-making (Siebold & Shea, 2001). Once the public relations professional is able to advise on ethics, some knowledge of ethical decision-making is a prerequisite, preferably with ethical training academically, professionally, or both (Wright, 1996). Gaining consistency of analysis requires a commitment by the organization to foster ethical decision-making and an organizational culture willing to support the research, arguments, and analyses that allow issues managers to engage in complex moral reasoning (Bowen, 2004b). That environment fosters not only the autonomy of the public relations function and its membership in the dominant coalition management but also the overall responsibility and excellence of the organization, leading to more trusting relationships between an organization and its publics. This approach extends the Excellence Theory by not only placing the public relations function in the dominant coalition and using the inherent ethics of symmetry but also serving as the ethical conscience of the organization. In other words, enhancing the ethical rectitude of the organization through building trust and consistency leads to enhancing overall organizational excellence.

Corporate Responsibility, Rectitude, Reflexivity, and Reflectivity

The ethics of the Excellence Theory apply not only to the conduct of public relations but also to how the organization plays a role in society with regard to its responsibilities and ethical obligations. How an organization then communicates with publics in that society, defining issues and framing messages, also has an ethical component. Morality is an integral part of business, and an organization has a responsibility to engage in its activities with rectitude. The Excellence Theory argued that business exists by permission of society (J. E. Grunig, 1992). DeGeorge (2010) argued, "Business is a social enterprise whose mandate and limits are set by society" (p. 7). As a voice on behalf of business and as a business unto itself, scholars believe that public relations can hold a positive social role (Heath & Li, 2010; Kent & Taylor, 2002) or can contribute in an ethical way toward society (Bowen, 2010a), especially in an increasingly complex global environment (Sriramesh & Verčič, 2003). Van Ruler and Verčič (2005) studied the positive social role for public relations and encouraged organizations to use reflective management to study their own roles, responsibilities, and intentions. Their paper concluded that the reflective management approach deserved a significantly expanded role for ethics in the public relations function.

Taking a consequentialist view, J. E. Grunig (1992) argued that publics arise because of the consequences organizations have on them as a matter of doing business. J. E. Grunig and Repper (1992) defined stakeholders and publics as connected to the organization through the consequences each has on the other, or when publics "recognize one or more of the consequences as a problem" (p. 124). The ethics of those consequences, J. E. Grunig and White (1992) argued, should "incorporate ethics into the process of public relations" as a dialogue. In combining consequentialism with the symmetrical worldview, the Excellence Theory provided a strong rationale for ethics as dialogue and strategic management. It went on to include a deontological justification of rhetoric by Cheney and Tompkins (1984) based on "guardedness, accessibility, nonviolence, and empathy" (as cited in J. E. Grunig & White, 1992, p. 58).

The role of public relations ethics in the Excellence Theory is to create an authentic dialogue between an organization and publics so that relationships can be formed and cultivated. Therefore, reflective or reflexive management is in concert with the goals of the symmetrical approach to ethics and with the dialogue of the Excellence Theory. The reflective or reflexive organization (Heath & Li, 2010) is willing to listen to the values and opinions of publics and is open to changing the way it does business in response to those publics. It considers its role in both the decisions it makes toward publics and in the role it plays in society. In that sense, the organization has reached the highest level of moral development (Kohlberg, 1969) in which it is autonomous and principled, acting from a basis of examined and rational self-awareness. We can say that the organization has become reflective when it reaches this highest level of moral development and examination.

A Role for Ethics: CSR in Creating Excellence

Reflective organizations engage in socially responsible behavior because they see it as an obligation or responsibility to do so. Corporate social responsibility (CSR, also known as social responsibility) has long been associated with community relations and with philanthropy. Contemporary approaches tend to focus on the use of CSR as a business strategy to maximize profit (e.g., Schreiber, 2011); however, the very definition of CSR precludes this: "CSR can be generally defined as the organization incurring responsibilities to society beyond profit maximization" (Dodd & Supa, 2011, p. 1). Thus, if an organization pursues good deeds only due to profit motives, it should not refer to its efforts as CSR because it is not engaging in CSR. Furthermore, the Kantian approach to ethics that Bowen (2004a) conceptualized in the development of the ethics principle in the Excellence Study establishes that "promoting one's own advantage should not be a deciding factor in a moral decision" (p. 74). In other words, an organization that is motivated to engage in CSR due to a return on investment is not making a moral decision by Kantian standards because it would be based on selfish motives rather than on pure moral intent.

Giving back to the community, with the sole goal of making money for shareholders, is only partly ethical. It is ethical in the sense that it is a duty-based decision because companies have a fiduciary duty to generate profit for share-holders. However, an organization that decides to give back to the community only due to a profit motive is not making a moral decision because it would be only treating the community as a means to an end, which is forbidden by the Kantian approach (Bowen, 2004a).

Companies that are solely motivated by profit for their community initiatives take a gamble that people will not uncover their inauthentic endeavors. For example, Unilever launched the award-winning Dove Campaign for Real Beauty, which involved a so-called CSR component, while also running misogynist advertisements that objectify women for its Axe brand. Contradictions such as these can invite publics to view the company as just treating women as a means to an end. A company that is truly committed to CSR will protect itself from these contradictions by embracing the same set of ethical values across all its brands.

In addition to a company having one of its brands discredit the CSR initiatives of the other, sole profit motives are also exposed through the decisions that an organization makes. For example, the term *greenwashing* was first inspired by hotels that encouraged the reuse of towels yet lacked recycling programs (Romero, 2008). Many employees and former employees engage in what is referred to as *positive or negative megaphoning* about a company's true commitment to CSR by sharing what they observe behind the scenes with external publics (see J.-N. Kim & Rhee, 2011, for the conceptualization, and Gallicano, 2011, for empirical evidence), meaning that it is imperative for an organization's CSR efforts to be authentic or undertaken from pure moral intent. It is also vital that a company's leadership demonstrates its commitment to CSR to set the tone for the organiza-tion and to symmetrically communicate about CSR efforts with employees (as well as external stakeholders; Spangler & Pompper, 2011).

Companies that are inauthentic with their so-called CSR efforts commonly endure intense criticism from activist publics on social media. In fact, activist publics can leverage enough support to forcefully pressure global companies to change their practices. For example, Greenpeace launched a brand-jacking video on YouTube in which it parodied a Nestlé Kit Kat commercial (Coombs & Holladay, 2012). With momentum from the video, activists controlled the content posted to Nestlé's Facebook fan page for more than two days due to the intense outrage people expressed. Although Nestlé initially refused to change how it sources palm oil, the activism culminated in the company's agreement to accommodate Greenpeace's requests (Coombs & Holladay, 2012).

Online criticism about inauthentic CSR can create a reputational crisis for an organization that becomes a prominent—and permanent—embarrassment on the company's Wikipedia page. Given that a company's Wikipedia page tends to be one of the first results in online searches for a company (if not the first), it can play a key role in shaping an organization's reputation. Prior to the Internet, negative coverage in a communication medium such as a newspaper was not widely reread by new audiences. Due to online sites such as Wikipedia, reputational crises (such as the one Nestlé endured) are inscribed into the collective public memory and freshly consumed regularly. In fact, research suggests that the coverage devoted to organizational crises and scandals on companies' Wikipedia pages has been escalating over time (DiStaso & Messner, 2010).

Social media, however, can be used powerfully for CSR efforts, especially given the ability to use social media to engage in symmetrical dialogue with stakeholders. Organizations have found success with engaging in dialogue with stakeholders and then adapting their business practices and initiatives (Bartlett, Tywoniak, & Hatcher, 2007). For example, My Starbucks Idea enables people to suggest ideas, vote on the suggested ideas they like best, and then hear the company's response and progress towards the ideas it selects (Starbucks Corporation, 2010). A large number of these ideas are about social responsibility and community building.

In addition to using social media to engage in dialogue about CSR efforts, social media can be used to create engagement around a company's CSR efforts. In fact, we propose that CSR is the missing key to companies' success with achieving engagement on their fan pages, which has generally been elusive (McCorkindale, 2010; Men & Tsai, 2012). Bowen (2010b) found ethics and CSR on Fortune 500 websites lacking symmetrical engagement with publics. Similarly, O'Neil (2012) found in her study of Fortune 500 companies that the large majority of companies do not use their fan pages to cultivate relationships with stakeholders through task sharing, such as helping to solve a problem of interest. In the wake of studies that have focused on failed attempts to create engagement, it is insightful to examine how a company's CSR campaign has resulted in tremendous engagement on its fan page. Milk-Bone focused its fan page on its CSR initiative to use a portion of proceeds from product sales to raise and train guide dogs for people who could benefit from assistance. The agency that launched the campaign estimated that the company received an astounding 20,000 likes and comments per fan page update, with a cumulative total of 6.3 million likes and comments during the campaign (DraftFCB, n.d.). In addition, the nonprofit organization it partnered with received

800% more web traffic during the first month of the campaign and recruited 300 new donors during the campaign. Through powerful storytelling, compelling multimedia, and the selection of a meaningful issue that resonates with the community, a company can engage stakeholders through a CSR initiative on its fan page.

A common concern with CSR promotion is creating a perception that the company is only motivated by the financial return. However, research suggests that many consumers approve of companies that clearly benefit from their CSR initiatives—as long as they believe the companies are also motivated by their commitment to serve the community (S. Kim & Lee, 2012). Research suggests that nonprofits are also supportive of the idea that companies will benefit from CSR initiatives and are satisfied when mutually beneficial partnerships can be achieved with shared control and governance (Rumsey & White, 2009).

Companies need to communicate their CSR efforts due to the business benefits of doing so, as well as the increasing demands for corporate accountability, ethics, and transparency that are involved in creating a higher level of expected—or demanded—CSR today than ever before (Dodd & Supa, 2011). DeGeorge (2010) called this changing mandate for organizations "the business ethics movement" (p. 10). Of course, the Excellence Theory posed ethical responsibility as an inherent feature of symmetry. It also had an emphasis on social movements in its contention that activism helps to make an organization more excellent by encouraging it to respond to environmental pressures from publics and work to solve the issues they raise (L. A. Grunig, J. E. Grunig, & Dozier, 2002). These features of the Excellence Theory are congruous with both ethics and CSR taking lead roles in the strategic management of an organization.

Ethics should drive and manage the CSR function of an organization (Werhane, 2007). The ethical values, mission statement, goals, and objectives of the organization indicate what type of corporate social responsibility initiatives will be strategic for the organization. Strategic CSR initiatives are those that relate to stakeholder groups that the company has power over (see Bivins, 2009), those that further enhance relationships with stakeholders who can affect the organization's success, or both. The role of the organization is not simply to be a good corporate citizen by engaging in philanthropic donations but to engage communities and build relationships, engendering trust based on ethical responsibility. In that way, the reflective organization uses its moral agency to become an ethically functional individual, in the sense of a corporation as an individual and also as a socially responsible citizen with its own moral autonomy. By acting ethically, the organization fulfills its moral obligation to society and its ethical obligations to itself, its industry, and the publics and stakeholders who interact with it (Singer, 1994).

Ethics refers to the overall values, approach, and driving paradigm of the organization with regard to what it considers moral or good (Weiss, 1994). Many organizations hold a deontological mission statement, based on duty and moral principle, such as Johnson & Johnson's (2012) Credo, outlining its responsibilities to four stakeholder groups (customers, employees, communities, and stockholders). Other organizations embrace a utilitarian paradigm of ethics based on maximizing good consequences or the greater good, such as Merck & Co.'s motto, "Medicine is for the people, not the profits."

Each organization derives its values from its leadership, mission, and management style: what is rewarded, what is valued, if and how the organization trains employees on ethics, and to what extent ethical considerations are discussed as a part of strategic management and issues management (Sims, 1994). Therefore, the ethical values system, whether deontological (duty and principle-based) or utilitarian (maximizing good consequences) should guide the CSR activities of the organization in accordance with that ethical values system. For example, a deontological organization would carry out CSR efforts it saw as associated with its duties, whereas a utilitarian organization would maximize good consequences to a public (or publics) with its CSR initiatives.

Consequentialism: Ideal Utilitarianism

Due to the consequence-based nature of many CSR initiatives, a brief discussion of ethical consequence-based theory is necessary. The main consequence-based theory is called utilitarian theory in the sense that it determines what is ethical based on the potential consequences (utility) of a decision (Mill, [1861] 1957). The outcomes of a decision should maximize good and minimize bad, as defined by whatever is deemed the good to be maximized in that decision. Act utilitarian theory looks at the specifics of the decision and seeks to maximize whatever good can be derived from various decision options while minimizing harm (Beauchamp & Bowie, 2004). Rule utilitarian theory examines the consequences of a decision based on the moral principle those consequences have upheld in prior situations and what principles are worth maximizing as potential outcomes, while minimizing bad consequences. The rule that maximizes a good moral principle while minimizing harms is determined ethical (DeGeorge, 2010).

Though both utilitarian frameworks are based on predicting the consequences of a decision, act utilitarianism is specific to a certain situation while rule utilitarianism looks for similar situations from the past and seeks to maximize the principle behind whatever drove those situations. The basic considerations are the same: to be ethical, a decision must maximize the positive outcomes and minimize the negative outcomes. This basic understanding is known as the utilitarian calculus (Mill, [1861] 1994) and can be understood best through what is known as the maxi-mins rule. According to the maxi-mins rule, that which is good should be maximized and that which is bad should be minimized (Biswas, 1997). By applying the maxi-mins rule to act or rule utilitarianism, the consequences on the greater good, to greater public interest, or the greater impacts on publics can be determined. Though there are many drawbacks of utilitarian theory, they have been written about elsewhere (Bowen, 2004a) and will not be discussed here. The purpose of the inclusion of this theory is to create a comprehensive model of reflective ethical symmetry (see Figure 11.1), encapsulating the Excellence Theory's reliance on consequence-based definitions of issues, publics, and stakeholders (J. E. Grunig & Repper, 1992), along with its consequentialist ethics (J. E. Grunig & White, 1992), as well as a deontological framework of doing one's moral duty to uphold universal moral laws, as called for in the generic principles of excellence (L. A. Grunig et al., 2002; Verčič et al., 1996) and later expanded upon theoretically and empirically (Bowen, 2000).

The model in Figure 11.1 is based on capturing the primary ethical concepts of the original Excellence Theory and the Excellence Theory as it has evolved, situated to continue to explain public relations excellence in the future. Organizational values and mission drive the framework of ethics an organization will choose in determining how to interact with publics, stakeholders, and society; what constitutes an issue; when an issue needs analyses; and so on. An ongoing process of dialogue with stakeholders and publics is an essential component of both defining issues and refining or adjusting the values and mission of the organization, as represented by the dotted lines in the model.

Organizations that make decisions from a deontological framework, such as Johnson & Johnson, would then use the right side of the model to implement an ethical analysis. This deontological flowchart in the model is based on Kantian deontology, examining autonomy, moral duty, principle, dignity and respect, pure intention (also known as good will; Kant, [1793] 1974), the exchange and dialogue of symmetry, and a responsibility to take universal moral actions that would hold true rationally, as a moral law, for all time, in all similar situations (Kant, 1948). The resulting analysis, based on Kant's categorical imperative (Kant, 1948), provides one of inordinate rigor when examining the responsibilities, obligation, duties, and values of organizational decisions.

Organizations that are more public interest-oriented or consequence-based in nature, such as Merck & Co., would use a utilitarian paradigm on the left side of the model. Once the utilitarian paradigm is selected as commensurate with organizational values, acts or rule utilitarianism must be chosen to analyze the issue. Organizations with stronger or codified values systems, codes of ethics, or systems of rules and principles tend to use a rule utilitarian approach when applying the maxi-mins principle. Organizations that hold more flexible values systems would look at the specifics of each situation individually, thereby using an act utilitarian system to apply the maxi-mins principle (Bakhtin, 1993). Rule utilitarian organizations would determine the universal principles to be maximized by examining prior cases. They would compare the consequences of certain principles (decisions) and compare the greater good created by those principles, concluding that the one creating the most good and least bad consequences is ethical.

Organizations employing the act utilitarian paradigm would look at the specific, detailed situation and determine a number of viable decision options (for example,

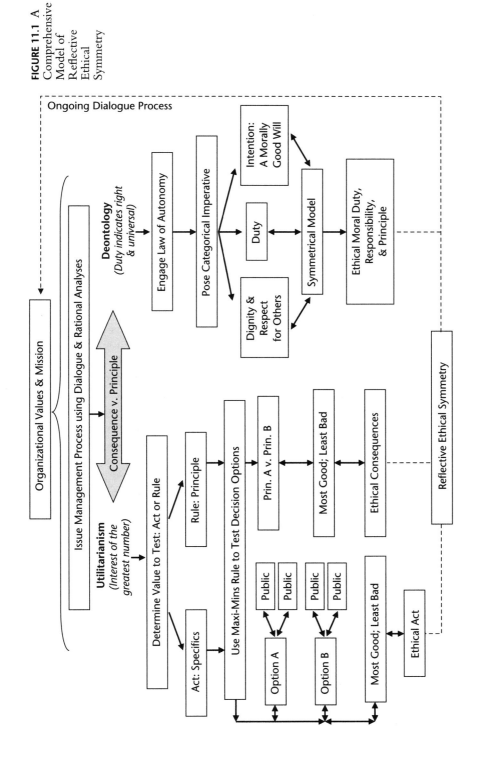

FIGURE 11.1 A Comprehensive Model of Reflective Ethical Symmetry

"Option A" versus "Option B"). The potential consequences of each decision option are weighed by their various outcomes on publics and subjected to the maxi-mins principle. Of the various decision options under consideration and the various outcomes they were each predicted to have on publics, that which is deemed ethical is the decision with the most good outcomes and the least bad outcomes; it is deemed the ethical act in that specific instance.

Using each of the three ethical analysis paradigms in the model (deontology, rule utilitarianism, and act utilitarianism) results in an ethically well-considered decision, based on values and dialogue, that we named reflective ethical symmetry. Normatively, it is best when more than one means of analysis can be used to examine an issue and weigh potential decisions based on both principle and consequence. The reflective ethical symmetry model captures both the best thinking of moral philosophers and the ethical tenets of the Excellence Theory. When used in a multiple analyses format, various definitions of what is ethical in the model ("ethical yardsticks") will undoubtedly result in divergent conclusions. However, those decisions should be better analyzed and considered both in their principle and in their consequences than decisions not employing such an ethical model as the backbone for analyses. Those analyses strengthen the diversity of perspectives and are the fodder for discussion with stakeholders and publics to ascertain their values and beliefs in relation to the issue at hand, using symmetrical dialogue. That strategy not only builds relationships but also increases trust by incorporating more of the values of publics into organizational decisions.

Although using opposite means of moral analyses can create divergent conclusions and opinions of how to resolve an issue, that outcome is not a negative one. Disparate conclusions can allow the organization to identify new decision alternatives to resolve the situation, obtain new insights, understand the values of a multiplicity of publics and stakeholders, or see the true value of resolving the issue in a certain manner. Disparate conclusions can be resolved by working to discover the "determining factor" (Baron, 1995) or the most important ethical consideration that overrides all others. That determining factor is either the moral principle to be maintained or the utility to be maximized with organizational decisions and policy.

The Future of Excellence

There is great promise for continued excellence by the Millennial generation of public relations employees, which includes those born in 1982 or later. In fact, 79% want to work for a socially responsible company (Cone, 2006), and 92% expressed that they would leave an employer who had different values than theirs (PricewaterhouseCoopers, 2008). Research shows that practitioners in their twenties and practitioners who have fewer than 10 years of experience are not likely to confront management about an unethical decision (especially as compared with senior practitioners), perhaps due to their lack of institutional power (Berger

& Reber, 2006; Curtin, Gallicano, & Matthews, 2011). Although many Millennials might not voice their concerns yet, most entry-level practitioners will be dissatisfied with their jobs if their employers make unethical decisions (Blum & Tremarco, 2008).

A study by Curtin, Gallicano, and Matthews (2011) provides several insights into the ethics of Millennial practitioners who work in public relations agencies, at least in the United States. They found that successful relationship-building with this group depends on a strong ethical vision that is enacted in everyday decision-making. Millennials' loyalty to their employers is compromised when they see unethical behavior and then see that top management does not reprimand employees for the behavior. Millennial practitioners disapprove of inflating credentials, overbilling clients, lying, and attempting to justify unethical acts, such as the excuse that "everyone does it."

The new generation of practitioners tends to value a deontological approach to decision-making, although a vocal minority prefers a utilitarian approach. Moreover, Millennial practitioners highly rated the six questions from the second step in Bowen's (2005) Kantian model for ethical decision-making. Curtin et al. (2011) modernized the wording of some of these questions, which was necessary for their survey. The questions, including the modern wording, are listed below, and the questions within the larger context of the new model can be seen in the deontological side of Figure 11.1:

- Should everyone else who is in a similar situation do the same thing I am about to do?
- If I were the customer (or other public), would I accept this decision?
- Am I proceeding with good intentions?
- Will the dignity and respect I have for myself and others be compromised by this decision?
- Have I faced a similar ethical issue before?
- Am I doing the right thing?

In their use of deontological reasoning, the Millennial generation uses transparency as a principle for determining what to do—perhaps because they are digital natives, and transparency is a rule that practitioners and publics emphasize in the digital realm. Asking these questions not only helps in the analyses of moral dilemmas but also helps by enabling organizations to act with transparent intentions, helping to build trust.

Generally speaking, the incoming generation of public relations practitioners has the foundational knowledge and attitudes necessary for ethical decision-making. As part of a public relations department with strong moral guidance and as part of an organization that is committed to moral decision-making, the future for excellence in public relations is in good hands to increase the level of moral and social responsibility in public relations practice and in the activities of organizations in which public relations acts as a corporate conscience.

References

Arthur W. Page Society (Ed.). (2007). *The authentic enterprise.* New York: Author.

Bakhtin, M. M. (1993). *Toward a philosophy of the act* (V. Liapunov, Trans.). Austin: University of Texas Press.

Baron, M. W. (1995). *Kantian ethics almost without apology.* Ithaca, NY: Cornell University Press.

Bartlett, J., Tywoniak, S., & Hatcher, C. (2007). Public relations professional practice and the institutionalisation of CSR. *Journal of Communication Management, 11*(4), 281–299.

Beauchamp, T. L., & Bowie, N. E. (2004). *Ethical theory and business* (7th ed.). Upper Saddle River, NJ: Pearson Prentice Hall.

Berger, B. K. (2005). Power over, power with, and power to public relations: Critical reflections on public relations, the dominant coalition, and activism. *Journal of Public Relations Research, 17*(1), 5–28.

Berger, B. K., & Reber, B. H. (2006). *Gaining influence in public relations: The role of resistance in practice.* Mahwah, NJ: Lawrence Erlbaum Associates.

Biswas, T. (1997). *Decision-making under uncertainty.* New York: St. Martin's Press.

Bivins, T. (2009). *Mixed media: Moral distinctions in advertising, public relations, and journalism.* New York: Routledge.

Blum, P. K., & Tremarco, V. Q. (2008). *High potential public relations professionals thrive on challenge: A study of employee turnover and retention in the public relations industry.* Gainesville, FL: Institute for Public Relations.

Bowen, S. A. (2000). A theory of ethical issues management: Contributions of Kantian deontology to public relations' ethics and decision making. Unpublished doctoral dissertation, University of Maryland, College Park.

Bowen, S. A. (2004a). Expansion of ethics as the tenth generic principle of public relations excellence: A Kantian theory and model for managing ethical issues. *Journal of Public Relations Research, 16*(1), 65–92.

Bowen, S. A. (2004b). Organizational factors encouraging ethical decision making: An exploration into the case of an exemplar. *Journal of Business Ethics, 52*(4), 311–324.

Bowen, S. A. (2005). A practical model of ethical decision making in issues management and public relations. *Journal of Public Relations Research, 17*(3), 191–216.

Bowen, S. A. (2006). Autonomy in communication: Inclusion in strategic management and ethical decision-making, a comparative case analysis. *Journal of Communication Management, 10*(4), 330–352.

Bowen, S. A. (2007). The extent of ethics. In E. L. Toth (Ed.), *The future of excellence in public relations and communication management: Challenges for the next generation* (pp. 275–297). Mahwah, NJ: Lawrence Erlbaum Associates.

Bowen, S. A. (2008a). Foundations in moral philosophy for public relations ethics. In T. L. Hansen-Horn, & B. D. Neff (Eds.), *Public relations: From theory to practice* (pp. 160–180). Boston: Pearson A and B.

Bowen, S. A. (2008b). A state of neglect: Public relations as corporate conscience or ethics counsel. *Journal of Public Relations Research, 20*(3), 271–296.

Bowen, S. A. (2009). What communication professionals tell us regarding dominant coalition access and gaining membership. *Journal of Applied Communication Research, 37*(4), 418–443.

Bowen, S. A. (2010a). The nature of good in public relations: What should be its normative ethic? In R. L. Heath (Ed.), *The Sage handbook of public relations* (2nd ed., pp. 569–583). Thousand Oaks, CA: Sage.

Bowen, S. A. (2010b). An examination of applied ethics and stakeholder management on top corporate websites. *Public Relations Journal, 4*(1).

Cheney, G., & Tompkins, P. K. (1984, March). Toward an ethic of identification. Paper presented at the Burke Conference, Philadelphia, PA.

Cone, C. (2006, October 24). *Civic-minded Millennials prepared to reward or punish companies based on commitment to social causes.* Press release. Retrieved from: http://www.csrwire.com/press/press_release/19346-Civic-Minded-Millennials-Prepared-to-Reward-or-Punish-Companies-Based-on-Commitment-to-Social-Causes.

Coombs, W. T., & Holladay, S. J. (2012). Fringe public relations: How activism moves critical PR toward the mainstream. *Public Relations Review, 24.* Retrieved from: http://dx.doi.org/10.1016/j.pubrev.2012.02.008.

Curtin, P. A., Gallicano, T. D., & Matthews, K. (2011). Millennials' approaches to ethical decision making: A survey of young public relations agency employees. *Public Relations Journal, 5*(2), 1–21.

DeGeorge, R. T. (2010). *Business ethics* (7th ed.). Boston, MA: Prentice Hall.

DiStaso, M. W., & Messner, M. (2010). Forced transparency: Corporate image on Wikipedia and what it means for public relations. *Public Relations Journal, 4*(2), 1–23.

Dodd, M. D., & Supa, D. W. (2011). Understanding the effect of corporate social responsibility on consumer purchase intention. *Public Relations Journal, 5*(3), 1–19.

DraftFCB. (n.d.). It's good to give. Retrieved from: http://www.facebook-sstudio.com/search/index?PublicSearchForm[query]=noble&yt0=Search#/gallery/submission/its-good-to-give.

Ferguson, M. A. (1984, August). Building theory in public relations: Interorganizational relationships. Paper presented at the annual meeting of the Association for Education in Journalism and Mass Communication, Gainesville, FL.

Gallicano, T. D. (2011). A critical analysis of greenwashing claims. *Public Relations Journal 5*(3), 1–21.

Gallicano, T. D., & Heisler, T. A. (2011). Relationship outcomes in an organization with a mechanical structure. *PRism, 8*(1), 1–15.

Goodman, E. C. (Ed.). (1997). *The Forbes book of business quotations.* New York: Black Dog & Leventhal.

Grunig, J. E. (1989, November). Symmetrical communication systems and excellent organizations: An integrative theory of communication and development. Paper presented at the Association for Advancement of Policy, Research, and Development in the Third World, San Juan, Puerto Rico.

Grunig, J. E. (1992). What is excellence in management? In J. E. Grunig (Ed.), *Excellence in public relations and communication management* (pp. 219–250). Hillsdale, NJ: Lawrence Erlbaum Associates.

Grunig, J. E., & Huang, Y. H. (2000). From organizational effectiveness to relationship indicators: Antecedents of relationships, public relations strategies, and relationship outcomes. In J. A. Ledingham & S. D. Bruning (Eds.), *Public relations as relationship management: A relational approach to the study and practice of public relations* (pp. 23–53). Mahwah, NJ: Lawrence Erlbaum Associates.

Grunig, J. E., & Repper, F. C. (1992). Strategic management, publics, and issues. In J. E. Grunig (Ed.), *Excellence in public relations and communication management* (pp. 117–157). Hillsdale, NJ: Lawrence Erlbaum Associates.

Grunig, J. E., & White, J. (1992). The effect of worldviews on public relations theory and practice. In J. E. Grunig (Ed.), *Excellence in public relations and communication management* (pp. 31–64). Hillsdale, NJ: Lawrence Erlbaum Associates.

Grunig, L. A., Grunig, J. E., & Dozier, D. M. (2002). *Excellent public relations and effective organizations: A study of communication management in three countries.* Mahwah, NJ: Lawrence Erlbaum Associates.

Heath, R. L., & Li, N. (2010). Community relations and corporate social responsibility. In R. L. Heath (Ed.), *The Sage handbook of public relations* (2nd ed., pp. 557–568). Thousand Oaks, CA: Sage.

Hon, L. C., & Brunner, B. (2002). Measuring public relationships among students and administrators at the University of Florida. *Journal of Communication Management, 6*(3), 227–238.

Jo, S., Hon, L. C., & Brunner, B. R. (2004). Organisation–public relationships: Measurement validation in a university setting. *Journal of Communication Management, 9*(1), 14–27.

Johnson & Johnson (2012). Our credo. Retrieved from: http://www.jnj.com/connect/about-jnj/jnj-credo/.

Kant, I. ([1793] 1974). *On the old saw: That may be right in theory but it won't work in practice* (E. B. Ashton, Trans.). Philadelphia: University of Pennsylvania Press.

Kant, I. (1948). *The groundwork of the metaphysic of morals* (H. J. Paton, Trans.). New York: Harper Torchbooks.

Kent, M. L., & Taylor, M. (2002). Toward a dialogic theory of public relations. *Public Relations Review, 28*(1), 21–37.

Ki, E.-J., & Hon. L. C. (2007). Testing the linkages among the organization–public relationship and attitude and behavioral intentions. *Journal of Public Relations Research, 19*(1), 1–23. doi:10.1207/s1532754xjprr1901_1.

Kim, J.-N., & Rhee, Y. (2011). Strategic thinking about employee communication behavior (ECB) in public relations: Testing the models of megaphoning and scouting effects in Korea. *Journal of Public Relations Research, 23*(3), 243–268.

Kim, S., & Lee, Y-J. (2012). The complex attribution process of CSR motives. *Public Relations Review, 38*(1), 168–170.

Kohlberg, L. (1969). Stage and sequence: The cognitive developmental approach to socialization. In D. A. Goslin (Ed.), *Handbook of socialization theory of research* (pp. 347–480). Chicago, IL: Rand McNally.

McCorkindale, T. (2010). Can you see the writing on my wall? A content analysis of the Fortune 50's Facebook social networking sites. *Public Relations Journal, 4*(3), 1–13.

Men, L. R., & Tsai, W.-H. S. (2012). Understanding public engagement on corporate social network sites (SNSs): Antecedents and motivations. Paper presented at the International Public Relations Research Conference, Miami, FL.

Mill, J. S. ([1861] 1957). *Utilitarianism.* New York: The Liberal Arts Press.

Mill, J. S. ([1861] 1994). Higher and lower pleasures. In P. Singer (Ed.), *Ethics* (pp. 201–205). Oxford: Oxford University Press.

O'Neil, J. (2012). An examination of how Fortune 500 companies and Philanthropy 200 nonprofits cultivate relationships using Facebook. Paper presented at the International Public Relations Research Conference, Miami, FL.

PricewaterhouseCoopers (2008). *Managing tomorrow's people: Perspectives from a new generation.* Retrieved from: http://www.pwc.com/managingpeople2020.

Romero, P. (2008, September 17). *Beware of green marketing, warns Greenpeace exec.* Retrieved from: https://abs-cbnnews.com/special-report/09/16/08/beware-green-marketing-warns-greenpeace-exec.

Rumsey, G. G., & White, C. (2009). Strategic corporate philanthropic relationships: Nonprofits' perceptions of benefits and corporate motives. *Public Relations Review, 35*(3), 301–303.

Ryan, M., & Martinson, D. L. (1983). The PR officer as corporate conscience. *Public Relations Quarterly, 28*(2), 20–23.

Ryan, M., & Martinson, D. L. (1985). Public relations practitioners, public interest and management. *Journalism Quarterly, 62*(Spring), 111–115.

Schreiber, E. (2011). *Shared values: A more sustainable approach to CSR.* Retrieved from: http://prsay.prsa.org/index.php/2011/09/07/pr-role-in-shared-values-csr/.

Siebold, D. R., & Shea, B. C. (2001). Participation and decision making. In F. M. Jablin & L. L. Putnam (Eds.), *The new handbook of organizational communication: Advances in theory, research, and methods* (pp. 664–703). Thousand Oaks, CA: Sage.

Sims, R. R. (1994). *Ethics and organizational decision making: A call for renewal.* Westport, CT: Quorum.

Singer, P. (Ed.). (1994). *Ethics.* Oxford: Oxford University Press.

Spangler, I. S., & Pompper, D. (2011). Corporate social responsibility and the oil industry: Theory and perspective fuel a longitudinal view. *Public Relations Review, 37*(3), 217–225.

Sriramesh, K., & Verčič, D. (Eds.). (2003). *The global public relations handbook: Theory, research, and practice.* Mahwah, NJ: Lawrence Erlbaum Associates.

Starbucks Corporation. (2010). My Starbucks idea: FAQ's. Retrieved from: http://my starbucksidea.force.com/ideafaq.

Taylor, M. (2010). Public relations in the enactment of civil society. In R. L. Heath (Ed.), *The Sage handbook of public relations* (2nd ed., pp. 5–15). Thousand Oaks, CA: Sage.

Van Ruler, B., & Verčič, D. (2005). Reflective communication management, future ways for public relations research. *Communication Yearbook, 29,* 239–273.

Verčič, D., Grunig, L. A., & Grunig, J. E. (1996). Global and specific principles of public relations: Evidence from Slovenia. In H. M. Culbertson & N. Chen (Eds.), *International public relations: A comparative analysis* (pp. 31–65). Mahwah, NJ: Lawrence Erlbaum Associates.

Weiss, J. W. (1994). *Business ethics.* Belmont, CA: Wadsworth.

Werhane, P. H. (2007). Corporate social responsibility/corporate moral responsibility: Is there a difference and the difference it makes? In S. May, G. Cheney, & J. Roper (Eds.), *The debate over corporate social responsibility* (pp. 459–474). Oxford: Oxford University Press.

Wright, D. K. (1989). Ethics research in public relations: An overview. *Public Relations Review, 15*(2), 3–5.

Wright, D. K. (1996). Communication ethics. In M. B. Salwen & D. W. Stacks (Eds.), *An integrated approach to communication theory and research* (pp. 519–535). Mahwah, NJ: Lawrence Erlbaum Associates.

12

GLOBALIZATION, PUBLIC RELATIONS, AND ACTIVISM FOR SOCIAL CHANGE

A Culture-Centered Approach

Mohan J. Dutta

Abstract

This chapter, utilizing the culture-centered approach (CCA) to public relations, puts forward the argument that obfuscating the vast inequities produced by neoliberal forms of governance and manipulating the top-down forms of power enacted by TNCs through discourses of participation, community engagement, liberty, and dialogue, public relations practices lie at the heart of neoliberal expansion, the production of communicative asymmetries, and the inequitable distributions of communicative opportunities globally. The critique of public relations as a rhetorical artifact serving the status quo creates openings for interrogating the interplays of power and control in public relations practices. In this backdrop, projects driven by the CCA are offered as dialogic openings for listening to the voices of the margins and for rendering impure the dominant categories of the mainstream that serve as the expert-driven justifications for erasure of subaltern voices. In summary, a culture-centered reading of public relations constructs public relations in resistance, in a framework of relating that engages the mainstream through disruptions of its assumptions and taken-for-granted logics.

Key Words

culture-centered approach, globalization, Global South, hegemony, neoliberalism, subaltern activism

Globalization, a phenomenon that has been depicted by the rapidly enhancing networks of global flow of goods, services, and labor across national boundaries, is established on the underlying economic principles of trade liberalization; privatization of resources; and minimization of public programs, tariffs, and subsidies (Dutta, 2011, 2012). These economic principles of globalization, captured in the concept of neoliberalism, and proposed in the form of the Bretton Woods Treaties to govern global markets, operate on the rhetoric of the free market, based on the assumption that promoting free markets globally ensures competition and growth, ultimately leading to the trickling down of economic wealth. Whereas neoliberal forms of governance have increasingly favored power and control in the hands of transnational corporations (TNCs), the promises of trickledown have not been materially realized across most of the globe (Dutta, 2011, 2012). Instead, neoliberal reforms carried out in the form of structural adjustment programs (SAPs) have simultaneously contributed to large-scale global inequities and disenfranchisement of the poor in the form of displacement, impoverishment, migration, unemployment, and increasing lack of access to public resources.

In this chapter, utilizing the culture-centered approach (CCA) to public relations, I put forth the argument that obfuscating the vast inequities produced by neoliberal forms of governance and manipulating the top-down forms of power enacted by TNCs through discourses of participation, community engagement, and dialogue, public relations practices lie at the heart of neoliberal expansion, production of communicative asymmetries (Grunig & Grunig, 1997), and the inequitable distributions of communicative opportunities globally (Dutta, 2009, 2012). It is particularly important to critically interrogate the role of public relations in crafting and reproducing frames that shape public attitudes and opinions embodying the individualistic values of neoliberalism put forth under the narratives of development, freedom, and liberty on a global scale. SAPs are promoted through value-driven campaigns directed at local elites and seeking to open up local markets through partnerships with local elites. For instance, in the wake of the Arab Spring, the United States Agency for International Development (USAID, 2002) spent large proportions of funding supporting US-based NGOs and local NGOs in shaping the political processes of Egypt and Tunisia. The funding was specifically allocated toward directed democracy promotion initiatives that serve as the broader public relations frameworks for pushing neoliberal governmentality, fostering favorable markets for US-based TNCs after opening up these markets to international trade. As noted in the USAID (2002) annual letter in reference to the role of the USAID within the context of the Arab Spring, development serves as a framework for articulating the values of privatization on a global scale:

> Within weeks of the revolution, we assisted the nation's transition to democracy by helping support an independent elections commission and provide training on electoral procedures. Last year, millions of Tunisians cast their votes in a historic and peaceful election—the first free election of the Arab Spring . . . As the events of the last year have shown us, the

development landscape is changing and we must change with it. The Arab Spring has ushered in new possibilities to empower the oppressed. Conflict and extreme poverty are increasingly becoming intertwined. And private sector investment in the developing world has outpaced foreign assistance. To respond to these changing tides, the development community must embrace more challenging roles.

The role of the US in supporting electoral commissions and providing training on electoral processes is tied to US-driven agendas of setting up political systems and political processes that enable neoliberal hegemony. This top-down nature of US aid that sought to leverage popular resistance in the context of the Arab Spring to push neoliberal values was particularly evident in the support of US-based political NGOs such as the National Endowment for Democracy (NED). The neoliberal agenda embodied in US funding for NED is well captured in the following excerpt from the State of the Union Speech of George Bush in 2004:

> As long as the Middle East remains a place of tyranny, despair and anger, it will continue to produce men and movements that threaten the safety of America and our friends. So America is pursuing a forward strategy of freedom in the greater Middle East. We will challenge the enemies of reform, confront the allies of terror, and expect a higher standard from our friends. To cut through the barriers of hateful propaganda, the Voice of America and other broadcast services are expanding their programming in Arabic and Persian—and soon, a new television service will begin providing reliable news and information across the region. I will send you a proposal to double the budget of the National Endowment for Democracy, and to focus its new work on the development of free elections, free markets, free press, and free labor unions in the Middle East. And above all, we will finish the historic work of democracy in Afghanistan and Iraq, so those nations can light the way for others, and help transform a troubled part of the world.
>
> *(Bush, 2004)*

Note here that whereas the communication activities of the primitive other (read undemocratic, and therefore, savage) are marked off as propaganda, the persuasion-based activities of the US in the Middle East (such as support for the Voice of America and for the National Endowment for Democracy) are framed as sources of reliable news and information. US support for NED activities in the Middle East are constituted in the simultaneous support for political freedom and the free market rationality of neoliberalism. Freedom in the political sphere is intrinsically tied to market freedom, i.e. the opening up of the markets in the Middle East. It is against this backdrop then that the NED serves the very specific function of pushing neoliberal reforms through the shaping of the public sphere and political processes in the Middle East and elsewhere.

Drawing upon postcolonial and Subaltern Studies theories, the CCA interrogates the role of public relations in the production of symbols that achieve the hegemony of neoliberal reforms through the circulation of specific knowledge claims that hide the material exploitations and inequities that are produced through neoliberal reforms globally. The taken-for-granted values of freedom, democracy, and liberty are interrogated for the specific forms of hegemonic configurations that they serve when it comes to policy-making and program planning on a global scale, especially as these public relations practices relate to the production of communicative asymmetries (Dutta, 2009; Grunig & Grunig, 1997). I make the argument that public relations practices of lobbying, policy-based knowledge production, community relations, and whitewashing are intrinsic to the reproduction of neoliberal hegemony on a global scale, while simultaneously generating the image of participation, democracy, and emancipation that are couched in a seemingly altruistic language of development. Therefore, it is through deconstruction that the CCA seeks to foster spaces for listening to the voices of those communities from the Global South that have otherwise been rendered both invisible and exploitable through the dominant discourses of public relations.

A culturally centered interrogation of public relations notes that the hegemony of neoliberal governmentality across nation-states on the global landscape is achieved through the global flow of communications, constituted in the form of strategic public relations activities engaged in by transnational corporations (TNCs), international financial institutions (IFIs) such as the International Monetary Fund (IMF) and the World Bank (WB), transnational policy organizations, national governments, think tanks, and various other knowledge-producing bodies that consolidate power through the very deployment of languages of participation and democratization (Dutta, 2011, 2012; Pal & Dutta, 2008a, 2008b). Public relations practices have emerged on the political economy of transnational capitalism as key actors in the management of public opinion, public policies, and resources at a global level, setting agendas, foregrounding specific issues, and fostering specific frames around these issues. They actively work on legitimizing, circulating, and reifying neoliberal governmentality across the globe, consolidating power in the hands of TNCs and reifying policies that reiterate the hegemony of the free market through the circulation of images that equate neoliberal reforms with development, structural adjustment with modernization, and privatization with growth (Dutta, 2009; Pal & Dutta, 2008a, 2008b). Through languages of democracy promotion, community relations, community empowerment, and nation-building, public relations practices often perform the fundamental role of pushing forth the capitalist agenda of neoliberalism that seeks to consolidate communicative opportunities in the hands of those with power (Dutta, 2009).

It is on the foundations of deconstruction that a culture-centered reading of public relations articulates entry points for alternative theorizing and praxis of public relations, rooted in culturally based epistemologies from the Global South that have historically been treated as backward and have been erased from the dominant discursive spaces of knowledge production and representation (de Sousa Santos, 2007; Shiva, 2000). Culture-centered theorizing of public relations foregrounds the resistive capacity of public relations practices that participate in dialogue with the subaltern sectors to co-create alternative representations of truth claims, thus rupturing the knowledge claims of the mainstream, and searching out alternative forms of economic, political, social, and cultural organizing that resist the market-based logic of contemporary globalization politics (Kim, 2008; Pal, 2008). In this sense, the re-envisioning of public relations lies at the heart of the transformations in inequitable structures at the local, national, and global levels. The assumptions embodied in the dominant structures and the accompanying public relations practices are rendered impure through the fostering of spaces for listening to alternative voices from elsewhere, questioning the values that are reified through mainstream public relations practices. These alternative rationalities then become the vortex of the politics of social change, directed at bringing about structural transformations across the globe.

Culture-Centered Approach: Public Relations and Social Change

The study of public relations and social change within the framework of the CCA attends to the public relations practices embodied in the dominant power structures that underlie the concentration of wealth in the hands of these dominant power structures, and simultaneously offers a communicative entry point for listening to the voices of disenfranchised communities at the margins. The concentration of wealth in the hands of dominant power structures is legitimated through the production of knowledge that justifies these inequities and asymmetries, achieved through powerful relationships of knowledge-producing structures with the sites of economic and political control. Knowledge itself becomes an instrument of public relations, inherently serving political and economic inequities that are perpetuated through communicative asymmetries. Therefore, social change is achieved through transformative politics that takes to task the messages, message frames, meanings, and communicative processes that undermine the subaltern sectors and frame them as primitive in order to justify carrying out the disenfranchisement of these sectors through policies and interventions that are directed at consolidating power in the hands of the local, national, and global elite (Dutta, 2011, 2012). The languages of freedom, democracy and participation etc. are paradoxically deployed to foster inequities and communicative asymmetries globally. Democracy becomes the buzz word for the imperial penetration of nation-states to set up neoliberal governance, as we witnessed in the example of Iraq (Dutta, 2009, 2011; Dutta-Bergman, 2005b).

The deconstruction of dominant structures offers the foundation for co-constructive journeys of solidarity with the grassroots that foreground opportunities for listening to subaltern voices from the Global South, thus offering the impetus for activist politics that is driven from the South toward the agenda of rendering accessible spaces for participation, engagement, and dialogue, and through the fostering of symmetrical opportunities for communication, rendering open possibilities of political and economic transformations. For instance, deconstructing the co-optive agendas of the National Endowment for Democracy (NED) offers critical insights into the functioning of initiatives of democracy promotion as the façade for imperial practices of the US in pushing neoliberal reforms in the Global South through the language of democracy. The languages of freedom and the market are manipulated on a mass scale to justify neo-imperial neoliberal interventions globally.

Knowledge and Hegemony

That the production of knowledge is essential to the achievement of hegemony is evident in the communicative processes of policy–TNC–academic linkages that lie at the heart of neoliberalization. Neoliberal reforms, articulated in principles of free market rationality, were conceived and reproduced within academic knowledge structures (with academics such as Milton Friedman and Von Hayek at the University of Chicago), think tanks such as the Free Enterprise Institute and the Mont Pèlerin Society, political structures, business structures, as well as global transnational organizations. At the core of carrying out the agendas of the transnational elite is the production of specific forms of knowledge that would be directed at adjusting policies and programming to ensure the consolidation of resources in the hands of the rich. In this sense, knowledge production is essentially a public relations exercise as it frames specific issues in specific formats to legitimize policies that produce inequalities. Reforms in the form of structural adjustments were initially shaped by academic experts interested in producing a specific form of political and economic organizing on a global scale. Similarly, academic experts often working for and with think tanks (especially academics in economics) have played pivotal roles in developing economic policies, simultaneously profiting enormously from these consulting roles.

Neoliberal reforms were carried out globally through the influencing roles of international financial institutions (IFIs) such as the World Bank (WB) and the International Monetary Fund (IMF), which were in turn shaped largely by the political influence of nation-states such as the US through leadership presence as well as through economic contributions to these institutions. Therefore, when neoliberal reforms were forced upon the Global South, they were often accomplished through the combination of terms attached to debts as well as knowledge-driven influences in academic, policy, and program circles. Elite actors within states that were going through economic reforms were often trained at powerful sites of knowledge production in the United States (such as the training of economists of Chile in principles of neoliberal reform at the University of Chicago). From public relations standpoints, US academics have played key roles in global surveillance and democracy promotion initiatives, on one hand, utilizing their academic knowledge to gather intelligence data on nation-states, and, on the other hand, utilizing US funding to develop global bases of support for the US.

Knowledge and Delegitimization

The production of knowledge in globalization politics is also then tied to the delegitimization of specific forms of knowledge in the Global South in order to establish neoliberal hegemony and to justify neoliberal interventions under the label of modernization. Framing is critical to the practice of public relations in ascertaining and maintaining the dominant structure, and in reproducing the asymmetries in globalization politics through specific claims to knowledge. Consulting firms, knowledge-producing bodies, and global funding agencies such as the McKinsey Company, the Global Fund, and the Bill and Melinda Gates Foundation carry out their agendas of knowledge production on the basis of the depiction of problems in the Global South that are then to be solved through interventions developed at the sites of power. Portrayals of poverty and malnutrition in the Global South become the basis for justifying neoliberal interventions. The irony of these interventions lies in the essential mismatch between their supposed objectives of poverty reduction, on one hand, and the large-scale inequities they produce on the other (Dutta, 2011).

Global interventions are constituted on the framework of needs in the Global South. These needs are depicted in the modernist language of development that depicts the Global South as primitive and backward. Essential then to the political economy of transnational development initiatives is the framing of the Global South as primitive and backward, in need of interventions that are manufactured and produced in the North/West. Large budgets, funding infrastructures, programs, and policies then are directed by these hegemonic structures, operating under the logic of offering privatized and civil society-based top-down solutions. The depiction of the backward sites of intervention in the Global South emerges as a quintessential instrument of control, fostering and perpetuating dichotomies that freeze the agency of individuals and communities from the Global South, and instead turn them into objects of targeting. The violence of the politics of interventions therefore lies in the disenfranchisement of Southern participants from discursive spaces and in the erasure of ways of knowing from the Global South. The delegitimization of local ways of knowing then becomes a tool for control, essentially creating markets for imperial goods and services that are predicated on the presumed universal appeal and superiority of these goods and services.

Funding Community Initiatives and Fostering Spaces for Reform

The community has emerged as a site of control in neoliberal interventions. Community relations activities have been manipulatively co-opted to serve specific neoliberal agendas that seek to align the community with the goals of transnational capital (Dutta, 2012; Dutta–Bergman, 2005a). Organizations such as the United States Agency for International Development (USAID) find civil society organizations in local communities across the globe in order to diffuse neoliberal values, thus rendering open the political and economic boundaries of nation-states in the Global South as markets for US-based TNCs. For instance, in the context of the Arab Spring, the US funding of NED worked to push neoliberal values in Tunisia and Egypt, seeking to align the political and economic policies of these countries along the lines of the interests of US-based TNCs on a global scale. Similarly, a US-funded organization, the International Republican Institute (IRI) serves as an international NGO that promotes neoliberal governance abroad through community relations activities, and through the deployment of strategic programs directed at inculcating neoliberal values in the Global South, with the ultimate goal of opening up the markets in the Global South to US TNCs (Sourcewatch, 2012).

The imperial configuration of nation-states (such as the US) emerges on the site of neoliberal governance as an influential player in the shaping of political and economic configurations through the funding of non-governmental organizations (NGOs) that are supportive of the goals of the imperial nation-states (read primarily the US). NGO funding has been at the heart of public relations strategies of influence, shaping values and aspirations in the Global South by controlling the agendas and objectives of civil society actors. The logics of free market capitalism and structural adjustment are globally articulated through the funding initiatives of international organizations who seek to foster community engagement precisely to co-opt the participatory potential of communities in order to serve neoliberal agendas on a global scale.

Listening to Voices at the Margins

CCA foregrounds the role of dialogue as an entry point for co-constructing knowledge from elsewhere that has historically been erased from the dominant spaces of knowledge production. Knowledge therefore is a resistive strategy, seeking to disrupt the values and the assumptions of the status quo. In co-creating entry points for social change, culture-centered public relations emphasizes the agency of local cultures in producing knowledge that is meaningful to the lived experiences of the local communities, and that is responsive to these lived experiences as entry points for constituting action on a global scale.

Culture is conceptualized here as dynamic, contextually situated, heterogeneous, and continually negotiated through communication. Culture is constituted through communicative and participatory processes, and is foregrounded in the voices of local communities. Therefore, the fostering of participatory spaces for communication lies at the heart of social change. The logics and underlying rules of these spaces are themselves created by community members; therefore, subaltern forms of communication serve as spaces for the enactment of localized agency in the Global South. In the politics of activism emerging from the Global South, these subaltern forms of communication interface with mainstream channels and spaces of communication where policies are formulated and programs are designed. For instance, in the face of the bauxite mining project set up by the British aluminium giant Vedanta in the Niyamgiri Hills of Odisha in India, the Dongria Kondh tribe, the indigenous tribe residing in the hills, organized through localized forms of communication such as songs, dances, and community-wide meetings, and simultaneously participated in mainstream spheres through protest marches at key sites, solidarity meetings at key public sites along with NGO workers, and organizing through online and social media to have a global presence. The networks of solidarity that were fostered locally also built networks at national and global levels, effectively organizing resistance in London, and utilizing social media platforms to mobilize letter writing and telephone campaigns in London, voicing protests at the shareholder meeting, and campaigning key political actors. The pressures that were created by the local movement leveraged local, national, and global structures, forcing the Government of India to regulate the mining operations of Vedanta in Niyamgiri.

Of particular relevance in the culture-centered approach is the relationship between culture and agency, the capacity of individuals and communities to enact their choices. Cultural scripts offer the templates for the enactment of resistive agency. In other words, agency becomes meaningful through the circulation of cultural symbols. In turn, cultures are made meaningful through the active processes of meaning making and interpretation that are central to the enactment of localized agency. Both culture and agency are situated amidst structures, the forms of institutional roles, relationships, and functions that constrain and/or enable the access to resources. In their resistance against Vedanta mining, Dongria Kondh leaders drew upon cultural symbols and relics to put forth a narrative of resistance.

Culture-centered public relations theory notes the active interplay among culture, structure, and agency in the creation and reproduction of meanings. Essential to the foregrounding of agency is the capacity of local communities to articulate their choices and to participate in processes of social change that bring about structural transformations. The act of listening to hitherto erased voices in discursive spaces creates the entry point for change, bringing forth alternative rationalities and challenging global, national, and local structures. Listening itself becomes a strategy for resistance as it seeks to transform the inequities of voice that are intrinsic to the mainstream structures of oppression.

The theorization of dialogue in the culture-centered approach turns toward the emancipatory capacity of "listening to the other" in bringing about structural transformations in global public spheres. It is through dialogue then that the public relations scholar/activist participates in the foregrounding of alternative rationalities in global platforms that challenge the hegemony of neoliberalism. For example, the dialogic co-constructions with farmers in India participating in the "Navdanya" movement creates alternative meanings of agriculture, foregrounding the rights of farmers to the seed, to retaining seeds, and to re-growing them the next season as opposed to the neoliberal co-optation of agriculture under the market framework of monoculture seeds to be purchased by farmers from TNCs. The framing of agriculture as a profit-making enterprise is resisted with the localized understanding of agriculture as a sustainable source of food for local communities. The right of the farmer to grow seeds and to retain and re-regrow them for the next season is an age-old cultural practice, and is put forth in the discursive space to oppose the concept of monoculture seeds that turn farmers into slaves of TNCs by connecting them to the market and by rendering the process of agriculture dependent on the capitalized markets for seeds where seeds become commodities.

Furthermore, the co-constructive role of public relations scholars/practitioners/ activists is directed toward the active participation along with local communities in projects of social change that seek to create alternative realities that challenge the political and economic rationalities of neoliberal governmentality. In the example above, the public relations researcher/practitioner/activist emerges as a collaborator with local communities in the Global South, in figuring out the rules and logics of the mainstream structures, and in utilizing these rules and logics to disrupt the knowledge claims made by the mainstream. The activist network of Navdanya conducts research on seed ownership and then utilizes this research as evidence to challenge the biopiracy of seeds by global agribusiness. Therefore, at the heart of the culture-centered approach is the active participation of the scholar/practitioner/activist in the co-creation of local knowledge and alternative rationalities that challenge the claims of universality in global spaces. At the same time, the legitimacy of local knowledge at global sites is articulated through the utilization of the very tools and strategies of control that are utilized by TNCs to co-opt and steal subaltern knowledge. The role of the public relations scholar/ practitioner/activist is redefined from one of serving the interests of transnational capitalism to one of actively participating in resisting global structures of oppression perpetuated by neoliberal hegemony. Attention is paid to the processes of resistance through which narratives of change are articulated at global sites.

Alternative Rationalities

Alternative rationalities are the rationalities of organizing economic and political systems that originate from outside the purviews of the global mainstream. These alternative forms of organizing challenge the logics of individualism that are widely present in neoliberal governance, and point toward frames of social justice and equity that originate from the participation of local communities that have been disenfranchised from spheres of decision-making. For instance, the organizing of farmers under the framework of the *La Via Campesina* movement draws attention to alternative rationalities of farming that emphasize sustenance and the food security needs of the poor. The *La Via Campesina* movement is a movement that involves farmers' representatives from four continents, paving the way for global organizing of farmers built on the leveraging of local organizing capacities at a global level to resist the neoliberal policies of agriculture that seek to turn agricultural resources over to the hands of global agribusiness and simultaneously disenfranchise local farmers.

The movement involves over 150 local and national organizations from 70 countries in Asia, Africa, Europe, and the Americas, and seeks to defend small-scale sustainable agriculture as a mechanism for promoting social justice and dignity by opposing corporate agriculture and transnational agro-corporations. The local rights of farming communities to food are offered as alternative rationalities that resist the profiteering rationality of neoliberalism. This emphasis on local sustenance as opposed to commoditization of agriculture is evident in the following depiction of the movement on its website:

> La Vía Campesina is the international movement which brings together millions of peasants, small and medium-size farmers, landless people, women farmers, indigenous people, migrants and agricultural workers from around the world. It defends small-scale sustainable agriculture as a way to promote social justice and dignity. It strongly opposes corporate-driven agriculture and transnational companies that are destroying people and nature.
>
> *(http://viacampesina.org/en/index.php?option=com_*
> *content&view=category&layout=blog&id=27&Itemid=44)*

Resistance to neoliberalism that concentrates power and control of agriculture in the hands of TNCs is offered by connecting a variety of disenfranchised groups, including peasants, farmers, landless people, indigenous communities, and migrants in a struggle for recognition and representation. Therefore, essential to resistance is the very struggle for recognition that is built on an alternative principle of participation of the margins as opposed to the top-down frameworks of the mainstream. The participation of farmers from the margins in the processes of change resists the top-down expertise-driven modes of decision-making in neoliberal governance.

The power consolidated in the hands of TNCs is resisted through the global networks of small and medium-sized farmers from across the world who have come together under the umbrella of *La Via Campesina*. *La Via Campesina* emerges as a symbol of resistance through the very nature of its organizing processes that disrupt the top-down rationality of neoliberal organizing that privileges experts. The promotion of global agribusiness under neoliberalism is resisted through these global linkages among farmers, represented through local and national organizations that are linked globally through *La Via Campesina*. Therefore, forms of local organizing emerge onto global spaces as entry points for social change. Under the title "Globalizing hope, globalizing the struggle," the movement notes its global resistance to neoliberalism:

La Vía Campesina is built on a strong sense of unity and solidarity between small and medium-scale agricultural producers from the North and South. The main goal of the movement is to realize food sovereignty and stop the destructive neoliberal process. It is based on the conviction that small farmers, including peasant fisher-folk, pastoralists and indigenous people, who make up almost half the world's people, are capable of producing food for their communities and feeding the world in a sustainable and healthy way.

(http://viacampesina.org/en/index.php?option=com_ content&view=category&layout=blog&id=27&Itemid=44)

Foregrounding the local capacity of farming, peasant, and indigenous communities to produce food challenges the neoliberal framing of agriculture under corporate control of TNCs through top-down agendas of change. Local participation emerges onto global networks of solidarity, depicting an organizing structure that is formed through the participation of farmer organizations at multiple levels of the social change process. The organizing of the movement is distributed into nine regions, with each region being represented by a man and a woman, who make up an International Coordinating Committee. The globally decentralized decision structure is connected through international conferences that emerge as sites of action as well as specific events of resistance. Examples of global events of resistance include International Women Day on March 8, International Day of Peasants' Struggle on April 17, and International Struggle Day against the WTO on September 10. Ultimately, culturally centered processes of change led through the participation of subaltern communities in the Global South offer entry points into possibilities for structural transformations globally.

Alternative Knowledge Claims

Because the oppression of subaltern communities is achieved through the erasure of subaltern participation from mainstream discursive spaces, subaltern struggles against oppression are also struggles for recognition and representation in these mainstream discursive spaces. Through these struggles for recognition and representation, subaltern activism seeks to disrupt the processes through which scientific knowledge claims are made, and also seeks to utilize the very structures of claims-making to articulate alternative knowledge claims that disrupt the political and economic hegemony of knowledge claims made through references to science. For instance, in the face of the large-scale agribusiness profiteering that takes place through the patenting of indigenous genetic material, resistance at national and global patenting sites has struggled to take back this genetic material by utilizing the frame of piracy. By demonstrating patenting as piracy through the use of evidence at the mainstream sites of dominant structures where these patents have been filed, activists from the Global South have regained the ownership of indigenous seeds in the hands of indigenous communities from the Global South. In these instances of struggles of patenting, resistance has been constituted through the disruption and utilization of those very same structures that have been utilized in order to delegitimize and steal subaltern knowledge as a source of TNC profiteering.

Similarly, the Movement of Landless Rural Workers (MST) in Brazil resists the neoliberal narrative of greed and acquisition by organizing local landless, slum-dwelling, and unemployed people to gain access to vast areas of unused land and to set up cooperatively based communities run by local community members through participation and democratic decision-making (Bell, 2012). The model of democracy modeled through the cooperatively run program is one that foregrounds the collective and highlights entry points for solidarity in governance. These local communities have established their localized forms of self-government, restorative justice, educational systems, legal processes, sustainable and ecologically sound agriculture, collective forms of production, and self-produced forms of local media. This logic of alternative knowledge claims is aptly noted in the voice of Ilda Martinez de Souza:

> My dream is to see real agrarian reform for all the land, so no child goes hungry, and no mother sheds tears because her son was murdered trying to steal a piece of bread. The pain of a mother is my pain. Every child is my child. I'm not mother to six. I am mother to thousands of youth, of children. I can't just listen to a mother in pain because her son was murdered in the favelas.
>
> *(http://truth-out.org/news/item/8382-without-firing-an-arm-we-created-a-revolution-land-reform)*

Evident in the understanding of agrarian reform is an alternative knowledge base that is built on the principles of empathy and collective ownership. For Ilda Martinez de Souza, the logic of the movement lies in her compassion for other mothers in pain. In her claim that she is not just a mother of six, but a mother to thousands of youth and children, she extends the basis of organizing to the broader collective. Noting the organizing principles of this narrative, she observes:

> This alternative is based on the dreams of each of us who comes to the countryside to be part of the land reform movement. "How is it that I want my life to be in the country?" We learn that people want a small house, they want to plant different foods, to have a pretty table, to always have enough milk for their children. And to see their kids study and play. That's what we discover slowly, traveling through the minds and dreams of each human being that becomes part of our settlements. We don't impose anything on them. We discover that we can share our dream with someone else, unite it with theirs, and begin to construct paradise together. We want to build

this paradise so our children and everyone who comes to the country can step on this land and be proud to say, "Here, we don't shed blood. Here, we don't wage war."

(http://truth-out.org/news/item/8382-without-firing-an-arm-we-created-a-revolution-land-reform)

The articulations of sharing dreams, collectively uniting with others, and constructing the economic system together as a collective lies at the heart of the organizing principles of MST. MST therefore emerges on the discursive spaces of neoliberal governance with an alternative framework of relationships, relationship management, and relating with multiple stakeholders. The principles of solidarity and community stand in resistance to top-down frames of ownership driven by conflict and competition. Ultimately, the multiple examples of subaltern public relations depict the principles of resistance through which communities at the margins of the Global South seek to disrupt the asymmetries that are produced by neoliberalism.

Conclusion

In conclusion, in this chapter, I sought to outline the culture-centered approach to public relations by highlighting the important role of subaltern participation in the Global South as an entry point to the activist politics of social change and structural transformation. The CCA is built on deconstructing the fundamental assumptions that run through the mainstream structures of political, economic, social, and cultural organizing globally. Demonstrating the role of knowledge as an instrument of public relations that produces asymmetries globally, the CCA suggests the importance of listening as an entry point to structural transformations. Essential therefore to a politics of social change is the fostering of alternative communicative spaces and communicative rationalities that disrupt the assumptions of the mainstream through practices of relating that are fundamentally resistive in nature. A culture-centered reading of public relations constructs public relations in resistance, in a framework of relating that engages the mainstream through disruptions. Deconstructing the façade of democracy promotion and the underlying agendas of capitalism and imperialist expansion that accompany these democracy promotion initiatives, the CCA seeks to listen to the voices of subaltern sectors in the Global South as avenues for structural transformations. In listening to these subaltern voices, culturally centered public relations workers develop relationships of solidarity with the Global South through which inequitable global policies are challenged. The participation of the subaltern sectors in organizing processes at the global margins disrupts the erasure of subaltern voices through the creation of communicative spaces, rules, and processes that serve as platforms for listening to subaltern voices from the Global South.

References

Bell, B. (2012). Without firing an arm, we created a revolution: Land reform. Truthout. Retrieved from: http://truth-out.org/news/item/8382-without-firing-an-arm-we-created-a-revolution-land-reform (accessed April 14, 2012).

Bush, G. W. (2004). State of the Union Speech. Washington, DC. Retrieved from: http://www.pbs.org/newshour/bb/white_house/jan-june04/sotu_text1_2004.html (accessed April 15, 2012).

De Sousa Santos, B. (2007). *Another knowledge is possible: Beyond Northern epistemologies.* London: Verso.

Dutta, M. (2009). Theorizing resistance: Applying Gayatri Chakravorty Spivak in public relations. In Ø. Ihlen, B. van Ruler, & M. Fredrikson (Eds.), *Social theory on public relations.* New York: Routledge.

Dutta, M. J. (2011). *Communicating social change: Structure, culture, agency.* London: Routledge.

Dutta, M. J. (2012). Critical interrogations of global public relations: Power, culture, agency. In K. Sriramesh (Ed.), *Culture and public relations.* New York: Routledge.

Dutta-Bergman, M. J. (2005a). Civil society and public relations: Not so civil after all. *Journal of Public Relations Research, 17,* 267–289.

Dutta-Bergman, M. (2005b). Theory and practice in health communication campaigns: A critical interrogation. *Health Communication, 18*(2), 103–112.

Grunig, J. E., & Grunig, L. (1997). Review of a program of research on activism: Incidence in four countries, activist publics, strategies of activist groups, and organizational responses to activism. Paper presented at the Fourth Public Relations Research Symposium, Managing Environmental Issues, Lake Bled, Slovenia.

Kim, I. (2008). Voices from the margin: A culture-centered look at public relations of resistance. Unpublished doctoral dissertation. Purdue University, West Lafayette, IN.

Pal, M. (2008). Fighting from and for the margin: Local activism in the realm of global politics. Unpublished doctoral dissertation, Purdue University, West Lafayette, IN.

Pal, M., & Dutta, M. (2008a). Public relations in a global context: The relevance of critical modernism as a theoretical lens. *Journal of Public Relations Research, 20,* 159–179.

Pal, M., & Dutta, M. (2008b). Theorizing resistance in a global context: Processes, strategies and tactics in communication scholarship. *Communication Yearbook, 32,* 41–87.

Shiva, V. (2000). *Stolen harvest: The hijacking of the global food supply.* Cambridge, MA: South End Press.

Sourcewatch. (2012). International Republican Institute. Retrieved from: http://www.sourcewatch.org/index.php?title=International_Republican_Institute#cite_note-1 (accessed April 15, 2012).

United States Agency for International Development (USAID). (2002). *Annual letter.*

13

THE EFFECTS OF ORGANIZATION–PUBLIC RELATIONSHIP TYPES AND QUALITY ON CRISIS ATTRIBUTES

Chun-ju Flora Hung-Baesecke and Yi-Ru Regina Chen

Abstract

Research on organization–public relationships (OPR) has been receiving extensive attention on the research agenda. The aim of this study is to assess the effects of OPR types that Hung developed on attribution of crisis responsibility through the mediation of OPR quality, based on Coombs and Holladay's situational crisis communication theory. Facebook was the studied organization in a survey for this research. Results showed OPR types affect OPR quality. Mutual communal OPRs positively affect all four relational outcomes of OPRs. The significant effects of OPR types and OPR quality on attribution of crisis responsibility to the organization were not found. Theoretical and practical implications are suggested.

Key Words

attribution, crisis responsibility, communal relationship, exchange relationship, type and quality of organization–public relationship, Facebook, social media

Introduction

The research on organization–public relationships (OPR) has been receiving extensive attention on the research agenda. Over the years, the topics surrounding OPR have been extended to measuring quality of relationships (Hon & J. Grunig, 1999; Huang, 2001; Y. Kim, 2001), relationship cultivation and maintenance (Hung, 2004, 2006; Ki & Hon, 2006; Rhee, 2004), its effects on an organization's reputation (Brønn, 2007; J. Grunig & Hung, 2002; Hong & Yang, 2009; Yang, 2007; Yang & J. Grunig, 2005), the exploration of the effects of OPR on publics' attitudes and behavioral intentions toward an organization (Ki & Hon, 2007), the discussion of employee relations (Rhee, 2004; H. Kim, 2007), and manufacturer–retailer relations (Jo, 2006). In addition, studies also further investigated the values of OPR. For example, quality and good relationships enhance organizational reputation (J. Grunig & Hung, 2002; Kim, 2001; Yang, 2007), contain economic values (Kim, 2001), are conducive to an organization's strategic management (Men & Hung, 2009; 2012) and its strategy implementation (Ni, 2006), mediate conflicts between an organization and its publics (Huang, 2001), and help establish a positive and favorable attitude toward an organization (Ki & Hon, 2007).

However, even though much focus has been on the cultivation and maintenance of relationships in achieving quality relationships, little has been explored on how the intention and motivation of an organization in developing relationships with its publics result in the choices of relationship cultivation strategies which lead to different relationship outcomes, and the quality of organizational reputation. Coombs (2000), Kim and Lee (2005) and Park and Reber (2011) contended that a positive organization–public relationship plays a significant role in an organization's reputation during the time of a crisis.

The aim of this study, therefore, is to explore how an organization's relationships with publics prior to a crisis affect the publics' perception in their evaluation on an organization's behaviors in a crisis, and how publics attribute a crisis to an organization. It aims to enrich public relations theory and research in the following ways: first, this study provides more substantive insights into the importance of relationship management prior to crises. J. Grunig (2001) contended that organizations usually can survive better in a time of crisis when they have already established long-term quality relationships with their publics, and when they view the publics' interest at least as important as their own. Yet, there has been little research into this topic. As the intangible values that public relations contributes to an organization are the quality of relationships with publics (Ni, 2009), we believe how an organization intends to cultivate relationships affects the publics' perception of their relationships with the organization, and how much they support an organization in difficult times. Second, this study helps bridge the gap of understanding as to why some organizations have better relationships with publics than others do. Since Hon and J. Grunig (1999) identified trust, control mutuality, relational satisfaction and relational commitment, and communal and exchange relationships as the relationship outcomes, quite a few scholars have adopted these indicators in their studies. However, communal and exchange relationships, the two types of relationships that explain the different degrees of expectations and concern for others in the relationship, may also lead to different levels of the four relational outcomes. Until now, none of the studies has explored this possible factor (i.e., OPR types) that may play a role in the differences in relationship quality. Thus, this study aimed to provide an understanding of how different types of relationships an organization develops result in various relationship outcomes and in the publics' evaluation of an organization's responsibility when it encounters a crisis.

Conceptualization

Organization–Public Relationships

Scholars have provided different definitions of organization–public relationships (OPR) (Broom, Casey, & Ritchey, 2000; Huang, 1998; Hung, 2005; Ledingham & Bruning, 1998). Taking the system theory perspective, Broom, Casey, and Ritchey (2000) defined OPR thus:

> Organization–public relationships are represented by the patterns of interaction, transaction, exchange, and linkage between an organization and its publics. These relationships have properties that are distinct from the identities, attributes, and perceptions of the individuals and social collectivities in the relationships. Though dynamic in nature, relationships can be described at a single point in time and tracked over time.
>
> *(p. 18)*

Huang (2008) contended that OPR could be considered either a subjective reality, objective reality, or a combination of both. As a result, one's perception of his or her relationships will affect how this person perceives some specific incident or event that an organization experiences.

Adopting studies by Clark and Mills (1979, 1993), Hung (2002) explained the nature of organization–public relationships so as to provide perspectives on why some organizations had better relationships than other organizations.

Types of Relationships

Hon and J. Grunig (1999) posited that, in an *exchange* relationship, each party gives benefits to the other only if the other has provided benefits in the past or will do so in future; while in a *communal* relationship, both parties provide benefits not for something in return but for the welfare of the other. Yet, the dynamics of OPR should not be only identified by these two types of relationships. As a result, in reviewing research done on OPR, we would like to adopt Hung's typology of OPR (2002, 2005).

Hung (2002, 2005) expanded these two types of relationships and identified an additional six types of organization–public relationships: (1) exploitive relationships; (2) manipulative relationships; (3) symbiotic relationships; (4) contractual relationships; (5) covenantal relationships; and (6) mutual communal relationships (for details, see Hung, 2005). These eight types of relationships were therefore developed along a continuum, with one end of the continuum highlighting "concern for self-interest" and the other highlighting "concern for others" (Hung, 2005, p. 416).

- *Exploitive relationships.* In this type of relationship, one party takes advantage of the other without considering the other party's interests or benefits or one party violates the norm of exchanging benefits with the other party (Clark & Mills, 1993; Hung, 2002).
- *Manipulative relationships.* According to Hung (2005), a manipulative relationship arises when an organization knows what the publics want, and still applies "pseudo-symmetrical approaches to communicate with publics to serve its own interest" (Hung, 2005, p. 408).
- *Symbiotic relationships.* In symbiotic relationships, different parties rely on each other for their common interests of surviving or goal attainment in the business environment. In Hung's (2005) study, a symbiotic relationship happens when different departments of an organization interact just for job requirements, without any specific consideration about exchanging or attaining each other's interests or benefits.
- *Contractual relationships.* In developing a relationship between an organization and its publics, both parties agree on what they should do in the relationships, such as making a contract. Yet, as Hung (2005) pointed out, contractual relationships cannot guarantee equal relationships as there are power imbalances in the process of negotiation of the obligations of both sides.
- *Covenantal relationships.* Besides exchange relationships, this is considered one type of OPR in the "win–win zone" in the continuum of OPR as both parties "commit to a common good by their open exchanges and the norm of reciprocity" (Hung, 2005, p. 398). This type of relationship can be developed when both the organization and its publics provide suggestions, criticisms, and insights while at the same time they also listen and provide responses to the other side (Hung, 2005).
- *Mutual communal relationships.* Mutual communal relationships are developed when both the organization and its publics expect the relationship to be communal and both parties show concern for the welfare of the other. This type of relationship can be achieved through cultivating the relationship over a period of time while both parties interact and understand each other more. Mutual communal relationships are also another type of relationship in the "win–win zone" in the continuum of OPR.

Relationship management is an ongoing dynamic process passing through the stages of antecedents, relationship cultivation and relationship outcomes. However, these three stages of relationship management are not separate, but connect and interplay with each other. The relationship types and outcomes that an organization intends to achieve decide the choice of relationship cultivation strategies; and the choice of relationship cultivation strategies in turn decides the quality of relationship and types of relationship. This entire process of relationship management is like a continuous developing loop. If constant efforts are made by organizations, the consequences of relationship management are long-term, quality relationships which can contribute to both the bottom line (L. A. Grunig, J. E., Grunig, & Dozier, 2002) and intangible benefits, such as reputation (e.g., J. E. Grunig & Hung, 2002; Yang & J. Grunig, 2005), and customer loyalty and satisfaction (Ledingham, 2003).

Men (2012) further built on the continuum of OPR types developed by Hung (2005) from the resource-based view. Her research indicated that exploitive, manipulative, and one-sided communal relationships are considered not feasible in corporations' business operations nowadays. The win–win zone (exchange, covenantal, and mutual communal relationships), as Hung (2005) identified in the continuum of types of OPR, is regarded as a strategic resource, conducive for a corporation to maintain or help it to attain its competitive advantage (Men, 2012).

In summary, with the type of OPR that an organization develops with its publics, it lays the foundation for whether an organization will receive the publics' support or trust during a crisis. Quality and win–win relationships are valuable resources for an organization that keeps the publics' interests in mind in the process of developing corporate competitive strategies. Thus, the publics, in return, will help an organization through a time of crisis.

Relationship Quality/Outcomes

Many studies have aimed to conceptualize or develop scales for evaluating or measuring the quality of relationships between an organization and its publics (Yang, 2007). Ferguson (1984) suggested the dimensions of dynamic vs. static, open vs. closed, mutual satisfaction, distribution of power, mutual understanding, and mutual agreement. Huang (1997), in adopting the interpersonal communication theory, proposed trust, control mutuality, commitment, and satisfaction as relationship outcomes. She later integrated the cultural elements of face and favor with the other four indicators in evaluating OPR outcomes (Huang, 2001). Ledingham and Bruning (1998) considered the relational outcomes as openness, trust, involvement, investment, and commitment. Hon and J. Grunig (1999) adopted Huang's (1997) relationship outcomes of trust, commitment, satisfaction, and control mutuality and developed two more indicators of communal and exchange relationships. Y. Kim (2001) identified trust, commitment, local and community involvement, and reputation as the indicators in evaluating relationship outcomes. Jo (2006) also included cultural context and developed the evaluation indicators of trust, control mutuality, commitment, satisfaction, face and favor, and personal networks. Among all these scholars' works, the indicators of relationship outcomes proposed by Hon and J. Grunig (1999) have been widely adopted in various studies (e.g., Brunner, 2000; Hon & Brunner, 2002; Hung, 2002, 2006; Ki & Hon, 2007; Ni, 2009). Extensive research has reported different findings on relationship outcome indicators. For example, Ki and Hon (2007) identified that the publics' perception of satisfaction has the strongest influence on the publics' support for an organization. Arnett, German, and Hunt (2003) confirmed that satisfaction significantly contributed to the public's identification with an organization in an exchange relationship context and proposed the following hypotheses (H1–H4):

H1 The types of OPRs in the win–win zone of the OPR continuum (exchange relationships, covenantal relationships, and mutual communal relationships) positively affect the public's perceived trust in an organization.

H2 The types of OPRs in the win–win zone of the OPR continuum (exchange relationships, covenantal relationships, and mutual communal relationships) positively affect the public's perceived commitment to an organization.

H3 The types of OPRs in the win–win zone of the OPR continuum (exchange relationships, covenantal relationships, and mutual communal relationships) positively affect the public's perceived control mutuality with the organization.

H4 The types of OPRs in the win–win zone of the OPR continuum (exchange relationships, covenantal relationships, and mutual communal relationships) positively affect the public's perceived satisfaction with an organization.

Attribution Theory and Crisis Management

Weiner's (1986) causal attribution theory provides a solid theoretical framework for developing effective crisis management for two reasons. First, people tend to engage in causal attribution processing when a negative, unexpected, or crucial event (such as a crisis) occurs in order to interpret the event and react to it (Weiner, 1986). Furthermore, people go through a common attribution process when making causal attribution to interpersonal events and organizational events (Moussavi & Evans, 1993). They ask "why the actor does this" as the basis for interpersonal attribution, while asking "who does this?" for organizational attribution (p. 83). Second, the purpose of crisis management is to minimize the negative impact of a crisis on the organization by responding to the crisis in the way that best meets the public's expectations. Attribution theory explains how people interpret the crisis and perceive the organization. This enhances the crisis manager's ability to predict people's expectations to organizational responses.

Adapting Weiner's (1986) attribution theory with empirical support, a model of situational crisis communication theory (SCCT) proposed by Coombs and Holladay (2002) has been widely employed in public relations research to investigate how a crisis can be effectively managed by selecting matched crisis communication strategies according to three factors: (1) people's interpretation of the crisis; (2) the crisis type; and (3) organizational performance (i.e., relationship history and the past crisis record). Most research results support the model's assumptions, positing that with more attribution of crisis responsibility to the organization (mediated by crisis types and organizational performance), more accommodative crisis strategies should be used to better manage the crisis, and the organization will be perceived more negatively during and after the crisis. Later, Jin, Pang and Cameron (2007) advocated exploring the effects of emotions to better understand how people evaluate crisis situations (causal attribution) so as to modify the selection of crisis response strategies.

OPR Effects on Crisis Management

Based on the relationship approach of public relations, OPRs are invaluable assets of an organization in various regards. Quality OPRs can foster support from the stakeholders to help achieve organizational goals during the good times and serve as a cushion to reduce negative impact on an organization in bad times. Following this rationale, public relations scholars have attempted to link relationship management and crisis management by examining the effects of OPRs on: (1) perception of the crisis (i.e., severity and responsibility); (2) perception of the crisis response strategies; (3) perception of the post-crisis OPR quality; and (4) the attitude of the organization involved. Marra (1998) argued for the importance of pre-crisis OPRs to the success of crisis communication and reduction of financial, emotional, and perceptual damage. Ulmer (2001) and Fearn-Banks (2002) further advocated that organizations should maintain quality OPRs throughout the crisis management process (i.e., pre-, current-, and post-crisis) by communicating with strategic publics in order to minimize the negative impact of the crisis. Past studies provide empirical evidence to support the above assertions. For example, the public in a favorable OPR was found to perceive less uncertainty associated with the crisis and have more potential supportive behavior than those in an unfavorable OPR (Kang, Garciaruano, & Lin, 2008; Ni, 2006; Ulmer, 2001). Unfavorable OPRs intensified attribution of crisis responsibility to the organization and damaged its reputation (Coombs & Holladay, 2001, 2002). In addition, the effects of OPR quality (favorable versus unfavorable) on crisis attribution differed from those of crisis history on the attribution even though the two constructs both represent an organization's performance history. Kim and Lee (2005) identified the positive effect of OPR quality on crisis perception with two components: crisis severity and crisis responsibility. A similar OPR effect on attributed crisis responsibility was found in Chen's (2009) study on web-users' responses to a well-known milk powder contamination case in Taiwan in 2008 and in Brown and White's (2010) study on students' responses to a university financial crisis scenario. However, Park and Reber's (2011) study did not support the previous results. Instead, they identified a link between OPR quality and attitude to the involved organization, which is in accordance with Ki and Hon's (2007) model.

The literature on OPR effects on perception of crisis response strategies and their effectiveness shows mixed results. Consistent with the findings of Coombs and Holladay (2004), Kim and Lee (2005) revealed that OPR quality contributes to trusting and acceptable responses to Benoit's (1995, 1997) image restoration strategies used during crises. Lee (2007) found no evidence supporting the effect of OPRs on attitude toward image restoration strategies selected based on the perceived OPR quality. Brown and White's (2010) findings showed that OPR quality significantly affected the effectiveness of three crisis response strategies on attribution of crisis responsibility: scapegoating, justification, and apology. However, crisis response strategies made no difference to the attribution of crisis responsibility among people in OPRs with same or similar quality. In other words, when an organization has unfavorable relationships with its key publics, crisis responsibility attributed to the organization would be the same regardless of the response strategy used. These mixed findings suggest that for organizations, pre-crisis OPRs are more essential to successful crisis management than any particular crisis response strategy.

As OPR quality has been commonly measured by the public's overall evaluation of the relationship (i.e., favorable versus unfavorable), when assessing its impact on crisis perception, scholars usually investigate the factors affecting post-crisis OPR quality by looking at the impact of factors on each indicator of OPR quality (i.e., relational outcomes). With empirical support, three factors have been identified: attribution of crisis responsibility, crisis response strategies, and pre-crisis OPR quality. Lee (2005, 2007) discovered the main positive effect of crisis attribution (i.e., causality) and crisis response ("no comment" strategy) perceived by consumers in Hong Kong on organizational trust after a crisis that positively affected their intention to purchase the organization's products. Huang (2008) revealed that concession-oriented crisis communication, mediated by crisis response forms, is a stronger predictor than crisis types and organization association for both trust in and commitment with the organization after a crisis. Roberts (2009) concluded that relationship history significantly affected all the dimensions of the OPR quality and corporate credibility after a crisis.

The above review indicates two gaps in crisis communication literature. First, little research has examined the effects of specific OPR types or of OPR quality (i.e., trust, satisfaction, commitment, and control mutuality) on perception of crises and of response strategies. Second, most research used experiments and did not test the actual OPRs between participants and an organization. As a result, this study investigated the effects of OPR types and quality on attribution of crisis responsibility. The final hypothesis (H5) and the research question (RQ) are as follows:

H5 OPR quality (i.e., all of the relational outcomes) negatively affects the public's crisis attribution to an organization.

RQ What is the relationship among OPR types, OPR quality, and attribution of responsibility in a crisis situation?

Method

Participants and Procedure

A quantitative survey was conducted with users of Facebook living in Hong Kong. Facebook was chosen for this study because of its strong visibility and huge user base in the community after only four years of existence. This study recruited participants by asking faculty for access to students in their classrooms at a university and by inviting active users on Facebook. The participants were purposely selected because, different from several studies that manipulated relationship and/or crisis status (Coombs & Holladay, 1996, 2001), this study measured actual types and quality of OPRs between Facebook and its users. Facebook is a social media site widely used among university students and local members who wish to connect their lives with their relatives and friends.

In total, 161 participants completed the study in March 2012 via online or paper questionnaires. Six cases were deleted from the dataset due to missing answers and a further four were removed as outliers based on the mahalanobis distance. Among the 151 participants, 75.5% (n = 114) of the participants were women and 24.5% (n = 37) men. About 72.8% (n = 110) of the participants were students. Participants aged 18–20 years old accounted for 31.8% (n = 48), 21–30 years old = 48.3% (n = 73), 31–40 years old = 13.9% (n = 21), and above 40 years old = 6% (n = 9). Participants were all Chinese with 101 (66.9%) from Hong Kong, 36 (23.8%) from Mainland China, 10 from Taiwan (6.6%), two from Singapore (1.3%), and two from Malaysia (1.3%). About 68.2% of the participants had a bachelor's degree (n = 103), followed by 13.9% with a master's degree (n = 21), 9.9% (n = 15) with college degrees or below, and 7.9% (n = 12) with a doctoral degree. Most participants used Facebook every day (n = 112; 74.2%) and their history of using Facebook was as follows: 3–5 years 38.4% (n = 58), 1–3 years 29.8% (n = 45), 5–8 years 17.9% (n = 27), less than one year 10.6% (n = 16), and more than eight years 3.3% (n = 5).

Measurements

The measurement items were mostly adopted from previous research (Hon & Grunig, 1999; Hung & Chen, 2009; McAuley, Duncan, & Russell, 1992; Yang & Grunig, 2005). The questionnaire used in this study contained four sections of questions. The first two sections measured participants' perceived relationship type with Facebook followed by their perceived quality of the relationship. In section three, participants received a fictitious news story about a Facebook crisis[1] including the scapegoating crisis response strategy of SCCT used by the company (see Appendix) and answered questions measuring their attribution of crisis responsibility after reading the article. The last section asked about participants' demographics. All measurements (except for the last part of the survey) used a

7-point Likert-type scale, with 1 indicating the lowest amount of the variable property (i.e., strongly disagree) and 7 indicating the highest amount (i.e., strongly agree). An initial exploratory factor analysis was performed on the items of each measure and those that poorly loaded on the factor were omitted. The effectiveness of the manipulation (news story on a human error crisis with a scapegoating strategy) was checked by a 1-item question, stating "Facebook's spokesperson blamed an employee, Steve Showen, for causing the problem." The reported mean score of this question was 6.2 (SD = 1.36).

1. *Instruments for independent variables.* Independent variables included five types of OPRs, out of the eight, that could possibly be formed between Facebook and its users. Items of exchange and communal OPRs were adapted from Hon and J. Grunig (1999), while items of symbiotic, covenantal, and mutual communal relationships were from Hung and Chen's (2009) study. The internal reliability tests yield .63 (Cronbach's alpha) for mutual communal OPRs, .78 for covenantal OPRs, .76 for communal OPRs, .61 for symbiotic OPRs and .62 for exchange OPRs.

2. *Instruments for mediators.* In this study, we treated communal and exchange OPRs as OPR types. Thus, OPR quality was assessed by the four relational outcomes—trust, relational satisfaction, relational commitment, and control mutuality—by using Hon and J. Grunig's (1999) measures. Cronbach's alphas were .76 (trust), .79 (satisfaction) .73 (commitment), and .68 (control mutuality).

3. *Instrument for the dependent variable.* Attribution of crisis responsibility to the organization was the dependent variable of this study by employing McAuley et al.'s (1992) scale with a Cronbach's alpha at .62.

Results

The effects of OPR types on attribution of crisis responsibility were fully or partially mediated, if at all, by OPR quality. LISEL 8.80 was used to develop a structural equation model (SEM) by analyzing covariances of latent variables and measured variables (Bentler, 1997; Müller, 1996; Yang, 2007). An SEM model (see Figure 13.1) was converged and tested for its data–model fit. Scholars are in the process of searching for the best assessment of data–model fit in a structural equation model (Loehlin, 1992). Due to the small size of the sample and the complexity of models, the goodness-of-fit indices used in this study were: (1) χ^2/df < 3; (2) RMSEA ≤ .06 and SRMR ≤ .10 (Hu & Bentler, 1999); and (3) CFI ≥ .90 instead of χ^2 (Kline, 2005; Ni & Wang, 2009; Yang & Grunig, 2005). According to the above criteria, the model fit the data acceptably (χ^2/df = 1.75, RMSEA = .06, SRMR = .10, CFI = .84).

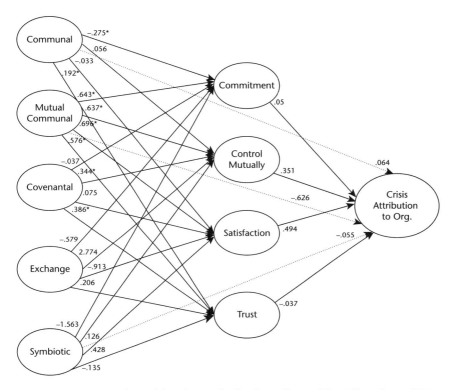

FIGURE 13.1 Structural Model with Standardized Loadings of the Effects from OPR Types on Quality of OPRs, and Their Effects on Attribution of Crisis Responsibility. The solid lines and dotted lines represent the mediation effects and the direct effects respectively.

$\star\ p < 0.5$

RQ: Relationships among OPR Types, OPR Quality, and Attribution of Crisis Responsibility

To answer the proposed research question, the SEM model showed that three out of the five OPR types and all four OPR quality dimensions have direct and indirect effects on the attribution of crisis responsibility to the organization even though the effects are weak. The model also revealed positive but weak effects of commitment, control mutuality, and satisfaction on the internal crisis attribution along with the negative effect of trust. Thus, H5 was not supported.

The model indicated that three OPR types significantly affect the quality of OPRs. Trust was positively affected by communal, covenantal, and mutual communal OPRs whereas commitment was positively affected by mutual communal OPRs, and negatively by communal OPRs. Control mutuality was positively influenced by covenantal and mutual communal OPRs whereas satisfaction was positively associated with mutual communal OPRs.

H1–H4, positing that OPRs in the win–win zone (i.e., mutual communal, exchange and covenantal) positively affect OPR quality, were partially supported according to the model. Mutual communal OPRs, as the most salient type, had significant positive effects on all four indicators of OPR quality. Exchange OPRs were the only win–win OPR type that did not have any significant contribution to OPR quality while communal OPRs contributed to trust.

Discussion

Effect of OPR Types

This study extends the relationship management research in the crisis context by empirically testing the effect of OPR types and OPR quality dimensions on crisis perception. Results better refine the understanding of OPRs and relationship management that provides insights for how OPRs act in crisis management. Several findings are worth discussing. First, mutual communal OPRs were found to significantly contribute to OPR quality and different OPR types affected a single OPR quality differently. Even though Hon and Grunig's (1999) study provided a possible implication on how the two types of relationships (i.e., exchange and communal) would produce different degrees of relational quality, studies thus far have not yet focused on this enquiry. The findings provide the theoretical implications that there do exist other OPR types—e.g., mutual communal OPRs—conducive to quality relationships. In addition, more studies are needed to fully identify how OPR types affect relational quality. Second, OPRs in the win–win zone did not necessarily have significant positive effects on OPR quality. The finding that exchange OPRs had no effects on OPR quality might be because the people in OPRs only fulfill the most basic need of relationship formation: to give and take. Relational quality can only be improved by fulfilling higher-level psychological needs, such as caring (Teven & Hanson, 2004). The finding that covenantal relationships were positively associated with control mutuality and trust reflects one of the current trends, public engagement, in public relations research and practices (e.g., Edelman Trust Barometer, 2009; Kang, 2012). The essence of a covenantal relationship is to encourage both organizations and publics engaging in discussions and communication to agree on what behaviors would benefit both sides. Engaging publics requires continuous listening and communication. In this approach, publics will think that organizations not only take publics' interests into the decision-making process, but also provide opportunities to raise concerns and questions.

Third, one type of OPR did not affect the four OPR quality indicators in the same direction. Communal relationships were negatively associated with commitment but positively associated with trust. This means, even when an organization strives to do whatever it can for the public without expecting the public to do anything in return, the public would not consider this act worthy of spending time and effort to maintain the relationship with the organization. In Hung's (2005) and Men's (2012) research findings, companies being interviewed also expressed their reluctance to develop communal relationships with the public as these companies did not consider communal relationships to be feasible in the business environment. However, even though participants probably would be unlikely to be committed to their relationships with a company applying the communal norm, they still think it is a company that they would trust inasmuch as the public's interests and benefits are likely to be protected by this company.

No Significant Effects on Crisis Attribution

No significant effects of OPR types or OPR quality on crisis attribution were found, as the model shows. The finding is consistent with Park and Reber's (2011) study. There are two possible explanations for this. First, Facebook users do not really consider they have formed a "relationship" with Facebook. Due to the nature and function of Facebook, even though most of the participants in this study use Facebook every day, there are no interactions between Facebook and its users. Thus, they might view Facebook as the tool for communication but not as an entity they need or can establish a relationship with. Second, users enjoy free services by Facebook; hence, the users might ask for little responsibility or low expectations toward Facebook.

Practical Implications

Based on the results, we suggest the following for public relations practitioners or crisis managers. First, to maximize the value of OPRs, it is beneficial for organizations to take the initiative to build OPRs with their key publics when they are not traditionally identified as an entity people can have relationships with. Second, following the above rationale, public relations managers should aim to establish mutual communal OPRs with their organizations' stakeholders before a crisis occurs to increase the quality of their OPRs. The type of OPR can be built by first engaging publics in dialogs and activities that convey the organization's concerns for the publics, and then empowering publics in the decision-making process to facilitate their concerns for the organization. Crowdsourcing is a technique widely used by companies to engage stakeholder in the decision-making in a win–win manner. Third, when a mutual communal approach is not feasible for an organization for any reason, public relations practitioners should first audit the organization's OPR quality and select the matched OPR type to cultivate with the stakeholders.

Limitations and Future Research Directions

This study has several limitations. First, it had a relatively small sample size due to the difficulty in recruiting. The SEM model was the first attempt to explore the relationship among pre-crisis OPR types, OPR quality dimensions, and crisis perception. Future research with a larger sample size should refine the model to further build the role of OPR types in crisis management. In addition, future research can test the effects of OPR types on OPR quality in the model by surveying various stakeholders (e.g., employees or the government) of Facebook. Second, it was limited to one type of crisis involving one organization. Although the one-crisis focus provided a better understanding of how OPR types and quality affect people's responses in that crisis situation, the possible response difference among crisis types and OPR types across organizations could not be examined. We propose future research to replicate the study to examine OPRs in crisis management for other crisis types or other organizations with which people tend to form other types of OPRs, such as NGOs or governments. Third, it used online questionnaires. Even though, based on the nature of the study's participants, an online medium should be their favorite platform to use when filling out a questionnaire, use of this medium might lower the generalizability of results due to difficulty in identifying repeated responses and inconsistent rigidity among participants in doing the online survey. Results should be validated by being compared with the data of future research through other collection methods.

Appendix

Crisis Manipulation: A Crisis with a Scapegoating Response Strategy

Facebook technician makes US$ 44M selling Hong Kong users' personal data.

2012-03-02 HKT 06:29

Reuters. Facebook today confirmed a previous CNN report that one of its technicians has sold Hong Kong users' personal data to several companies, supposedly the purposes of targeted advertisements. Facebook revealed Senior Technician Steve Showen to be the man responsible for the incident with internal investigations showing that he had sold 2 million user records to eight companies between 2008 and 2010, getting paid a total of US$ 44 million. The data sold include user names, gender, dates of birth, and email addresses. In addition, a list of the names of merchant web sites that users visited, as well as the times of their visit was also sold. Most importantly, some posts made by Hong Kong celebrities were sold to two weekly magazines, which were then circulated online.

A Facebook spokesperson said:

> Facebook is deeply saddened by the behavior of Steve Showen, who has trampled upon the core beliefs of what we are all about. We have terminated his employment contract and have already initiated legal actions against him. Our own investigation has confirmed that Showen acted alone. Facebook

has stepped up the access security of our storage system, which keeps our users' personal information. We are also reviewing operating procedures for our employees. Our staff handbook now has more stringent guidelines to prevent similar incidents from happening. Facebook has always been committed to ensuring the privacy of its users. We stand for providing a convenient platform for global users to maintain contact and share every moment of their lives with their friends.

Statistics show that 53 per cent of Hong Kong people are users of Facebook, which is currently the most frequently used social networking site in the city. It is also one of the websites to hold large amounts of personal information. It is difficult to assess just how much aggravation and inconvenience this incident has caused Facebook users. The scale of this incident is said to be comparable to the 2010 incident involving the operator of the "Octopus" cash card system.

Note

1   The Facebook crisis story provided to participants in this study was a fabricated one and participants were informed of this after completing the survey.

References

Arnett, D. B., German, S. D., & Hunt, S. D. (2003). The identity salience model of relationship marketing success: The case of nonprofit marketing. *Journal of Marketing, 68,* 89–105.

Benoit, W. (1995). *Accounts, excuses and apologies: A theory of image restoration strategies.* Albany: State University of New York Press.

Benoit, W. (1997). Image repair discourse and crisis communication. *Public Relations Review, 23,* 177–180.

Bentler, P. M. (1997). *EQS: Structural equations program manual.* Encino, CA: Multivariate Software.

Brønn, P. S. (2007). Relationship outcomes as determinants of reputation. *Corporate Communication: An International Journal, 12*(4), 376–393.

Broom, G. M., Casey, S., & Ritchey, J. (2000). Concept and theory of organization–public relationships: An update. In J. A. Ledingham & S. D. Bruning (Eds.), *Public relations as relationship management: A relational approach to the study and practice of public relations* (pp. 3–22). Mahwah, NJ: Lawrence Erlbaum Associates.

Brown, K. A., & White, C. L. (2010). Organization–public relationships and crisis response strategies: Impact on attribution of responsibility. *Journal of Public Relations Research, 23,* 75–92.

Brunner, G. (2000). Measuring students' perceptions of the University of Florida's commitment to public relationships and diversity. Unpublished doctoral dissertation. Gainesville, FL.

Chen, Y. T. (2009). The influence of web site performance on needs for crisis communication in the case of toxic milk powder: The mediation effect of organization–public relationship. Unpublished master's thesis, Shih Hsin University, Taipei, Taiwan.

Clark, M., & Mills, J. (1979). Interpersonal attraction in exchange and communal relationships. *Journal of Personality and Social Psychology, 37,* 12–24.

Clark, M. S., & Mills, J. (1993). The difference between communal and exchange relationships: What it is and is not. *Personality and Social Psychology Bulletin, 19,* 684–691.

Coombs, T. (2000). Crisis management: Advantages of a relational perspective. In J. A. Ledingham & S. D. Bruning (Eds.), *Public relations as relationship management* (pp. 73–93). Mahwah, NJ: Lawrence Erlbaum Associates.

Coombs, W. T., & Holladay, S. J. (1996). Communication and attributions in a crisis: An experimental study in crisis communication. *Journal of Public Relations Research, 8,* 279–295.

Coombs, W. T., & Holladay, S. J. (2001). An extended examination of the crisis situation: A fusion of the relational management and symbolic approaches. *Journal of Public Relations Research, 13*(4), 321–340.

Coombs, W. T., & Holladay, S. J. (2002). Helping crisis managers protect reputational assets: Initial tests of the situational crisis communication theory. *Management Communication Quarterly, 16,* 165–186.

Coombs, W. T., & Holladay, S. J. (2004). Reasoned action in crisis communication: An attribution theory-based approach to crisis management. In D. P. Miller & R. L. Heath (Eds.), *Responding to crisis: A rhetorical approach to crisis communication* (pp. 95–115). Mahwah, NJ: Lawrence Erlbaum Associates.

Edelman Trust Barometer (2009). Retrieved from: http://edelmaneditions.com/wp-content/uploads/2010/11/edelman-trust-barometer-full-report-2009.pdf.

Fearn-Banks, K. (2002). *Crisis communications: A casebook approach* (2nd ed.). Mahwah, NJ: Lawrence Erlbaum Associates.

Ferguson, P. (1984, August). Building theory in public relations: Interorganizational relationships as a public relations paradigm. Paper presented to the Association for Education in Journalism and Mass Communication, Gainesville, FL.

Grunig, J. E. (2001). The role of public relations in management and its contribution to organizational and societal effectiveness. Speech delivered in Taipei, May 12.

Grunig, J. E., & Hung, C. J. F. (2002, March). The effect of relationships on reputation and relationships on reputation: A cognitive, behavioral study. Paper presented at the Conference of Public Relations Society of America, Educator's Academy, Miami, FL.

Grunig, L. A., Grunig, J. E., & Dozier, D. (2002). *Excellent public relations and effective organizations: A study of communication management in three countries.* Mahwah, NJ: Lawrence Erlbaum Associates.

Hon, L., & Brunner, B. R. (2002). Measuring public relationships among students and administrators at the University of Florida. *Journal of Communication Management, 6*(3), 227–238.

Hon, L., & Grunig, J. E. (1999). *Guidelines for measuring relationships in public relations.* Singapore: The Institute for Public Relations.

Hong, S. Y., & Yang, S. U. (2009). Effects of reputation, relational satisfaction, and consumer–company identification on positive word-of-mouth intentions. *Journal of Public Relations Research, 21*(4), 381–403.

Hu, L., & Bentler, P. M. (1999). Cutoff criteria for its indices in covariance structure modeling: Sensitivity to underparameterized model misspecification. *Psychological Methods, 3,* 424–453.

Huang, Y. H. (1997). Public relations strategies, relational outcomes, and conflict management strategies. Unpublished doctoral dissertation, University of Maryland, College Park.

Huang, Y. H. (1998, August). Public relations strategies and organization–public relationships. Paper presented at the annual conference of the Association for Education in Journalism and Mass Communication, Baltimore, MD.

Huang, Y. H. (2001). OPRA: A cross-cultural, multiple-item scale for measuring organization–public relationships. *Journal of Public Relations Research, 13,* 61–90.

Huang, Y. H. (2008). Trust and relational commitment in corporate crises: The effects of crisis communicative strategy and form of crisis response. *Journal of Public Relations Research, 20,* 297–327.

Hung, C. J. F. (2002). The interplays of relationship types, relationship cultivation, and relationship outcomes: How multinational and Taiwanese companies practice public relations and organization–public relationship management in China. Unpublished doctoral dissertation, University of Maryland, College Park.

Hung, C. J. F. (2004). Cultural influence on relationship cultivation strategies: Multinational companies in China. *Journal of Communication Management, 8*(3), 264–281.

Hung, C. J. F. (2005). Exploring types of organization–public relationships and their implications on relationship management in public relations. *Journal of Public Relations Research, 17*(4), 393–426.

Hung, C. J. F. (2006). Towards the theory of relationship management: How to cultivate quality relationships? In E. L. Toth (Ed.), *The future of excellence in public relations and communication management: Challenges to the next generation.* (pp. 443–476). Mahwah, NJ: Lawrence Erlbaum Associates.

Hung, C. J. F., & Chen, Y. R. (2009). Types and dimensions of organization–public relationships in greater China. *Public Relations Review, 35,* 181–186.

Jin, Y., Pang, A., & Cameron, G. T. (2007). Integrated crisis mapping: Towards a publics-based, emotion-driven conceptualization in crisis communication. *Sphera Publica, 7,* 81–96.

Jo, S. (2006). Measurement of organization–public relationships and their implications for relationship management in public relations. *Journal of Public Relations Research, 17*(3), 225–248.

Kang, H., Garciaruano, K. J., & Lin, Y. H. (2008, March). Factors affecting E-mail rumor belief and activity: The effects of type of rumor and organization–public relationships. Paper presented to the 11th Annual International Public Relations Research Conference, Miami, FL.

Kang, M. (2012, March). Understanding public engagement: Conceptualization and measurement. Paper presented to the 15th Annual International Public Relations Research Conference, Miami, FL.

Ki, E.-J., & Hon, L. C. (2006). Relationship maintenance strategies on Fortune 500 company web sites. *Journal of Communication Management, 10*(2), 27–43.

Ki, E.-J., & Hon, L. C. (2007, May). Reliable and valid relationship maintenance strategies measurement. Paper presented at the 2005 Annual Conference of the International Communication Association, San Francisco.

Kim, H. (2007). A multilevel study of antecedents and a mediator of employee–organization relationships. *Journal of Public Relations Research, 19*(2), 167–197.

Kim, Y. (2001). Searching for the organization–public relationship: A valid and reliable instrument. *Journalism and Mass Communication Quarterly, 78*(4), 799–810.

Kim, Y., & Lee, E. (2005, May). The impact of the organization–public relationship on perceptions toward the crisis and image restoration strategies. Paper presented at the annual meeting of the International Communication Association, New York.

Kline, R. B. (2005). *Principles and practices of structural equation modeling* (2nd ed.). New York: Guilford.

Ledingham, J. A. (2003). Explicating relationship management as a general theory of public relations. *Journal of Public Relations Research, 15*, 181–198.

Ledingham, J. A., & Brunig, S. D. (1998). Relationship management and public relations: Dimensions of an organization–public relationship. *Public Relations Review, 24*(1), 55–65.

Lee, B. K. (2004). Crisis audience-oriented approach to crisis communication: A study of Hong Kong consumers' evaluation of an organizational crisis. *Communication Research, 31*, 600–618.

Lee, B. K. (2005). Hong Kong consumers' evaluation in an airline crash: A path model analysis. *Journal of Public Relations Research, 17*, 363–391.

Lee, E. (2007, May). Organization–public relationships and crisis communication. Paper presented at the annual meeting of the International Communication Association, San Francisco.

Loehlin, J. C. (1992). *Latent variable models: An introduction to factor, path, and structural analysis* (2nd ed.). Hillsdale, NJ: Lawrence Erlbaum Associates.

Marra, F. (1998). Crisis communication plans: Poor predictors of excellent crisis public relations. *Public Relations Review, 24*, 461–474.

McAuley, E., Duncan, T., & Russell, D. (1992). Measuring causal attributions: The revised causal dimension scale (CDII). *Personality and Social Psychology Bulletin, 18*, 566–573.

Men, L. J. R. (2012). Revisiting the continuum of types of organization–public relationships: From a resource-based view. *Public Relations Journal, 6*(1).

Men, L. J. R., & Hung, C. J. F. (2009, August). Exploring the value of organization-public relationships in strategic management: A resource-based view. Paper presented at the Public Relations Division of the Annual Convention of Association for Education in Journalism and Mass Communication, Boston, MA.

Men, L. J. R., & Hung, C. J. F. (2012). Exploring the roles of organization–public relationships in the strategic management process: Towards an integrated framework. *International Journal of Strategic Communication, 6*, 151–173.

Moussavi, F., & Evans, D. A. (1993). Emergence of organizational attributions: The role of a shared cognitive schema. *Journal of Management, 19*, 79–95.

Müller, R. O. (1996). *Basic principles of structural equation modeling: An introduction to LISREL and EQS*. New York: Springer.

Ni, L. (2006). Relationships as organizational resources: Examining public relations impact through its connection with organizational strategies. *Public Relations Review, 32*, 276–281.

Ni, L. (2009). Strategic role of relationship building: Perceived links between employee–organization relationships and globalization strategies. *Journal of Public Relations Research, 21*, 100–120.

Ni, L., & Wang, Q. (2009). Anxiety and uncertainty management in an intercultural setting: The impact on organization–public relationships. *Journal of Public Relations Research, 23*(3), 269–301.

Park, H., & Reber, B. H. (2011). The organization–public relationship and crisis communication: The effect of the organization–public relationship on public's perceptions of crisis and attitudes toward the organization. *International Journal of Strategic Communication, 5*, 240–260.

Rhee, Y. (2004). The employee–public–organization chair in relationship management: A case study of a government organization. Unpublished doctoral dissertation, University of Maryland, College Park.

Roberts, C. (2009). An experimental investigation into the effect of crisis response strategies and relationship history on relationship quality and corporate credibility. Unpublished master's thesis, University of South Florida.

Teven, J. J., & Hanson, T. L. (2004). The impact of teacher immediacy and perceived caring on teacher competence and trustworthiness. *Communication Quarterly, 5,* 39–53.

Ulmer, R. (2001). Effective crisis management through established stakeholder relationships. *Management Communication Quarterly, 14,* 590–615.

Weiner, B. (1986). *An attributional theory of motivation and emotion.* New York: Springer-Verlag.

Yang, S. U. (2007). An integrated model for organization–public relational outcomes, organizational reputation, and their antecedents. *Journal of Public Relations Research, 19,* 91–121.

Yang, S. U., & Grunig, J. E. (2005). Decomposing organizational reputation: The effects of organization–public relationship outcomes on cognitive representations of organizations and evaluations of organizational performance. *Journal of Communication Management, 9,* 305–325.

14

PUBLIC RELATIONS HISTORIOGRAPHY

Perspectives of a Functional-Integrative Stratification Model

Günter Bentele

Abstract

The chapter discusses some problems of public relations historiography: the beginning of public relations, the social, organizational and other criteria related to this beginning and the subsequent development of public relations. This is still a matter of considerable debate and different logics and approaches exist concerning these problems. Relating to these problems, two different types of public relations historiography may be distinguished: the fact- and event-based approach and the model and theory-based approach. A functional-integrative stratification model is developed. Stratification models are well known in biology, psychology and geography, but until now they have been unknown in communication and public relations research.

Key words

communication, functional-integrative historiography, profession, public relations, stratification model

Introduction

This chapter discusses some important problems of public relations historiography, i.e., the way(s) in which PR history is written. While public relations research focusing on excellent communication management (J. E. Grunig & L. A. Grunig, 2008) is growing internationally, it is more important than ever to understand the roots of the field and its basic concepts, as well as its cultural and historical boundaries. The chapter argues from a European, especially from a German perspective.

What kind of problems arise in public relations historiography? At first glance there are above all content-related problems: When did PR really begin? Did public relations already exist in ancient Greece and Rome or in the Middle Ages or did PR only come into being during the industrial age? What meaningful criteria should apply in determining the beginning of PR? What criteria should be established in order to discuss public relations from a historical standpoint in the first place? Is the concept 'public relations' sufficient and clear enough? Is it primarily the existence of particular tools of communication or communication technologies, or is the beginning of PR only defined by the basic socio-historical and socio-economic conditions? This seems to be a crucial question (Ronneberger & Rühl, 1992). What precisely is to be understood by 'PR precursors'? Is there a prehistory of public relations and a 'real' PR history, as most textbooks written in the United States see it? What criteria can be given for distinguishing between the various periods? Do these criteria apply globally, for each continent and each country, or are they only valid for certain continents, countries and historical periods? In Germany during the Nazi period, for example, was there such a thing as industrial public relations (albeit under a different name), or was this period a PR-free one, that is, was everything absorbed by propaganda activities, which had nothing to do with public relations? Did public relations exist in the German Democratic Republic (GDR) or in other Eastern European countries, formerly socialist or communist countries, albeit with a basic socialist understanding? The answer especially to the last two questions seems to be crucial to PR historiography in that already here it becomes clear that any PR historiography presupposes, first, a conceptual preconception of public relations – in this case an acceptable differentiation between PR and propaganda – and that, second, it becomes clear that the history of PR cannot be considered independently of different forms of societies, political and economic systems, and the structure of 'the public sphere'.

The aim of this chapter is to discuss some of these questions and to consider some theoretical and meta-theoretical reflections on the assumptions, problems and types of public relations historiography before a *functional-integrative stratification approach* is presented, one which can better cope with the existing problems – such is our claim at least – than previous approaches.

A Brief Look at Contemporary Public Relations Historiography

When we look at the situation of public relations historiography, we can describe the situation as follows. Only in one country, the United States, does public relations historiography seem to be at a more advanced stage: there are some specialized professorships in PR and there are regular articles about public relations history in different scholarly journals. In all other countries, the situation is not as advanced. In many other countries, the writing of the history of public relations still seems to be in its infancy. An important new period began in 2009 when Tom Watson began to organize the annual 'International History of PR Conference' in Bournemouth, United Kingdom (see http://www.blogs.bournemouth.ac.uk/ historyofpr). A closer look at the papers presented at these conferences leads to the conclusion that it makes sense to distinguish between three different types of studies in public relations history:

1. *National PR histories of a rather descriptive nature.* Research on the historical development of public relations, especially in single countries. Examples include L'Etang (2004) for the United Kingdom or Kunczik (1997) for Germany. Among the shorter versions are history chapters, especially in American textbooks. This is a type of public relations history with general, global coverage (Cutlip, 1994, 1995). But these examples are in fact more or less national PR histories, which focus on the United States. A very short overview of examples of national public relations history for many countries is given by Sriramesh and Verčič (2009) and Van Ruler and Verčič (2004).

2. The second type of studies includes papers that focus on *specific aspects*, for example, the historical development of individual firms like Krupp, Siemens, AEG or other organizations. Also research in the history of parts of the professional field, such as PR agencies (Nöthe, 1994) or communal public relations (Liebert, 1995). Case studies show only the historical development of smaller segments of the professional field, but they can nonetheless also provide deeper insights into the field as a whole. A special subtype of these publications includes studies of famous practitioners (Ewen, 1996), such as Edward L. Bernays (Tye, 1998) and Ivy Lee (Hiebert, 1966) in the United States, or Carl Hundhausen (Lehming, 1997) and Albert Oeckl (Oeckl, 1964; Mattke, 2006) in Germany.

3. The third type of publications reflects *various problems of public relations historiography on a meta-theoretical or methodological level*. Approaches to public relations historiography are discussed as well as different periodization models, etc. Examples include Bentele (1997), L'Etang (2008), Hoy (2002), Raaz and Wehmeier (2011), and Lamme and Russell (2010).

Two Approaches to PR Historiography

This short look at the international literature and a review of most of the existing works on PR history as well as PR historiography have led me to distinguish between two different approaches to PR historiography:

1. the approach consisting of a *fact- or event-based PR historiography*;
2. the approach consisting of a *model and theory-based historiography*.

I introduced this distinction for the first time in Bentele (1997). It was taken up by Hoy (2002), Hoy, Wehmeier and Raaz (2007), Wehmeier, Raaz and Hoy (2009), and Raaz and Wehmeier (2011). But in contrast to Hoy (2002), who does not distinguish two different types of historiography, but rather three types: (1) fact-/event-oriented type; (2) the periodizing type; (3) the model/theory-oriented type). In my opinion, the second, periodizing type is merely a subtype of the fact-oriented type of historiography.

The Fact- and Event-Based Approach

At present, the fact- and event-based PR historiography still constitutes the most widespread approach. At the same time, it often represents the initial phase of a historical preoccupation with most varied phenomena. The approach is simple: Facts about communication practices, which had previously only been cited and published in a scattered way, are collected and arranged in chronological-historical sequence. An example of such a method is the chapter 'Milestones in the History of Public Relations', in the *Encyclopedia of Public Relations* by Heath (2005, pp. 915–918), which builds on material collected for a website by Kirk Hallahan. The milestones begin with the year 1800 BC and end – because of the year in which the *Encyclopedia* was published – in 2002. It concentrates mainly on PR history in the United States. Similar examples, which focus mainly on Germany, can be found in Szyszka (1997) and Liebert (2003). In the field of historical research this type of historical writing corresponds to the older method of 'historicism', the classic type of historical writing in the 19th century, which was based primarily on events which were derived from sources, which in turn had to be understood. However, in the 20th century, under the influence of the emerging social sciences, 'structural historiography' established itself in the field of history in a critical departure from historicism. This type of historical writing concentrates mainly on examining how social and economic structures evolve over lengthier periods of time.

As applied to PR history, the astonishment of laypeople, but also of PR practitioners, is often considerable when it can be demonstrated that PR phenomena, that is, typical PR tools or PR methods in politics or the economy, are nothing new; in other words, that they at least have ancient 'roots' or precursors which can often be traced back as far as the Greek polis.

If, beyond such collections of facts, attempts at systematization become discernible which in general lead to chronological tables and also types of periodization, then one can speak quite reasonably of the existence of a PR historiography. To that end, as a rule, understandable and specifiable criteria for defining the periods have to exist. An example of this first type of historiography is Bernays (1923), who was arguably the first person to comprehensibly divide the development of American PR into periods and describe it. Probably the most widely used textbook in the United States, *Effective Public Relations*, is based on this periodization. It was published in a first edition in 1952 and its following editions (e.g., Cutlip, Center, & Broom, 1994; Broom, 2009) offer subdivisions into phases to which one can ascribe almost canonical value. Here, for example, the distinction is made between an early history of PR and the history of PR, strictly speaking, and the later is in turn subdivided into six or seven periods. The criteria for such a subdivision into periods admittedly are not precisely indicated.

This fact-based approach fundamentally lacks any theoretical grounding. It does not entirely do without a theoretical preconception, however. In this approach, too, it is at least necessary to assume a particular concept of 'public relations' in order to be able to gather facts on the development of the phenomenon at all. Since the understanding of PR varies widely, in this approach, which has until now been the most widely diffused, inconsistencies emerge in part within the historical descriptions and in part divergent approaches also emerge within the same type of PR historiography. Among the examples are the two (mutually exclusive) views according to which, first, PR is as old as the history of humankind itself and, second, PR is of only recent date, i.e., only began with industrialization (Ronneberger & Rühl, 1992) or only *strictu sensu* at the beginning of the 20th century (Cutlip, Center, & Broom, 1994; Broom, 2009). Nevertheless, the fact-based approach is still utilized widely. In a recent attempt to construct a 'new theory of public relations history', Lamme and Russell (2011) describe 'public relations' over a period of approximately 2,000 years as it involves various areas of society (religion, education, etc.), without giving any substantial reasons for their 'method' of beginning the history of public relations so long ago.

The Model or Theory-Based Approach

The approach consisting of model-driven and theory-based PR historiography is directly linked with James E. Grunig's 'four models of public relations'. This distinction between four different types or models of PR (publicity, information, asymmetric communication, and symmetric communication) is interpreted by Grunig and Hunt (1984) not only systematically, but also historically. The four models of PR or the entire diagram (Grunig & Hunt, 1984, p. 22) are viewed, to be sure, as a simplification of complex reality but at the same time, through the introduction of distinguishing criteria (for example, communications objectives, communications structure, underlying communications model, etc.), it becomes transparent and – as a kind of ideal type – useful as an aid in understanding and reconstructing actual PR activities.

The historical interpretation was originally also given by Grunig and Hunt (1984, p. 25) by a subdivision into phases: the publicity type is placed mainly in the phase between 1850 and 1900; the information model begins around 1900; the beginning of the asymmetric communications model is placed around 1920; and that of the symmetrical communications model is placed much later, in the 1960s and 1970s. This – model-based – subdivision of periods is not further specified or elaborated.

It is clear that a PR historiography which has models of this type as its starting point is much more grounded in theory than the simpler type of fact-based PR historiography. The method of this type of historiography is alongside and based on a collection of facts, mainly a systematization of historical facts. The aim is not only the description of the development but rather – going beyond this – the explanation of historical developments. In addition to functions specific to the professional field of PR, this type of historiography also obviously has social scientific functions. The limits of this approach of course lie in the quality and the empirical validity of the underlying models. In an unpublished manuscript, J. E. Grunig (1996) goes one step further. He describes PR historiography and PR scholarship themselves in their social contexts, which definitely have an influence on the character of the historiography. For example, traditional PR historiography is described, as 'linear', 'male dominated', 'white dominated', and 'U.S. dominated' (Grunig, 1996, p. 7). In his new approach, J. E. Grunig no longer views PR history as a linear process leading from the publicity model to the symmetrical communications model, but rather these models are conceptualized as 'magnifying lenses' for describing the previous development and – this being an explicit claim – for explaining it. According to this line, the history of public relations is pursued as a *history of ideas*, and this procedure is specified by distinguishing the historical elements that make up the 'idea' of PR. Historical elements that constitute the broad 'notion' of public relations include, for example, the idea that human communication is generally an alternative to force and violence. This is, according to J. E. Grunig (1996, p. 116), the most basic idea of public relations and means that the PR function in organizations emerges when the environment or growth in the size and power of an organization makes it necessary. This also explains why and when a specific management function dealing with public relations develops; that the fundamental idea of symmetrical PR communication can only be achieved through the process of developing a profession; and that – contrary to PR historiography up to this point, i.e., the mid-1990s – a diversity of practical approaches to practising public relations is observable.

As shown by the comparison of both approaches in Table 14.1, the second type includes a clearly defined theoretical foundation for public relations historiography. It is also defined by a clear method (meta-theoretically, reflective systematization) and the transparent aim of describing and explaining the evolution of PR ideas, practices, and structures of the professional field from a socio-historical point of view. Apparently most problems involving PR historiography – as they were described in the first section – can only be addressed and solved in the framework of model and theory-based approaches. This is valid also for the decision concerning the historical point in time from which one can even speak of public relations, how and based on what factors and influences public relations has developed. The following section will introduce a theoretical model which could be seen as a basic model for a globally applicable public relations historiography and can therefore also serve as a model for comparative research on the history of public relations.

TABLE 14.1 Two Approaches to Public Relations Historiography

	Fact- and Event-Based Approach to PR Historiography	Model and Theory-Based Approach to PR Historiography
Distinguishing Criteria:		
Methods	a) Collection of facts, historical sequence b) Subdivision into phases; periodization	a) Concept and theory-driven collecting; systematization b) Structural-historical method
Objectives	Description	Description and explanation
Theoretical basis	None, historical order	Concepts, typologies, theories
Functions	Attractiveness for the occupational field, social scientific beginnings	Social scientific functions; contribution to the professionalization of the occupational field
Examples	Bernays, 1923; Cutlip, Center, & Broom, 1994; Broom, 2009; Oeckl, 1964; etc.	Grunig & Hunt, 1984; Grunig, 1996; Bentele, 1997, etc.

Functional-Integrative Stratification: Preconditions and Elements

Some Preconditions and a Different Perspective

A fundamental and actual historical precondition for a stratification approach is that public relations – just like other forms of public communication – have evolved historically from interpersonal forms of human communication. But public relations cannot be understood as being identical with communication: public relations are a certain *type* of communication. Second, public relations in the sense of systematic communication management – this is an additional precondition – is historically and currently always associated with the production of organizational-internal and/or organizational-external *public communication*. Two basic requirements can be derived from these preconditions: First, public relations historiography can basically only be pursued meaningfully in the context of the history of communication and, second, only in the context of the development of public communication. PR historiography would lose out on essential insights if it ignored these contexts. Given these positions, PR historiography is diminished if it views itself primarily as a form of historiography that concentrates on famous persons or companies.

If public relations history is only understood as part of the more general history of public communication, logically then there is a close connection with the professional history of journalism. In this context of a kind of co-evolution of two professional fields, it would seem somewhat implausible to assume that first the professional field of journalism would have developed and only then the professional field of public relations.

Functional-Integrative Stratification

What can be understood by the term 'functional-integrative stratification'? I would like to designate this term as a theoretical perspective that is based on the 'stratification principle', a fundamental principle of the social evolution of communication and communications systems. The perspective of functional-integrative stratification can – so the argument goes – also prove fruitful for the historiography of public relations. The evolution of public relations is in this perspective first examined *functionally*, i.e., in the context of related (e.g., journalism, advertising) and overarching social systems (politics, economics, culture, science, etc.). With that, in addition to descriptions – as common in the fact- and event-based approach – patterns of explanation are also made available. Second, the evolution of PR is viewed as an *integrative* co-evolution, that is, public relations is seen as an integral part of the history of human communication as well as of the history of 'the public sphere'. Third, the stratification model designates an important evolutionary principle, one which until now has not been thought about or used in the history of communication. This approach is *per definitionem* genetic, i.e., development-based, since we are dealing with historical reconstructions. The approach attempts to place insights from systems theory, communication theory and evolutionary theory in relation to one another (for this combination, see also Luhmann, 1995).

Stratification models have been used until now mainly in geography, biology, psychology and philosophy. Geographic stratification models show different strata from different periods, if we look at the Earth using the model of a longitudinal cut. Philosophical, biological and psychological stratification models are not so well known. Sincce philosopher Nicolai Hartmann (1935–1950) developed an ontological stratification model, more precise stratification models are being used today, mostly in evolutionary biology and developmental psychology. Riedl (1980), for example, presents a model in which biological evolution, beginning with quarks and atoms and continuing through molecules, biomolecules, cells, tissue, organ animals, animals, human individuals, groups, and societies all the way to civilizations and cultures, is conceived as a development of layers, whereby one layer overlays another, and at the same time genetically older layers are 'contained' within genetically more recent layers. The younger layers are built on the older layers and contain the latter material – or at least their principles. The phylogenetic evolution of biological organs (the nervous system, for example), but also the ontogenetic evolution of mental abilities and capacities (for example, emotions), can be understood with the aid of stratification models (Schmidt, 1977). For all that, stratification is not the only evolutionary principle: differentiation and hierarchization are likewise fundamental principles. Furthermore, evolution can at the same time perfectly well be understood as a sequence of phases. An interesting issue for research would be to work out the mutual dependencies and links between these various principles.

The stratification approach is largely unknown in the history of communication and media research and is seldom used. Nevertheless, a sort of prominent precursor for this approach does exist: Wolfgang Riepl. As long ago as 1913, Riepl, a German historian and newspaper editor, based on studies of the circulation of news in ancient Greece and Rome, formulated his so-called 'law of complementarity':

> On the other hand, there exists to a certain extent as a basic law of the evolution of communications that the most simple means, forms, and methods, once they have become ensconced and are found to be usable, cannot be lastingly supplanted or set into disuse by even the most perfect and highly developed means, forms, and methods, but instead continue to maintain themselves alongside the latter, the only requirement being that they have to search for other tasks and areas of application.
>
> *(Riepl, 1913, p. 5; translation by the author)*

Oral communication was indeed stifled and its structural environment was modified by the emergence of writing but not entirely rejected. Through the development of communication technology – in this case the telephone – oral communication regained lost terrain. Further examples can be easily found: Through the development of the printing press, human handwriting has disappeared just as little as painting has suffered extinction because of the development of photography or photography has become extinct because of the advent of film. Television has neither driven out films nor theatre nor the daily newspaper, although – seen in terms of society as a whole – the functional losses of the older media were and are clearly ascertainable. Television – understood as a technical and social system – 'layers itself' on top of older media as functional systems, and the latter, first, maintain themselves as independent media but, second, find themselves incorporated into the new medium as integral parts, as 'sublayers'. Similar things have happened with the development of online communication: oral and written communications media, stationary and moving images, and, moreover, the old telephone technology, are integrated with one other.

Not only for biological and psychological development but also – and that is my argument – for the development of communication, a 'principle of stratification' can be meaningfully assumed. This principle can be provisionally formulated as follows: media, communication patterns and communication systems that have formed within anthropogenesis and human history and that have shown themselves to be successful are preserved within the overall evolution, often as autonomous systems. Crucial media or communications systems (communication, language) form the basis and the precondition – the lower layers – of more recently emerging media and systems. And it is possible to describe some important principles of development: Differentiation of the entire system, subsystems becoming independent, hierarchization of the entire system and linking of subsystems are principles of development which are closely tied to stratification.

The Stratification Model as a Basis of a PR Historiography?

What can be deduced for the historical development of public relations from the development principle of 'stratification'?

First of all, it should be noted that the transfer of models which are effectively used in biology or psychology to social sciences and communication and media research in general, as well as public relations research in particular, have nothing to do with a naïve 'biologism'. It is important to note the differences between biological and social processes and structures. However, an evolutionary development can also been assumed in societies. In the same way that the originally purely biological concept of 'autopoiesis', for example, has been made fruitful for social systems by Luhmann (1995), 'stratification' as a development principle can be useful in reconstructing social-communicative developments.

The existence of *information and communication processes* is the – logical and historical – precondition of the existence of public relations processes. All PR processes are communication processes but not the reverse. The 'communications layer' has been preserved in PR, just as in other forms of communication. But communication is likewise the precondition of or the 'base layer' for other types of communication which have evolved historically: written communication (for example, in the form of written correspondence), theatrical, musical or dance communication, telephone communication, as well as mass communication of the most diverse forms.

The first delimiting criterion and one which at the same time marks a historically verifiable 'layer boundary' is that of the *public structure of communication*. Along these lines, Ronneberger and Rühl (1992) have described the characteristic feature 'public communication' as one of the three 'constitutive principles' of public relations. But this is still not sufficient, since there are too many forms or types of public communication.

The next – logical – delimiting criterion is the necessary *link to organizations*. The communicators responsible for PR communication are organizations which conduct their own communication, be it as social systems that communicate internally or externally or by engaging someone from outside (e.g., PR agencies) to handle this function.

Within such a developmental model, it would only be logical if PR were to initially emerge as a communications *function* of social organizations (e.g., governmental organizations) before becoming autonomous in the form of regular vocational or professional activities, organizational departments, etc. It can probably be assumed that a general historical rule has developed: in the first stage, it became necessary to communicate publicly and internally for (small) organizations and the owners themselves communicated functionally, whereas in later stages the communication function became independent and autonomous departments developed. This can be reconstructed on the basis of individual historical examples (Wolbring, 2000).

It is quite logical that within this historical process *basic procedures* and *communication tools* have been developed, which are still valid today, before one could even speak of a separate form of communication called 'public relations'. This can and should be examined historically. Within the evolution of public communication a large number of tools were developed and used separately, before a large range of these tools were aggregated, so to speak, into a 'toolbox' by a particular group of experts, i.e., members of the public relations profession. While the tools of media relations must have developed in close contact with journalism, it frequently happened that public speeches, written communications tools like newsletters, or even complex tools such as sponsoring were used and implemented by individuals or organizations at a very early stage without one necessarily having to speak of 'public relations' in the sense of a professional field.

At another stage of development, *organizational forms* for an independent PR function emerge within political or economic organizations. As a German example, the attempts in Prussia at the end of the 18th century to convey regular information to newspapers (Groth 1927, p. 37), the establishment of the 'Ministerial Newspaper Office' and of the 'Literary Cabinet' of the Prussian government in 1816, and again in 1841, can be mentioned. In the corporate world, Alfred Krupp looked for a 'litterateur' (*'Literat'* in the original German job announcement in 1866), whose duties were to observe the outside world and to inform the world outside (Bentele & Wehmeier, 2009; Wolbring, 2000).

Having as one's main occupation organizational communication and at the same time seeing this as a distinguishing feature of a particular historical layer is something that could be observed at the latest since the beginning of the 19th century. One can assume that typical occupational patterns (work routines, typical sets of tools) gradually developed through the assignment of duties within the respective departments. In the 20th century an occupational field and thus a profession develop in several – partly by fostering education and awarding degrees.

The emergence of PR as a regular vocation was decisively influenced by one particular factor that has not yet been addressed here: the development of *mass communication*. It can generally be assumed that the expanded activities of the media and their expanded influence – through mass diffusion – together with the expanded influence of government authorities and companies nonetheless also involved increased risks for institutions (for example, through negative reporting). Institutions presumably reacted to the greater influence of economically independent and influential media through increased PR activities, for example, by establishing industrial public relations departments as early as the 1870s. It has also been shown particularly in the public relations history of the United States that –

mainly business-critical – media activities of so-called 'muckraking journalism' led to the activities of corporate PR and thus to the establishment of independent PR consultants and PR agencies (Ewen, 1996; Grunig & Hunt, 1984; Hiebert, 1966).

Part of the logic of this development is also the fact that in some areas early on, overall at the beginning of the 1950s, a *professional self-conception* developed. In Germany, the establishment of a professional association, the German Public Relations Association (German acronym: DPRG), followed in 1958. This development is linked to a growing process of *professionalization*. In this the emergence of a social subsystem of public relations can be observed as a final phase of public relations history – for the time being. This subsystem of public relations can be viewed as a subsystem of public communication and has important functions in society as a whole. It can be characterized by certain social functions, labour organizations, professional roles, professional decision-making programmes as well as by a mixture – typical of this social system – of methods, procedures and tools (Bentele, 1997). The contours of a theory outlined in this way have indeed become clearer since the essential contribution by Ronneberger and Rühl (1992).

Figure 14.1 shows the attempt to depict the entire development leading from communication to the public relations system in a stratification model. A crucial aspect of this view – this needs to be stressed again – is that the model describes not only a *sequence of phases* in the sense of a succession but also a *layered development*, i.e., that the early layers in evolutionary terms are 'contained' in the more recent

Layers				**Criteria**
			Public relations, developing into a social system [20th and 21st century]	Profession as a structured *social system*
		Public relations (PR as an occupational field and as a profession) [19th and 20th century]		PR as *main occupation* and the emergence of specialized departments influencing the *mass media system*
	Organizational communication (functional PR, PR tools) [End of Middle Ages, Modern Age]			Organizations begin with functional public communication
	Public communication [Ancient World, Middle Ages]			Communication in *public* settings
Interpersonal communication (various communications functions) [Human History]				*Communications* as the oldest precondition for PR

FIGURE 14.1 Stratification Model for the Evolutionary History of PR

layers. Interpersonal (human) communication is thus seen as the historically first, basic 'layer' out of which certain forms of public communication and, in particular, media-facilitated public communication (= journalism) have developed.

The basic communication functions (for example, information on particular facts, self-depiction, and persuasion) are contained in all forms of interpersonal communication, whether linguistic or non-linguistic.[1] Thus, although figures of rhetoric can already be identified in the ancient world and although religious buildings like medieval cathedrals also fulfil communication functions such as representation, one is still not obliged to speak of 'public relations'. But these functions are preserved in more recent layers and they take new forms, such as in the field of corporate media and social media communication

The *structures of the public sphere*, regulated both by politics (national and international law) and economics (market demands), also influence the development of public relations. Likewise, the emergence of the professional field of journalism in connection with the emergence of the mass media occurs in close interaction with the development of public relations. In the representative medieval public sphere this included insignia (badges, weapons), non-verbal signs (sign systems) such as clothing, hairstyle, forms of greeting, gestures and rhetorical figures, which through their use and on the basis of medieval power relationships constituted a strict code of 'noble' behaviour (Habermas, 1989). In the age of the emerging bourgeois public sphere, initially the non-publicly accessible *Briefzeitungen* ('letter newspapers') and correspondence (e.g., the Fugger newspapers) had established themselves as the means of communication, even before the public press, i.e., truly publicly accessible newspapers, appeared at the end of the 17th century. As a rule, political institutions and organizations in the ancient world, just like the analogous institutions of the Middle Ages (royal houses, the court, the great commercial traders of early capitalism), instrumentalized or even initiated various media before they emancipated themselves into economically and organizationally independent mass media.

Perspectives

The stratification model for the history of public relations, as outlined in this chapter, can be utilized in various ways. Most importantly, scholars can combine the two most recent layers (PR as a social system; PR as an occupational field and as a profession) using periodization models, as they are known. This has been demonstrated for public relations in Germany (Bentele & Wehmeier, 2009), but can also be applied to the large body of historical knowledge in the United States or the United Kingdom.

By using this model, it is no longer necessary to speak of 'public relations' as beginning with the history of humankind or at least in ancient times. This should be discussed in relation not only to European, but also to American or Asian settings, as well as in relation to different countries. The approach would have the desired results if it provides a stimulus for a more internationally focused, comparative research in public relations historiography.

Note

1   In linguistics and philosophy of language, these communication roles of language are today generally accepted. Karl Bühler (1934) considered language to be a tool, an 'organon', having communicative functions: the functions of expression, depiction and appeal. Language signs always express something about the speaker, they express the views of the speaker. In addition, they depict something, i.e., refer to circumstances outside of language, and 'appeal' to the person who receives the language signs, i.e., they attempt to provoke effects of an emotional or cognitive nature. All three of these basic functions obviously also apply to texts which are produced and diffused by PR practitioners or journalists. PR texts contain pieces of information about the producers themselves or the particular organizations (expressive function). They refer to circumstances (descriptive function) and they affect recipients in various ways (appeal function).

References

Bentele, G. (1997). PR-Historiographie und funktional-integrative Schichtung. Ein neuer Ansatz zur PR-Geschichtsschreibung [PR historiography and functional-integrative stratification]. In P. Szyszka (Ed.), *Auf der Suche nach einer Identität. PR-Geschichte als Theoriebaustein* [In search of identity: PR history as a building block for PR theory] (pp. 137–169). Berlin: Vistas.

Bentele, G., & Wehmeier, S. (2009). From literary bureaus to a modern profession: The development and current structure of public relations in Germany. In K. Sriramesh & D. Verčič (Eds.), *The global public relations handbook: Theory, research and practice* (Expanded and rev. ed., pp. 407–429). New York: Routledge.

Bernays, E. L. (1923). *Crystallizing public opinion.* New York: Boni and Liveright.

Broom, G. M. (2009). *Cutlip and Center's effective public relations* (10th ed.). Upper Saddle River, NJ: Pearson Prentice Hall.

Bühler, K. (1934). *Sprachtheorie: Die Darstellungsfunktion der Sprache* [Theory of language]. Jena, Germany: G. Fischer.

Cutlip, S. M. (1994). *The unseen power: Public relations: A history.* Hillsdale, NJ: Lawrence Erlbaum Associates.

Cutlip, S. M. (1995). *Public relations history: From the 17th to the 20th century. The antecedents.* Hillsdale, NJ: Lawrence Erlbaum Associates.

Cutlip, S. M., Center, A. H., & Broom, G. M. (1994). *Effective public relations* (7th ed.). Englewood Cliffs, NJ: Prentice Hall.

Ewen, S. (1996). *PR! A social history of spin.* New York: Basic Books.

Groth, O. (1927). *Die Zeitung. Ein System der Zeitungskunde (Journalistik)* [The newspaper: A system of newspaper research, vols 1–4]. Mannheim, Germany: Bensheimer.

Grunig, J. E. (1996). The history of an idea. Unpublished paper (draft for the historical chapter of a new edition of *Managing Public Relations*). Washington, DC.

Grunig, J. E., & Grunig, L. A. (2008). Excellence Theory in public relations: Past, present, and future. In A. Zerfass, B. van Ruler, & K. Sriramesh (Eds.), *Public relations research: European and international perspectives and innovations* (pp. 327–347). Wiesbaden, Germany: VS Verlag für Sozialwissenschaften.

Grunig, J. E., & Hunt, T. (1984). *Managing public relations.* New York: Holt, Rinehart and Winston.

Habermas, J. (1989). *The structural transformation of the public sphere: An inquiry into a category of bourgeois society.* Cambridge, MA: MIT Press [originally published in 1962 as *Strukturwandel der Öffentlichkeit. Untersuchungen zu einer Kategorie der bürgerlichen Gesellschaft,* Darmstadt and Neuwied, Germany: Luchterhand].

Hartmann, N. (1935–1950). *Ontologie. 4 Bände: 1. Zur Grundlegung der Ontologie, 2. Möglichkeit und Wirklichkeit, 3. Der Aufbau der realen Welt: Grundriß der allgemeinen Kategorienlehre, 4. Philosophie der Natur: Abriß der speziellen Kategorienlehre* [Ontology, vols 1–4]. Berlin: Walter de Gruyter.

Heath, R. L. (2005). *Encyclopedia of public relations.* Thousand Oaks, CA: Sage.

Hiebert, R. E. (1966). *Courtier to the crowd: The story of Ivy Lee and the development of public relations.* Ames: Iowa State University Press.

Hoy, P. (2002). Ansätze und Probleme einer PR-Historiography [Approaches and problems of a PR historiography]. Unpublished master's thesis, University of Leipzig.

Hoy, P., Wehmeier, S., & Raaz, O. (2007). From facts to stories or from stories to facts? Analysing public relations history in public relations textbooks. *Public Relations Review, 33*(2), 191–200.

Kunczik, M. (1997). *Geschichte der Öffentlichkeitsarbeit in Deutschland* [History of public relations in Germany]. Köln: Böhlau.

Lamme, M. O., & Russell, K. M. (2010). Removing the spin: Toward a new theory of public relations history. *Journalism Communication Monographs, 11*(4), 281–362.

Lehming, E.-M. (1997). *Carl Hundhausen: sein Leben, sein Werk, sein Lebenswerk. Public Relations in Deutschland.* [Carl Hundhausen: His life, his work, his lifework]. Wiesbaden, Germany: DUV.

L'Etang, J. (2004). *Public relations in Britain: A history of professional practice in the 20th century.* Mahwah, NJ: Lawrence Erlbaum Associates.

L'Etang, J. (2008). Writing PR history: Issues, methods and politics. *Journal of Communication Management, 12*(4), 319–334.

Liebert, T. (1995). History of municipal public relations in Germany (from its roots up to the Weimar Republic). Paper presented at the Bledcom International Public Relations Research Symposium, Bled, Slovenia, 6–9 July.

Liebert, T. (2003). *Der Take-off von Öffentlichkeitsarbeit* [The take-off of public relations]. Leipziger Skripten für Public Relations und Kommunikationsmanagement, No. 5. Leipzig, Germany: University of Leipzig.

Luhmann, N. (1995). *Social systems.* Stanford, CA: Stanford University Press [originally published in 1985 as *Soziale Systeme. Grundriss einer allgemeinen Theorie.* Frankfurt; Germany: Suhrkamp].

Mattke, C. (2006). *Albert Oeckl. Sein Leben und Wirken für die deutsche Öffentlichkeitsarbeit.* [Albert Oeckl: His life and his work for German public relations]. Wiesbaden; Germany: VS Verlag für Sozialwissenschaften.

Nöthe, B. (1994). *PR-Agenturen in der Bundesrepublik Deutschland* [PR agencies in West Germany]. Münster: Agenda.

Oeckl, A. (1964). *Handbuch der Public Relations. Theorie und Praxis der Öffentlichkeitsarbeit in Deutschland und der Welt* [Handbook of public relations: Theory and practice in Germany and in the world]. Munich: Süddeutscher Verlag.

Raaz, O., & Wehmeier, S. (2011). Histories of public relations: Comparing the historiography of British, German and US public relations. *Journal of Communication Management, 15*(3), 256–275.

Riedl, R. (1980). *Biologie der Erkenntnis. Die stammesgeschichtlichen Grundlagen der Vernunft* [Biology of knowledge: Foundations of reason]. Berlin: Parey.

Riepl, W. (1913). *Das Nachrichtenwesen des Altertums mit besonderer Berücksichtigung der Römer* [News systems in ancient times with special emphasis on the Romans]. Berlin: Teubner.

Ronneberger, F., & Rühl, M. (1992). *Theorie der Public Relations. Ein Entwurf* [Theory of public relations: An outline]. Opladen, Germany: Westdeutscher Verlag.

Schmidt, H.-D. (1977). *Allgemeine Entwicklungspsychologie* [General developmental psychology]. Berlin: VEB Deutscher Verlag der Wissenschaften.

Sriramesh, K., & Verčič, D. (Eds.). (2009). *The global public relations handbook: Theory, research and practice* (Expanded and rev. ed.). New York: Routledge.

Szyszka, P. (Ed.). (1997). *Auf der Suche nach einer Identität. PR-Geschichte als Theoriebaustein* [In search of identity: PR history as a building block for PR theory]. Berlin: Vistas.

Tye, L. (1998). *The father of spin.* New York: Crown Publishers.

Van Ruler, B., & Verčič, D. (Eds.). (2004). *Public relations and communication management in Europe: A nation-by-nation introduction to public relations theory and practice.* Berlin: Mouton de Gruyter.

Wehmeier, S., Raaz, O., & Hoy, P. (2009). PR-Geschichten. Ein systematischer Vergleich der PR-Historiografie in Deutschland und den USA [PR histories: A systematic comparison of PR historiographies in Germany and the United States]. In A. Averbeck-Lietz, P. Klein, & M. Meyen (Eds.), *Historische und Systematische Kommunikationswissenschaft. Festschrift für Arnulf Kutsch.* [Historical and systematic communication science: Festschrift for Arnulf Kutsch] (pp. 309–330). Bremen, Germany: Edition Lumiére.

Wolbring, B. (2000). *Krupp und die Öffentlichkeit im 19. Jahrhundert: Selbstdarstellung, öffentliche Wahrnehmung und gesellschaftliche Kommunikation* [Krupp and the public sphere: Self-presentation, public perception and societal communication]. Munich: C.H. Beck.

15

ORGANIZATIONAL CONTEXTS AND STRATEGIC IMPACTS

On Power and Mediation

Dejan Verčič and Ana Tkalac Verčič

Abstract

The Excellence Theory explains how public relations contributes to organizational success and which organizational contexts enables that contribution. This chapter links the Excellence Theory of public relations with theories of the network society, communication power (Castells) and mediation of everything (Livingstone). Situational theory of publics (J. Grunig) is in synch with mass self-communication theory (Castells), both underlining the power of symmetry in communication. Excellent organizations nurture symmetrical internal communication to cultivate an organic, inclusive culture. They nurture symmetrical external communication to cultivate trusting relationships with groups and organizations in their environments. These live their separate, yet interrelated and interdependent identities. Similar to an agora in Old Greece, a forum in Old Rome, a coffeehouse and a reading club in Habermasian 18th-century European public sphere, communication is the public space for social media. Public relations is where management and communication meet.

Key Words

communication management, Excellence Theory, mediation, network society, symmetrical communication

This chapter comments on the organizational contexts of "the excellence in public relations and communication management" and its strategic impacts. By "excellence etc.," we mean valued practices that are favored over less-than-excellent, mediocre or simply bad practices in the ways organizational leaders manage interrelationships and interdependencies with social environments, inside and outside organizations—as described in the Excellence Theory of public relations and communication management of J. Grunig (1992a), Dozier, L. Grunig and J. Grunig (1995), and L. Grunig, J. Grunig and Dozier (2002). The Excellence Theory explains "the value of public relations to an organization" and "characteristics of a public relations function that increase its value" (J. Grunig & L. Grunig, 2008, p. 327). These generic principles have been described in Chapter 12 on globalization in this volume.

The Excellence Theory is philosophically ameliorating in its underlying assumption that humans and societies (and organizations between them) can change for the better, and that public relations can be a positive force in that process. Excellence in public relations and communication management is enabled by organic organizational cultures favoring employee/membership participation (in contrast to mechanic organizational cultures favoring authoritarianism/submission) and dynamic environments nurturing social (stakeholder, publics) activism (in contrast to static and statist environments founded on massive apathy). That does not mean that the principles of excellent public relations cannot be applied in less favorable conditions; only that under more favorable conditions (i.e. an organic culture, with a dynamic environment) an excellent practitioner in an excellent department can be more valuable to an organization than under less favorable conditions (i.e. a mechanic culture, with a static environment). The Excellence Theory is politically liberal in its foundations in human rights and liberal democracy.

In this chapter, we will show how the Excellence Theory fits with two of the most intriguing themes in contemporary social research: the network society and communication power work of Manuel Castells (2007) and the mediation of everything (Livingstone, 2009).

Excellence, Power and Mediation

Small organizations can develop in interpersonal relationships, in interpersonal communication. At a certain point of their growth they become too big for that: large organizations formalize power and/or generalize trust, relationships become impersonal and communication-mediated. Modern communication technology, from the telegraph through the press to radio and film, and the need of governments and businesses to monitor, influence, control and use it, were the impetus for the birth of modern public relations practice in the 19th and the 20th centuries (for Austria, see Nessmann, 2004; for Germany, see Bentele & Junghänel, 2004; Bentele & Wehmeier, 2009; for the UK, see White, L'Etang, & Moss, 2009). Mediatization of society is the habitat for public relations; but public relations develops its full potential only when it understands that mediatization is about mediation. Mediated communication greatly extends human environments, making large organizations and societies possible; indeed, the current global society would be impossible without the constituting help of modern information, communication and transportation technology. But mediated communication is only a surrogate for interpersonal communication; it is literally between communicating humans. This is evident in social media: even friends when chatting or tweeting do it using crutches in the form of Facebook, LinkedIn or Twitter.

Public relations emerged with the intention to exercise power through the mass media to control the minds of the masses, i.e. openly as propaganda:

> The conscious and intelligent manipulation of the organized habits and opinions of the masses is an important element in democratic society. Those who manipulate this unseen mechanism of society constitute an invisible government which is the true ruling power of our country.
>
> *(Bernays, [1928] 2005, p. 37)*

But its initial promises were fantastically inflated: media rarely control people; media are usually used by people, not the other way around. (An omnipotent propaganda approach to public relations has largely been abandoned by public relations scholars as being an unethical practitioner pitch-line, while it still exists in critical sociology commenting on public relations, e.g. Mahew, 1997; see also Stanton, 2009). This is accelerated with social media and their applications on mobile platforms. *Nota bene:* students today don't use (read, listen or watch) traditional, off-line media (press, radio or television)—all their mediated communication about the wider world around them comes through social media. This, of course, is not universally valid yet as we are reminded by scholars such as Sriramesh and Rivera (2010) of the presence of the Digital Divide which determines how "networked" a society is, which depends on the level of economic development—poverty, literacy, and other cultural factors.

Social media embody the network society with communication as its public space (Castells, 2007, p. 258). It is here that power as "the relational capacity that enables a social actor to influence asymmetrically the decisions of other social actor(s) in ways that favor the empowered actor's will, interests, and values" (Castells, 2009, p. 10) meets counter-power as "the capacity by social actors to challenge and eventually change the power relations institutionalized in society" (Castells, 2007, p. 248). This is where social movements and activists exploit the Internet and wireless communication networks with mass self-communication, "self-generated in content, self-directed in emission, and self-selected in reception by many that communicate with many" (p. 248). In the language of the Excellence Theory: publics are communicatively self-generated social actors organizing to solve problems emerging for them as results of organizational behaviors (L. Grunig, 1992a). It is this counter-power that is forcing organizations to organize their responses to challenges of interrelationships and interdependencies—organizations are dependent on their (social) environments. Public relations becomes a managerial function to populate boundaries and public relations practitioners—boundary spanners (L. Grunig, 1992b). Mediatization requires managed mediation: mediated (mass) communication is a surrogate for interpersonal communication in the face of increasing size and complexity—it has a fundamental deficit over the original that needs to be filled in with work: public relations work. "Public relations is where management and communication meet" (Van Ruler, Tkalac Verčič & Verčič, 2008, p. 4).

The network society, mass self-communication and unstable balances between power and counter-power (*TIME*'s Person of the Year 2011 was *The Protester*—from 26-year-old street vendor Mohhamed Bouazizi who set himself on fire in the Tunisian town of Sidi Bouzid, to millions protesting in Alexandria, Cairo, Madrid, Athens, New York, Moscow, Tibet, Ljubljana . . .; Andersen, 2011) structurally favor symmetrical internal communication (J. Grunig, 1992b), attention to power structures in public relations departments (L. Grunig,1992c), organic organizational cultures (Sriramesh, Grunig, & Buffington, 1992), and cultural sensitivity externally in dealing with the social surroundings (Sriramesh & Grunig, 1992). Some approaches to management of interrelationships and interdependencies are better than others.

Public relations has only recently recognized the problem of the extension of its principles originating in the US. Following Chapter 12 on globalization and public relations in this volume, Verčič, L. Grunig and J. Grunig (1996) proposed the use of nine excellence principles of public relations as global principles and adjusted their use around the world using specific (localized) applications determined by five environmental variables. Sriramesh and Verčič (2009) collapsed these five variables into three factors: (1) a country's infrastructure (composed of the political system, the economic system and the level of development, the legal system and social activism); (2) the media environment (with media control, media diffusion and media access being critical); and (3) societal culture. The notion of culture and public relations has been taken further by Sriramesh and Verčič (2012), although its goods were already present in Sriramesh (2004), Van Ruler and Verčič (2004), and Sriramesh and Verčič (2003). Tkalac Verčič, Verčič and Sriramesh (2012) have recently strongly advocated the need to study cross-national and cross-cultural perspectives of internal communication as well—a field that currently is being viewed predominantly with a one-size-fits-all perspective.

From a network perspective, we can either see dominant networks (often backed by organizations) and resisting communes (often self-generated publics, people communicating to solve problems created for them by the dominant networks), or a society of multiple identities able to communicate because the only common value they have is the value of communication: "The global culture is the culture of communication for the sake of communication" (Castells, 2009, p. 38).

Let us now move from the most complex, global level, to lower levels. As much as organizations embody domination, so also do they produce counter-power that questions their practices and sometimes their very existence. This comes with costs that can be reduced as much as an organization resembles a network in which actors participate voluntarily and willfully. This is exactly what the Excellence Theory calls the organic culture and the use of symmetrical communication inside an organization: communication has a value in itself because it is an enabling mechanism that makes networks and organizations possible. This value of communication extends beyond the borders of an organization because organizations exist to make changes to their environments and this very *raison d'être* constitutes environments and creates reactions in them: to be challenged from an environment means for an organization that it is making a difference for that environment—if, and to what degree, that change is positive or negative is something to be communicatively (mutually) defined. Exactly because in such contexts where there are no universally accepted predefined values and institutions a need exists for knowledgeable and skillful mediation, that is the *raison d'être* for public relations.

Although relationships between public relations, networks, communication power and mediation have been highlighted by the speed of globalization and the need for cross-cultural cooperation, they were already present in the notion of the reflective communication management approach to public relations proposed by Van Ruler and Verčič (2005, p. 266):

> Communication management is engaged in constructing society by making sense of situations, creating appropriate meanings out of them and looking for acceptable frameworks and enactments. This reflective communication management approach sees communication management concerning itself with maximizing, optimizing or satisfying the process of meaning creation, using informational, persuasive, relational and discursive interventions to solve managerial problems by coproducing societal (public) legitimation.

Successful organizations build social foundations on which they can thrive; or they form parasitic relations to society, which they exploit.

Discussion

Contemporary global society emerged out of Western modernization that produced Western civilization (Debeljak, 2012), and its fundamental characteristic is interdependence (Levy, 1996). Management as a social function emerged in that context to ensure rationality, i.e. efficiency, and public relations to ensure adaptation, i.e. effectiveness (Verčič & Grunig, 2000). Public relations as a purposeful human activity aimed at mediating power and counter-power can, through the choices of its practitioners and their patrons, contribute to the betterment of the world or the reproduction of existing and even the production of new forms of oppression.

There is a certain level of progressivism in this line of argumentation. We know that the notion of development and progress in human affairs has been largely discredited by the postmodernists. But there is more than enough empirical evidence that individuals of the human species live longer, healthier and less violent lives than ever before (Pinker, 2011). And notwithstanding the current depressing economic and political climate in the Western world, there is a good chance that our lives will continue to get better (Diamandis & Kotler, 2012)—but progress is not an automatic ride, it is a man-made condition. And at the center of that condition is communication. The Excellence Theory provides the heuristics for conceptualization and the use of communication power in a globalized world.

References

Andersen, K. (2011). The protester. *Time*, Dec. 14. Retrieved from: http://www.time.com/time/specials/packages/article/0,28804,2101745_2102132,00.html.

Bentele, G., & Junghänel, I. (2004). Germany. In B. van Ruler & D. Verčič (Eds.), *Public relations and communication management in Europe: A nation-by-nation introduction to public relations theory and practice* (pp. 153–168). Berlin: Mouton de Gruyter.

Bentele, G., & Wehmeier, S. (2009). From literary bureaus to a modern profession: The development and current structure of public relations in Germany. In K. Sriramesh & D. Verčič (Eds.), *The global public relations handbook: Theory, research, and practice* (Expanded and rev. ed., pp. 407–429). New York: Routledge.

Bernays, E. L. ([1928] 2005). *Propaganda*. Brooklyn, NY: Ig Publishing.

Castells, M. (2007). Communication, power and counter-power in the network society. *International Journal of Communication, 1,* 238–266.

Castells, M. (2009). *Communication power.* Oxford: Oxford University Press.

Debeljak, A. (2012). In praise of hybridity: Globalization and the modern Western paradigm. In K. Sriramesh & D. Verčič (Eds.), *Culture and public relations: Links and implications.* New York: Routledge.

Diamandis, P. H., & Kotler, S. (2012). *Abundance: The future is better than you think.* New York: Free Press.

Dozier, D. M., Grunig, L. A., & Grunig, J. E. (1995). *Manager's guide to excellence in public relations and communication management.* Mahwah, NJ: Lawrence Erlbaum Associates.

Grunig, J. E. (Ed.). (1992a). *Excellence in public relations and communication management.* Hillsdale, NJ: Lawrence Erlbaum Associates.

Grunig, J. E. (1992b). Symmetrical system of internal communication. In J. E. Grunig (Ed.), *Excellence in public relations and communication management* (pp. 531–575). Hillsdale, NJ: Lawrence Erlbaum Associates.

Grunig, L. A. (1992a). Activism: How it limits the effectiveness of organizations and how excellent public relations departments respond. In J. E. Grunig (Ed.), *Excellence in public relations and communication management* (pp. 503–530). Hillsdale, NJ: Lawrence Erlbaum Associates.

Grunig, L. A. (1992b). How public relations/communication departments should adapt to the structure and environment of an organization . . . and what they actually do. In J. E. Grunig (Ed.), *Excellence in public relations and communication management* (pp. 467–481). Hillsdale, NJ: Lawrence Erlbaum Associates.

Grunig, L. A. (1992c). Power in the public relations department. In J. E. Grunig (Ed.), *Excellence in public relations and communication management* (pp. 483–501). Hillsdale, NJ: Lawrence Erlbaum Associates.

Grunig, J. E., & Grunig, L. A. (2008). Excellence theory in public relations: Past, present, and future. In A. Zerfass, B. van Ruler, & K. Sriramesh (Eds.), *Public relations research: European and international perspectives and innovations* (pp. 327–347). Wiesbaden: VS Verlag für Sozialwissenschaften.

Grunig, L. A., Grunig, J. E., & Dozier, D. M. (2002). *Excellent public relations and effective organizations: A study of communication management in three countries.* Mahwah, NJ: Lawrence Erlbaum Associates.

Levy, M. J., Jr. (1996). *Modernization and the structure of society, Vol. 2: The organizational contexts of societies.* New Brunswick, NJ: Transaction Publishers.

Livingstone, S. (2009). On the mediation of everything: ICA presidential address 2008. *Journal of Communication, 59,* 1–18.

Mahew, L. (1997). *The new public: Professional communicators and the means of social influence.* New York: Cambridge University Press.

Nessmann, K. (2004). Austria. In B. van Ruler & D. Verčič (Eds.), *Public relations and communication management in Europe: A nation-by-nation introduction to public relations theory and practice* (pp. 13–27). Berlin: Mouton de Gruyter.

Pinker, S. (2011). *The better angels of our nature: The decline of violence in history and its causes.* London: Penguin.

Sriramesh, K. (Ed.). (2004). *Public relations in Asia: An anthology.* Singapore: Thomson Learning.

Sriramesh, K., & Grunig, J. E. (1992). Societal culture and public relations. In J. E. Grunig (Ed.), *Excellence in public relations and communication management* (pp. 597–614). Hillsdale, NJ: Lawrence Erlbaum Associates.

Sriramesh, K., Grunig, J. E., & Buffington, J. (1992). Corporate culture and public relations. In J. E. Grunig (Ed.), *Excellence in public relations and communication management* (pp. 577–595). Hillsdale, NJ: Lawrence Erlbaum Associates.

Sriramesh, K., & Rivera, M. (2010). ICTs and web sites: A study of corporate and non-profit web sites five years apart. Paper presented at the 13th International Public Relations Research Conference, Miami, FL, March 10–14.

Sriramesh, K., & Verčič, D. (Eds.) (2003). *The global public relations handbook: Theory, research, and practice.* Mahwah, NJ: Lawrence Erlbaum Associates.

Sriramesh, K., & Verčič, D. (2009). A theoretical framework for global public relations research and practice. In K. Sriramesh & D. Verčič (Eds.), *The global public relations handbook: Theory, research, and practice.* Expanded and revised ed. (pp. 3–21). New York: Routledge.

Sriramesh, K., & Verčič, D. (Eds.). (2012). *Culture and public relations: Links and implications.* New York: Routledge.

Stanton, R. C. (2009). On Mahew: The demonization of soft power and the validation of the new citizen. In Ø. Ihlen, B. van Ruler, & M. Fredriksson (Eds.), *Public relations and social theory: Key figures and concepts* (pp. 212–230). New York: Routledge.

Tkalac Verčič, A., Verčič, D., & Sriramesh, K. (2012). Internal communication: Definition, parameters, and the future. *Public Relations Review, 38,* 223–230.

Van Ruler, B., Tkalac Verčič, B., & Verčič, D. (2008). Public relations metrics: Measurement and evaluation – an overview. In B. van Ruler, A. Tkalac Verčič, & D. Verčič (Eds.), *Public relations metrics: Research and evaluation* (pp. 1–18). New York: Routledge.

Van Ruler, B., & Verčič, D. (Eds.). (2004). *Public relations and communication management in Europe: A nation-by-nation introduction to public relations theory and practice.* Berlin: Mouton de Gruyter.

Van Ruler, B., & Verčič, D. (2005). Reflective communication management: Future ways for public relations research. In P. J. Kalbfleisch (Ed.), *Communication yearbook 29* (pp. 239–273). Mahwah, NJ: Lawrence Erlbaum Associates.

Verčič, D., & Grunig, J. E. (2000). The origins of public relations theory in economics and strategic management. In D. Moss, D. Verčič, & G. Warnaby (Eds.), *Perspectives on public relations research* (pp. 9–58). New York: Routledge.

Verčič, D., Grunig, L. A., & Grunig, J. E. (1996). Global and specific principles of public relations: Evidence from Slovenia. In H. M. Culbertson & N. Chen (Eds.), *International public relations: A comparative analysis* (pp. 31–65). Mahwah, NJ: Lawrence Erlbaum Associates.

White, J., L'Etang, J., & Moss, D. (2009). The United Kingdom: Advances in practice in a restless kingdom. In K. Sriramesh & D. Verčič (Eds.), *The global public relations handbook: Theory, research, and practice.* Expanded and revised ed. (pp. 381–406). New York: Routledge.

16

INSTITUTIONALIZATION, ORGANIZATIONS, AND PUBLIC RELATIONS

A Dual Process

Anne Gregory, Emanuele Invernizzi, and Stefania Romenti

Abstract

In this chapter, the concept of institutionalization is addressed as a dual process. First, and as originally conceived, institutionalization theory is applied to organizations and seeks to articulate how they become socially accepted and successful, with their existence and activities legitimized. Second, institutionalization is applied to public relations as a function to examine whether it is becoming institutionalized within organizations, recognized as important for organizational life and success, and to what extent it has become a strategic function of the organization itself.

The chapter consists of four parts. First, the basic concepts of old and new institutionalization theory are discussed with a number of themes identified, in order to explore the process that organizations go through to be recognized as legitimate. This sets the scene for a discussion, in the second section, of the institutionalization of the public relations function within organizations using a number of empirical studies as an evidence base to demonstrate progress. Part three considers how the institutionalization of public relations supports the institutionalization of the whole organization within the economic and social context. Finally, the fourth section draws conclusions from these considerations, opening up pointers to areas for further progress and research.

Key Words

communication, institutionalization theory, isomorphism, legitimacy, organizations, public relations, strategic practice

Introduction

In his paper summarizing his life-long work in developing theory on public relations as a management function, James Grunig, (2006) concluded that "the greatest challenge for scholars now is to learn how to institutionalize strategic public relations as an ongoing, accepted practice in most organizations" (p. 151). This chapter is a response to that challenge as the basic concepts of institutionalization theory are introduced, the development of public relations is considered, and some pointers are given for the future. The dual process mentioned in the title refer to, first, the process of acceptance that organizations go through in order to be viewed as legitimized in society and second, the contribution of public relations to that legitimizing (or institutionalizing) process. To cover the second area, the chapter examines how the public relations function itself is being institutionalized in organizations and then how it, in turn, contributes to the institutionalization of organizations.

Institutionalization and Organizations

Institutionalization theory is wide-ranging and concerns how organizations obtain and maintain legitimacy and thereby secure their license to operate. The underpinning concept of institutionalization is that organizations adapt to and take on the norms of society around them in order to achieve acceptance by conforming to what is expected of them. Simply put, they do this through a two-pronged process of being pressured into conformity and voluntarily taking on societal norms. Once institutionalized, organizations then have a level of freedom to act to further their own ends and objectives within the bounds of those norms.

Basic Principles of Old Institutionalism

The origins of institutional theory can be traced to Selznick (1948) in a seminal work entitled "Foundations of the Theory of Organization." During subsequent years the theory and its implications have been studied by authors from different disciplines such as sociology (Powell & Di Maggio, 1983), economics (Scott, 1995, 2004), and by organizational theorists (Meyer & Rowan, 1977).

From its origins, older institutional theory focused its attention "on the role of social influence for social conformity in shaping organizations' actions. Because organizations are assumed to be approval-seeking, they are susceptible to social influence" (Berrone, Gelabert, Fosfuri, & Gomez-Mejia, 2007, p. 3). The theory therefore highlights the role of social and institutional pressures in influencing the way organizations operate. These pressures encourage and sometimes force organizations to adapt to the social environment for two reasons. First, and defensively, in order to reduce the uncertainties within their operating environment since they are broadly aligned to societal norms and expectations and therefore are less likely to encounter opposition, and second, and more positively, to obtain approval and legitimacy for their actions.

One of the more interesting concepts that emerges from this theory is that legitimacy is a social construction (Deephouse, 1996). Legitimacy is in fact "a generalized perception or assumption that the actions of an entity are desirable, proper, or appropriate within some socially constructed system of norms, values, beliefs, and definitions" (Suchman, 1995, cited in Tilling, 2004, p. 2). An organization becomes empowered to act if it embodies the values prevailing in the surrounding environment (Pfeffer & Salanick, 1978, cited in Deephouse, 1996). Being given the permission to act indicates its actions are deemed legitimate and legitimacy is an essential precursor to an organization becoming an institution. An organization that is given permission to act makes a contribution to society and is seen to add value. For example, an institutionalized organization may take a leadership role and thus add value in more ways than are just commercial—Kindle has revolutionized not only the way that books are consumed, but stimulated new readership with the social implications associated with that. As Selznick (1957) argues, organizations become institutions as they are "infused with value beyond the technical requirements of the task at hand" (p. 17).

According to Scott (2004), institutions are a set of relatively stable and organized practices, embedded in structures of meaning and resources that give stability and meaning to social life. This definition indicates that institutions have some key features. Institutions are united by rules and practices that prescribe appropriate behaviors for specific actors in specific situations. The structures of meaning, purpose, and relationships provide a common direction and in turn justify and reinforce existing codes of behavior. By preserving habits and socially accepted behaviors, each institution crystallizes an organizational character. Since the formation of that character happens at the level of each single organization, it assures a degree of inter-organization differentiation/heterogeneity. Finally, resources create the capacity for action. Institutions both empower and limit their members by making them more or less able to act in accordance with accepted and enduring rules which are particular to itself.

If an institution is a social model that has achieved a certain status, institutionalization denotes the process of achieving this (Jepperson, 2002). The process of institutionalization involves regularizing and systematizing patterns of activities to a point where they become recognized as the accepted norm, are standardized and embedded. However, it has to be noted that although they insist on the importance of legitimation and routinized practices, old institutionalization scholars accept change as an inherent component of the process by which organizations try to adapt themselves to the environment.

From Old to Neo-Institutionalism

In the 1970s, a stream of studies separated from old institutionalism and these led writers such as Meyer and Rowan (1977), followed by Powell and Di Maggio (1983). This new approach became known as neo or new institutionalism. If for old institutional theory the impetus for institutionalization are the pressures that the local community exert on the organization where it operates (what is called the physical environment), neo-institutionalism introduces the concept of an organizational field, where the pressures to conform are exerted by the inter-organizational environment, not the physical one.

The organizational field is an area of recognized institutional life characterized by fluid and indistinct boundaries, but with a dense and stable network of communication. All those organizations within an organizational field are both the object and the subject of pressures, and the final result is isomorphism, that is, they become similar. This isomorphic tendency is different from what happens in old institutional theory. In neo-institutionalism, the process of institutionalization within a field tends to reduce strategic and structural diversity among different organizations, neutralizing differences among them. This is known in the literature as organizational isomorphism (Powell & Di Maggio, 1983). They tend to adapt to the practices in their field and to "adopt structures, strategies and similar processes" (Berrone et al., 2007, p. 1). This increased organizational homogeneity is also accompanied by the dynamics of persistence (that is, persisting with the accepted way of doing things), because the strategies that the company has assimilated through the isomorphic process are in and of themselves stabilizing (Powell & Di Maggio, 1983). The persistence and stability of these business practices drive organizations to make choices that turn out to be sub-optimal, because of what are called sunk costs. This means that the social and psychological costs associated with changing the habits and routines of the organization are regarded as being too great compared with the perceived benefits. This prevents the organization from seeking economically feasible or even better alternatives (Oliver, 1997).

Having looked at the theory of institutionalization, this chapter now turns to an examination of the contribution of public relations to the institutionalization process. To do this it will first explore how the function of public relations has itself begun to gain legitimacy, or to be institutionalized within organizations, and then it will address how public relations contributes to the institutionalization of organizations.

Institutionalization and Public Relations

A number of empirical studies have confirmed that the role of the public relations function has become increasingly important within organizational settings. Furthermore, its strategic contribution to the success of organizations has recently been recognized by Chief Executives, other members of the dominant coalition, and other managerial functions (Arthur W. Page Society, 2007; Gregory, 2011; Invernizzi, & Romenti, 2009; Murray & White, 2004; Zerfass, Verhoeven, Tench, Moreno, & Verčič, 2011).

This trend has been measured by such indicators as the rising number of public relations/communication departments within organizations; the number of people employed in public relations/communication; the amount of budget allocated to the department; reporting lines to C-Suite executives; the number of senior public relation/communication practitioners on the Board; the degree of involvement of the most senior public relations/communication practitioner in strategic decision-making processes; the perceived importance of proposals by the public relations/communication department to CEOs; the perceived importance of the role of public relations generally by top management; the level of integration with other functions; and the evaluation methods for measuring the contribution of public relations.

Data obtained from recent studies in the United States (Swerling, Thorson, Tenderich, & Ward, 2012), Europe (Zerfass et al., 2011; Invernizzi, Muzi Falconi, & Romenti, 2009), Italy (Invernizzi & Romenti, 2009), and the UK (CIPR, 2011; Gregory, 2011) show similar trends about the growing institutionalization of the public relations function.

The Rising Number of Communication Departments

The increasing importance of the public relations function within organizational structures is evidenced by the growth in distinct departments responsible for communication programs. Empirical data clearly show that public relations activities are being concentrated within a single department. In Italy, for example, the percentage of communication departments has increased steadily throughout the past few years from 55% in 2004, to 78% in 2008, to 86% in 2011 (Invernizzi & Romenti, 2009). Furthermore, the function has broadened its range of responsibility at a managerial level in terms of specialized initiatives, tasks, and reference stakeholders. In 2011, in Europe, for example, 83% of the most senior practitioners were responsible for all or at least three communication activities and stakeholders groups (Zerfas, et al., 2011). The growing remit and seniority of public relations have also been noted in the UK (Gregory, 2011; Rogers, 2010) where it was found that, compared with 2005, more strategic activities were being undertaken such as branding, reputation management, and communications planning and strategy development. In the US (Swerling et al., 2012), as well as significant new activity in social media, public relations departments are steadily taking over responsibility for customer relations and internal communications from marketing and HR respectively.

The Number of People Employed in the Public Relations Department

The economic problems of the beginning of the second decade of the 21st century have depressed growth in the profession in some parts of the world such as the UK, but the underlying trend is upwards (CIPR, 2011; Gregory, 2011). In other countries, for example, Italy, more public relations/communication staff have been recruited, indicating that organizations are prepared to invest more in resources in order to carry out complex projects and initiatives (Invernizzi, 2011).

The Amount of Budget Allocated to the Department

The higher levels of funding now being made available to public relations/communication activities indicates the level of confidence placed in the public relations function by senior resource managers. An appropriate budget allows public relations/communication departments to plan long-term strategies and to employ necessary resources, such as consultancy assistance to accomplish their objectives more efficiently (Invernizzi, 2011; Swerling et al., 2012).

Reporting Lines to C-Suite Executives

The direct reporting line of any function is a measure of its organizational importance. Increasing numbers of public relations/communication functions are reporting to the Chief Executive, Chair of the Board, or other C-Suite executives and this attests to the organizational power now attributed to the public relations function. The maintenance of a reporting line to C-suites represents a common trend in all empirical research: in Italy, 74% of communication departments report directly to the CEO, COO, or Chairman (Invernizzi, 2011); while in the US this percentage is 57% (Swerling et al., 2012). In Europe, 60% of communication directors report directly to the CEO.

The Involvement of the Senior Practitioner in Strategic Decision-Making Processes

Senior public relations practitioners are more involved in strategic decision-making processes as their numbers increase on executive and full boards. In the American context, 60% of communication professionals are invited to attend board-level strategic planning meetings (Swerling et al., 2012). In Europe, this percentage is approximately 78% (Zerfass et al., 2011). These opportunities allow practitioners to gain access to strategic information and actively participate and influence organizational decisions. Italian professionals, for example, contribute to defining organizational strategies (85%) and business processes (76%) (Invernizzi, 2011).

The Perceived Importance of Proposals by Public Relations/Communication Departments to CEOs

An indicator that CEOs assign credibility to and recognize the crucial role of senior public relations practitioners is when they are given equal opportunity with other senior managers to express their opinions on important issues. In the Italian context, the assessments given by communication directors are taken into account by top management in 93% of cases (Invernizzi, 2011). Similarly, in Europe, 78% of communication professionals are considered seriously by the CEO (Zerfass et al., 2011) and in the US the percentage is 69% (Swerling et al., 2012).

The Perceived Importance of the Role of Public Relations Generally by Top Management

There is increasing evidence that top management are recognizing the importance of public relations and communication more generally. The advances in communication technology and the effects of globalization are making organizations and their leaders more accountable and the demands for transparency and corporate responsibility are becoming irresistible (Arthur W. Page Society, 2007). Indeed, the role of communication is being seen as "mission critical" (Gregory, 2011) and a growing number of CEOs are requiring their advice on reputational and other potentially high-risk areas (Rogers, 2010). A note of caution has to be sounded here though, and one that is a potential threat to the further institutionalization of public relations. Those CEOs who do understand the strategic potential of public relations and who wish to see it institutionalized within their organizations also complain of the lack of professionals who are able to operate at the level at which they want them to (Murray & White, 2004; O'Neill, 2008).

The Level of Integration with Other Functions

The degree of integration and coordination between the public relations department and other organizational functions, such as finance, marketing and human resources, denotes the increasing recognition and acceptance of public relations function's role and capabilities by other departments (Invernizzi, 2011; Swerling et al., 2012). Furthermore, public relations has a vital leadership and educative role to play in assisting other organizational functions to be "communicatively competent" in a world that is increasingly connected and where the implications of those connections are fraught with risk (requiring buffering strategies) and opportunity (requiring bridging strategies) (Meznar & Nigh, 1995).

Evaluation Methods for Measuring the Contribution of Public Relations

The evaluation of public relations activities has been considered crucial for its institutionalization. Robust evaluation not only provides evidence that it adds value to the organization as a function and enables it to secure resources (Murray & White, 2004), but it also validates its strategic role in the eyes of the C-Suite (Invernizzi & Romenti, 2009; Swerling et al., 2012). In the US, the amount of budget that organizations allocated to measurement and evaluation increased from 4% in 2009 to 9% in 2011 (Swerling et al., 2012). Communication activities have been measured extensively also in Italian companies, mostly by analyzing qualitative parameters such as media content quality (86%), reputation quality (83%), and relationship quality (74%) (Invernizzi, 2011).

Implications for the Institutionalization of the Public Relations Function: Helping to Institutionalize the Organization

In order for an organization as institutionalized means that it has had to and continues to take into account the expectations of stakeholders, and the institutional and social pressures from the external environment when pursuing its long-term interests. Helping organizations to achieve isomorphism provides the public relations function with a strategic role, played at the increasingly fragile and porous boundary between the organization and its reference environment (White & Verčič, 2001). In their privileged position of observing and interpreting the context in which an organization operates, communication professionals enact the "strategic–reflective" role (Van Ruler, Verčič, & Balmer, 2002; Invernizzi, 2004). In this role, the public relations function collects information from the environment, interprets it, and offers a strategic contribution to organizational decision-making processes as option choices are formulated. Public relations prompts management to formulate strategies and processes aligned with the dynamic social context and with the expectations of stakeholders, rather than just considering organizational interests. The interpretation of the information gathered, and the attribution of sense and meaning to it, are part of the process that Weick (1995) defined as organizational sense-making. By including public relations in the dominant coalition, the process of sense-making gains a more holistic and articulated position, which combines organizational interests as well as those of stakeholders.

Old and new institutional theory focuses on the relational framework in which organizations are situated and on the structures of their inter-organizational relationships (Scott, 1995). Recognizing public relations as a strategic practice means underlining its role in maintaining the relational framework within which organizations are embedded. Grunig (2006) argues that public relations should be institutionalized as a bridging activity, which builds linkages with stakeholders to develop and transform organizations. He observes that unfortunately public relations is conceived more often as an activity that protects organizations from change—as a buffering activity. The process of institutionalization of public relations is important because the relationship-building work in which it is involved helps the institutionalization of complex organizations.

The overview presented in the first part of this chapter prompts three other insights about the contribution that public relations can make to the institutionalization of organizations.

Institutions and Culture: The Role of Internal Public Relations

The work of Meyer and Rowan (1977) recognized that an organization is not only a technical system of structures, processes, resources, and activities, but comprises cultural elements including the expressive and symbolic aspects of human behavior. These symbolic and cultural elements, such as beliefs, rules, and roles, when institutionalized, are able to influence organizational forms independent of resources and technical expertise (Meyer & Rowan, 1977). Leaders set, maintain, or change the culture of an organization (Schein, 1985), although clearly everyone within it plays a part. Internal communication, especially that initiated by managers, is crucial in the development of culture, and although it is socially constructed, it is an integral part of objective reality for organizational members (Rouleau & Balogun, 2011). Cultural systems affect the social sphere and affect the meanings that are attributed to social structures. Organizational structure is not only a rational set of components, but it also reflects the myths and symbols in the social environment. Many organizational models are based on cultural systems whose effectiveness relies on sharing values among organizational members (Scott, 2004). Hence, communications enacted through the day-by-day interactions of organizational members are the real vehicle through which cultural values are shared. Indeed, the construction of culture happens where symbols and meanings are publicly expressed and this is done substantively through communication and the language used inside an organization (Alvesson, 2002).

Normative Isomorphism and Public Relations

Powell and Di Maggio (1983) argue that isomorphism can be created by three types of institutional forces:

- *regulative*, based on legislation, sanctions, and industry regulations (coercive isomorphism);
- *normative*, driven by shared values and norms which derive from education and professional standards (normative isomorphism);
- *mimetic*, based on imitation of other organizations' behaviors and practices (mimetic isomorphism).

Normative isomorphism is an important concept for public relations because it is linked to professionalization. Professionalization consists of the collective efforts of people in the same occupation to define the conditions and methods of their work, and to lay a foundation and cognitive status of legitimacy so that they can achieve professional autonomy.

Two aspects of professionalization are important sources of isomorphism. The first is that universities and training centers are crucial for engendering norms which are shared by managers and staff through relatively standardized management and occupational curricula. The second is the development of professional networks and cross-organizations (professional associations) through which professional norms diffuse rapidly. These two factors help to create groups of people who have an orientation and a way of thinking which is so similar as to neutralize the differences between organizations. There are some obvious examples of this. Doctors have professional norms and appeal to accepted rules of practice and conduct which are significantly more influential than those of the organizations for whom they work, likewise lawyers and accountants. A result of isomorphism is that to attract the best professionals, organizations seek to offer them the same or better benefits and the same or better services as those offered by their competitors (Powell & DiMaggio, 1983).

The discussion on professionalization also merits reference to the way in which public relations as a profession is seeking institutionalization. Public relations has long suffered from an image problem associated with suspect practices and spin doctoring and indeed, there is still debate about whether it is really a profession (Millar & Dinan, 2008; Pieczka & L'Etang, 2006). The actions of the professional bodies from around the world (for example, the Public Relations Society of America, the Public Relations Institute of South Africa, the Public Relations Society of New Zealand, and the Swedish Institute of Public Relations) in establishing Codes of Ethics, supporting university and professional education, contributing to the body of knowledge, and attempting to describe and proscribe the practice are all such professionalizing attempts. The formation of the Global Alliance, an umbrella organization consisting of over 60 professional associations from across the globe, represents an inter-organizational network which is institutionalizing in purpose. Perhaps the apotheosis of the institutionalizing process can be seen to be the awarding of a Royal Charter to the UK Institute of Public Relations in 2005, where the Institute is now recognized constitutionally as the representative body for the profession, regulating it in the public interest and having the constitutional right to be consulted by government and the UK institutions on matters concerning the profession.

Institutions, Sense-making, and Public Relations

Scott (2004) contends that scholars over-emphasize homogeneity among organizations as a result of the institutionalization process. He points out that organizations can and do respond to the surrounding environment in different ways.

According to Powell (2007), in early studies on neo-institutional theory, emphasis was placed on the fact that institutional pressures obliged organizations to comply with the expectations of the organizational field of which they were members. In subsequent studies, attention has been focused instead on the complexity and variety of organizational responses. Institutionalization is thus seen as a process whose form may depends on the relative power of actors who try to govern it. In introducing the concept of action, Scott (2004) acknowledges the variety of interactive, intentional, managerial processes that occur between actors within an organizational field. He observes that organizational responses to institutional and social pressures are different, because pressures are interpreted differently, and this impacts on the creation and negotiation of the meanings of signals coming from the environment (Scott, 2004). Public relations can play an important role in attributing meanings to the pressures coming from the organizational field and making judgments about their strength and importance.

The reputation of an organization can be taken as a measure of how influential an actor is in a field. The most common measures of corporate reputation, for instance, by the Reputation Institute, Harris Interactive, and the *Financial Times*, help public relations to interpret what the social environment thinks of the organization. Because it is largely perception-based, these reputation measures are in fact a summation of evaluations by different stakeholder groups about the organization, its management, its business conduct, and its ability to be responsive to its operating environment.

Institutions, Innovation, and Public Relations

Exploring the theme of isomorphism and similarity/uniformity among companies in the organizational field is inherent in neo-institutionalism. Deephouse (1999) highlights the tension that exists between the need to look like other companies to gain legitimacy, and the need to be different to gain competitive edge. He introduces strategic balance theory, according to which the organization should develop a strategy that balances the need to gain legitimacy while at the same time innovating for competitive differentiation and success (Deephouse, 1999).

Old institutional theory embraced the concepts of change and heterogeneity which encourages innovation. "Institutional pressures can be a source of competitive advantage as they establish the boundaries within which organizations can be creative and innovative" (Berrone et al., 2007, p. 15). Ayuso, Rodriguez, and Ricart (2006) argue that organizations that achieve an effective balance between innovation and isomorphism are those which develop dynamic capabilities (Teece, Pisano, & Shuen,1997). Of particular relevance is the ability to enter into dialogue with stakeholders in order to access their knowledge (stakeholder dialogue) and the ability to assimilate the insights gained from the dialogue and turn them into innovation (stakeholder knowledge integration). Both of these contribute to developing the dynamic capability of sustainable innovation, which in turn enhances social legitimacy because it is based on a continuous interaction between the organization and stakeholders, which also contributes to institutionalization.

This implies that the organization should not remain impassive to external influences, transfixed within inter-organizational networks, which can create inertia, but respond to external stimuli in a strategic manner (Hoffman & Ventresca, 2002; Lawrence, 1999; Oliver, 1991, 1997). "Innovating within the limits established by the institutional context allows companies to conform to social demands while searching for competitive advantage" (Berrone et al., 2007, p. 5). Organizations have to develop responses which both prevent failure and meet social expectations. Hence, they must identify a combination of key resources and capabilities which enable them to address social demands and gain legitimacy, vital for survival and organizational success (Berrone et al., 2007). Organizations derive legitimacy "when organizational practices are congruent with the broader social system" (Andriof & Waddock, 2002, p. 31). Among the rules or social values "which produce a strong social legitimacy" are, for example, standards on child labor and environmental protection. Adopting a broader perspective, corporate social responsibility (CSR) practices develop legitimization because they support organizations to become "good citizens" within their social environment. CSR practices, embedded in strategic actions and everyday business conduct, demand that organizations conduct their business in a way that respects regulations, produces safe and efficient goods and services, creates jobs and prosperity, supports technological developments, and meets environmental standards, ethics, and labor and human rights. Institutional theories have been analyzed in relation to environmental topics in particular. Berrone et al. (2007) show how regulatory environmental pressures and regulations induce firms to develop innovative solutions in order to meet expectations and gain legitimacy: "A key prediction of institutional theory applied to environmental issues refers to the gain of legitimacy" (p. 3).

Because of their impact on the natural environment, companies are under intense scrutiny by stakeholders. It follows that to avoid scandals and criticism, they should seek legitimacy by reducing their environmental impact.

Institutional pressures not only force corporate actions in the environmental arena, but also create business opportunities.

> In order to seize these opportunities, companies need to develop novel and increasingly complex technologies that reduce or eliminate toxic waste . . . In this context, innovation in environmentally-related issues is essential to create capabilities that enable companies to seize market opportunities for sustainable development.
>
> *(Berrone et al., 2007, p. 6)*

Environmental innovations are company-specific and difficult to imitate. The value produced by these innovations is both a potential economic gain and a means to obtain legitimacy by conforming to social expectations. "By innovating in environmentally-related issues, companies that respond to the external legitimacy demands secure their survival and, at the same time, create unique resources and capabilities that are difficult to be imitated" (p. 6).

Conclusion

The empirical research conducted in different parts of the world indicates that the process of institutionalization of public relations as a strategic management function is (1) an important phenomenon; (2) not yet established; but (3) growing and will continue into the future.

The theories of institutionalization explain the reasons for this phenomenon. They tell us:

- why it is important: because of institutional and organizational isomorphism, as Grunig (2006) also reminds us;
- that the phenomenon is in progress but not yet established. The concept of normative isomorphism raises the question about the preparedness of the professional community in terms of the awareness, skills, and abilities required to perform the strategic role required;
- that the phenomenon is growing and will continue in the future because public relations can help organizations to develop an organizational culture, helps to give meaning and significance to environmental pressures, and points to the business opportunities inherent in organizational change.

References

Alvesson, M. (2002). *Understanding organisational culture*. London: Sage.

Andriof, J., & Waddock, S. (2002). Unfolding stakeholder engagement. In J. Andriof, S. Waddock, B. Husted, & S. S. Rahman (Eds.), *Unfolding stakeholder thinking* (pp. 19–42). Sheffield: Greenleaf Publishing.

Arthur W. Page Society (2007). *The authentic enterprise*. New York: Arthur W. Page Society. Retrieved from: www.awpagesociety.com.

Ayuso, S., Rodriguez, M. A., & Ricart, J. E. (2006). Using stakeholder dialogue as a source for new ideas: A dynamic capability underlying sustainable innovation. Working Paper 633, IESE Business School, University of Navarra, Spain.

Berrone, P., Gelabert, L., Fosfuri, A., & Gomez-Mejia, L. R. (2007). Can institutional forces create competitive advantage? Empirical examination of environmental innovation. Working Paper 723, IESE Business School, University of Navarra, Spain.

CIPR (2011). *State of the PR profession benchmarking survey*. Conducted for the Chartered Institute of Public Relations by ComRes. London: CIPR. Retrieved from: www.cipr.co.uk/sites/default/files/CIPR%20Membership%20Survey%20Report.pdf.

Deephouse, D. L. (1996). Does isomorphism legitimate? *The Academy of Management Journal*, *39*, 1024–1039.

Deephouse, D. L. (1999). To be different, or to be the same? It's a question (and theory) of strategic balance. *Strategic Management Journal*, *20*, 147–166.

Gregory, A. (2011). The state of the public relations profession in the UK: A review of the first decade of the twenty-first century. *Corporate Communication: An International Journal, 16,* 89–104.

Grunig, J. E. (2006). Furnishing the edifice: Ongoing research on public relations as a strategic management function. *Journal of Public Relations Research, 18,* 151–176.

Hoffman, A. J., & Ventresca, M. J. (2002). *Organizations, policy and the natural environment.* Stanford, CA: Stanford University Press.

Invernizzi, E. (2004). RP e comunicazione aziendale. *Sviluppo & Organizzazione, 204,* 69–88.

Invernizzi, E. (2011). Strategic communication for organisational and entrepreneurial development. Keynote speech at Sinergie Euprera Congress, Corporate Governance and Strategic Communication, Milan, Italy, 10–11 November.

Invernizzi, E., Muzi Falconi, T., & Romenti, S. (Eds). (2009). *Institutionalising PR and corporate communication.* Milan, Italy: Pearson.

Invernizzi, E., & Romenti, S. (2009). Institutionalization and evaluation of corporate communication in Italian companies. *International Journal of Strategic Communication, 3,* 116–130.

Jepperson, R. L. (2002). The development and application of sociological neoinstitutionalism. In J. Berger & M. Zelditch Jr. (Eds.), *New directions in contemporary sociological theory* (pp. 229–266). New York: Rowman & Littlefield.

Lawrence, T. (1999). Institutional strategy. *Journal of Management, 25,* 161–188.

Meyer, J. W., & Rowan, B. (1977). Institutional organizations: Formal structure as myth and ceremony. *American Journal of Sociology, 83,* 340–363.

Meznar, M. B., & Nigh, D. (1995). Buffer or bridge? Environmental and organisational determinants of public affairs activities in American firms. *Academy of Management Journal, 38,* 975–996.

Millar, D., & Dinan, W. (2008). *A century of spin: How public relations became the cutting edge of corporate power.* London: Pluto Press.

Murray, K, & White, J. (2004). *CEO views on reputation management: A report on the value of public relations as perceived by organisational leaders.* London: Bell Pottinger.

Oliver, C. (1991). Strategic responses to institutional forces. *Academy of Management Review, 16,* 145–179.

Oliver, C. (1997). Sustainable competitive advantage: Combining institutional and resource based views. *Strategic Management Journal, 18,* 697–713.

O'Neill, S. J. (2008). *World class communications: The view from primary care trust chief executives.* Report for Centre of Public Relations Studies. Birmingham: Multi Communications.

Pfeffer, J., & Salancik, G. R. (1978). *The external control of organizations: A resource dependence perspective.* New York: Harper & Row.

Pieczka, M., & L'Etang, J. (2006). Public relations and the question of professionalism. In J. L'Etang & M. Pieczka (Eds.). *Public relations: Critical debates and contemporary practice* (pp. 423–433). Mahwah, NJ: Lawrence Erlbaum Associates.

Powell, W. W. (2007). The new institutionalism. In S. R. Clegg & J. Bailey (Eds.), *The international encyclopedia of organization studies* (pp. 975–979). Thousand Oaks, CA: Sage Publishers.

Powell, W. W., & Di Maggio, P. J. (1983). The iron cage revisited: Institutional isomorphism and collective rationality in organizational fields. *American Sociological Review, 48,* 147–160.

Rogers, D. (2010). The Freud supremacy. In *PR Week, 2010 top 150 PR consultancies.* London: Haymarket.

Rouleau, L., & Balogun, J. (2011). Middle managers, strategic sense making, and discursive competence. *Journal of Management Studies, 48,* 953–982.

Schein, L. K. (1985). *Organisational culture and leadership.* San Francisco, CA: Jossey-Bass.

Scott, W. R. (1995). *Institutions and organizations.* Thousand Oaks, CA: Sage.

Scott, W. R. (2004). Institutional theory: Contributing to a theoretical research program. In K. G. Smith & M. A. Hitt (Eds.), *Great minds in management: The process of theory development* (pp. 460–484). Oxford: Oxford University Press.

Selznick, P. (1948). Foundations of the theory of organization. *American Sociological Review, 13,* 25–35.

Selznick, P. (1957). *Leadership in administration.* New York: Harper & Row.

Suchman, M. C. (1995). Managing legitimacy: Strategic and institutional approaches. *Academy of Management Review, 20,* 571–610.

Swerling, J., Thorson, K., Tenderich, B., & Ward, N. (2012). *Seventh communication and public relations generally accepted practices study.* Strategic Communication and PR Center, USC Annenberg, USA. Retrieved from: http://ascjweb.org/gapstudy.

Teece, D. J., Pisano, G., & Shuen, A. (1997). Dynamic capabilities and strategic management. *Strategic Management Journal, 18,* 509–533.

Tilling, M. V. (2004). Some thoughts on legitimacy theory in social and environmental accounting. *Social and Environmental Accounting Journal, 24,* 3–7.

Van Ruler, B., Verčič, D., & Balmer, M. T. (2002). *The Bled manifesto on public relations.* Ljubljana: Pristop.

Weick, K. E. (1995). *Sensemaking in organizations.* Thousand Oaks, CA: Sage.

White, J., & Verčič, D. (2001). An examination of possible obstacles to management acceptance of public relations contribution to decision making, planning and organisation functioning. *Journal of Communication Management, 6,* 194–200.

Zerfass, A., Verhoeven, P., Tench, R., Moreno, A., & Verčič, D. (2011). *European Communication Monitor 2011: Empirical insights into strategic communication in Europe. Results of a survey in 43 countries.* Brussels: EACD/EUPRERA, Helios Media.

17

STRATEGIC COMMUNICATION

Pillars and Perspectives of an Alternative Paradigm

Derina R. Holtzhausen and Ansgar Zerfass

Abstract

Professional communication in and between organizations and their stakeholders continues to be researched from a multitude of theoretical perspectives. In communication science, public relations and organizational communication have evolved as multi-faceted paradigms with different starting points and foci, but overlapping questions, concepts and explanations. In business administration and marketing science, concepts such as integrated (marketing) communications, corporate reputation and corporate communications are broadly discussed. While every concept provides valuable insights, none of them has been able to establish itself as an overall paradigm for theory and practice. While this might not be a desirable end at all, it makes sense to find common ground by accentuating the common and core attributes of professional communication—the use of communications to reach the overarching goals of a specific organization or social actor. This is at the center of *strategic communication,* a concept used more and more often to guide research and inspire study programs around the world. This chapter will review the current state of the strategic communication discipline through an analysis of theoretical approaches to the field at three levels: (1) the macro level, which pertains to philosophical and meta-theoretical applications; (2) the meso level, which refers to theoretical analyses at the organizational level of practice; and (3) the micro level, which addresses the application of theories to understand how communication takes place in the strategic context. Based on this analysis, the chapter will conclude with suggestions how additional theoretical applications can extend the field.

Key Words

public sphere, stakeholders, strategic communication, strategy

Introduction

The field of communication practice continues to have a naming and perhaps even an identity crisis. Public relations, which has been influenced worldwide by the work of J. E. Grunig and L. A. Grunig (2008), is a contested term. According to the annual European Communication Monitor survey of communication managers working in companies, non-profit, governmental organizations and agencies in 43 countries, the term often has negative connotations in the mass media. This damages the reputation of professionals and decreases trust in the practice. Consequently, only a minority (46.7%) of those working in the field still regard public relations as a suitable label (Zerfass, Verhoeven, Tench, Moreno, & Verčič, 2011, pp. 18–29). At the same time the differences between public relations, marketing communications, corporate communications and organizational communication continue to be hotly debated (see, for instance, Christensen & Cornelissen, 2011). Add to that mix, health communication, political communication, environmental communication, business communication and all the other communication focus areas, it is apparent that naming the field remains a problem.

From the onset the development of strategic communication as an academic discipline has been an interdisciplinary project rather than merely creating a catch-all name for communication practice (Hallahan, Holtzhausen, Van Ruler, Verčič, & Sriramesh, 2007). Globally, communication is practiced in many different contexts and called by different names. This chapter builds on the original Hallahan et al. article and proposes the following definition for strategic communication:

> Strategic communication is the practice of deliberate and purposive communication a communication agent enacts in the public sphere on behalf of a communicative entity to reach set goals.

Goals can be as diverse as winning market share, wining a political campaign, building a positive reputation, or effecting social change. Communicative entities can "cover the full spectrum of economic and social sectors, such as trade and industry politics, nonprofit, government agencies, activist groups, and even celebrities in the sports and entertainment industries" (Holtzhausen, 2008, p. 4849).

The study of strategic communication has been consistent with the above definition and has focused on the following attributes of communication practice across disciplines and in many different contexts:

- Practice is deliberate and intentional.
- It desires a certain outcome.

- It involves one or more practitioners communicating on behalf of a communicative entity.
- It involves communication in the public sphere.

Thus, the study of strategic communication has consistently endeavored to find commonalities in the various disciplines above to see how research in these fields informs academics and practitioners alike on communicating deliberately, on behalf of another, and in the public sphere. For instance, a researcher who does research on message strategies in political campaigns might very well inform us on how these message strategies might be used in health communication or business communication, or not.

Another area of focus has been to bring different stakeholders into the communication field. Thus, instead of focusing on only publics, consumers or political constituents, strategic communication's focus is on stakeholders more broadly and includes them in the strategic communication process. That does not mean that they are treated equally but rather that they are all considered in the process. Strategic communication therefore suggests a broader knowledge of stakeholders than those traditionally addressed in individual communication disciplines. Perhaps one of the most glaring exclusions is the body of knowledge from consumer behavior, which is seldom considered in corporate communication, public relations, or organizational communication.

The strategic communication discipline embraces theoretical approaches at three levels: the macro level, which pertains to philosophical and meta-theoretical applications; the meso level, which refers to theoretical analyses at the organizational level of practice; and the micro level, which addresses the application of theories to understand how communication takes places in the strategic context (J. E. Grunig, 1992; Holtzhausen & Verwey, 1996). It is important to note that theory application more often than not involves two or more of these dimensions. For instance, cultural attributes in society affect how communication at the micro level takes place; organizational structure might affect the ability of the practitioner to communicate effectively internally and externally; and political systems might affect organizational culture and subsequent strategic communication. The chapter will analyze these levels and, based on this, will conclude with suggestions how additional theoretical applications can extend the field.

The Parameters of the Field

One of the first efforts to define the field came in an article by Hallahan et al. (2007), which has now become one of the seminal and most-cited articles in strategic communication research. The original vision defined strategic communication as "the purposeful use of communication by an organization to fulfill its mission" (p. 3) and stressed the *professional nature* of the field, namely, that it involves a practitioner who is charged with supervising or managing communication or communicating on behalf of a communicative entity. This professional communicator is not necessarily educated as such but nonetheless serves as a communication *agent*, who has legal and contractual obligations.

A second characteristic of the communication professional is that he/she represents any *entity that wishes to communicate* in the public sphere. This permits bringing a variety of divergent entities into the fold, not only corporations. Even though Christensen and Cornelissen (2011) argue that the root meaning of *corporate* lies in the word *corpus*, which assumes collectivity, it is important to note that a corporation is a legal entity and more than the sum of its collective actions (Zerfass, 2010, pp. 248–278). Furthermore, it excludes individual entities such as sports stars, entertainers, or politicians who employ strategic communicators on their behalf. One can argue that there are considerable differences between being the communication agent for a corporation with its hierarchical and bureaucratic structure and an individual who either runs for election or needs to communicate in a crisis, which is often the case when individuals require strategic communication. Additionally, new communication technologies have now enabled individuals or small groups of activists to communicate in the public sphere without the typical constraints of corporations.

If communication in the *public sphere* is one of the attributes of strategic communication, it excludes many areas of communication studies, such as how individuals in organizations communicate with each other or how communication constitutes organization (organizational communication), how doctors communicate with patients or vice versa (health communication), how lobbyists communicate with legislators behind closed doors (a form of political communication), or how relationships are formed through daily interaction (some aspects of public relations or marketing communications), to mention only a few. This component implies a communication process that is not one-to-one but involves many people with divergent ideas, and is continuous and dynamic.

While in the past printed media and television were the main vehicles for communication in the public sphere, new media technologies now allow for many communication vehicles that all shape organizational identities in the public sphere. This leads to one of the most controversial attributes of strategic communication, namely, *goal orientation,* because it invokes images of manipulation, management power and control, and corporate dominance of the public sphere. However good or bad, communicating with a specific purpose has to remain part of the field and has to remain an area of focus in strategic communication. At the same time, new approaches to communication and its role in organizing have also opened up new approaches to communication strategy and goal attainment.

Theory Application in Strategic Communication

As mentioned, the purpose of the strategic communication focus is not to develop a single perspective on the field but it is rather an interdisciplinary project to see how different theoretical strands can inform the field. An analysis of theory application in the *International Journal of Strategic Communication* (Holtzhausen & Zerfass, 2011b) showed that a wide range of theories were used to explain strategic communication over the first five years of the publication of this journal. Organization theory was the most applied (n = 17, 24.6%) followed by communication theory (n = 14, 20.3%) and then a host of other theoretical approaches. Thus, one could argue that the interdisciplinary thrust of strategic communication has been successful and that the field is defining itself with theories beyond the reigning debate of whether organizational communication can inform corporate communication or whether corporate communication is the same as public relations. Instead of narrowing fields of communication practice to levels of potential implosion, looking at it in the context of *strategic* has opened its theoretical scope considerably.

Macro-level Applications

The public sphere remains a central and defining concept in strategic communication. From a philosophical perspective, strategic communication does not have a good reputation in the context of the promotion of democratic speech. From Habermas (1979, 2006) to Lyotard (1992), strategic communication is associated with an abuse of power and the exclusion of less powerful voices in the public sphere. But both these authors, with Foucault (1988), also argue that strategic communication is the tool that allows the less powerful to reach their own goals through communication in the public sphere.

The public sphere is receiving renewed interest because of new technologies that allow more participation and allow ordinary citizens to set their own agendas, often bypassing media gatekeepers. The Internet in particular has become the great communication equalizer, and structural properties, such as organization size or type, no longer matter in determining the weight of an argument. To communicate strategically means to argue for legitimacy of a viewpoint in the public sphere (Bentele & Nothhaft, 2010). Arguments that are deemed illegitimate are viewed as self-serving, not deserving of being in the public sphere, and therefore private.

Discussions of the public sphere also link strategic communication and the concept of publics as articulated in the Situational Theory of Publics (STP) in the public relations field (J. E. Grunig & Hunt, 1984). The STP was based on Dewey's (1984) concept of publics that form and organize in the public sphere based on levels of problem recognition, level of involvement and constraint recognition. Grunig argued that publics formed through the rational communication behavior of people in the public sphere (symmetrical communication behavior) versus the earlier notion of public relations practices where demographic and psychographic information was used to manipulate people (asymmetrical communication) (Self, 2010).

There is much criticism of aspects of Habermas's and Dewey's approaches to the public sphere. The central argument is about power and dialogue, namely, people with less power do not shape the dialogue or the consensus (Holtzhausen, 2012). Rather than dialogue, the postmodern approach of a dialectic based on conflict and difference is a better way to ensure full and democratic participation in the public sphere. New communication technologies facilitate this more than ever. No longer are the media gatekeepers the only agenda setters but through the strategic use of communication and the strategic use of an array of technology, individuals, activists, and corporations of all shapes and sizes can state their case in the public sphere.

This introduces the concept of public as a process that is continuously shaped through communication. It becomes "*an act of public*" (Self, 2010, p. 89; italics in the original). To be active in the public sphere and to successfully participate in the act of being public, strategic communication has become more essential than ever before. Communicators have to understand how to shape their messages, how to reach an array of fragmented and continuously fragmenting audiences through a wide variety of possible communication technologies (Holtzhausen, 2012). The public sphere of the 21st century has not come about because of strategic communication but has made it essential to be a strategic communicator to effectively and actively participate in the public sphere.

A case in point is the Feldner and Meisenbach (2007) study, which used a Habermasian perspective to analyze how activists successfully used a website to challenge the legitimacy of the Walt Disney Company during a management and leadership crisis. The study showed that powerful organizations' legitimacy can be challenged if statements made in the public sphere are viewed as truthful, righteous and sincere. The study also showed how activists who are knowledgeable in the use of technology and strategic message design can effectively communicate in the public sphere and bring about change.

The use of language is another central issue in philosophical approaches to strategic communication, particularly in the way language shapes meaning. In one of the earliest efforts to establish a philosophical foundation for strategic communication practice, Malcolm, McDaniel, and Langett (2008) proposed four philosophical bridges to integrated marketing communication (IMC) based on communicative theory. The first is the Aristotelian bridge of rational information to communicate with customers. The second is a phenomenological bridge that draws on customers' senses, experiences and intuition to build a brand. The narrative bridge connects with customers through story-telling; and the dialogic bridge connects with customers through open communication channels. These four bridges are particularly useful when analyzing the organization–consumer relationship and also provide a useful application to other areas of strategic communication.

The focus on language is an important development for the field of communication practice in general because it challenges the assumptions of fixed meaning inherent in the transmission model and even the fixed borders of organizations. This is particularly evident in the concept of emergence, which proposes that meaning is shaped through the use of language and emerges from daily practice (Christensen & Cornelissen, 2011; Hallahan et al., 2007; King, 2010). For instance, organizational boundaries shift constantly, depending on who is talking about it and strategy emerges through the daily practices of organizational members. We permanently live in a "discursive condition" (Ermarth, 2001, p. 206) and our perceptions, meanings and identities are shaped in between different discourses.

This focus on and interpretation of the role of language in both strategizing and the communication process itself have important implications for strategic communicators because it implies that we can never create a message that is understood in exactly the same way by all constituents. This is far removed from the transmission model of communication (Shannon & Weaver, 1949) that implied we send messages through a limited number of relatively controlled media that are understood by all who hear them in the same way. These messages are then interpreted and responded to in an orderly fashion. This new understanding of communication seriously challenges cause-and-effect communication in the strategic communication process. As with Habermas's ideal communicative action, consensus and subsequent cause-and-effect are only possible when everybody in the communication process has equal power and the same understanding and worldview (Holtzhausen, 2012).

One of the earliest and most significant developments in public relations theory building was the understanding that turbulent environments create unique conditions that affect an organization's ability to communicate (L. A. Grunig, 1986). This has important implications for systems theory approaches to organizational communication, which has been one of the most applied meta-theoretical approaches to the study of communication practice. Systems theory and its subsequent modern spin-offs, chaos and complexity theories, are based on the concept of wholeness, of a system that can organize itself and again emerge in a stable form after a chaotic incident. One of the earliest applications of complexity theory to strategic communication was in the context of change communication (Ströh, 2007). The study suggested change in complex systems changes the role of the organizational communicator to one of communication leadership that creates opportunities for self-organizing and the emergence of strategic change.

Similarly, Nothhaft and Wehmeier (2007) proposed a socio-cybernetics approach to managing communication with publics in a complex and turbulent environment through "context-control" (p. 166). This approach also emphasizes the role of communication managers in creating a favorable environment in which trust and a good reputation can emerge, albeit in the organization's external environment. One can argue that institutional theory is an offspring of systems theory because it explores the relationship between organizational environments and their subsequent effect on organizational processes. For instance, Sandhu

(2009) proposed institutional theory as a framework for many levels of strategic communication application and analysis, particularly economic, historic and political institutionalism. Similarly, Holtzhausen and Zerfass (2011a) found that the political systems in Eastern and Western Europe, the United States and South Africa differently impacted strategic communication practice. In the European context, the balance between the political system and organizations was more balanced than that in South Africa, which favored the social environment over corporations, and that of the United States, which favored the organization.

However, these theories make a distinction between an organization's internal and external environments and accept a distinct boundary between the internal and external environment. This is a notion that is increasingly being contested in fields such as organization theory and organizational communication theory because of the argument that people and communication are the organization and that an organization does not exist beyond that context. This concept also is problematic for strategic communication and although it does not challenge the intent and focus of strategic communication, the implications of emergent strategy and communication pose new challenges to strategic communicators.

Meso-level Applications

Perhaps one of the most important concepts at the organizational level is that of strategy or the strategic process. Strategic planning is typically associated with the Management By Objectives (MBO) process, which is typically associated with rational decision-making (Hatch, 1997). This also is mostly the process taught to students in communication management courses in public relations, advertising and management, and emphasizes a linear process of SWOT analysis, goal setting, measurable outcomes and action plans (see, for instance, Austin & Pinkleton, 2006; Percy & Elliot, 2009).

The strategic planning and communication process has many critics who believe it privileges management discourse and is a control mechanism that promotes the blind acceptance of organizational goals (see Holtzhausen, 2012, for a review of the critique of strategic communication). It is, however, never a good approach to view the strategic process in such basic terms and does not do justice to its usefulness and complexity. As a result, there are several scholars who have proposed alternative approaches to these traditional viewpoints. In an analysis of strategic processes used in organizations, Sloan (2006) came up with ten different approaches but said they have the following attributes in common: "a will to win; an element of competition; a process or framework to win; an extended time horizon; determination of a broad and major aim; unifying intent; decisions about resource allocation" (p. 4).

As mentioned, emergent strategy (Quinn, Mintzberg, & James, 1991) is increasingly viewed as a positive alternative to traditional perspectives of strategic planning as rational, linear and executed by top management. Emergent strategy is based on prior experience that informs the organization of future trends and scenarios and legitimates and values the actions and decisions of stakeholders at all levels of the organization. Several scholars value both approaches, namely a leadership role as well as respect and inclusion of other stakeholders (Canales & Vilà, 2005; Heracleous, 2003; Rughase, 2006). After a comprehensive review of the literature, Hafsi and Howard (2005) concluded that strategy research takes place at the intellectual and practical levels and identified five areas that inform the intellectual domain:

(i)   strategy as a leader's statement;
(ii)   strategy as a community's statement;
(iii) strategy as a guiding track;
(iv)   strategy as the building of competitive advantage;
(v)   strategy as a relationship with the environment (p. 243).

This allows for a much more complex and non-linear interpretation of the concept, which has important implications for strategic communication. If, as Nothhaft and Wehmeier (2007) suggested, the role of the organizational communicator is to create an environment that facilitates communication, this expands the role of the communicator in the strategic planning process to ensure inclusion of communities, consumers, and other stakeholders. Thus, instead of only identifying publics that can harm an organization, as in the public relations process, the strategic communicator is responsible for a 360-degree inclusion of all stakeholders before strategy can be executed. Furthermore, if strategy is a unifying action with a variable timeframe, as Sloan (2006) suggested, a strategic communication campaign never has a beginning and an end. In fact, one might not even be able to talk about a campaign as such but rather a continuous process that emerges every day and has to be reconsidered every day.

Such an approach to strategy would require a special kind of leadership. Leadership research in strategic communication was conducted at two levels. One area of focus has been on how the communication abilities of organizational leaders could facilitate organizational change, as Nothhaft and Wehmeier (2007) suggested. Zerfass and Huck (2007) introduced the concept of communication leadership, which emphasized the importance of change leadership and the ability to create an environment that encourages innovation by "shaping the meaning of new ideas, technologies, processes, products, and services within social relationships" (p. 120).

Communication skills of leaders also were examined and proved to be a vital component of leadership communication. Van Woerkum and Aarts (2011) suggested active listening is an important component of organizing. Using projective hearing theory, the researchers argued active hearing on the part of leaders provides immediate feedback in a variety of daily situations that can facilitate change management. Supervisory communication, consisting of positive relationship communication, upward openness communication, negative relationship communication, and job-relevant communication, also proved to be important attributes for employees' commitment to work groups (Bakar & Connaughton, 2010).

A second level of leadership analysis was research that focused on the leadership qualities of communication managers. Drawing on public relations leadership studies, Werder and Holtzhausen (2009, 2011) found communication managers did not support a transactional leadership style but rather one that was both transformational and inclusive. They argued these leadership styles were influenced by the requirements of the environment existing in and created by communication practice. Their study supported the organizational communication perspective that communicative ability was "the essential component of inspiration and change" (Eisenberg, Goodall, & Tretheway, 2007, p. 280).

One of the most interesting outcomes of meso-level research in strategic communication was confirmation of the strategic role of communication practitioners, which draws on organization theory applications in the field. In three different studies conducted on three continents, the strategist role strongly emerged (Tindall & Holtzhausen, 2011; Verhoeven, Zerfass, & Tench, 2011; Werder & Holtzhausen, 2011). These studies confirmed strategic communicators have problem-solving skills and environmental scanning expertise, participate in the strategic planning process, are part of the strategic planning team and consider strategic implications during problem solving.

An interesting development in strategic communication research was the concern for employees in the communication process, mostly informed by organizational communication literature. In this line of research the focus was again on the role of language in strategic communication but in this case on its strategic use in the organization's internal environment, if such a division can still be made. King (2010) used a discourse analysis approach to show how internal communication strategies emerged through an internal memo and defined emergent communication as "a communication construct derived from the interaction between reader/hearer response, situated context, and discursive patterns" (p. 19). This discursive approach also is evident in the work of Garner (2009), who argued that employees used dissent strategically for sense-making purposes rather than organizational change. He held that dissent was an important aspect of employee communication that helped employees to "feel more satisfied at work and helping organizations better use employee feedback" (p. 34).

A related area of research focused on the role of culture and society on employee communication. Employees' decisions to remain silent during times of organizational crises were mostly driven by cultural norms that exist in the employee's "own peer, social, and reference groups" (Shaia & Gonzenbach, 2007, p. 148). Sociocultural factors also would enable communication practitioners to "shape, sustain and transmit organizational culture over time and through space" (Ristino, 2008, p. 54). The four dimensions of communicating culture—

personification, socialization, enculturation and adaptation—provide practitioners with a method for defining organizational reality. The sociocultural model "describes how communication practitioners, through the skillful and artful use of symbols and language, shape, sustain and transmit organizational culture for both internal and external actors in the environment" (p. 70).

Lastly, while the integration of communication functions in organizations remains a serious concern for researchers (e.g. Zerfass, 2008; Christensen & Cornelissen, 2011), little research has been done internationally on either the status or benefits of integration apart from regional studies in the German-speaking countries (Bruhn, 2006). Einwiller and Boenigk (2012) identified significant contributions to business effectiveness in a large sample of small and medium-sized companies with integrated communication functions in Switzerland. Along this line, Ragas and Roberts (2009) showed how Chipotle in the United States used a synergized effort between public relations, brand management, corporate social responsibility, and marketing to create an effective strategic communication campaign rather than viewing these functions as competing organizational forces. While Chipotle's communication functions remained separate, they could collaborate to strengthen the brand through multiple communication efforts.

Micro-level Applications

Not surprisingly, the crisis communication genre found a perfect home in strategic communication. It is a *genre* of strategic communication because it pertains to many different phases and outcomes of a crisis, which justifies a thorough discussion of strategic communication perspectives in this context. Interestingly, crisis communication has, with a few notable exceptions, been addressed at the micro level, namely in the context of the communication between a communicative entity and its stakeholders. Because of the wide variety of theory applications, it is helpful to review crisis communication in the context of the different phases of a crisis, from prevention through to reputation management.

One of the mainstays of crisis communication management is the need for preventative crisis planning and sensible communication at the risk management stage. This has become one of the focus areas for strategic communication researchers. Because communicators do not know how their messages are understood or reacted to, communication about possible emergencies or terror attacks should have components of two-way symmetry in the planning stage (Botan & Penchalapadu, 2009). Message strategies are viewed as particularly important in this stage. Communicators who plan safety campaigns should be sensitive to the possibilities of creating an environment of intolerance that might actually lead to violence (Veil & Mitchell, 2010). They should create a balance in their strategic communication messages between warnings that are actually taken seriously and promote tolerance. To be prepared for national disasters, organizations should also communicate within a network of similar or related organizations and agencies, and messages and actions should be understood within the same cultural-cognitive frame (Frandsen & Johansen, 2009). For instance, hospitals should ensure that other hospitals and health organizations and agencies share the same preparedness plans to "ensure maximal communication and cooperation during terrorist events" (Matusitz, 2007, p. 169).

Crisis communication also is the ideal context to study the concept of *publics*, which generally refers to a group of people who becomes active against a communicative entity (for a comprehensive discussion of the term, see J.-N. Kim, Grunig, & Ni, 2010). This sets publics apart from the concept of stakeholders, who have a vested interest in the communicative entity but do not necessarily have a problem. Thus publics often are involved in the crisis situation. The behavior of publics is studied through the Situational Theory of Publics (STP). One of the latest extensions of this theory is to reconceptualize the communicative behavior of publics in the problem-solving process (J.-N. Kim et al., 2010; Ni & Kim, 2009). With this study, Kim, Grunig, and Ni hoped to extend the ability of communicators to segment publics through a better understanding of their communicative action. This is a valuable approach for strategic communicators because it focuses on how publics use information in the problem-solving process through information acquisition, selection and transmission.

The public relations focus on relationship building was also applied to crisis situations. One significant finding indicated that relationships alone do not determine publics' perceptions of a crisis and that crisis-response strategies are inherently important to crisis management (Park & Reber, 2011). In general, the study of relationships has not contributed a great deal to the field of strategic communication because of the lack of focus on communication in the relationship building process *per se*. One of the few exceptions is a study by Ki and Hon (2009) who focused on how relationships can be cultivated in the strategic communication process through access to information and assistance; courteous, continuous and positive communication; task sharing; and most importantly, assurances of the stakeholders' importance to the institution.

Yet another area where public relations theory informs strategic communication is in the contexts of image restoration and reputation management. In an overview of 18 years' worth of crisis communication literature, S. Kim, Avery, and Lariscy (2011) found organizations' main aim with image repair is preserving their reputation rather than considering the best interests of the public. Rather than providing instruction and appropriate information to ensure public safety, organizations' first concern was for their own image. A unique application of crisis communication that shows the breadth of application of strategic communication was a study that focused on communication during the recall of defective products (Courtright & Smudde, 2010). Although crisis communication during or as a result of a defective product is not uncommon, crisis communication in the context of marketing communication is not widely discussed and this is an area of research that in future deserves more focus.

A newly introduced area to the study of strategic communication is that of legitimacy and authenticity of communication in a global context. This also relates to issues of cultural identity and the influence of social culture on strategic communication. Impressions of legitimacy are essential to successful strategic communication but can differ globally between geopolitical regions such as the West and the Middle East, between stages of modernity or social development, and even between closely aligned neighbors, such as Sweden and Denmark (Holmström, Falkheimer, & Nielsen, 2010). Similarly, perceptions of authenticity can often bridge many local and global cultural divides and can be a useful tool in nation-building and brand-building at the local level and brand and country reputation building globally (Molleda & Roberts, 2008).

Yet another area of strategic communication research at the micro level is corporate social responsibility (CSR) and researchers consistently argue that CSR should be a part of business objectives. Coombs and Holladay (2012) took a distinctly strategic communication approach to the field and argued that it should be a function of strategic communication and not of public relations due to perceptions that CSR is merely organizational spin. Yet another finding that takes CSR out of the purely public relations terrain is the study by Werder (2008) that tested the Theory of Reasoned Action on advertising and marketing literature in the context of CSR. One of the most interesting findings of this study was that cause-related marketing was the most influential CSR strategy in terms of shaping consumers' beliefs about an organization. Werder, following Kotler and Lee (2005), suggested the level of involvement of consumers through the purchasing process enhanced their personal experience of contributing to a social cause and improved their perceptions of the organization. This is yet another example of how strategic communication can bridge otherwise highly insulated approaches to the study of communication phenomena. The integration of public relations and marketing concepts in the study of CSR seems to be one such case, as the previously mentioned Ragas and Roberts (2009) study showed.

Other areas where strategic communication made an impact at the micro level are in public diplomacy and country reputation, health communication and political communication. Traditionally these domains are viewed as independent communication domains, as is evident in the different divisions in national and international communication associations. However, through strategic communication these domains have found some common ground. In health communication, strategic communication was specifically studied in the crisis context. In two instances, researchers from Africa found that well-focused and well-planned strategic communication campaigns were essential to successfully communicate during public health scares (Akpabio, 2008; Kiwanuka-Tondo, Hamilton, & Jameson, 2009). Bowen and Heath (2007) similarly found that inconsistent and unmanaged information campaigns led to confusion and misinformation. From these studies it appears that strategic communication has found a niche in health communication, particularly in the context of health campaigns.

Strategic communication literature in the context of political communication is somewhat more diverse and runs the gamut of political advertising in election campaigns in Korea (Chen & Kim, 2011), to civic participation in the political process in the United States (Zhang & Seltzer, 2010), and political communication consulting in Europe (Hoffman, Steiner, & Jarren, 2008). Another area where strategic communication was studied in the context of political communication was in the use of social media (Sweetser & Lariscy, 2008). The use of social media in political campaigns will likely become an important focus area for the field.

Studies of the impact of technology on strategic communication were mostly conducted in the context of corporations. For instance, Hughes and Porter (2007) found working in high-tech environments enhanced the status and power of communication practitioners and Catalino's (2007) prediction that corporate blogs will become a permanent fixture of the strategic communication mix came true. Websites also were shown to be efficient and cost-effective tools to raise funds for non-profits (Ingenhoff & Koelling, 2010) and a previously mentioned study showed how activists successfully challenged the Disney Corporation through the clever use of a website (Feldner & Meisenbach, 2007).

One final example of how strategic communication is used in studies across many communication disciplines is the case of public diplomacy and country reputation. In addition to the previously mentioned study of the successful relaunch of Columbian coffee globally and locally (Molleda & Roberts, 2008), Molleda (2011) conducted a content analysis of international news agencies' coverage to analyze how blame is shifted globally through news coverage. Countries with low country reputation are more vulnerable to be blamed for transnational incidents.

Strategic communication is also receiving increasing attention in public diplomacy. Fitzpatrick, Kendrick and Fullerton (2011) found that information and policy dimensions were the most important factors that determined attitudes to the United States, more so than local culture and values. Strategic communication on CSR initiatives by U.S. companies in Romania also contributed to public diplomacy efforts of the United States (White, Vanc, & Coman, 2011), showing that nonstate actors can play an important role in the diplomatic efforts of their country of origin.

Future Directions

The above review of strategic communication literature is by no means exhaustive. The aim of this review was to determine the status of the field and to see where researchers and academics are focusing their attention. It also was an effort to determine if strategic communication is a paradigm or domain for the study of communication practice different from other existing fields.

This chapter might not come up with a definitive answer to that question except to say that strategic communication is a *process* that is used in many different communication fields, including public relations, corporate communication, health communication, and all the other fields of practice mentioned above. One of the areas where it might be used least is, ironically, organizational communication as practice. It might well be that strategic communication has limited usefulness for many of these disciplines. For instance, public relations keeps its focus on publics rather than on stakeholders. That is a very important distinction because publics have a limited use in strategic communication and definitely do not define the field. Similarly, not all health communication is strategic and not all strategic communication is health related. At the same time, strategic communication is used for very specific purposes in these two fields. One can argue that strategic communication is not there to replace any other communication discipline but rather to expand our understanding of how the process of communicating strategically shapes and is shaped at the three levels of analysis. An excellent example of how the different areas of practice inform us about strategic communication is the role of the communication strategist that emerged from three studies on three continents that also included advertising practitioners (Holtzhausen & Zerfass, 2011a).

The vision for strategic communication Hallahan et al. (2007) set for the field was neither to replace other fields of practice nor to become part of a naming war. The vision was to look across areas of practice and find theoretical and practical commonalities that can be analyzed and studied. The overview in this chapter shows the vision for the field is well on its way to being realized.

There are, however, some major challenges. For instance, at the macro level, the use of strategic communication in the promotion of capitalism and a free market philosophy has not been addressed. Another under-researched area relating to strategic communication at the macro level is how activists strategically use social media to become active and change society. At the same time, strategic communication as a defined field of study is relatively new and there is still a great deal of work to do. New media technologies have now forever changed our ability to communicate in the public sphere, which in turn will lead to many new opportunities for research. This relates not only to political and social issues but also to marketing, sales, and CSR where new technology changes the way consumers make product choices, interact with marketers, make charitable contributions, and many more.

This also is true for strategic communication research at the meso level, where one of the most neglected areas is the impact of communication technology on strategic communication. One area in particular that needs attention is how communication in alternative structures such as networks and virtual organizations challenges strategic communicators, not only in terms of information dissemination but also in terms of shaping organizational culture and including many different and diverse voices. One of the biggest challenges to strategic communicators at the meso level is the concept of emergence and how to harness the power of all viewpoints in the strategic communication process. Yet another challenge is the concept of the borderless organization and the notion that meaning is shaped in the process of communicating, or in the in-between of communication. This truly challenges notions of control and rationality of formal communication. Here too a lot of work is needed.

At the micro level there still is a shortage of literature on strategic communication in the context of marketing and branding and of consumers as stakeholders. Consumer behavior is well established in marketing and strategic message strategies in that area have great potential for future research. Here too the impact and use of social media in strategic communication will become a major future focus area for strategic communication researchers. While the study of strategic communication in many different areas of practice has begun, it is still in a fledgling stage and it will be interesting to see how research in different domains of practice will unfold.

Strategic communication not only offers multiple possibilities for research and education, but it is also attractive for practitioners working in communications. When asked to value alternative concepts to describe the various internal and external communication activities by an organization in the largest empirical study on the profession worldwide, 61.3% of 2,209 respondents favored "strategic communication," which is slightly less than "corporate communications" (67.9%), but clearly more than "communication management" (55.7%), "public relations" (46.7%), "integrated communications" (45.9%), and "organizational communication" (32.6%) (Zerfass et al., 2011, p. 26). Interestingly, the support for corporate communications differs widely between professionals working in various types of organizations, while strategic communication is equally appealing to the whole field and might be a term that unifies the debate and shapes a new identity for the future. Obviously, the acceptance of a concept neither means that the core idea has been internalized, nor that it is really practiced. But the accordance between theory and practice offers many opportunities to advance the paradigm of strategic communication within the near future.

References

Akpabio, E. (2008). Management of "killer" Indomie scare and impact on consumer confidence: A case study. *International Journal of Strategic Communication, 2*(4), 244–252.

Austin, E. W., & Pinkleton, B. E. (2006). *Strategic public relations management: Planning and managing effective communication programs* (2nd ed.). Mahwah, NJ: Lawrence Erlbaum.

Bakar, H. A., & Connaughton, S. L. (2010). Relationship between supervisory communication and commitment to workgroup: A multilevel analysis approach. *International Journal of Strategic Communication, 4*(1), 39–57.

Bentele, G., & Nothhaft, H. (2010). Strategic communication and the public sphere from a European perspective. *International Journal of Strategic Communication, 4*(2), 93–116.

Botan, C. H., & Penchalapadu, P. (2009). Using sense-making and coorientation to rank strategic communication in state Emergency Operations Plans (EOPs). *International Journal of Strategic Communication, 3*(3), 199–216.

Bowen, S., & Heath, R. L. (2007). Narrative of the SARS epidemic and ethical implications for public health crises. *International Journal of Strategic Communication, 1*(2), 73–91.

Bruhn, M. (2006). *Integrierte Kommunikation in den deutschsprachigen Ländern. Bestandsaufnahme in Deutschland, Österreich und der Schweiz* [Integrated communications in the German-speaking countries: An inventory in Germany, Austria, and Switzerland]. Wiesbaden, Germany: Gabler.

Canales, J. I., & Vilà, J. (2005). Strategy effects on managerial action. In S. W. Floyd, J. Roos, C. D. Jacob, & F. W. Kellermanns (Eds.), *Innovating strategy process* (pp. 33–46). Malden, MA: Blackwell Publishing.

Catalino, C. S. (2007). Megaphones to the internet and the world: The role of blogs in corporate communications. *International Journal of Strategic Communication, 1*(4), 247–262.

Chen, H.-T., & Kim, Y. (2011). Attacking or self-promoting? The influence of tone of advertising and issue relevance on candidate evaluations and the likelihood of voting for an emerging challenger in Korea. *International Journal of Strategic Communication, 5*(4), 261–280.

Christensen, L. T., & Cornelissen, J. (2011). Bridging corporate and organizational communication: Review, development and a look to the future. *Management Communication Quarterly, 25*(3), 383–414.

Coombs, W. T., & Holladay, S. (2012). *Managing corporate social responsibility: A communication approach.* Malden, MA: Wiley-Blackwell.

Courtright, J. L., & Smudde, P. M. (2010). Recall communications: Discourse genres, symbolic charging, and message design. *International Journal of Strategic Communication, 4*(1), 58–74.

Dewey, J. (1984). The public and its problems. In J. A. Boydston & B. A. Walsh (Eds.), *John Dewey: The later works, 1925–1953 (Vol. 2: 1925–1927).* Carbondale: Southern Illinois University Press.

Einwiller, S., & Boenigk, M. (2012). Examining the link between integrated communication management and communication effectiveness in medium-sized enterprises. *Journal of Marketing Communications, 18*(5), 335–361.

Eisenberg, E., Goodall, H. L. J., & Tretheway, A. (2007). *Organizational communication. Balancing creativity and constraint* (5th ed.). Boston: Bedford/St. Martin's.

Ermarth, E. D. (2001). Agency in the discursive condition. *History and Theory, 40,* 34–58.

Feldner, S. B., & Meisenbach, R. J. (2007). SaveDisney.com and activist challenges: A Habermasian perspective on corporate legitimacy. *International Journal of Strategic Communication, 1*(4), 207–226.

Fitzpatrick, K., Kendrick, A., & Fullerton, J. (2011). Factors contributing to anti-Americanism among people abroad: A retrospective view from the frontlines of U.S. public diplomacy. *International Journal of Strategic Communication, 5*(3), 154–170.

Foucault, M. (1988). Power and sex. In L. D. Kritzman (Ed.), *Michael Foucault: Politics, philosophy, culture* (pp. 110–124). New York: Routledge.

Frandsen, F., & Johansen, W. (2009). Institutionalizing crisis communication in the public sector: An explorative study in Danish municipalities. *International Journal of Strategic Communication, 3*(2), 102–115.

Garner, J. T. (2009). Strategic dissent: Expressions of organizational dissent motivated by influence goals. *International Journal of Strategic Communication, 3*(1), 34–51.

Grunig, J. E. (1992). The development of public relations research in the United States and its status in communication science. In H. Avenarius & W. Armbrecht (Eds.), *Ist Public Relations eine Wissenschaft?* [Is public relations a science?] (pp. 103–132). Opladen, Germany: Westdeutscher Verlag.

Grunig, J. E., & Grunig, L. A. (2008). Excellence theory in public relations: Past, present, and future. In A. Zerfass, B. van Ruler, & K. Sriramesh (Eds.), *Public relations research.*

European and international perspectives and innovations (pp. 327–347). Wiesbaden, Germany: VS Verlag für Sozialwissenschaften.

Grunig, J. E., & Hunt, T. (1984). *Managing public relations*. Fort Worth, TX: Holt, Rinehart & Winston.

Grunig, L. A. (1986, September). Environmental and organizational response: Contemporary cases of collective behavior. Paper presented at the 15th annual conference of the North American Association for Environmental Education, Eugene, OR.

Habermas, J. (1979). *Communication and the evolution of society*. Boston: Beacon Press.

Habermas, J. (2006). Political communication in media society: Does democracy still enjoy an epistemic dimension? The impact of normative theory on empirical research. *Communication Theory, 16*(4), 411–426.

Hafsi, T., & Howard, T. (2005). Reflections on the field of strategy. In S. W. Floyd, J. Roos, C. D. Jacobs, & F. W. Kellermanns (Eds.), *Innovating strategy process* (pp. 239–246). Malden, MA: Blackwell Publishing.

Hallahan, K., Holtzhausen, D. R., Van Ruler, B., Verčič, D., & Sriramesh, K. (2007). Defining strategic communication. *International Journal of Strategic Communication, 1*(1), 3–35.

Hatch, M. J. (1997). *Organization theory: Modern, symbolic, and postmodern perspectives*. Oxford: Oxford University Press.

Heracleous, L. (2003). *Strategy and organization: Realizing strategic management*. Cambridge: Cambridge University Press.

Hoffman, J., Steiner, A., & Jarren, O. (2008). Unravelling the muddle of services and clients: Political communication consulting. *International Journal of Strategic Communication, 2*(2), 100–114.

Holmström, S., Falkheimer, J., & Nielsen, A. G. (2010). Legitimacy and strategic communication in globalization: The cartoon crisis and other legitimacy conflicts. *International Journal of Strategic Communication, 4*(1), 1–18.

Holtzhausen, D. R. (2008). Strategic communication. In W. Donsbach (Ed.), *The international encyclopedia of communication* (vol. 10, pp. 4848–4855). Malden, MA: Blackwell.

Holtzhausen, D. R. (2012). *Public relations as activism: Postmodern approaches to theory and practice*. New York: Routledge.

Holtzhausen, D. R., & Verwey, S. (1996). Towards a general theory of public relations. *Communicare, 15*(2), 25–56.

Holtzhausen, D. R., & Zerfass, A. (2011a). The status of strategic communication in 48 countries. *International Journal of Strategic Communication, 5*(2), 71–73.

Holtzhausen, D. R., & Zerfass, A. (2011b, May). Strategic communication: A concept at the center of applied communication? Paper presented at the Preconference "Strategic communication – A concept at the center of applied communications," International Communication Association, Annual Conference, Boston, MA.

Hughes, J., & Porter, L. V. (2007). High-tech persuaders: Proximity to innovation and communicators' roles, status, and power. *International Journal of Strategic Communication, 1*(4), 227–245.

Ingenhoff, D., & Koelling, A. M. (2010). Web sites as dialogic tools for charitable fundraising NPOs: A comparative study. *International Journal of Strategic Communication, 4*(3), 171–188.

Ki, E.-J., & Hon, L. C. (2009). Causal linkages between relationship cultivation strategies and relationship quality outcomes. *International Journal of Strategic Communication, 3*(4), 242–263.

Kim, J.-N., Grunig, J. E., & Ni, L. (2010). Reconceptualizing the communicative action of publics: Acquisition, selection, and transmission of information in problematic situations. *International Journal of Strategic Communication, 4*(2), 126–154.

Kim, S., Avery, E. J., & Lariscy, R. W. (2011). Reputation repair at the expense of providing instructing and adjusting information following crises. *International Journal of Strategic Communication, 5*(3), 183–199.

King, C. (2010). Emergent communication strategies. *International Journal of Strategic Communication, 4*, 19–38.

Kiwanuka-Tondo, J., Hamilton, M., & Jameson, J. K. (2009). AIDS communication campaigns in Uganda: Organizational factors and campaign planning as predictors of successful campaign execution. *International Journal of Strategic Communication, 3*(3), 165–182.

Kotler, P., & Lee, N. (2005). *Corporate social responsiblity: Doing the most good for your company and your cause.* Hoboken, NJ: John Wiley & Sons.

Lyotard, J.-F. (1992). Answering the question: What is postmodernism? In C. Jencks (Ed.), *The postmodern reader* (pp. 138–150). London: Academy Editions.

Malcolm, S. B., McDaniel, H. C., & Langett, J. (2008). Philosophical bridges for IMC: Grounding the practice. *International Journal of Strategic Communication, 2*(1), 19–30.

Matusitz, J. (2007). Improving terrorism preparedness for hospitals: Toward better interorganizational communication. *International Journal of Strategic Communication, 1*(3), 169–189.

Molleda, J.-C. (2011). Advancing the theory of cross-national conflict shifting: A case discussion and qualitative content analysis of a transnational crisis' newswire coverage. *International Journal of Strategic Communication, 5*(1), 49–70.

Molleda, J.-C., & Roberts, M. (2008). The value of "authenticity" in "glocal" strategic communication: The Juan Valdez campaign. *International Journal of Strategic Communication, 2*(3), 154–174.

Ni, L., & Kim, J.-N. (2009). Classifying publics: Communication behaviors and problem-solving characteristics in controversial issues. *International Journal of Strategic Communication, 3*(4), 217–241.

Nothhaft, H., & Wehmeier, S. (2007). Coping with complexity: Sociocybernetics as a framework for communication management. *International Journal of Strategic Communication, 1*(3), 151–168.

Park, H., & Reber, B. H. (2011). The organization–public relationship and crisis communication: The effect of the organization–public relationship on publics' perceptions of crisis and attitude toward the organization. *International Journal of Strategic Communication, 5*(4), 240–260.

Percy, L., & Elliot, R. (2009). *Strategic advertising management.* Oxford: Oxford University Press.

Quinn, J. E., Mintzberg, H., & James, R. M. (1991). *The strategy process: Concepts, contexts, and cases.* Englewood Cliffs, NJ: Prentice Hall.

Ragas, M. W., & Roberts, M. S. (2009). Communicating corporate social responsibility and brand sincerity: A case study of Chipotle Mexican Grill's 'Food with Integrity' program. *International Journal of Strategic Communication, 3*(4), 264–280.

Ristino, R. J. (2008). The sociocultural model of public relations/communication management practice: A critical-cultural perspective. *International Journal of Strategic Communication, 2*(1), 54–73.

Rughase, O. G. (2006). *Identity and strategy.* Cheltenham: Edward Elgar Publishing, Inc.

Sandhu, S. (2009). Strategic communication: An institutional perspective. *International Journal of Strategic Communication, 3*(2), 72–93.

Self, C. (2010). Hegel, Habermas, and community: The public in the new media era. *International Journal of Strategic Communication, 4*(2), 78–92.

Shaia, J. S., & Gonzenbach, W. J. (2007). Communications with management in times of difficulty and crisis: Silence explained. *International Journal of Strategic Communication, 1*(3), 139–150.

Shannon, C. E., & Weaver, W. (1949). *The mathematical theory of communication.* Urbana: University of Illinois Press.

Sloan, J. (2006). *Learning to think strategically.* Burlington, MA: Elsevier.

Ströh, U. (2007). Relationships and participation: A complexity science approach to change communication. *International Journal of Strategic Communication, 1*(2), 123–137.

Sweetser, K. D., & Lariscy, R. W. (2008). Candidates make good friends: An analysis of candidates' uses of Facebook. *International Journal of Strategic Communication, 2*(3), 175–198.

Tindall, N. T. J., & Holtzhausen, D. R. (2011). Toward a roles theory for strategic communication: The case of South Africa. *International Journal of Strategic Communication, 5*(2), 74–94.

Van Woerkum, C., & Aarts, N. (2011). Organizing by projective hearing: The active use of a passive sense. *International Journal of Strategic Communication, 5*(3), 171–182.

Veil, S., & Mitchell, K. (2010). Terror management theory: Promoting tolerance in campus safety campaigns. *International Journal of Strategic Communication, 4*(4), 207–224.

Verhoeven, P., Zerfass, A., & Tench, R. (2011). Strategic orientation of communication professionals in Europe. *International Journal of Strategic Communication, 5*(2), 95–117.

Werder, K. G. P. (2008). The effect of doing good: An experimental analysis of the influence of corporate social responsiblity initiatives on beliefs, attitudes, and behavioral intention. *International Journal of Strategic Communication, 2*(2), 115–135.

Werder, K. G. P., & Holtzhausen, D. R. (2009). An analysis of the influence of public relations department leadership style on public relations strategy use and effectiveness. *Journal of Public Relations Research, 21*(4), 404–427.

Werder, K. G. P., & Holtzhausen, D. R. (2011). Organizational structures and their relationship with communication management practices: A public relations perspective from the United States. *International Journal of Strategic Communication, 5*(2), 118–142.

White, C., Vanc, A., & Coman, I. (2011). Corporate social responsibility in transitional countries: Public relations as a component of public diplomacy in Romania. *International Journal of Strategic Communication, 5*(4), 281–292.

Zerfass, A. (2008). Corporate communication revisited: integrating business strategy and strategic communication. In A. Zerfass, B. Van Ruler, & K. Sriramesh (Eds.), *Public relations research: European and international perspectives and innovations* (pp. 65–96). Wiesbaden, Germany: VS Verlag für Sozialwissenschaften.

Zerfass, A. (2010). *Unternehmensführung und Öffentlichkeitsarbeit. Grundlegung einer Theorie der Unternehmenskommunikation und Public Relations.* [Corporate management and public relations: A theory of corporate communication and public relations] (3rd rev. ed.). Wiesbaden, Germany: VS Verlag für Sozialwissenschaften.

Zerfass, A., & Huck, S. (2007). Innovation, communication, and leadership: New developments in strategic communication. *International Journal of Strategic Communication, 1*(2), 107–122.

Zerfass, A., Verhoeven, P., Tench, R., Moreno, A., & Verčič, D. (2011). *European Communication Monitor 2011: Empirical insights into strategic communication in Europe. Results of a survey in 43 countries.* Brussels: EACD/EUPRERA.

Zhang, W., & Seltzer, T. (2010). Another piece of the puzzle: Advancing social capital theory by examining the effect of political party relationship quality on political and civic participation. *International Journal of Strategic Communication, 4*(3), 155–170.

18

THE PRETORIA SCHOOL OF THOUGHT

From Strategy to Governance and Sustainability

Estelle de Beer, Benita Steyn, and Ronél Rensburg

Abstract

In the past two decades South Africa has contributed to the global search for excellence in communication management, initiated by the Excellence Study in Public Relations and Communication Management. This chapter describes the development of what has come to be known as the Pretoria School of Thought – a scientific worldview on strategic communication management shared by researchers, lecturers and postgraduate students in the academic field of Communication Management at the University of Pretoria.

The foundation of the Pretoria School of Thought is based on the differentiation between 'strategic communication management' and 'communication management' taking place on different organizational levels. Theoretical pillars include the corporate communication 'strategist' role at the top management (macro/environmental) level, contributing to the development of the organization's enterprise strategy; and the redefinition of the historic 'manager' as a role played at the middle management (meso/functional) level, focusing on the development of corporate communication strategy linked to enterprise strategy.

The next wave of thinking in the Pretoria School of Thought includes the conceptualization of strategic communication management in the triple context environment, providing a research area within which contemporary scientific and pragmatic questions can be addressed. Its assumption is that the most value is added at the strategic level, taking into account the changing environment within which organizations operate with specific reference to governance and sustainability.

Key Words

Pretoria School of Thought, strategic communication management paradigm, communication strategist role, enterprise strategy, corporate communication strategy, sustainability, governance, King Report on Governance 2009, reflective paradigm

Introduction

Spurred by the movement in the early 1980s to search for the characteristics of excellently managed corporations (Peters & Waterman, 1982), the Excellence Study in Public Relations and Communication Management was launched in 1985 (Grunig, 1992a). The resultant Excellence Theory (Dozier, Grunig & Grunig, 1995) provided the impetus for a global search for excellence in communication management that started in the 1990s and still continues.

South Africa (SA) contributed to this movement by further exploring the value-added contribution that communication management could make to the organization. The worldview that resulted has come to be known as the *Pretoria School of Thought* (De Beer, 2010) – a paradigm that focuses on the conceptualization of communication management in the strategic context of the organization. A significant early contribution has been the differentiation between 'strategic communication management' and 'communication management' taking place on different organizational levels (Steyn, 2007, pp. 139–141) – as manifested in the conceptualization and empirical verification of the corporate communication[1] 'strategist' role at the top management (macro/environmental) level, and the redefinition of the historic 'manager' as a role played at the middle management (meso/functional) level (Steyn, 2000a, 2000b, 2000c).

The strategic positioning of communication management in the organization has gained momentum with the latest research in the field (Gregory & Willis, forthcoming July 2013; Grunig, 2006, 2009; Invernizzi, 2008; Steyn & De Beer, 2012a). The institutionalization of strategic communication management within the triple context environment – people, planet and profit – is a seminal perspective that is shaping the theoretical and pragmatic thinking in the field of communication management (De Beer & Rensburg, 2011a, 2011b; Muzi Falconi, 2010; Rensburg & De Beer, 2003; Steyn, 2009, 2011; Steyn & De Beer, 2012b; Steyn & Niemann, 2008, 2010; Stockholm Accords, 2010).

The practice of including stakeholders in the organization's decision-making processes has highlighted the role of strategic communication management in identifying the legitimate expectations of organizational stakeholders through research; providing this information to the strategic management team and the board; and giving feedback to stakeholders in the integrated report (IoD, 2009; Steyn & De Beer, 2011).

Early Beginnings of the Pretoria School of Thought

Communication science as a discipline has been offered at various SA universities in the humanities since 1968, with public relations and organizational communication as specialization areas. However, at the University of Pretoria (UP) only Marketing has been taught (since 1970), as a field of study within the Department of Business Economics (now Business Management).

When decision-makers at UP announced at the beginning of the 1990s that a degree in corporate communication was to be initiated, Gustav Puth drove the positioning debate towards the management sciences (as advocated by Argenti, 1996). The reasoning was that corporate communication is a functional terrain similar to marketing, finance and human resources, and a broad management background would enable practitioners to better understand the business world and the 'language it speaks' (Hatfield, 1994).

At the time, this perspective on the academic roots of corporate communication was in contrast to most academic views, not only in SA but worldwide (Argenti, 1996; Botan & Hazleton, 1989; Brody, 1991; Grunig & Hunt, 1984). It was, however, the view of Puth that the positioning in the humanities did not produce the unique body of knowledge necessary for the advancement of the profession. Corporate communication was therefore to be regarded as a management discipline and students at UP were to be prepared for management positions.

In 1993, the first undergraduate students enrolled in the degree BCom (Communication Management) at UP. It was a separate field of study in the newly formed Department of Marketing and Communication Management, situated in the Faculty of Economic and Management Sciences. Puth, first head of the Department, can be considered as the 'father' of communication management in South Africa. Ronél Rensburg, head of the Department from 2000 to 2009, was instrumental in arranging an international evaluation of the Communication Management division by Larissa Grunig in 2000. The various text books authored/edited by Puth and by Rensburg are still widely used in SA.

The first Honors and Master's degrees in Communication Management were offered at UP in 1995, the emphasis being on the management and strategic perspective of corporate communication (rather than the technician or skills-oriented perspective common to the field). The textbooks *Excellence in Public Relations and Communication Management* (Grunig, 1992a) and *Manager's Guide to Excellence in Public Relations and Communication Management* (Dozier, Grunig, & Grunig, 1995) were core sources in the postgraduate courses in Communication Management.

Foundations of the Pretoria School of Thought

The Excellence Study (Grunig, 1992a) created intense interest and discussions in the Master's classes in Communication Management at UP, especially the concept of communication excellence. The Excellence Study's empirical findings indicate two prerequisites for an organization to practise 'excellent' communication (Dozier et al., 1995, pp. 11–17):

- The corporate communication manager must have the *knowledge* to play a managerial role, especially knowledge of strategic management and two-way symmetrical communication.
- In addition, there must be *shared expectations* between the corporate communication function and top management on the role that communication should play in the organization.

These findings triggered a two-phase research project in Communication Excellence at UP in 1997, conducted by three staff members, namely, Groenewald (1998), Steyn (2000a) and De Beer (2001).

Phase 1: Knowledge Base of Corporate Communication Managers

Groenewald (1998) determined that communication managers in SA organizations perceived management, strategic communication and management communication skills to be significantly more important in their positions than technical communication skills. However, the effectiveness of their training in the former was significantly lower than their training in technical communication skills. Based on her empirical findings, Groenewald developed a model for Communication Management training and suggested further research on a strategic role for corporate communication.

Steyn addressed the lack of strategic communication and management skills among corporate communication managers by:

1. conceptualizing the role of the corporate communication 'strategist' and redefining the historical roles of the 'manager' and 'technician' (Steyn, 2000a);
2. conceptualizing corporate communication strategy and developing a model for its implementation (Steyn, 2000a, 2000c; Steyn & Puth, 2000).

Phase 2: Shared Expectations between Top Management and the Corporate Communication Manager

De Beer (2001) determined communication managers' perceptions of senior management's expectations of excellent communication in SA organizations. A major finding was that it is the perception of communication managers that senior management expect them to make a strategic contribution to organizational decision-making, by playing the corporate communication manager role.

Steyn (2000b) furthermore quantitatively determined 'CEO normative role expectations' as well as 'CEO perceptions of the role performance' of the most senior corporate communication practitioner, with regard to the 'strategist', 'manager' and 'technician' roles.

Theoretical Pillars of the Pretoria School of Thought: A Strategic Communication Management Paradigm

In 2000, a research programme in the fledgling field of Strategic Communication Management was initiated by Steyn. Various staff members and students contributed during the next decade, planting the seeds that eventually became known as the Pretoria School of Thought.

Teaching and research at UP represent a 'strategic communication management' paradigm (scientific worldview), its central concepts being '*role*' (specifically of the strategist), and '*levels of strategy formulation*' (specifically the contribution of corporate communication to the development of the enterprise strategy at top management level).

Strategic communication management[2] assumes corporate communication to be a strategic management function with a mandate to function at the strategic (macro or societal or environmental) level. In its strategic role, corporate communication assists an organization (or institution) to adapt to its societal and stakeholder environment by feeding intelligence with regard to strategic stakeholders[3] (and their concerns/expectations), societal issues and the publics[4]/interest groups that emerge around the issues, into the organization's strategy formulation processes (Steyn, 2007). According to Grunig, Grunig and Dozier (2002, pp. 143, 383), this is the 'full-participation' approach to strategic corporate communication where the function is 'empowered', i.e. involved *before* strategic decisions are made.

Three Roles for Corporate Communication: Differentiating Strategist from Manager and Technician

Steyn's (2000a) initial conceptualization of three roles was based on Van Riel's mirror and window function of corporate communication (1995, p. 2).

- Steyn broadened the *mirror* function to the 'monitoring of relevant environmental developments and the anticipation of their consequences for the organization's policies and strategies, especially with regard to relationships with stakeholders and other interest groups in society'. These activities constitute the role of the *strategist* (Steyn, 2000a; Steyn & Puth, 2000).
- The *window* function was broadened to 'the preparation and execution of a communication policy and strategy, resulting in messages that portray all facets of the organization in a transparent way' (Steyn, 2000a; Steyn & Puth, 2000). The manager develops a corporate communication strategy and strategic plan while the technician implements it through plans and programmes.

In order to contribute most to organizational effectiveness, Grunig (in Grunig, 1992b, p. 3) sees corporate communication as being practised on the *macro* (strategic/societal/environmental) level (the strategist); the *meso* (functional/ divisional) level (the manager); and the *micro* (implementation/operational) level (the technician).

Meta-Theoretical Framework: Three Roles for Corporate Communication

The meta-theoretical framework for three roles (strategist, manager and technician) was constructed from a synthesis of seven approaches (Steyn, 2003a):

1. *Dialogic approach* (Gadamer, 1985), a dialogue or conversation between organization and stakeholders/societal interest groups.
2. *Open systems approach* to organizational effectiveness (Grunig, 1992a). The strategist acquires information from the environment to facilitate organizational adaptation to stakeholder views/societal norms; the manager and technician disseminate (provide) information on organizational positions/ policies/strategies.
3. *Ecological (boundary spanning) approach* (Everett, 1993). The strategist scans the environment and provides intelligence for strategic decision-making processes and adaptation. The manager develops core themes/messages (corporate communication strategy) to address strategic issues and stakeholder expectations/ values, which the technician communicates to strategic stakeholders/relevant societal interest groups.
4. *Corporate social responsibility/responsiveness approach* (Sethi, cited in Carroll, 1996) (issues management). The strategist identifies strategic, social and other issues for consideration in strategy development. The manager identifies the consequences on stakeholders/societal interest groups, and decides what must be communicated. The technician implements the strategy by developing communication plans and activities.
5. *Corporate community approach* (Halal, 2000), where management facilitates joint problem solving/collaboration with stakeholders. The strategist keeps top management informed of stakeholder expectations/values – enabling mutually beneficial relationship building.
6. *New institutional approach to the organization* (Rumelt, Schendal, & Teece, 1994), where society is viewed as the source of rules, standards, expectations, etc. The strategist brings societal values/norms to the organization's attention in order to adapt organizational strategies. The manager and technician communicate the identity of the 'adapted' organization to stakeholders/interest groups – obtaining legitimacy and a licence to operate.
7. *Excellence approach* to communication management (Dozier et al., 1995; Grunig, 1992a), stabilizing relationships with strategic stakeholders; identifying/

managing interest groups and activists; and reducing conflict/uncertainty in strategic decision-making.

The meta-theoretical framework for the three corporate communication roles mentioned was constructed mainly based on US literature and did not include European approaches to corporate communication (which were subsequently included).

A Societal Approach to Corporate Communication

The BledCom 2002 Symposium (Slovenia) on the theme 'The Status of Public Relations Knowledge in Europe and Around the World' highlighted theoretical developments in corporate communication *outside* the USA. A contribution by Rensburg on an African perspective on the Bled Manifesto culminated in a chapter in the first edition of *The Global Public Relations Handbook* (Rensburg, 2003).

This conference had a major influence on the Pretoria School of Thought. The Bled Manifesto (Van Ruler & Verčič, 2002, p. 16) explicated the European societal approach to corporate communication as a strategic process of viewing an organization from an 'outside' perspective, showing a special concern for broader societal issues. Legitimacy and public trust in the organization are central concepts in this approach and an organization's inclusiveness, preserving its 'licence to operate', is of primary concern (Verčič, Van Ruler, Bütschi, & Flodin, 2001, p. 382).

Four Roles/Dimensions for Corporate Communication

The Bled Manifesto also highlighted the four dimensions/roles that emerged from the European Body of Knowledge (EBOK) project (Verčič et al., 2001). Considered to be the most important, the reflective role has to do with analyzing changing standards, values and norms in society and pointing these out to organizational decision-makers so that they can adjust the standards and values of the organization regarding social responsibility and legitimacy. The other three European roles were the managerial, operational and educational roles (Verčič et al., 2001).

Although an undefined concept in Europe, the reflective role appeared to be similar to the strategist role conceptualized and verified in SA.

Comparative Analysis: SA Strategist Role Versus European Reflective Role

In a comparative analysis conducted by Steyn and Bütschi (2003), the three SA roles (strategist, manager and technician) were found to be theoretically similar and practically identical to three of the EBOK roles (reflective, managerial and operational).

Based on the four EBOK roles and the comparative analysis which found Steyn's three roles similar to three of the EBOK roles, Steyn and Green (2006) reconceptualized the strategist role to include a reflective dimension; developed measurement items for EBOK's four roles; and subsequently empirically verified four roles in SA. In Table 18.1, the purified items for the role of the PR strategist/reflectionist that resulted from this research can be viewed. The four items in boldface are from Steyn's original strategist index (Steyn, 2000b).

Between 2003 and 2009, various postgraduate studies were conducted on the role of the strategist (Le Roux & Steyn, 2006; Steyn & Everett, 2009) – some of them including the reflective dimension (Van Heerden & Rensburg, 2005; Steyn & Green, 2006).

TABLE 18.1 Purified Items for the Role of the PR 'Strategist/Reflectionist'

Factor Loadings	PR 'Strategist/Reflectionist' = Factor 2 (Cronbach's Alpha 0.91)
0.78	*Advise top management of societal values/norms so that company strategies can be adjusted accordingly
0.77	*Enlighten top management on societal expectations for socially responsible behaviour
0.74	*Make top management aware of the importance of accommodating perspectives (in society) different from their own
0.73	**Act as an 'early warning system' to top management before issues in the societal environment erupt into crises for our company**
0.70	*Influence top management's decisions to ensure that our company is regarded by society as being trustworthy
0.69	*Ensure a balance between organizational goals and the well-being of society
0.64	**Initiate dialogue with pressure groups in the societal environment that are limiting the company's autonomy (e.g. environmentalists/consumer advocates/legislators)**
0.64	*Ensure that top management balances the quest for the realization of organizational goals with respect for the natural environment (the planet)
0.62	**Explain to top management the impact of their behaviour (obtained through research) on key stakeholders (e.g. the media/investors/customers)**
0.59	**Act as an advocate for key stakeholders by explaining their views to top management**

Note: *New items that added a reflective dimension to Steyn's PR 'Strategist' index.
Source: Steyn and Green (2006).

The Reflective Paradigm for Corporate Communication

Another European scholar also influenced the Pretoria School of Thought considerably. Anchored in social systems theory, Holmström (1996) developed a reflective paradigm for corporate communication with *mutual reflection* as its core concept and social responsibility at the core of its practice. In this approach, the organization sees itself in the larger societal context, the ultimate objective being to generate social trust.

Reflective and Expressive Tasks for Corporate Communication

Mutual reflection consists of both a reflective and expressive task for corporate communication (Holmström, 1996, pp. 97–98):

- The *reflective* task is inward communication: selecting information on what is considered socially responsible behaviour in society and encouraging organizational members to balance their behaviour in accordance with expectations.
- The *expressive* task is outward communication, providing regular, widely distributed information (based on reflection) on the organization to help strengthen public trust in it.

Comparative Analysis: SA Mirror/Window Function Versus European Reflective/Expressive Task

In a comparative analysis conducted by Steyn and Bütschi (2003), the South African *mirror* function was found to be very similar to the European *reflective* task and the *window* function also shared similarities with the *expressive* task.

Reflective Paradigm Added to the Meta-Theoretical Framework for the Three SA Roles

Based on the comparative analyses outlined and the assumptions of the reflective paradigm, the latter was selected as the overarching paradigm for the research on Strategic Communication Management conducted in the Pretoria School of Thought.

Levels of Strategy Formulation

Another important pillar of the Pretoria School of Thought is the explication of corporate communication's contribution to organizational strategy formulation, described in detail in Steyn (2000c, 2003b); Steyn (2007); and Steyn and Niemann (2008, 2010). This contribution can be summarized as making inputs to the enterprise strategy at top management level (the role of the strategist); developing corporate communication strategy at the middle management level (the role of the manager); and developing operational strategy at the implementation level (the role of the technician).

Corporate Communication Strategy

In response to requests from industry, Steyn conceptualized corporate communication strategy (2000a) and developed a model for its implementation (2000c) through a longitudinal action research project conducted from 1999 to 2003 at UP. It was also based on findings of her research among chief executives (CEOs), *inter alia* that it was revealed that the development of corporate communication strategy supporting the corporate strategy was CEOs' highest expectation of the function (2000b). The model formed the core of *Corporate Communication Strategy*, the first textbook devoted solely to the strategic management of corporate communication (Steyn & Puth, 2000).

Between 2000 and 2006, the model for developing corporate communication strategy was applied to different contexts by postgraduate students at UP, for example, community development (Steyn & Nunes, 2001); government (Steyn & Green, 2001); the Internet (Steyn, Grobler, & Cilliers, 2005); and banking (Prinsloo, 2005; Worrall, 2005).

The conceptualization and operationalization of corporate communication strategy are discussed in detail in Steyn (2003b). It is further elaborated upon by Steyn (2007), where the concepts of 'deliberate' and 'emergent' communication strategy are introduced.

The Enterprise Strategy

The role of the communication strategist includes co-responsibility for developing the enterprise strategy (Steyn & Niemann, 2010), which addresses the organization's relationship with society as well as its political and social legitimacy. The enterprise strategy answers the question of what the organization *should* be doing (Freeman, 1984) and acts as a framework within which other, more specific types of strategies operate. It is also known as a societal role strategy (Freeman, 1984), bridging strategy, social strategy, institutional strategy, and the strategy level that achieves non-financial goals (Steyn & Niemann, 2008, 2010). The authors regard enterprise strategy as being similar to Botan's concept of integrative grand strategy (in Botan & Hazleton, 2006, p. 234).

In the corporate communication literature, the concept of the enterprise strategy was introduced as the strategy level at which corporate communication practitioners could or should make a strategic contribution at the top management level, i.e. in Steyn (2000a, 2003a, 2007, 2009); Steyn and Puth (2000); Prinsloo (2005); Worrall (2005); and Steyn and Niemann (2008, 2010).

Although the enterprise strategy is often not formally stated in organizations, it manifests by way of mission and vision statements, codes of conduct or ethics, approach to stakeholders, multi-stakeholder dialogue, ethical conduct, symmetrical communication, committees on social audits, and corporate philanthropy.

Strategic Reflection as the Core Concept of a Strategic Communication Management Paradigm

The findings of an analysis of the various roles studies conducted in the Pretoria School of Thought since the beginning of the decade (Steyn, 2009) indicated the purpose of corporate communication as being *reciprocal strategic reflection,* consisting of both a reflective and expressive task (as conceptualized by Holmström, 1996). The strategic role of corporate communication (as the reflective task/mirror function) is therefore *strategic reflection.* Based on this finding, Steyn (2009) relabelled her original PR 'strategist' role (which now includes a reflective dimension) as the 'reflective strategist'.

The 'reflective strategist' acts as an advocate for key stakeholders by explaining their views to management; makes the latter aware of the impact of their behaviour/organizational policies and strategies on key stakeholders and societal interest groups; and acts as an early warning system before issues in the environment erupt into crises.

Furthermore, the 'reflective strategist' influences management to adapt strategies to societal/stakeholder values, norms and expectations, balancing the quest for the realization of organizational goals with respect for the natural environment (the planet) and its inhabitants (the people). Management is made to understand that public trust is not earned by simply changing outward communication to signify responsibility – an organization actually has to behave accordingly.

Strategic Role of Corporate Communication: Contributing to Enterprise Strategy Development, Governance and Sustainability

Steyn and Niemann (2008) reported the empirical findings of a study that formed the foundations of a normative model for enterprise strategy development subsequently suggested. The model indicates that the enterprise strategy is developed at the macro organizational level within the context of *enterprise governance* (including enterprise relationship and enterprise risk governance), as well as social/ environmental *sustainability and responsibility* (Steyn & Niemann, forthcoming.

From this perspective, the reflective strategist:

- brings about shifts in organizational thinking necessary for implementation of a triple bottom line approach, and provides social and environmental intelligence;
- obtains input about/conveys concern and sensitivity to, *societal responsibility, sustainability and good governance;* and assists with their achievement;

- employs a reflective perspective to corporate reputation by *monitoring the environment* to identify *reputation and other strategic risks*, and addresses them through *communication strategies*;
- assists senior management to identify *strategic goals and stakeholder/societally responsive strategies*;
- oversees the *communication strategy* development process with stakeholders and other societal interest groups so that it is transparent and ethical; assists in *building relationships* with stakeholders; obtains legitimacy; and fosters social cohesion between business and society.

Theoretical Pillars of the Pretoria School of Thought: A Sustainability and Governance Approach to Strategic Communication Management

Early research by De Beer (2001) and Steyn (2000b) focused on 'shared expectations', the middle sphere of the Communication Excellence Factor identified in the Excellence Study (Dozier et al., 1995, p. 7). The concept of shared expectations (consisting of departmental power, the demand–delivery loop and the manager/adviser roles), initiated questions about the level at which corporate communication has value for the organization.

The *demand-delivery loop* construct remains of interest to De Beer (in progress), particularly the demands of top management in a changing triple context environment and the ability of the communication function to deliver on those demands. Previous research indicated that, apart from top management's demands for communication excellence, there was also a clear demand for communication practitioners to have *business knowledge* (Groenewald, 1998; Steyn, 2000b, 2003a). These are important variables in De Beer's research (in progress) on the conceptualization of communication management in a strategic organizational context. It started in 2003 with a research paper at the BledCom Conference (Rensburg & De Beer, 2003) entitled 'Reputation management and stakeholder engagement: An integrated approach to future corporate governance in South Africa.'

Delivering on the demands of top management requires new thinking in the field of communication management. A suggested point of departure is Van Riel and Fombrun's concepts of the *business and communication cycle* (2007, p. 60). It is imperative for communication professionals to understand the business cycle (the corporate strategy, business activities and financial performance) as well as the communication cycle (corporate communication, corporate reputation and supportive behavior towards the organization). In contemporary organizations, the business cycle has been extended to include the triple bottom line of environmental, social and financial considerations.

De Beer and Rensburg (2011b) state that an increasing number of organizations view *corporate responsibility* as integral to their systems of governance. It is their contention that a new approach to (strategic) communication management is needed to support the triple context domain in which contemporary business, government and civil society have to operate. A fundamental element of sustainability is the phenomenon of communication in all its manifestations.

The Triple Context: A Next Wave of Thinking

Measuring organizational performance against the triple bottom line has inevitable implications for communication management. If the organization is held accountable by its stakeholders for how it reaches its strategic goals in this environment, then the communication management function must also perform against those expectations.

As part of a qualitative research study (De Beer, in progress) on how communication should be managed on a macro level, De Beer became part of the research team for the King Report on Governance for South Africa (IoD, 2009), also known as King III. The King Committee, with its ten subcommittees, was led by Professor Mervyn King, SC. With its three pillars of sustainability, governance and strategy, King III (IoD, 2009) provides guidance on governance to companies listed on the Johannesburg Stock Exchange (JSE) and also serves as an example of best practice for the government and NGO sectors.

The first meetings of the King III Committee took place in 2007. De Beer was part of the Committee for Compliance and Stakeholder Relationships, which was responsible for writing King III's Chapter 6: 'Compliance with Laws, Rules, Codes and Standards', as well as Chapter 8: 'Governing Stakeholder Relationships'. She also served briefly on the Committee for Integrated Reporting and Disclosure, which wrote Chapter 9: 'Integrated Reporting and Disclosure'.

With the Excellence Theory as the foundation for her research, De Beer (in progress) explored the demand-delivery loop of expectations for the duration of the writing of the Report and was confronted with the typical business and communication demands of top management, in practice and in theory. Intense deliberations on the inclusive stakeholder approach to corporate governance culminated in a separate chapter in King III on the governing of stakeholder relationships – its core concepts being corporate reputation, stakeholder and shareholder relationships and communication. During the public comment phase of the King III draft, the conceptualization of Chapter 8 was confirmed by Toni Muzi Falconi of Italy – an academic and communication professional with a specific interest in the 'governing of stakeholder relationships' (see Muzi Falconi, 2010).

After the launch of King III in 2009, Muzi Falconi brought together a team of academics and practitioners from around the world (including the authors of this chapter) to compile the Stockholm Accords (2010) – a guiding document for the profession that contains concepts from King III. De Beer facilitated one of the six virtual groups, namely, the governance working group, while Rensburg co-facilitated a session on communicators' contribution to sustainability during the Global Alliance's World Public Relations Forum in Stockholm, where the final text of the Accords was approved. The Accords considered the business concepts of sustainability, governance and management; the communication concepts of internal and external communication; and the coordination of internal and external communication.

Sustainability and Governance: Two New Perspectives in the Communication Management Domain

Sustainability and governance, as they appear in King III (IoD, 2009) and in the Stockholm Accords (2010), can be considered as two new approaches to strategic communication management. The terminology of sustainability is mostly used with respect to corporate responsibilities such as corporate environmental responsibility, corporate social responsibility, corporate business responsibility and corporate governance (Campbell & Mollica, 2009, pp. xv–xvi). Responsible business behaviour furthermore constitutes the consciousness that an organization can do well in the long run by paying attention to the environment and the society in which it operates. Other similar concepts include corporate social responsibility/ investment/performance (CSR/CSI/CSP) and corporate citizenship (CC). John Elkington's (1999) concept of the triple bottom line (TBL) – people, planet and profit – captures this idea.

Rensburg, De Beer and Coetzee (2008) address the above-mentioned perspective in referring to public relations (corporate communication) strategy as the nexus that binds stakeholder relationships and corporate reputation, to work towards corporate sustainability – a core focus of the Pretoria School of Thought. This should be supported by the integration and alignment of communication activities, processes and systems in organizations.

Van Tulder and Van der Zwart's (2006, p. 142) view on the shift of CSR from a largely instrumental and managerial approach to one aimed at managing *strategic networks* (where longer-term relationships with stakeholders are prominent in strategic decision-making), also influenced the Pretoria School of Thought because of its similarity to the inclusive stakeholder approach to corporate governance – a dominant principle in King III. From this perspective organizations can stay in touch with the new responsibilities of 'legitimacy' and a 'licence to operate' only through the systematic and structural exchange of facts, opinions and values through strategic stakeholder dialogue and a process that has clear accountability mechanisms (O'Brien, 2009, p. xviii).

During the drafting of King III (IoD, 2009), it became clear that top management expects the communication management function to contribute to the governing of stakeholder relationships and to assist in reporting in the integrated report on how the legitimate expectations of stakeholders are addressed. Gao and Zhang's (2006) argument that genuine dialogue concerns a two-way process where stakeholders are not merely consulted or 'listened to' but also 'responded to' guided further research in the field of communication management. Stakeholder engagement is about organizations using leadership to build relationships with stakeholders and hence improve their overall performance, accountability and sustainability.

The Pretoria School of Thought supports the view that corporate governance deals with managing and being accountable for the full range of corporate responsibilities, as stated by Campbell and Mollica (2009, p. xiv). As such, it provides guidance for the corporate communication function when developing its strategies, policies and activities. Furthermore, Katsoulakos and Katsoulacos (2007, pp. 356, 359) state that corporate governance reflects the way companies specifically address legal responsibilities and provides the foundations upon which CSR and corporate sustainability practices can be built to enhance responsible business operations. They argue for the integration of corporate responsibility principles and stakeholder approaches into mainstream strategy.

According to King III (IoD, 2009, pp. 7–9), the ultimate compliance officer is the organization's stakeholders who will let the board know by their continued support whether they accept the departure from a recommended practice (see also Friedman & Miles, 2006, pp. 1–2). Against this background, the board is ultimately responsible to its stakeholders. This inclusive stakeholder approach to governance considers, weighs and promotes the interests of all the organization's stakeholders, thus ensuring their cooperation and support. In this way, the organization creates trust between itself and its internal and external stakeholders, without whom it cannot operate sustainably (IoD, 2009, pp. 20–21). If the organization is run ethically, it earns the necessary approval – its licence to operate – from those affected by and affecting its operations (p. 21). This approach contributes to a positive corporate character, corporate personality and corporate identity, culminating in a positive brand image and corporate reputation.

Meta-Theoretical Framework for Strategic Communication Management in a Triple Context Environment

De Beer's theoretical framework for responsible strategic communication management, with specific reference to the governing of stakeholder relationships, contributes to the debate about the institutionalization of strategic communication management in the organization (De Beer, in progress; De Beer & Rensburg, 2011b, p. 211). She suggests that communication management approaches, such as stakeholder relationship management, can assist an organization in achieving its objectives – even to the point of becoming objectives in themselves. The major concepts of her framework are sustainability, governance, strategy, communication, stakeholder relationships and corporate reputation.

Based on the shared expectations between managers and communicators (as identified in the Excellence Study) and the inclusive stakeholder approach to governance, De Beer (in De Beer & Rensburg, 2011b, p. 214) suggests sustainability and governance as two new approaches to the strategic management of communication at the macro level in a triple context environment, which ultimately results in the governing of stakeholder relationships.

Pragmatic Implications for the Reflective Communication Strategist

In a strategic context (the environmental/societal level of the organization), decisions are taken that could influence the organization and its role in society. Success in the interaction between the organization and society typically ensures the long-term survival of the organization. The communication management function is particularly suited to play the role of boundary spanning. Conducting environmental scanning and obtaining information about the legitimate expectations of stakeholders and the publics/interest groups that develop around issues (through formal and informal research) are some of the main value-added contributions that the function, and in particular the reflective communication strategist, can make in the contemporary organization. Providing communication intelligence to top management and the board before top-level strategies are developed and then reporting in the integrated report on how stakeholder expectations have been addressed, can be considered as the current demand that top management has of the communication function and on which the latter should deliver (Steyn & De Beer, 2012a).

In its strategic role, corporate communication represents the needs, interests and desires of the organization's various stakeholders and interest/advocacy groups to management and explains management's perspectives to them – opening a dialogue between an organization and its stakeholders, as well as the societal advocacy groups it affects. This perspective alludes to the demand from top management for the communication management function to determine the legitimate expectations of stakeholders, publics and activists through formal and informal research, and to report about it to top management for consideration in top level strategies. The results of the mutual adjustments between the organization and its stakeholders/publics/activists are reported in the organization's integrated report to stakeholders and social groups.

Conclusion

Scholars and postgraduate students at UP, who contributed to the Pretoria School of Thought, not only have influenced the communication management domain on a national level but have also made significant contributions on an international level. The focus on the management and governance of communication on the strategic level of the organization provides a research area within which answers to contemporary scientific and pragmatic questions can be addressed.

As the research agenda of this scientific worldview (paradigm) is extended to include business perspectives, theoretical and practical applications will manifest that could benefit communication professionals on all levels in the organization. Conveying this scientific knowledge in classrooms and boardrooms has become an imperative for scholars in the field. The newly established Centre for Communication and Reputation Management (CCRM) at UP is also an instrument for the dissemination of this knowledge.

The triple context environment will influence strategic communication management in its broadest sense. Not only will it influence its conceptualization in the strategic organizational context, but it will also challenge the paradigms and theories of contemporary public relations. The inclusion of multidisciplinary concepts such as sustainability and corporate governance in the institutionalization debate in the field could, among others, assist with determining the level at which communication management has value – a core focus in the search for excellence in communication management. It is the view of the Pretoria School of Thought that the calls made by boards and top management for the communication management function to play a more strategic role in business and society could lead to a spiral of excellence in the demand-delivery loop of shared expectations, resulting in a function and discipline that could create value in all dimensions of the triple context environment.

Notes

1   'Corporate communication' and 'communication management' are used in this chapter because of the negative connotation of the term 'public relations'. Most communication professionals in Europe favour *corporate communication, strategic communication* and *communication management* as labels for the profession, a trend also prevalent in other countries (Zerfass et al., 2011).
2   Strategic communication management principles are as relevant to government and NGO communication as they are to corporate communication.
3   People or groups are stakeholders when they are affected by the decisions/behaviour of an organization or when their decisions/behaviour affect the organization (Grunig & Repper, 1992, p. 125).
4   Publics form when stakeholders (or other interest groups) recognize one of more of the consequences of organizational behaviour as a problem and organize to do something about it (Grunig & Repper, 1992, p. 124).

References

Argenti, P. A. (1996). Corporate communication as a discipline: Toward a definition. *Management Communication Quarterly, 10*(1), 73–97.

Botan, C. H. (2006). Grand strategy, strategy, and tactics in public relations. In C. H. Botan & V. Hazleton (Eds.), *Public relations theory II* (pp. 223–247). Mahwah, NJ: Lawrence Erlbaum.

Botan, C. H., & Hazleton, V. (1989). *Public relations theory*. Hillsdale, NJ: Lawrence Erlbaum.

Botan, C. H., & Hazleton, V. (Eds.). (2006). *Public relations theory II.* Mahwah, NJ: Lawrence Erlbaum.

Brody, E. Q. (1991). Response to IPRA's latest gold paper: How and where should public relations be taught? *Public Relations Quarterly, Summer,* 45–47.

Campbell, T., & Mollica, D. (2009). *Sustainability: The library of corporate responsibilities.* Burlington: Ashgate.

Carroll, A. B. (1996). *Business and society: Ethics and stakeholder management* (3rd ed.). Cincinnati, OH: South-Western College.

De Beer, E. (2001). The perception of top communicators of senior management's expectations of excellent communication in SA organisations. Unpublished master's thesis, MA (Communication Management), University of Pretoria, SA.

De Beer, E. (2010, September). The Pretoria School of Thought. Presentation during the AGM of the Council for Communication Management (CCM), SACOMM Conference, University of Johannesburg, South Africa.

De Beer, E. (in progress). The conceptualisation of strategic communication management in a triple context environment. Doctoral dissertation, PhD (Communication Management) to be submitted at the University of Pretoria, SA.

De Beer, E., & Rensburg, R. (2011a). Playing by the rules: How South Africa's King III Report could shape communication worldwide. Special Report on Africa. *Communication World, March/April.*

De Beer, E., & Rensburg, R. (2011b). Towards a theoretical framework for the governing of stakeholder relationships: A perspective from South Africa. *Journal of Public Affairs, 11*(4), 208–225.

Dozier, D. M., Grunig, L. A., & Grunig, J. E. (1995). *Manager's guide to excellence in public relations and communication management.* Mahwah, NJ: Lawrence Erlbaum.

Elkington, J. (1999). *Cannibals with forks: The triple bottom line of 21st century business.* Oxford: Capstone.

Everett, J. L. (1993). The ecological paradigm in public relations theory and practice. *Public Relations Review, 19*(2), 177–185.

Freeman, R. E. (1984). *Strategic management: A stakeholder approach.* Boston: Pitman.

Friedman, A. L., & Miles, S. (2006). *Stakeholders: Theory and practice.* Oxford: Oxford University Press.

Gadamer, H. G. (1985). *Truth and method.* London: Sheed and Ward.

Gao, S. S., & Zhang, J. J. (2006). Stakeholder engagement, social auditing and corporate sustainability. *Business Process Management Journal, 12*(6), 722–740.

Gregory, A., & Willis, P. (forthcoming July 2013). *Strategic public relations leadership.* London: Routledge.

Groenewald, J. M. (1998). Die ontwikkeling van 'n model vir kommunikasiebestuursopleiding [The development of a model for communication management training]. Unpublished master's thesis, MCom (Communication Management), University of Pretoria, SA.

Grunig, J. E. (Ed.). (1992a). *Excellence in public relations and communication management.* Hillsdale, NJ: Lawrence Erlbaum.

Grunig, J. E. (1992b). Communication, public relations, and effective organizations: An overview of the book. In J. E. Grunig (Ed.), *Excellence in public relations and communication management* (pp. 1–28). Hillsdale, NJ: Lawrence Erlbaum.

Grunig, J. E. (2006). Furnishing the edifice: Ongoing research on public relations as a strategic management function. *Journal of Public Relations Research, 18*(2), 151–176.

Grunig, J. E. (2009). Paradigms of global public relations in an age of digitalisation. *PRism, 6*(2). Retrieved from: http://praxis.massey.ac.nz/prism_on-line_journ.html (accessed 2 May 2010).

Grunig, J. E., Grunig, L. A., & Dozier, D. M. (2002). *Excellent public relations and effective organizations*. Mahwah, NJ: Lawrence Erlbaum.

Grunig, J. E., & Hunt, T. (1984). *Managing public relations*. New York: Holt, Rinehart & Winston.

Grunig, J. E., & Repper, F. C. (1992). Strategic management, publics and issues. In J. E. Grunig (Ed.), *Excellence in public relations and communication management*. Hillsdale, NJ: Lawrence Erlbaum.

Halal, W. E. (2000). Corporate community: A theory of the firm uniting profitability and responsibility. *Strategic Leadership, 28*(2), 10–16.

Hatfield, C. R. (1994). Public relations education in the United Kingdom. *Public Relations Review, 20*(2), 189–199.

Holmström, S. (1996). An intersubjective and a social systemic public relations paradigm. Master's dissertation, University of Roskilde, Denmark.

Invernizzi, E. (2008, October). Towards the institutionalization of PR/CC in Italy (1994–2008). Presentation at a plenary session of the EUPRERA Congress, IULM University, Milan.

IoD (2009). *King Report on Governance for South Africa 2009 (King III Report)*. Institute of Directors, Johannesburg. Retrieved from: http://www.iodsa.co.za/products_reports. asp?CatID=150 (accessed 14 May 2011).

Katsoulakos, T., & Katsoulacos, Y. (2007). Strategic management, corporate responsibility and stakeholder management. *Corporate Governance, 7*(4), 355–369.

Le Roux, T., & Steyn, B. (2006). Exploring practitioner constraints in advancing to more senior corporate communication roles. *Communicare, 25*(1), 23–58.

Muzi Falconi, T. (2010). *Global stakeholder relationship governance*. Miami: Institute for Public Relations. Retrieved from: http://www.instituteforpr.org/wp-content/uploads/ Global_Stakeholder_Relationship_Governance.pdf (accessed 2 May 2011).

O'Brien, J. (2009). *Corporate business responsibility: The library of corporate responsibilities*. Burlington, VA: Ashgate Publishing.

Peters, T. J., & Waterman, R. H., Jr. (1982). *In search of excellence*. New York: Warner.

Prinsloo, P. W. F. (2005). A framework for the formulation of corporate communication strategy in a financial services organization: A case study. Research report, MPhil (Communication Management), University of Pretoria, SA.

Rensburg, R. (2003). Public relations in South Africa: From rhetoric to reality. In K. Sriramesh & D. Verčič (Eds.), *The global public relations handbook* (pp. 145–178). Mahwah, NJ: Lawrence Erlbaum.

Rensburg, R., & De Beer, E. (2003, July). Reputation management and stakeholder engagement: An integrated approach to future corporate governance in South Africa. Paper delivered at the 10th International PR Research Symposium, Lake Bled, Slovenia.

Rensburg, R., De Beer, E., & Coetzee, E. (2008). Linking stakeholder relationships and corporate reputation: A public relations framework for corporate sustainability. In A. Zerfass, B. Van Ruler, & K. Sriramesh (Eds.), *Public relations research: European and international perspectives and innovations* (pp. 385–396). Wiesbaden: VS Verlag für Sozialwissenschaften.

Rumelt, R., Schendel, D. E., & Teece, D. J. (Eds.). (1994). *Fundamental issues in strategy: A research agenda*. Boston, MA: Harvard Business School.

Steyn, B. (2000a). Strategic management roles of the corporate communication function. Unpublished master's thesis, MCom (Communication Management), University of Pretoria, SA. Retrieved from http://upetd.up.ac.za/thesis/submitted/etd-06192012-162416/unrestricted/00front.pdf (accessed 26 October 2012).

Steyn, B. (2000b). CEO expectations in terms of PR roles. *Communicare, 19*(1), 20–43.

Steyn, B. (2000c). Model for developing corporate communication strategy. *Communicare, 19*(2), 1–33.

Steyn, B. (2003a, July). A conceptualisation and empirical verification of the '*strategist*', (redefined) '*manager*' and '*technician*' roles of public relations. Paper presented at the 10th International PR Research Symposium, Lake Bled, Slovenia.

Steyn, B. (2003b). From strategy to corporate communication strategy: A conceptualisation. *Journal of Communication Management, 8*(2), 168–183.

Steyn, B. (2007). Contribution of public relations to organizational strategy formulation. In E. L. Toth (Ed.), *The future of excellence in public relations and communication management. Challenges for the next generation* (pp. 137–172). Mahwah, NJ: Lawrence Erlbaum.

Steyn, B. (2009). The strategic role of public relations is strategic reflection: A South African research stream. *American Behavioral Scientist, 53*(4), 516–532.

Steyn, B. (2011). Değişen iş ve halka ilişkiler paradigmaları [Changing business and public relations paradigms]. In Ç. Karakaya Şatir (Ed.), *Halkla ilişkilerden stratejik halkla ilişkilere* [From public relations to strategic public relations] (pp. 1–31). Istanbul, Turkey: Nobel Yayınevi.

Steyn, B., & Bütschi, G. (2003, July). Reflective public relations: A commentary on conceptual and empirical similarities and differences between South African and European research. Paper delivered at BledCom 2003, Lake Bled, Slovenia.

Steyn, B., & De Beer, E. (2012a). Strategic role of public relations in the process of 'integrated reporting': An exploratory study. *Sinergie, 88* (May to Aug), 53–72.

Steyn, B., & De Beer, E. (2012b). Conceptualising strategic communication management (SCM) in the context of governance and stakeholder inclusiveness. *Communicare, 31*(2), 29–55.

Steyn, B., & Everett, T. (2009). International comparative study indicates different PR roles in South Africa and the UK, using the same measuring instrument. *Trípodos, 24*, 95–105.

Steyn, B., & Green, M. (2001). Investigating strategic management roles of the corporate communication function in the Department of Housing. *Communicare, 20*(2), 1–35.

Steyn, B., & Green, M. (2006, September). Dominant coalition of recently privatised South African telecommunications service provider expects 'reflectionist' and 'educationist' roles of public relations practitioners. Paper delivered at the 8th Annual EUPRERA Conference, Carlisle, UK.

Steyn, B., Grobler, A. F., & Cilliers, B. (2005). A theoretical framework for the concept of 'Internet strategy'. *Communicare, 24*(1), 20–48.

Steyn, B., & Niemann, L. (2008, October). Institutionalising the strategic role of corporate communication/public relations through its contribution to enterprise strategy and enterprise governance. Paper delivered at the 10th Annual EUPRERA Conference, Milan, Italy.

Steyn, B., & Niemann, L. (2010). Enterprise strategy: A concept that explicates corporate communication's strategic contribution at the macro organisational level. *Journal of Communication Management, 14*(2), 106–126.

Steyn, B., & Nunes, M. (2001). Communication strategy for community development: A case study of the Heifer Project South Africa. *Communicatio, 27*(2), 29–48.

Steyn, B., & Puth, G. (2000). *Corporate communication strategy*. Sandown, SA: Heinemann.

Stockholm Accords. (2010). *Final Text*. Retrieved from: http://www.stockholmaccords.org/accords-text (accessed 15 May 2011).

Van Heerden, G., & Rensburg, R. (2005). Public relations roles empirically verified among public relations practitioners in Africa. *Communicare, 24*(1), 69–88.

Van Riel, C. B. M. (1995). *Principles of public relations.* Hertfordshire, UK: Prentice Hall.

Van Riel, C. B. M., & Fombrun, C. J. (2007). *Essentials of corporate communication.* London: Routledge.

Van Ruler, B., & Verčič, D. (2002, July). *The Bled Manifesto on public relations.* Prepared for BledCom 2002, held in conjunction with EUPRERA, Lake Bled, Slovenia.

Van Tulder, R., & Van der Zwart, A. (2006). *An international business–society management: Linking corporate responsibility and globalisation.* London: Routledge.

Verčič, D., Van Ruler, B., Bütschi, G., & Flodin, B. (2001). On the definition of public relations: A European view. *Public Relations Review, 27,* 373–387.

Worrall, D. N. (2005). The contribution of the corporate communication and marketing functions to strategy formulation: A case study within a financial services institution. Research report, MCom (Communication Management), University of Pretoria, SA.

Zerfass, A., Verhoeven, P., Tench, R., Moreno, A., & Verčič, D. (2011). *European Communication Monitor (ECM) 2011. (Chart Version).* Brussels: EACD, EUPRERA. Retrieved from: http://www.communicationmonitor.eu.

19

THE GRUNIG LEGACY TO ACADEMIC STUDIES AND PROFESSIONAL PRACTICE IN LATIN AMERICA

Maria Aparecida Ferrari

Abstract

This chapter outlines the introduction and trajectory of the theories developed by James Grunig and Larissa Grunig in Latin America and describes the reception and incorporation of those innovative ideas by the researchers in the region. Today, it is an indisputable fact that these authors have left a deep and lasting footprint on the region's academic sphere and professional market. From the first days of their introduction to this part of the world, the models of practice of public relations and the Excellence Theory have become an essential component of the research and studies conducted in Latin American countries. The chapter details the phases of transposition of the theoretical legacy and the personal engagement of both authors in the process, and demonstrates that, notwithstanding the cultural differences, their teachings have succeeded in changing the public relations approach in this vibrant part of the world.

Key Words

environmental scanning, Excellence Theory, James Grunig, Larissa Grunig, Latin America, public relations

Introduction

A significant part of the public relations academic world recognizes James E. Grunig and Larissa A. Grunig as renowned scholars whose work constitutes a reference in the practice of modern public relations.

Latin America did not "discover" James Grunig and Larissa Grunig until the 1990s; since then, however, their research and theories have boosted and renewed the programs in the Social Communications area in several Latin American universities, either by supporting the development of academic research projects or by helping shape professionals in both *Lato* and *stricto sensu* programs in the region.

In Latin America, the first contact with the research work conducted by the Grunigs dates back to 1993, during the 1st International Communication and Public Relations Congress that I organized at the Catholic University in Santiago, Chile (Figure 19.1). At that event, Dr. Otto Lerbinger, from the University of Boston, lectured on the role of models for the practice of public relations developed by Grunig and Hunt in 1984. From that point on, the Grunig's work was gradually introduced to the region either through my translations into Portuguese of their material or by the adoption of his original title, *Managing Public Relations*, by James Grunig and Todd Hunt. From Chile, the work reached Brazil and, successively, the other Latin American countries in my attempts to disseminate those new theories.

Looking back on the almost two decades that have elapsed since my first contact with the Grunigs, it is hard to pinpoint which have been the most enriching moments that I have spent with James and Larissa Grunig: whether the treasured

FIGURE 19.1 Maria Aparecida Ferrari and Larissa A. Grunig, During the 1st Brazilian Congress of Researchers on Organizational Communication and Public Relations—ABRAPCORP, April, 2007

personal contact with two very considerate and always available friends, or the countless hours of professional guidance and collaboration with the two scholars. Perhaps the most accurate would be to accept the impossibility of dissociating the human and the professional dimensions, as they are mutually nourishing and complementary. The following is my personal testimonial on the legacy of James E. Grunig and Larissa Grunig to Latin America.

The Public Relations Scene in Latin America before the Introduction of Grunig's Theories

The development of public relations in Latin America took a different course than that in the United States, considered the "cradle" of the profession. In Latin America, the practice was virtually imposed as the newly arrived multinational companies transposed onto the region the organizational structures from the parent company, which included the public relations department. Brazil was the first country to practice the activity of public relations at the Canadian Light Company in São Paulo in 1914. Later on, in the 1930s, companies such as Unilever, Siemens, Swift, Ericsson, Bayer, AGFA, Price Waterhouse, Goodyear, Citibank and Kodak were established in Argentina. In the same period, in Venezuela, the activity of public relations was launched with the installation of Shell. In Chile, public relations activities saw the light in 1952 with the installation of Braden Copper, an American mining company. In Uruguay, the activity was introduced in the 1950s in the military, namely the Army, the Navy and the Air Force. Bolivia, Colombia and Peru were late starters, with the establishment of press departments at the public administration level only in the 1970s.

The inception of the activity in the region can be divided into two stages: the first, between the 1930s and the 1950s, took place as the region experienced the first wave of industrialization; the second phase occurred between the 1960s and the 1970s. In both cases, the inception of the activity was conditioned to the models and techniques practiced in the US, England, France, etc. One of the reasons for that is the distribution by the larger international publishing houses of foreign titles in the area, which were adopted as the base for the practice of public relations. Another factor that explains the "import" phenomenon was the feeble capacity of the local associations and the lack of university-level education in public relations at the time.

According to Grunig, Ferrari and França (2011), at that time, the Latin American professionals adopted the Portuguese and Spanish translations of foreign works that oriented the communication community abroad, such as *Relações Públicas: casos e problemas*, by Bertrand R. Canfield, an American professor, which was published in Brazil in two volumes by Editora Pioneira in 1961, and published in Argentina, in Spanish as *Relaciones Públicas: principios, casos, problemas*, in 1962 by Editorial Mundi. Almost at the same time, a second title was published both in Spanish and Portuguese: it was *Relaciones Públicas*, by the Frenchmen Jean

Chaumely and Denis Huisman, by Editorial Universitaria, in Buenos Aires (Eudeba), in 1964. In Brazil, the text was published in Portuguese. In Peru, the Catholic University published *Relaciones Públicas*, by the American professor Howard R. Stephenson in 1960.

Because there were no specific university-level programs in the field at the time, as the activity of public relations was introduced to the region, the positions that became available in the area were absorbed by a variety of professionals from different fields of specialization: lawyers, engineers and business administrators functioned as public relations professionals in the newly installed PR departments in the businesses that were being established between 1940 and 1960. Those professionals had to resort to short courses abroad to improve their knowledge of the discipline.

In Brazil, the first initiatives were taken by the Business Department of the Universidade de São Paulo; by FGV (Fundação Getúlio Vargas); by Idort (Institute for the Rational Organization of Labor); and by the Catholic University in Rio de Janeiro (PUC-RJ). The programs were taught by a series of invited foreign lecturers such as Harwood L. Childs, Eric Carlson and Neville Sheperd, who visited Brazil and other countries in the region. In Peru, short courses were given by Howard R. Stephenson in 1958 and 1959, under the sponsorship of the Catholic University. Other initiatives to promote the formal education of the professionals in the area were also seen in Argentina, Uruguay and Chile.

In the 1960s, a sequence of events helped boost the practice of public relations in the region, namely: (1) the arrival of multinational companies equipped with more modern management models and including the PR Department in their organizational charts; (2) the establishment of Public Relations Associations in several countries in the region; and (3) the publication of the first specialized titles on public relations.

The setting-up of public relations departments in the organizational structures of the multinational companies signaled the region's first contact with the activity, which was obviously exercised from the point of view of a culture which was different from the Latin American culture. The local professionals, nonetheless, had no alternative but to absorb and apply this model as their only reference on which to base this newly introduced practice.

The creation of the Public Relations Associations in almost all of the Latin American countries in the 1950s and 1960s had a common objective, namely, to bring together and develop the professionals as well as to encourage the practice.

Starting with the inception of ABRP, the *Brazilian Public Relations Association of Public Relations* in 1954, other countries followed suit and created their own associations: the *Colegio de Relacionistas Públicos* in Venezuela (CRPV), in 1956; the *Asociación Argentina de Relaciones Públicas* (AARP), in Argentina in 1958; the *Asociación Uruguaya de Relaciones Públicas* (AURP), in Uruguay in 1962; the *Asociación Paraguaya de Profesionales de Relaciones Públicas* (APPRP), in Paraguay in 1963; and the *Centro de Relaciones Públicas de Colombia* (CERP), in Colombia in 1963.

This process culminated with the creation in Mexico City of the *Federación Interamericana de Asociaciones de Relaciones Públicas* (FIARP) on September 26, 1960, whose purpose was to assemble all of the national organizations "to foster the image of the profession and to promote education in public relations through the advancement and standardization of public relations education and practice," as stated in Article 5 of the institution's bylaws.

Finally, two pioneer publications in the 1960s in the area of public relations, at a time when the field was under the influence of American and then European authors, are worthy of note: in 1963, Cândido Theobaldo de Souza Andrade published *Para Entender Relações Públicas* (1968), and in the same year *Relaciones Públicas: fundamentos científicos y aplicaciones prácticas,* by Fernando Fernández Escalante, reached the shelves in Argentina. Additionally, in Colombia, Samper Gnecco published *Las Relaciones Públicas: ¿qué son y para qué sirven? Un análisis de treinta casos reales,* in 1963. Later on, other titles begin to appear: Francisco Flores Bao's *Relaciones Públicas: Ciencias de la integración humana* (1978) in Peru; *Semillas del Éxito, Técnicas de Relaciones Humanas y Relaciones Públicas* (1985) by Jaime Humerez Estrada in Bolivia; in Chile, *Las Relaciones Públicas en Chile* (1989) by Bárbara J. Délano A.; and in Venezuela, *Manual de Teorías y Técnicas Magistrales de las Relaciones Públicas* (1979) by Juan Merchán López.

Prevailing Views on Public Relations in Latin America between the 1960s and the 1980s

Until the 1980s, the practice of public relations in Latin America was dominated by the views of Ivy L. Lee, recognized as one of the pioneers of the profession in the USA. The American influence left therefore a deep imprint on the practice of public relations in the Latin American organizations, which resorted to concepts and tools which at times proved to be clearly foreign to the regional and local cultural context. Eventually it became evident to some researchers that for decades both professionals and scholars had focused primarily on the *whats* and *hows* of public relations, while failing to formulate their own theories which took into account the relevance of the activity to the local organizations as well as to the society at large.

Even today, certain distortions deriving from the transposition of this "inherited model" persist, confirming the results of my research from 2000 and 2010 that revealed that many companies continue to be more concerned about "publicity," that is, their visibility in the media, considering that this type of exposure is their most effective communication model, and continue to dismiss the need to analyze the context and the consequences that changes to that context may have on their business. Grunig (Grunig et al., 2011) had already pointed out that the same phenomenon was seen in the USA, where public relations were often defined by their techniques rather than by their strategic value. Many public relations professionals mastered the art of preparing press releases, preparing a media coverage plan, writing speeches, flyers or yearly activity reports, thus fulfilling their role as "technicians" rather than "strategists."

Starting in the 1980s, the School of Communication and Arts at the Universidade de São Paulo, Brazil, became the pioneer in Latin America in offering both master's and doctoral programs in public relations. In fact, it is still the only institution in the entire region offering the doctoral degree. This has had a bearing on the development of a critical mass, as both programs required the production of research and scientific projects in the area. It was only natural, therefore, that the bibliographic production in Brazil soon developed more than that of other countries in the region.

A review of the public relations literature in the whole of Latin America, however, shows that only a few local authors have developed their own theories, independent of the American and/or the European influence.

An analysis of all the titles published in all the Latin American countries in the field reveals that most works consist simply of a re-examination of foreign literature. Most titles are actually "primers" that deal with communication techniques— the *how to do*, while others are translations of works that introduce public relations from a foreign perspective. In the latter case, a frequent practice is the introduction of "cases" from other countries. One of the most frequently cited "cases" discussed by the Latin American students in their courses has been and still is the crisis experienced by Johnson & Johnson in 1982 as a result of the Tylenol incident. This is an indication that even the examples were transposed from the foreign reality, in the absence of research on local cases.

One of the authors who published specialized literature in the field is Roberto Porto Simões, from Brazil, who introduced innovative public relations concepts (1995) and defined public relations as "conflict management," and for whom conflict was an ever-present element in the organization, where the public relations professional played a management role to ensure the legitimacy of the organization's decisions. This was quite a revolutionary concept at the time, considering that, without exception, all literature between 1960 and 1970 had adopted the definition formulated in the Mexico Agreement, according to which

> the practice of the Public Relations profession requires planned action supported by research, systematic communication and planned participation in order to raise the levels of understanding, solidarity and cooperation between a public or private organization and the social groups associated to it, through the interaction of their legitimate interests with a view to fostering mutual development and the development of the community to which they belong.
>
> *(Andrade, 1993, p. 42)*

The Introduction of the Grunig Model to Latin America

Grunig's concepts were introduced to Latin America in the early 1990s. While I was living and working in Chile (1992–1997), I organized the 1st International Congress of Communication and Public Relations at the Pontificia Universidad Católica de Chile in 1993, at which Professor Otto Lerbinger, from Boston University, was the keynote speaker. Among other topics, Professor Lerbinger examined the models of public relations practice formulated by James E. Grunig and Todd Hunt, as published in their book, *Managing Public Relations* from 1984. The models were well received by the audience in general and triggered my special interest, as they assigned different levels of the practice of public relations according to the context of the organization and the degree of development in the country in question.

As a professor in the Public Relations program at the University of Viña del Mar at that time, I contacted Professor James Grunig, and that was the starting point of a friendship that has only deepened throughout the years. What struck my attention as a researcher the most was the ease and lucidity with which Professor Grunig explained his research work and his willingness to make his material available for dissemination in Latin America.

In 1994, I visited Professor James Grunig for the first time at the Communications Department at the University of Maryland, USA; that first encounter marked the beginning of a relationship characterized by studies and research which surpassed the boundaries of the academy and developed into intense cooperation. After that, I returned to the Communication Department of the University of Maryland in 1998 and again in 1999. The latter visit was for a more extensive period during which I completed my doctoral thesis.

By the second half of 1990, *Managing Public Relations* (Grunig, 1984) and *Excellence in Public Relations and Communication Management* (Grunig, 1992) had already been introduced and been adopted in their original English version in the programs under my coordination, both in Chile and in Brazil.

Another important event was the publication by Editora Gestión in 2000 of the Spanish version of *Managing Public Relations*, by Grunig and Hunt, which received the title of *Dirección de Relaciones Públicas*, as a translation by Jordi Xifra, and which was distributed in all Spanish-speaking countries. Those publications assured the ample dissemination of the content of Grunig's work among academics, students and professionals in the field of public relations throughout Latin America.

The vision expressed by James Grunig and his team of researchers combined theory and practice; it also addressed strategies and techniques, aspects which at the time were at the core of the debate among professionals and the academy. Grunig's concepts were the first to outline the major trends in the field, stressing his ideas that public relations is a profession based on academic knowledge and that its practitioners play the role of strategic advisors.

Latin American researchers, scholars and professionals alike were especially attracted to Grunig's views as expressed in his texts, where he suggests that public relations should be oriented according to universal principles of strategy, symmetry and diversity, which entail that the professionals carry out the task of analysis of scenarios—what he calls *environmental scanning*—before planning communication actions.

In 1997, Margarida Kunsch launched *Relações Públicas e Modernidade,* dedicating one chapter to the discussion of the work conducted by the Grunigs and the team of researchers from the University of Maryland, which I had translated into Portuguese for that publication.

A Welcome and Frequent Guest to Latin America

I arranged for James Grunig to visit Latin America for the first time in 2000, starting his tour in Brazil, specifically to teach a course to a group of graduate students at the Communication School at the Universidade de São Paulo (ECA/USP). He was also the keynote speaker at the yearly International Communication Congress organized by ABERJE, the Brazilian Association of Business Communication.

This was James Grunig's first contact with Brazilian executives and communication directors. In addition to his lecture commitments, Grunig paid a visit to the Public Relations Director of Petrobras, Brazil's flagship company, in Rio de Janeiro.

After this first visit to Brazil, the scientific journals made it a habit to print interviews, conferences and theories formulated by James Grunig and his team. Furthermore, researchers, educators and students began to adopt his work in their research and practice. From that point on, his visits to Latin America became more frequent.

In 2004, James Grunig and Larissa Grunig attended the International Public Relations Congress organized by the University of Viña del Mar in Chile. This was an opportunity for educators and students to come into contact with the authors and discuss their theories and views with them. James Grunig also met with executives in the area of communication to learn about the local practices.

In 2006, Professor James Grunig was invited to the 1st International Public Relations Congress organized by the University San Martín de Porres, in Lima, Peru. In the publicity material prepared for the Congress, Grunig was referred to as the "Pope of Public Relations," an acknowledgment of his expertise and position as the most prominent researcher today in the field of new public relations theory. During the Congress, in addition to giving the keynote speech, Grunig was invested with the title of *Doctor Honoris Causa* by the Universidad San Martín de Porres.

In 2007, Dr. Grunig attended the 2nd International Public Relations Congress organized by the same university in Lima, Peru, also in the capacity of keynote speaker. That same year, Larissa Grunig was one of the two keynote speakers—alongside Linda Putnam from the University of Texas—at the 1st Brazilian Congress of Researchers on Organizational Communication and Public Relations organized by ABRAPCORP, in São Paulo, Brazil (Figure 19.1). A spin-off of the Congress was the publication of a book including texts by both authors, and which promoted the further dissemination the theories formulated by both scholars.

In 2008, James Grunig and Larissa Grunig returned once again to Latin America as keynote speakers of the 3rd International Public Relations Congress held by the same university in Lima, Peru.

In August 2009, James Grunig returned to launch his first book in Portuguese, in co-authorship with Maria Aparecida Ferrari and Fábio França, *Relações Públicas: teoria, contexto e relacionamentos* (Figure 19.2). The book represented the validation of Grunig's work; now available in the national language, the highly updated content became more easily accessible to all students in all university and graduate courses in Brazil. A significant advantage of the book was the application of the theories formulated by Grunig and his team of researchers to the Latin American context; it also made possible the application and verification of the universal principles and concepts in this particular socio-political-economic reality. The book has been well received among professionals, educators and students, and is now in its second updated and expanded 2011 edition. The response to the publication demonstrates the extent of James Grunig's influence and the continued importance of his concepts for the studies on public relations.

FIGURE 19.2 James E. Grunig, Maria Aparecida Ferrari and Fábio França at the Launch of Their Book in Portuguese. São Paulo, August 1, 2009

In Barranquilla, Colombia, in 2011, James Grunig took part in the 1st Congress for Strategic Communication and Public Relations organized by the Universidad del Norte. Grunig was once again the keynote speaker and was eagerly received by all the professionals and academics attending the event.

Theory Applied to Scientific Research

The Grunigs' innovative theories changed the paradigms in the teaching of public relations in all courses in the Latin American countries, as they toppled the classical model that until then had been adopted by the academy.

Cultural differences between the USA and Latin America notwithstanding, the models for the practice of public relations introduced by Grunig and Hunt (1984) were gradually introduced and tested in different countries in the region to measure and assess the degree of maturity and development of public relations in the organizations. Additionally, the principles extracted from the Excellence Theory have become a new source of inspiration for researchers and professionals trying to identify and compare communication processes in place.

Bibliometric research carried out by Kunsch (2011) confirmed James E. Grunig as the international author in the area of public relations most frequently quoted in all master's and doctoral theses in Brazil over the past 10 years. Even in a scenario of limited formal research in the remaining countries in the region, the new titles published by local authors have consistently cited the work conducted by James Grunig and his team. The same applies to undergraduate and graduate programs in Latin American universities which recognize the groundbreaking character of his work and include the research conducted by Grunig in the content of their public relations-specific courses.

One of the first to use the theories formulated by James and Larissa Grunig and the Maryland team was Roberto Penteado in his master's dissertation, "Effects of public relations roles and models on Brazilian organizations committed to quality," developed at the University of Florida in 1996. In 2000, at the Universidade de São Paulo, I defended my doctoral thesis on the "Influence of organizational values in defining the practice and the role of the public relations professionals: a comparative study of organizations in Brazil and Chile."

It is safe to say that the work developed by James Grunig has transformed the way public relations are understood and has led to a more strategic practice that assures benefits for both parties, namely, the organization and their publics. The emphasis Grunig places on the analysis of scenarios (environmental scanning), as well as his concern for the development and fostering of strategic relations with the intent to seek excellence in public relations have cast a new light on the practice of Latin American communicators seeking to raise their level of specialization in the area. The following statement captures the essence of Grunig's theory:

The value of Public Relations at the societal level results from the cumulative impact of what it does at the program, functional, and organizational levels. The value of Public Relations at the societal level is the long-term impact of good relationships identified at the organizational level and cultivated at the program level. As a result, research on the quality of relationships also can be used to establish the contribution of Public Relations to society.

(Grunig, 2010, p. 96)

Influence on the Region's Bibliography

For years, the sum of the work conducted by James Grunig and his Maryland team were disseminated through books, contributions to other titles, and articles published in scientific journals. But Latin America would have to wait until 2000 to see the Spanish translation of *Managing Public Relations*, as *Dirección de Relaciones Públicas*.

And it was only in 2009, with the publication of the work in Portuguese, that the ideas formulated by Grunig and his Maryland team attained a more ample and deserving dissemination among students, educators and the professional community at large.

James Grunig has also contributed with specific articles to a series of collective publications in the region, such as *Las nuevas Relaciones Públicas*, published by the Universidad San Martín de Porres, in Lima, Peru, in 2010, which includes a chapter by James Grunig on public relations research, status and perspectives.

Together with Larissa Grunig and Maria Aparecida Ferrari, James Grunig wrote a chapter on Perspectives of the Excellence Study for organizations, published in *Campos Acadêmicos e Aplicados de múltiplas Perspectivas*, edited by Margarida Kunsch, in São Paulo, 2009.

In addition to the works referenced, Grunig's name has been attached to a number of other texts and interviews in scientific journals throughout the region. His views have attracted the attention of most researchers and professionals, be it for the consistency of his findings, or for his concepts which raise public relations to a function of management of communication of an organization to its publics. The typology of publics developed by Grunig and Hunt in 1984 underpins the maturity of the concept and underlines its relevance vis-à-vis the formulation of strategies indispensable to the establishment of actions aimed at securing the support, understanding and acceptance of the publics in question.

In conclusion, it is worth noting that in Brazil as well as in all other Latin American countries, Dr. James E. Grunig is highly regarded and respected by the academic and professional communities, who are inspired by his enthusiasm and value his profound knowledge of public relations and his enormous ability to gather a team of researchers around his idea, and join in the effort to continue heralding the legitimacy of public relations as a valuable core function in all organizations and institutions.

The Grunig legacy has without any doubt changed the course of public relations in the region. His work has provided us with the compass that helped orient us, professionals and academics alike, in the right direction, and his theories have helped pave the way to achieving the organization's objectives with symmetry, coherence and ethics.

Acknowledgments

In closing, I would like to express my personal gratitude for James Grunig's disposition to become my mentor and inspiration since the early moments of our professional contact, and for the privilege of enjoying the friendship and comradeship of both James and Larissa despite the geographical distance!

References

Andrade, C. R. S. (1993). *Para entender Relações Públicas*. São Paulo, Loyola.

Ferrari, M. A. (2000). A influência dos valores organizacionais na determinação da prática e do papel dos profissionais de relações públicas: estudo comparativo entre organizações do Brasil e do Chile. Doctoral thesis, São Paulo, ECA-USP.

Grunig, J. E., & Hunt, T. (1984). *Managing Public Relations*. New York: Holt, Rinehart & Winston.

Grunig, J. E. (1992). *Excellence in Public Relations and Communication Management*. Hillsdale, NJ: Lawrence Erlbaum.

Grunig, J. E. (2010). La investigación en las relaciones públicas: estado actual y nuevas perspectivas. In *Las nuevas Relaciones Públicas* (pp. 69–111). Lima, Peru: Universidad San Martín de Porres.

Grunig, J. E., Ferrari, M. A., & França, F. (2009). *Relações Públicas: teoria, contexto e relacionamentos*. São Caetano do Sul: Difusão.

Grunig, J. E., Ferrari, M. A., & França, F. (2011), *Relações Públicas: teoria, contexto e relacionamentos*. 2ª. edição revisada e ampliada. São Caetano do Sul: Difusão.

Grunig, J. E., Gorpe, S., Noguero, A., & Solórzano, E. H. (2010). *Las nuevas Relaciones Públicas*. Universidad San Martín de Porres, Editorial USMP.

Grunig, J. E., & Hunt T. (1984). *Managing public relations*. New York: Holt, Rinehart & Winston.

Kunsch, M. N. K. (1997). *Relações Públicas e Modernidade*. São Paulo: Summus.

Kunsch, M. N. K. (2011). *Comunicação Organizacional e Relações Públicas: perspectivas dos estudos Latino-Americanos*. São Paulo: Revista ALAIC.

Penteado, R. (1996). Effects of public relations roles and models on Brazilian organizations committed to quality. Master's dissertation, University of Florida.

Simões, R. P. (1995). *Relações Públicas: Função política*. 3rd edn. São Paulo: Summus.

20

THE PROCESS OF CONDUCTING THE EXCELLENCE STUDY

A Personal Reconstruction of Leadership

David Dozier and Louis C. Williams, Jr.

Abstract

This chapter provides a behind-the-scenes review of the Excellence Study, the single most influential study of the practice of public relations and communication management. Dozier and Williams provide a personalized and subjective review of the interplay of personalities and organizational cultures as this massive research project unfolded between 1985 and 2002, and argue that James Grunig's leadership was essential to the successful execution of the project. In addition, Dozier and Williams identify a number of challenges that James Grunig had to overcome, in order to shepherd the three-nation collection of survey data, the conduct of 25 follow-up case studies, and the publication of three widely cited books.

Key Words

challenges, Excellence Study, funding, James Grunig, Larissa Grunig, IABC Research Foundation, leadership

Introduction

Arguably, one of the major accomplishments of James Grunig's prolific and influential career in public relations is his leadership of the Excellence Study. James Grunig served as principal investigator of the project. This chapter provides a highly personalized and subjective reconstruction of the Excellence Study, examining the process of project execution from an insider's perspective. David Dozier was a member of the original Excellence Study research team; with James and Larissa Grunig, Dozier co-authored the three books generated by the Excellence Study. Lou Williams, chairman of L.C. Williams & Associates, Inc., chaired the sponsoring organization, the International Association of Business Communicators (IABC) Research Foundation.

The Excellence Study in a Nutshell

James Grunig provides a more detailed description of the Excellence Study elsewhere in this book. In this section, we describe the Excellence Study as a process. The concept for the study was born in an early 1984 brainstorming session of the IABC Research Foundation Board of Directors. Various ideas for possible studies were floated one after another; no one seemed satisfied. Then, Foundation Board member Richard Charlton, who had been quiet for some time, came up with "The Big Idea." Everyone in the room will remember the moment.

"We're always trying," Charlton said, "to convince people we add value to our organizations. We need to respond to that. Why don't we take a shot at a study that answers all of the questions about the work we do. Let's do the definitive study, one that PROVES our value." On that day, the Excellence Study was born. The rest of the all-day meeting was devoted to how to make that happen, and what it might cost. Little did the group realize that, in the end, the Excellence Study would be a truly mammoth undertaking, costing $400,000 and spanning three countries. Immediately after that meeting, John Bailey, then president of IABC, and Williams worked with staff to create an appropriate request for proposals. Five teams responded to that RFP. Ultimately, the team headed by James Grunig, now professor emeritus at the University of Maryland, College Park, was awarded the grant by a unanimous vote.

By 1990–1991, survey data had been collected from 327 organizations in the United States, Canada, and the United Kingdom. Subsequent to that, follow-up case studies were conducted with 25 organizations from the original 327. Organizations were selected because they scored either very high or very low on a scale of excellence generated through quantitative analysis of the survey data.

The Excellence Study generated three books. Edited by James Grunig and published in 1992, *Excellence in Public Relations and Communication Management* detailed the theoretical underpinnings of the Excellence Study. The *Manager's Guide to Excellence in Public Relations and Communication Management* (1995), co-authored by David Dozier, Larissa Grunig, and James Grunig, provided initial findings of the Excellence Study and was targeted to the practitioner community. Written by Larissa Grunig, James Grunig, and David Dozier, *Excellent Public Relations and Effective Organizations: A Study of Communication Management in Three Countries* (2002) provided a comprehensive analysis of data generated by the Excellence Study.

The three books, plus the numerous studies spawned by the Excellence Study, have exerted a profound impact on scholarship in public relations. In the Spring of 2012, a Google Scholar search indicated that the three Excellence Study books have been cited over 2,100 times by other scholars. Even today, a new generation of public relations practitioners and educators continue to learn from the Excellence Study and its findings.

Our Purpose in Reconstructing Excellence

Our purpose here is to describe our personal recall of the process of conducting the Excellence Study. Rather than a detailed historical accounting of the facts and events of the 15-year project, we seek to summarize the important lessons learned from implementing a project of this magnitude. In all important respects, the Excellence Study was a spectacular success. The IABC Research Foundation directors and members of the research team wanted the Excellence Study to exert a major impact on the field. That was the intention of the IABC Research Foundation when it sent out a request for proposals. Members of the research team recognized the potential. However, we can safely say that the impact of the Excellence Study exceeded everybody's expectations.

That said, the Excellence Study had to overcome a number of significant challenges along the journey from the initial request for proposals in 1984 to the publication of the third Excellence Study book in 2002. James Grunig's leadership was central to overcoming those challenges. The purpose of identifying those challenges is to assist those undertaking similar large-scale projects to learn from those challenges and deal with them proactively.

The perspectives detailed in this chapter are not official positions generated by the leadership at the IABC Research Foundation or the Excellence Study research team. Rather, they are the perspectives of the authors alone, based on very subjective recollections of events transpiring over nearly three decades. We define some of the major challenges faced by the Excellence Study. Those challenges were many. They were large challenges and, in retrospect, inherent in the undertaking. Illuminating those challenges is an important part of the Excellence Study story.

The Players

The International Communication Association (ICA) held its annual conference in Hawaii in May 1985. James and Larissa Grunig, who had recently married, met briefly with David Dozier at the ICA conference in Honolulu. James Grunig had just received word that the IABC Research Foundation had funded the research proposal, which James Grunig had developed with the team's input. The news elated the team members. At the same time, there was a collective gulp: the project was a massive undertaking.

James Grunig, the Excellence Study's principal investigator and team leader, was already established as a major scholar in the field. James Grunig earned his doctorate in mass communications from the University of Wisconsin in 1968; at the onset of the Excellence Study, he was a tenured full professor in the College of Journalism, University of Maryland. His textbook, *Managing Public Relations* (1984), which he co-authored with Todd Hunt, had been published the year before. From the outset of the Excellence Study, James Grunig already was internationally acclaimed as one of the top scholars and theoreticians in public relations.

Larissa Grunig and David Dozier, however, were untenured assistant professors at the University of Maryland and San Diego State University, respectively. Larissa Grunig earned her doctorate from the University of Maryland and was hired there as an assistant professor at the outset of the Excellence Study. Prior to that, Larissa Grunig had served on the faculty in the communications department at Washington State University. Dozier earned his doctorate in communication research from Stanford University. Before moving to San Diego State in 1980, Dozier worked for about two years as a public information officer for a community development corporation in central California, a Latino-run corporation with close ties to the United Farm Workers union. For Larissa Grunig and David Dozier, the Excellence Study would become one of the major scholarly accomplishments of their careers, based on frequency of citations by other scholars.

William Ehling, a full professor and an established scholar of public relations at Syracuse University, brought an economist's perspective to the Excellence team. Jon White, the only non-American on the team, split his time over the course of the project in Canada and the United Kingdom as a teacher and consultant. With a doctorate in psychology from the London School of Economics and Political Science, Jon White brought a uniquely psychological perspective to the Excellence Study.

Fred Repper was the only practitioner on the Excellence team. He had recently retired as vice president of public relations for Gulf States Utilities, an electric power company based in Beaumont, Texas. At the onset of the Excellence Study, Repper was working as a private public relations consultant. An enthusiastic supporter of public relations research in general, and the Excellence Study in particular, his keen insights into the practice would prove invaluable to the team.

In addition to the six ongoing team members, several others at the University of Maryland and San Diego State University also contributed to the Excellence Study. They included Jody Buffington, Linda Childers Hon, Judith K. Myer, Kenneth D. Plowman, and Krishnamurthy Sriramesh from the University of Maryland, and Troy Anderson, Jane Ballinger, Valerie Barker, Brian Ferrario, Danielle Hauck, Nancy Lowden, Susie Maguire, JoNell Miettinen, James Ritchey, Natalie Walsh, and Kimberly J. White from San Diego State University.

However, the research team constituted only half the players that made the Excellence Study happen. The leadership of the IABC Research Foundation board Chairs and IABC itself played a major role with fundraising, with monitoring the progression of the study, and helping with the distribution of research findings to the practitioner community. And, while one might think that fundraising would be, if not easy, at least systematic and organized, nothing could be further from the truth. It was chaotic from the start.

First and foremost, most people found it hard to believe that such a study could actually be done. And the price tag scared everyone. The IABC Research Foundation had been founded only two years earlier. Although the Foundation had funded some excellent work—the Velvet Ghetto (Cline et al., 1986) study, for example—no one at the Foundation really understood how difficult it would be to raise funds, as well as deal with the differing personalities and ways of doing business in the practitioner and academic communities. The largest previous project had been in the $4,000 range. The Excellence Study was 100 times that.

Williams and James Grunig made several trips to New York and elsewhere to secure funding. Hundreds of personal calls were made. Williams and James Grunig gave innumerable speeches and pleas for help to the membership, to the IABC executive board, and to IABC chapters and districts. And when help did come, it didn't come in large chunks. It is fair to say that the study was mostly funded by rank and file members; it was gifts of $5 or $10 that were by far the greatest number. Hundreds of those came in over the time of the study. Chapters held fundraisers that garnered $100 or $200. Districts made $500 or $1,000 gifts. Foundation board members who made paid speeches donated their honorariums to the cause. A few corporations did stand up and gave gifts of $2,500; one corporation even gave $10,000 (the largest donation by far).

By the time the last book was published in 2002, 10 different Foundation chairs and over 150 Foundation board members had dealt with the issue of funding and support. Chairs included Lou Williams, Wilma Mathews, Fred Halperin, Carolyn Douglas, Maire Simington, Vicci Rodgers, Barbara Puffer, Charles Pizzo, David Kistle, John Gerstner, and Tamara Gillis. Each of them had a different personality and approached the problems in different ways. Each faced challenges that threatened not only to stall the project, but also possibly destroy it.

Perhaps foremost among that group was Wilma Mathews, who happened to chair during a period when IABC finances were, to say the least, dicey. She faced an angry IABC executive board time after time with bad news: progress toward project completion was slow and funding was extremely difficult to come by. Support from the association's leadership seemed to slip away. Worse, the IABC chair decided during Mathews' tenure that the Foundation should be a freestanding organization; the Foundation should totally fund all of its activities and administration without any IABC contribution. That meant that contributions that previously went directly to projects were diverted to paying administrative support expenses to the association. Even a request to place a line on annual billing statements to the IABC membership was turned down as "inappropriate."

It seemed that each of the Foundation chairs was faced with a different problem, each more contentious than the last. Support from the IABC executive board wavered time and time again. Board members became concerned that the project, which was supposed to last five or six years, might never be completed. Some felt that money spent went down a rat hole. How, they asked, were they to explain that to various constituencies? Despite these challenges, each of the Foundation chairs made leadership contributions that eventually led to completion of the project.

One other complication that created difficulties for the researchers and fundraisers was the changeover in IABC staff and volunteers. Six different presidents and 18 different chairs guided IABC over the study period. Staff responsibilities were handled by a never-ending parade of coordinators. This turnover created many communication issues which, in turn, caused misunderstandings and mistrust among all parties involved. These were genuine distractions. Williams recalled a meeting with Barbara Puffer, the incoming chair in 1997, begging her to try to work hard to mend fences between all the various forces: IABC staff, the research team, and the Foundation board. To her credit, she provided smooth collaboration for a couple of years. Major contributions came from Fred Halperin, who worked tirelessly on the Excellence Study, as did Maire Simington, Vicci Rodgers, and Carolyn Douglas.

To say that not all IABC leaders supported the project would be an understatement. Many thought it was a foolish waste of time and money. They had their own priorities. The Excellence Study seemed such a long shot to successfully execute. And what would it matter in the end?

Fortunately, those who opposed the project were outvoted. Williams, who worked with each of these people over the entire span of the project, found himself more than once in the middle of disagreements over the research process, its length, and expensive nature of such a large-scale project. At the same time, Williams encouraged the research team for more speed. There were some difficult meetings in those 18 years, where tempers flared, egos were bruised, and hard words were spoken. Some meetings included both high tension and high enjoyment. One particular meeting happened in 1987, when the team from IABC (Williams and Jean Cormier) and the research team met to discuss concern about deadlines, but also grappled with what the project should be called, when completed. By a unanimous vote, Excellence in Public Relations and Communication Management won the day. Within a very short time, the project came to be called simply The Excellence Study. Why that title? Both teams wanted to tie into what was in the mid-1980s the most visible and highly popular book on managing organizations: *In Search of Excellence: Lessons from America's Best-Run Companies* (Peters & Waterman, 1982). Obviously, the book's title couldn't be used, but using the word "excellence" seemed a fair way to describe the ultimate objective of the project: discovering what works best in the field of public relations and communication management.

In retrospect, Williams believes that the final product made it all worthwhile; he counts the research team among his best friends to this day.

The Challenges of Organizational Cultures

One major challenge that James Grunig needed to address was the diversity of organizational cultures that overlapped in the Excellence Study. One cultural tension was how public relations education was regarded then at the University of Maryland.

Challenges at the University of Maryland

James and Larissa Grunig were on the faculty of the College of Journalism, University of Maryland. In many university journalism programs around the United States, a common conflict occurs among faculty members. At some universities, such as Columbia University and the University of California at Berkeley, the journalism faculty is strongly oriented to a professional studies model. Faculty are hired on the basis of prior distinguished careers in journalism, public relations, and other areas of mass communication; such professors often see their role exclusively as that of training future journalists, public relations, and other professional tracks.

At other universities, the journalism faculty is strongly oriented to a social science model of scholarship and instruction. Faculty are hired on the basis of strong academic preparation, with doctorates from top research universities; such professors often see their role as conducting original scholarship that benefits the practice. Ideally, journalism programs (often the academic units for public relations professional training) embrace both paradigms and work synergistically. Sometimes, the conflict between the so-called "green eyeshade" faculty and the so-called "Chi-Square" faculty devolves into wasteful infighting. Such was the challenge that James Grunig faced in the College of Journalism at the University of Maryland. The conflict was eventually resolved when the public relations program at the University of Maryland moved to the communication department.

Challenges on the Research Team

On the Excellence team, James Grunig had to marshal the strengths of a diverse group of scholars and practitioners. Larissa Grunig and Dozier were untenured at the outset, although Dozier received tenure and promotion to associate professor shortly after the Excellence Study was funded. As junior faculty, Larissa Grunig and Dozier needed to generate refereed articles in such journals as *Public Relations Review*. A long-term research project was unlikely to generate any immediate scholarly publications.

William Ehling was a tenured full professor at Syracuse University, so he didn't necessarily feel the same imperative for scholarly publications in the immediate future. However, Ehling had his own ideas about public relations theory and argued them forcefully (but respectfully) in those early meetings of the research team.

From the funding of the project in 1985 to the publication of the first Excellence book in 1992, Jon White moved from Mt. Saint Vincent University in Canada to the Cranfield School of Management in the UK. He later became a management and education consultant. Trained as a psychologist, White came at the Excellence Study from that perspective.

As a practitioner, Fred Repper had little interest in the different academic perspectives that eventually coalesced into what would become the Excellence Theory. His interest was ensuring that the research stayed focused on the three core research questions of most relevance to practitioners: First, when and why are the efforts of communication practitioners effective? Second, how do organizations benefit from effective public relations? Third, why do organizations practice public relations in different ways?

From 1985 to 1990, the research team met on several occasions to hammer out the underlying theories that would answer the three research questions both conceptually and practically. One memorable team meeting was held in the summer home of James and Larissa Grunig on the central Oregon coast. The team members used the hot, bubbling water in the Grunigs' jacuzzi to stimulate their thinking on the theoretical underpinnings of the Excellence Study.

The Excellence Study postulated that excellent public relations is more likely to occur in a participative organizational culture. James Grunig applied that principle to the internal operations of the research team. The two well-established professors worked in a participative, collegial fashion with the two junior professors, the management consultant, and the retired public relations vice president to ensure that the whole of the Excellence Study was greater than the sum of its parts.

The best evidence of this participative collaboration is *Excellence in Public Relations and Communication Management* (Grunig, 1992). In the beginning, the book was conceptualized by the research team as a simple literature review. Some 666 pages later, the book grew into the theoretical building blocks of what would become the Excellence Theory. In his Preface to this book he edited, James Grunig referenced the previously unpublished but frequently referenced "beating your head against the wall" theory (p. xiii). According to the theory, it feels good to finish editing a book in the same way that it feels good to stop banging your head against the wall over and over again. He allowed, however, that "this book will be a seminal book in the history of public relations" (p. xiii). His prediction was prescient. A Spring 2012 search of citations showed that *Excellence in Public Relations and Communication Management* had been cited 1,144 times by other public relations scholars. Among James Grunig's extensive list of publications, only *Managing Public Relations* (1984), the public relations textbook that he wrote with Todd Hunt, has been cited more frequently than the initial Excellence Study book.

The project came together with the launch of the mailed survey in 1990–1991. James Grunig had painstakingly assembled the questionnaire, with the help of the research team. Survey data collection was coordinated from the University of Maryland and San Diego State University. The unsung heroes of this Herculean effort were Linda Childers Hon and Krishnamurthy Sriramesh, then doctoral candidates at the University of Maryland, and JoNell Miettinen, then a master's degree candidate at San Diego State. Their task was to collect 1,700 variables from 327 organizations in the U.S., Canada, and the U.K. They used a 21-page questionnaire sent to top public relations practitioners, a 7-page questionnaire sent to CEOs or a close associate in the dominant coalition, and a 7-page questionnaire distributed to a sampling of regular employees. As previously noted, "the Excellence Study's extensive, multiphase collection strategy made this the survey from hell" (Dozier, L. A., Grunig, & J. E. Grunig, 1995, p. 245).

As principal investigator, James Grunig was responsible for managing the bicoastal data collection strategy. In 1990–1991, collecting survey data by mail was the only viable method, given the length and multiplicity of questionnaires. Data then needed to be entered by hand into a statistical data analysis software package, checked for quality, and analyzed.

Challenges of Academic/Practitioner Cultures

Perhaps the greatest challenge that James Grunig faced was differences in the cultural values of the IABC Research Foundation and the research team. Three core and interrelated challenges were (1) perceptions of time; (2) the scope of project deliverables; and (3) the use of academic prose. Differences in perceptions of time were especially problematic because of the progressive fundraising strategy that the IABC Research Foundation needed to employ. As noted above, the IABC Research Foundation did not have sufficient reserves to fund the entire project. Instead, fundraising would proceed sequentially. The research team would provide a particular research product deliverable, usually coordinated with the annual international conference of the International Association of Business Communicators. The annual conference provided an ideal venue to report the latest findings of the Excellence Study; the deliverable provided impetus for the next round of fundraising. This was a fine idea in the abstract. The problem, however, was twofold. First, very few people were present to hear reports made at the IABC international conferences; very few others heard about the deliverables. Second, with no savings to depend on, the Foundation was forced to stay one step ahead of the sheriff. No one ever knew when the next $10 would come in, or from where. That meant that the researchers were forced to make do with, to put it kindly, less than sufficient support to get their job done. Travel, computer expenses, and so forth were often provided as a "loan" to the Foundation, with the hope that the researchers would get it back over time.

To make matters worse, Larry Ragan of *Ragan Reports*, an important public relations trade publication, decided he didn't like the concept or execution of the Excellence Study. This critique occurred midway during the research project, just after publication of one of the major books. Ragan wrote several scathing articles, bemoaning the "academic" nature of the work, and how it would never have a positive impact on practitioners. Ragan was not alone. A gadfly columnist named Mickey Dover joined Ragan; Dover delivered his own (negative) take on the project. Both of these were blows to fundraising and the morale of all involved. Fighting the media relations battle took a toll on support; this struggle probably added an additional two years invested in responding to the criticisms and overcoming misperceptions created.

Cultural Differences in Perceptions of Time

Because public relations practitioners work with media and media deadlines, practitioners have an acute sensitivity to deadlines. If a news release or other collateral material is promised by noon on Friday, the practitioner commits a venal sin to deliver that information an hour late. It's a cardinal sin to deliver that information on Monday. A practitioner's professional reputation is closely tied to his or her ability to meet deadlines. Put bluntly, missing a deadline is considered unprofessional in the practitioner community.

Time is perceived very differently in the academic community. This is especially true when the product is an important scholarly publication. In addition, none of the members of the research team were working full-time on the Excellence Study. Demands of the Excellence Study competed with the demands of teaching, advising students, and other research projects. In an academic culture, perceptions of time are much more flexible and elongated. For example, an untenured faculty member's performance may be reviewed annually or less often, depending on the institution. An (untenured) assistant professor typically serves five to seven years on probation, before applying for promotion to associate professor and tenure. Unlike the 24-hour news cycle of the practitioner culture, dissemination of a peer-reviewed academic article can take over a year from date of submission to actual publication.

This disconnect regarding perceptions of time is best illustrated by the deadline for the first Excellence book. The research team originally set a deadline of March 31, 1987, for completion of the manuscript. As previously noted, the book was published in 1992. A number of factors delayed completion of the manuscript. Dozier, for instance, was diagnosed with cancer; a regimen of surgery, chemotherapy, and radiation was required to beat the disease.

As noted above, these cultural differences regarding perceptions of time created real challenges for the IABC Research Foundation. Each deliverable from the research team needed to be synched with fundraising efforts. When deliverables were not provided in a timely manner, fundraising efforts were compromised. These timing issues aggravated conflicts between the IABC Research Foundation and the IABC executive board.

Cultural Differences in Scope of Deliverables

As the Excellence Study progressed, the research team became increasingly aware of the groundbreaking nature of the study. Planning for the first Excellence book, for example, began with a rather narrow scope but soon expanded in breadth and depth. As James Grunig (1992) noted in the Preface:

> What started out as a routine review of the literature turned out to be a massive effort to build theory . . . In some chapters, we have integrated research that has been available to public relations for some time. In other chapters, we have built new theory from the related disciplines of sociology, psychology, management, marketing, women's studies, philosophy, anthropology, and communication.
>
> *(pp. xiii–xiv)*

In other words, the scope of work spelled out in the original research proposal was expanded by the research team into what the team regarded as a "seminal book in the history of public relations" (Grunig, 1992, p. xiii).

At the IABC Research Foundation, nobody objected to funding a seminal work. But because the scope of work had been expanded to something much larger than originally proposed, the completion of the first book took longer than expected. The practitioners' cultural imperative to meet deadlines here conflicted with the desire of the research team to produce a work that would impact public relations theory and practices for decades to come.

Cultural Differences in Use of Academic Prose

One of the recurring challenges in academic/practitioner communication is, frankly, communication. From an academic's perspective, college-educated practitioners ought to be able to read and understand the extant literature in public relations theory and research. In fact, one of the core tenets of any profession is a specialized "body of theory developed through research" (Cutlip, Center, & Broom, 2006, p. 125) that any professional worthy of the name should learn through formal education. When practitioners complain about jargon in academic journals such as *Public Relations Review* or the *Journal of Public Relations Research*, academics are miffed. How can you call yourself a professional, an academic might ask a practitioner, if you are ignorant of the science beneath the art of the practice?

From the practitioner's perspective, academics often seem pompous, ponderous, and purveyors of passively constructed sentences. How can you train the next generation of professional communicators, a practitioner might ask an academic, if you are such an incompetent communicator yourself?

James Grunig was well aware of this cultural tension between academics and practitioners. In reporting the findings of the Excellence Study, he saw the need to address two distinct audiences using two different communication strategies. Dozier had worked as a journalist for several years; he volunteered to be the lead author on a condensed version of the research findings for practitioners.

The IABC Research Foundation also made an important contribution to bridging the "communication gap." An editorial advisory panel, made up of working practitioners, was assembled. The panel included Robert Berzok, Kathleen Bourchier, Cheryl Greene, Lester Potter, Vicci Rodgers, Maire Simington, Nancy Welch, and Lou Williams.

The first book to report research findings was the *Manager's Guide to Excellence in Public Relations and Communication Management* (Dozier, Grunig, L. A., & Grunig, J. E., 1995). Because of the brevity of the book (258 pages), the authors were able to provide this deliverable on time. More importantly, the editorial advisory panel proved invaluable. As Dozier acknowledged at the beginning of the book, 15 years as a professor had dulled his capacity for active construction, terse sentences, and lucid examples.

One instance of sound editorial advice stands out, 16 years after the fact. Like all good academics, the authors of the *Manager's Guide* initially included a description of the research methodology before any report of findings. One member of the advisory panel suggested moving the methodology to an appendix and "cut to the chase." In the published *Manager's Guide*, the methodology appears in an appendix.

Another seven years passed before the third Excellence book was published. *Excellent Public Relations and Effective Organizations* (2002) provided a comprehensive analysis of the quantitative and qualitative data collected in the Excellence Study. In the 653-page book, Chapter 1 detailed the Excellence Theory and grounded that theory with supporting data. *Excellent Public Relations and Effective Organizations* (2002) reached the other important audience: the public relations academic community. By informing faculty and graduate students, the third Excellence book also communicates to the practitioner audience indirectly. The findings of the Excellence Study help provide the theoretical foundation for educating the next generation of practitioners.

James Grunig and the Excellence Study

It is safe to say that the Excellence Study would not have come to fruition without the leadership of James Grunig. In 1985, the IABC Research Foundation decided to take a big chance and fund a big study. That study would answer key questions relevant to the practice and contribute substantially to the body of knowledge. Despite the criticism heaped on the IABC Research Foundation for taking that $400,000 gamble, the Excellence Study, under James Grunig's leadership, was a singularly wise investment in the future of the practice. In fact, that gamble continues to provide return on investment. As the findings of the Excellence Study and the principles of the Excellence Theory diffuse into the content of introductory public relations textbooks, the benefits of the study—and James Grunig's leadership—continue to accrue.

References

Cline, C. G., Masel-Walters, L., Toth, E. L., Turk, J. V., Smith, H. T., Johnson, N. (1986). *The velvet ghetto: The impact of the increasing percentage of women in public relations and organizational communication.* San Francisco: IABC Foundation.

Cutlip, S. M., Center, A. H., & Broom, G. M. (2006). *Effective public relations* (9th ed.). Upper Saddle River, NJ: Pearson Prentice Hall.

Dozier, D. M., with Grunig, L. A., & Grunig, J. E. (1995). *Manager's guide to excellence in public relations and communication management.* Mahwah, NJ: Lawrence Erlbaum.

Grunig, J. E. (Ed.). (1992). *Excellence in public relations and communication management.* Hillsdale, NJ: Lawrence Erlbaum.

Grunig, J. E., & Hunt, T. (1984). *Managing public relations.* New York: Holt, Rinehart & Winston.

Grunig, L. A., Grunig, J. E., & Dozier, D. M. (2002). *Excellent public relations and effective organizations: A study of communication management in three countries.* Mahwah, NJ: Lawrence Erlbaum.

Peters, J. P., & Waterman, R. H., Jr. (1982). *In search of excellence: Lessons from America's best-run companies.* New York: Warner Books.

21

THE INFLUENCE OF EXCELLENCE

A Citation Analysis of the Excellence Study in PR Scholarship, 1992–2011

Yi-Hui Christine Huang and Joanne Chen Lyu

Abstract

The present study aims to use citation analysis to present a relatively comprehensive and systematic picture of the influence of the Excellence Study on scholarship. Specifically, it has the following objectives: (1) to explore the citations of the Excellence Study and identify its shifts over the past 20 years (from 1992 to 2011); (2) to identify the topics of the journal articles citing the Excellence Study; (3) to investigate the influence of the Excellence Study in terms of geography and language; and (4) to explore how the Excellence Study has been applied by various disciplines and fields.

A total of 1,862 citations of the Excellence Study were recorded, including 1,477 English works and 385 non-English works in 24 languages. Major findings were (1) The wide impact of the Excellence Study is borne out by the quantity of citations in various types of works, including journal articles, books, book chapters, conference papers, and dissertations/theses over the past two decades; (2) the total numbers of English citations are many more than that of non-English citations, though the gap between them is narrowing; (3) journal publishers from 15 countries and book publishers from 14 countries have published works citing the Excellence Study; and (4) the disciplines citing the Excellence Study include advertising and PR, business and economics, communications, public administration, sociology, law, and philosophy.

Key Words

bibliometrics, citation, discipline, Excellence Study, Google Scholar, public relations, Web of Science

The Excellence Study and the Purpose of the Study

When a study reaches a certain stage of development, its researchers reflect on its history, evaluate its present status, and contemplate what the future will look like (So, 1988). Theories are no different. This aim of this study is to examine the status and influence of the Excellence Theory, which has been considered the dominant theoretical paradigm in the field of public relations since the 1980s (Botan & Taylor, 2004).

In 1985, a research team headed by James Grunig, including Larissa Grunig, David Dozier, Jon White, William Ehling, and Fred Repper, began the Excellence Study (short for Excellence in Public Relations and Communication Management), which was sponsored by the IABC Research Foundation of the International Association of Business Communicators (L. A. Grunig, J. E. Grunig, & Dozier, 2002). This 15-year study of excellence in public relations and communications management in the USA, the UK, and Canada produced an explanation of the value of public relations to an organization and a set of theoretical principles describing how the public relations function should be organized, structured, and practiced in an organization (J. E. Grunig, & L. A. Grunig, 2002). Ultimately, the Excellence Study produced what Fleisher (1995) called "generic benchmarking"— identifying critical factors for success across different types of organizations.

The Excellence Study was issued in a series of three books: (1) *Excellence in Public Relations and Communication Management*, published in 1992 (Grunig, 1992), together with (2) *Manager's Guide to Excellence in Public Relations and Communication Management* (Dozier, L. A. Grunig, & J. E. Grunig, 1995), and (3) *Excellent Public Relations and Effective Organizations: A Study of Communication Management in Three Countries* (L. A. Grunig, J. E. Grunig, & Dozier, 2002). The conceptual framework for the Excellence Theory was detailed in Grunig's (1992) edited volume, the first of the three works to advance the theory. The second and third books then reported the empirical results, both quantitative and qualitative, resulting from the study. The research team concluded that public relations increases organizational effectiveness when it builds long-term relationships of trust and understanding with the strategic public constituents of the organization. Moreover, the Excellence Study also found that the use of the two-way symmetrical model, either alone or in combination with the two-way asymmetrical model, would be more likely to result in such relationships than would the other models, such as the press agentry and the public information models.

Exploring the state of public relations research, Botan and Taylor (2004) concluded that Grunig's symmetric perspective, the key concept in the Excellence Study, served as the dominant theoretical paradigm in public relations from roughly the late 1980s to the early 2000s. They further specified that the most prominent trend in public relations over the past 20 years has been its transition from a functional perspective to a co-creational one, a key concept in the perspective of symmetrical communication. A functional perspective, prevalent during the early years of public relations research, sees publics and communication as the means for achieving organizational goals, while a co-creational perspective sees publics as co-creators of meaning and communication (Botan & Taylor, 2004). Examples of co-creational research include the shift to organizational–public relationships, community theory, co-orientation theory, accommodation theory, and dialogue theory, but the most thoroughly researched co-creational theory is the symmetrical/Excellence Theory (Botan & Taylor, 2004, p. 652).

Previous bibliometric analysis also has demonstrated the influence of the Excellence Study in public relations research. Pasadeos, Berger, and Renfro's (2010) bibliometric study, which examined the public relations scholarship published between 2000 and 2005, found that the largest category of works cited was classified as the "Excellence Theory." Specifically and in terms of the three books resulting from the Excellence Study, an earlier bibliometric study examining the works between 1990 to 1995 showed the foundational Excellence Study text, i.e., *Excellence in Public Relations and Communication Management: Contributions to Effective Organizations* published in 1992, ranked eighth among the most cited works, with the top seven most cited works all being published before 1989 (Pasadeos, Renfro, & Hanily, 1999). In the more recent study on citation in public relations scholarship between 2000 to 2005, Pasadeos, Berger, and Renfro (2010) found that the first book of the Excellence Study occupied the second position among the most cited public relations works; the second book on the Excellence Study, *Manager's Guide to Excellence in Public Relations and Communication*, ranked fourth; and the third book, *Excellent Public Relations and Effective Organizations: A Study of Communication Management in Three Countries*, is the tenth most cited work in the field of public relations. Summing up the findings, Pasadeos, Berger, and Renfro concluded that the Excellence Theory, as the dominant theoretical perspective in the field (Dozier, L. A. Grunig, & J. E. Grunig, 1995; Grunig, 1989, 1992; J. E. Grunig & L. A. Grunig, 1992; Grunig et al., 2002), facilitated a prominent change in the public relations field: the increase in a focus on the development of public relations theory.

Viewed from the perspective of an academic discipline, public relations has been considered a sub-field of communications discipline, which often contributes to its perception as an "interdisciplinary clearinghouse" for other fields (Craig, 1999). This implies that the field of communications research in its broadest sense is influenced by multiple disciplines outside the field (Barnett, Huh, Kim, & Park, 2011). Additionally, its specific sub-area disciplines (public relations, journalism, etc.) are tied to a variety of other disciplines such as psychology, sociology, and anthropology (Pasadeos & Renfro, 1992). With the recent emergence of public relations as an area of scholarly pursuit, Pasadeos and Renfro (1992) raised the question of the extent to which public relations has been able to loosen its natural bonds to other disciplines and develop its own body of knowledge. Meanwhile, as Broom (2006) has warned, the field of public relations does not really benefit from "operating in a closed system," and researchers certainly "need to see our publications cited by scholars in other fields" (p. 149). On the other hand, however, when a new field or discipline such as public relations matures to a certain point, it may begin to influence others. To examine the extent to which the Excellence Study is influencing other disciplines/fields may shed valuable light on the discussion.

2012 marked the 20th anniversary of the publication of *Excellence in Public Relations and Communication Management*, the first seminal work in the study of PR excellence. The present study aims to use citation analysis to present a relatively comprehensive and systematic picture of the influence of the Excellence Study on scholarship. Specifically, it has the following objectives: (1) to explore the citations of the Excellence Study and identify its shifts in the past 20 years (i.e., from 1992 to 2011); (2) to identify the topics of the journal articles citing the Excellence Study; (3) to investigate the scope of influence of the Excellence Study in terms of geography and language; and (4) to explore how the Excellence Study has been applied by various disciplines/fields.

Method

A citations analysis, which used Google Scholar to locate the citations, was undertaken in this study. This section will first introduce the citation analysis, which will be followed by the rationale for why this study chose Google Scholar over Web of Science as its information source. A detailed depiction of this study's research method, which includes coding items, coding criteria, coding scheme, and inter-coding reliability, will then be presented.

Citation Analysis

Eugene Garfield first outlined the idea of a united citation for scientific literature in 1955. According to Garfield (1979, p. 1), "Citations are the formal, explicit linkages between papers that have particular points in common." The advantages of citation indexing include the ability to rank and evaluate literature according to how it is cited and who is citing it. Additionally, the automation of citation analysis eliminates the bias that human analysis can introduce, and observing collections of citations can help one form a highly accurate view of the key literature in a field in a relatively short period of time (Garfield, 1979; Noruzi, 2005).

The use of citation counts for evaluating research is based on the assumption that citations are a way of giving credit to and recognizing the value, quality, and significance of an author's work (Borgman & Furner, 2002; van Raan, 1996). A heavily cited published work must be considered important by a large number of scholars within a discipline or across disciplines (Pasodeos, Renfro, & Hanily, 1999).

Although So (1988) argued that citation counts say nothing of the quality of a cited work and that they do not reveal an author's intention in citing a certain work, it has also been suggested that citation counts are good approximations of quality (Cole & Cole, 1973), for citation counts have been found to correlate with scientific productivity, peer judgment of performance (Bayer & Folger, 1966; Koenig, 1983), and other measures of quality (Cole & Cole, 1973; Gordon, 1982; Summers, 1984). Furthermore, they are able to provide researchers and administrators with a reliable and efficient indicator for assessing the research performance of authors, projects, programs, institutions, and countries, as well as the relative impact and quality of their work (Cronin, 1984; van Raan, 2005). Besides, periodic studies of citation patterns not only provide a map of publishing activity within a discipline, but also help identify shifts in the relative impact of publications, institutions, and schools of thought, as well as links across disciplines (Pasadeos & Renfro, 1992).

Why Not Use the Web of Science?

The Web of Science (WoS), which comprises the three ISI citation databases, has been used for decades as a starting point and often as the only tool for locating citations and/or conducting citation analyses (Meho & Yang, 2007). Nevertheless, critics note the following limitations of the Web of Science database: (1) it covers mainly English-language journal articles published in the United States, the United Kingdom, and Canada; (2) it is limited to citations from journals and papers indexed in the ISI database; (3) it provides different coverage for research fields; (4) it does not count citations from books, most conference proceedings, and other non-ISI sources; and (5) it has citing errors such as homonyms, synonyms, and inconsistency in the use of initials and in the spelling of non-English names (Lewison, 2001; Reed, 1995; Seglen, 1998).

Among the disadvantages, exclusive inclusion of SSCI journals and the resulting lack of citation counts from books, conference proceedings, and other non-ISI sources create the most serious problems for future research. Consider, for example, the *Journal of Public Relations Research*, a core PR journal. Although it began publication in 1992, the SSCI database only began including it in 2008. This means articles published in the *Journal of Public Relations Research* before 2008 will not be taken into consideration by researchers if ISI is the sole information source.

Introduction of Google Scholar

The major competitor of the Web of Science in the field of citation analysis and bibliometrics is Google Scholar (GS) (Meho & Yang, 2007), which is the scholarly search tool of the world's largest and most powerful search engine (Beel & Gipp, 2009). Aiming to provide a single repository for scholarly information, GS enables users to search for peer-reviewed papers, theses, books, preprints, abstracts, and technical reports in many academic areas (Sadeh, 2006). Meho and Yang's (2007) comparison of WoS, Scopus, and GS also found that GS stands out in its coverage of conference proceedings as well as international, non-English language journals. GS indexes a wide variety of document types, some of which may be of significant value to researchers (Meho & Yang, 2007).

In terms of citation indexing, Noruzi (2005) argued that GS provides most of the advantages of other citation indexes. Compared to WoS, which primarily indexes refereed journal articles, GS sometimes finds citations which are in journals and conference proceedings not indexed in WoS, especially those in continental European languages (Noruzi, 2005). In addition, the automated citation index generated by Google Scholar is a multidisciplinary index covering virtually all sciences and disciplines and is not limited to a single language, country, field, or discipline (Noruzi, 2005). Accordingly, there is no bias of subjective selection of journals when using GS (Noruzi, 2005). This characteristic becomes even more important when the aim of the study is to explore the interdisciplinary citation of certain authors or works. GS, however, has its disadvantage and the biggest one is duplicate citations, e.g., a citation published in two different forms, such as preprint and journal article, will be counted as two citations (Meho & Yang, 2007).

Choice of GS as the Database for this Present Study

The advantage of GS over ISI is obvious and GS is used as the information source for the present study for the following reasons. First, one aim of this study is to explore the influence of three seminal books on the Excellence Theory; therefore, GS data with no limitation on refereed, high-quality journals and conference proceedings will be a better choice than ISI, which indexes only journal articles in its databases. As Meho and Yang (2007) note, GS could be very useful in showing evidence of broader international impact than those found in WoS. Second, in most cases, Google Scholar presents a more complete picture of impact than the Thomson ISI Web of Science (Harzing & Van der Wal, 2008), especially in the Social Sciences, Arts and Humanities, and Engineering. These disciplines in particular seem to benefit from Google Scholar's better coverage of citations in books, conference proceedings, and a wider range of journals (Harzing & Van der Wal, 2008). Third, this study endeavors to examine the trans-disciplinary application of the theory; therefore, the automated multidisciplinary citation index generated by Google Scholar, insofar as it breaks through disciplinary and geographic boundaries, is better able to serve the purpose of the study. Fourth, and also reflecting this study's purpose, one advantage of Google Scholar is its ability to include the non-English citations in one dataset. This study develops several measures, which will be explained more completely in a future section, in order to ensure the reduction of duplicate citations in Google Scholar to their smallest possible frequency.

Research Method of This Study

The titles of the three books including the Excellence Study were the terms used in the search:

- *Coding items*. In the current study, English citations and non-English citations are dealt with in distinct ways. English citations were coded according to (1) publication type of citing work, including journal article, book, book chapter, conference paper, dissertation/thesis, and other sources; (2) publication name; (3) year of publication; and (4) country of publisher (only for journal article, book, book chapter, dissertation/thesis). All non-English citations were coded according to (1) publication type; (2) year of publication; and (3) the language used.

- *Coding criteria*. *Publication type* was categorized as journal article, book, book chapter, conference paper, dissertation/thesis, or other sources. Other sources mainly refer to works labeled as working papers, discussion papers, research papers, and online journal articles. Application materials, proposals, drafts, unpublished manuscripts, course outlines, and teaching materials were not included in the study. Since the search was conducted using the Google Scholar database, newspapers, magazines, and government documents, which were included in some citation analyses (e.g., Pasadeos & Renfro, 1992) did not appear in the search results, therefore, these were not included in the study either. For a *book*, if a book has more than one edition, only the first edition will be coded. For a *book chapter*, the name of the book is coded as the publication name. If Google Scholar counts an edited book and one of its chapters as two citations, we eliminated the citation of the book. Two chapters of one edited book are counted as two citations. For a *conference paper*, it is possible that a journal article has been developed from a conference paper, and the journal article and its former version (i.e., conference paper) are counted by Google Scholar as two different citations; in this instance, we coded the results as two citations just as Google Scholar does. As to the *country of publisher*, for journal article, book, and book chapter, this term refers to the country where the publisher of the journal or book is. Few books were published simultaneously in several countries; all the countries were coded. For a *dissertation/thesis*, it refers to the country in which the dissertation/thesis was submitted. For the *language*, the function of "google translate" in Google was used for identification. Google Scholar updates its database periodically; searches for this study ended on February 20, 2012.

- *Inter-coder reliability and issue of duplicate citations*. Given that for most coding items in citation analysis, a reliability check was unnecessary because no coder judgment was needed (Pasadeos, Berger, & Renfro, 2010), this study conducted inter-coder reliability to ensure the data quality. Twenty percent of the total sample of 1,862 citations was coded to check for coder reliability.

Two coders were given instructions on how to generate the data and code in Excel files separately. For English citations, the inter-coder agreement was 98% for the publication type. In the non-English part, the inter-coder agreement was 91% for the publication type and 92% for the publication year.

Intensive manual cleaning was adopted to address the potential problem of duplicate citation in GS raised by Libris (Sadeh, 2006). Two steps were taken in this study to avoid duplicate counting. First, the duplicate problem was highlighted before coding in the coding instructions to alert the coder's attention. Second, the data were manually rechecked twice after coding: first by a research assistant and then by one of the authors. Additionally, accuracy checks of a random sample (15%) were conducted by one of the authors. Five items (approximately 0.27%) were found to be coded incorrectly and were corrected.

Results and Discussion

A total of 1,862 citations, including 1,477 English works and 385 non-English works were recorded. Of the English citations, 714 works cited the first book published in 1992; 347 works cited the second book published in 1995; and 416 works cited the third book published in 2002. Publication year could not be identified in seven search results so they were treated as missing data. Of the non-English citations, 228 works cited the first book; 75 works cited the second book; and 82 works cited the third book. Publication year could not be identified in 13 search results.

Types of Citations

Table 21.1 and Table 21.2 show the frequency of different publication types in the periods 1992–1996, 1997–2001, 2002–2006, and 2007–2011. The 2007–2011 total of 958 citations is 41.9% greater than the 2002–2006 total of 675 citations, more than five times the 1997–2001 total of 177 citations, and nearly 30 times the 1992–1996 total of 32 citations.

The English and non-English results demonstrate a similar pattern in Excellence Study citations in the following aspects: (1) all types of works show a sustained increase in citation over the past 20 years (English conference papers, however, remain stable between the third and fourth five-year periods); (2) there is a sharp citation increase between the second (1997–2001) and third five-year (2002–2006) periods; (3) after the second five-year period, journal citations increase at the fastest speed, followed by dissertation/thesis citations. After the noticeable increase between the second (1997–2001) and third five-year (2002–2006) periods, journal citations maintain the highest growth rate in the fourth five-year period. The increase may be due to the fact that the third book was published in 2002, which made the Excellence Theory more comprehensive. Moreover, the increase also

TABLE 21.1 Excellence Study Citations by Types of English Work

| Cited work | Number of Times Cited | | | | |
| | 1992–1996 | 1997–2001 | 2002–2006 | 2007–2011 | Total |
	(N=29)	(N=155)	(N=541)	(N=745)	(N=1470)
Journals	18	103	239	348	708
Books	7	9	30	44	90
Book chapters	2	18	58	83	161
Conference papers	0	9	90	87	186
Dissertations/theses	2	12	107	142	263
Other sources	0	4	17	41	62

TABLE 21.2 Excellence Study Citations by Types of Non-English Work

| Cited work | Number of Times Cited | | | | |
| | 1992–1996 | 1997–2001 | 2002–2006 | 2007–2011 | Total |
	(N=3)	(N=22)	(N=134)	(N=213)	(N=372)
Journals	2	5	42	79	128
Books	1	9	26	46	82
Book chapters	0	2	7	8	17
Conference papers	0	0	10	15	25
Dissertations/theses	0	2	38	53	93
Other sources	0	4	11	12	27

reflects that trend along with the theory evolving and maturing. The Excellence Study extends its impact into refereed academic journals that are usually under blind peer-reviews. Nevertheless, it should be noted that there is a big difference with respect to citation numbers between the English and non-English parts. First, it is evident that English is the dominant language in academic research. The total number of English citations is much higher than that of non-English citations, even though the gap between them is constantly reducing. In the first five-year period (i.e., 1992–1996), English citations are almost ten times all non-English citations combined, while the ratio falls to three and a half to one in the period between 2007–2011.

Nevertheless, when looking at the ratio of "book citations" to "total citations," there is a stunning contrast between the non-English and English parts. This ratio of book citations to total citations in the non-English sample (82/372) is much higher than that in its English counterpart (90/1470). Moreover, during the past 20 years, in all non-English citations, book citations as a whole rank third, behind citations in journals and dissertations/theses. If book and book chapter citations are combined into one type, however, this category exceeds dissertation/thesis in frequency, ranking second, although journal citations still rank first. We may conclude that the impact of the Excellence Study on books and book chapters in non-English citations, relative to other publication types, is much more prominent than that in English-language citations.

Most Citing Journals

Journal publications are considered to represent "actual work" done in a certain field (So, 2010, p. 232) inasmuch as journals cover various aspects and interests of research in a field. Because of the stable and consistent nature of journal publications, longitudinal data generated from this source can help discern the changes that have taken place over time. Given the important role journals play in the dissemination of scholarship, English journals citing the Excellence Study were sorted in ascending order in accordance with citing times. In order, the top ten journals (with several ranked the same) are the *Journal of Public Relations Research*, *Public Relations Review*, the *Journal of Communication Management*, the *International Journal of Strategic Communication*, *Public Relations Journal*, the *Journal of Promotion Management*, *Corporate Communications: An International Journal*, the *Journal of Public Affairs (Communication: South African Journal for Communication Theory and Research)*, the *Journal of Business Ethics (Journal of Marketing Communications, Corporate Reputation Review)*, and the *Journal of Mass Media Ethics*. The citations by these top ten journals account for almost two-thirds (66%) of all English journal citations.

Since the second five-year period (i.e., 1992–1996), the *Journal of Public Relations Research* has become the journal that cites the Excellence Study most in each five-year period. During the past 20 years, citations by the *Journal of Public Relations Research* and *Public Relations Review*, two SSCI journals indexed under the category of public relations, make up 36% of all English journal citations and 55% of the top ten journal citations.

Of the 13 journals ranking in the top ten, six journals' publishers are located in the UK and five journals' publishers are located in the US. There is only one journal published in the Netherlands and one in South Africa. Publishers' location will be examined and discussed in detail in a later part. More information about the top ten journals is listed in Table 21.3.

Disciplines Citing the Excellence Study Most Frequently

One objective of this study is to explore the citations of the Excellence Study across various disciplines. To achieve this aim, we identified the disciplines to which the top ten journals belong for two reasons. First, compared to other publication types such as books or conference papers, the specific disciplinary focus of journals can be identified more systematically through Ulrich's Periodicals Directory or ISI. As

TABLE 21.3 Journals that Cited the Excellence Study the Most

Journals and Citations	Country of Publisher	1992–1996	1997–2001	2002–2006	2007–2011	Total
1. Journal of Public Relations Research	US	0	30	67	57	154
2. Public Relations Review	UK	11	26	24	42	103
3. Journal of Communication Management	UK	0	2	32	17	52
4. International Journal of Strategic Communication	US	0	0	0	28	28
5. Public Relations Journal	US	0	0	0	22	22
6. Journal of Promotion Management	US	0	1	9	11	21
7. Corporate Communications: An International Journal	UK	0	2	6	8	16
8. Journal of Public Affairs	UK	0	0	4	11	15
Communication: South African Journal for Communication Theory and Research	South Africa	0	3	7	5	15
9. Journal of Business Ethics	The Netherlands	0	0	5	6	11
Journal of Marketing Communications Corporate	UK	1	9	0	1	11
Reputation Review	UK	0	0	7	4	11
10. Journal of Mass Media Ethics	US	0	2	3	4	9
Citation sum of the top 10 journals		12	75	164	216	468
Citation sum of all English journals		18	103	239	348	708
Sum of the top 10 journals/sum of all English journals (percentage)		67	73	69	62	66

previously indicated, citations in the top ten journals account for 66% of all English journal citations. Therefore, these ten should provide an acceptable representation of English journals.

Different databases have different standards of discipline categorization for journals. This study used Ulrich's Periodicals Directory, a standard library directory and database providing information about journals and other serial publications. Ulrich's Periodicals Directory was chosen over ISI because it makes available more uniform and comprehensive criteria compared to ISI, which offers subject categories for only four journals of the 13 journals that rank in the top ten.

Table 21.4 lists the disciplines to which the 13 journals belong, with discipline information offered from both Ulrich's Periodicals Directory and ISI. In the list, "Advertising and PR," "Business and Economics," and "Communications" are the top three disciplines of journals citing the Excellence Study.

To examine the influence of the Excellence Study upon various academic disciplines, Excellence Study citations by the top ten journals were analyzed at the discipline level. Basing on the disciplinary categorization in Table 21.4, each discipline was assigned one credit for one journal article. *Public Relations Review* provides a good illustration. One article in *Public Relations Review* will give one credit to "Advertising and PR" and one to "Business and Economics." We then totaled the credits of each discipline to generate the information in Table 21.5. With the exception of the discipline of Sociology, which slightly decreased from the third five-year period to the fourth five-year period, the data indicate that all other disciplinary foci, i.e., Advertising and PR, Business and Economics, Communications, Public Administration, Law and Philosophy, have continually increased over the past 20 years. Nevertheless, it is noticeable that the cumulative credits of Advertising and PR, Business and Economics, and Communications are far larger than other disciplines.

Key Themes in the Top Ten Journals

Another objective of this study is to identify the topics of journal articles that cite the Excellence Study. Key words of article citations in the top ten journals were coded and analyzed for two reasons. First, the key words of a journal article indicate its central concepts. Second, of the various publication types coded, journals are the only ones that would systematically provide key words.

Nevertheless, it should also be noted that key words are not featured in all journals. Of the 13 journals ranking in the top ten, key word information could be retrieved from only eight journals. The eight journals with key words are *Public Relations Review, Journal of Communication Management, Journal of Promotion Management, Corporate Communications: An International Journal, Communication: South African Journal for Communication Theory and Research, Journal of Business Ethics, Journal of Marketing Communications,* and *Corporate Reputation Review.* Also, some

TABLE 21.4 Journals Citing the Excellence Study

No.	Journals	ISI	Ulrich
1	Journal of Public Relations Research	Communication	Advertising and PR
2	Public Relations Review	1. Business 2. Communication	1. Advertising and PR 2. Business and Economics
3	Journal of Communication Management		1. Business and Economics-Management 2. Communications
4	International Journal of Strategic Communication		1. Business and Economics 2. Communications
5	Public Relations Journal		Advertising and PR
6	Journal of Promotion Management		1. Advertising and PR 2. Business and Economics-Management
7	Corporate Communications: An International Journal		1. Business and Economics-Management 2. Communications
8	Journal of Public Affairs		Public Administration
	Communication: South African Journal for Communication Theory and Research		Sociology
9	Journal of Business Ethics	1. Business 2. Ethics	1. Business and Economics 2. Law
	Journal of Marketing Communications		1. Business and Economics-Marketing and Purchasing 2. Communications
	Corporate Reputation Review		Business and Economics-Management
10	Journal of Mass Media Ethics	1. Communication 2. Ethics	1. Philosophy 2. Sociology

TABLE 21.5 Disciplines Citing the Excellence Study

Cited Discipline	Percentage of all Citations				
	1992–1996	1997–2001	2002–2006	2007–2011	Total
Advertising and PR	11	57	100	132	300
Business and Economics (including Management, Marketing and Purchasing)	12	40	83	117	252
Communications	1	13	38	54	106
Public Administration	0	0	4	11	15
Sociology	0	5	10	9	24
Law	0	0	5	6	11
Philosophy	0	2	3	4	9

journals only provide key words in certain back issues. For example, *Public Relations Review* was launched in 1976, but its articles contain key words only after 2004; similarly, *Communication: South African Journal for Communication Theory and Research* was launched in 1975, while its key words only began appearing in 2007.

A total of 932 key words were recorded, which, based upon the overarching themes behind the key words, were later divided into a number of sub-themes and finally 13 key themes, i.e., public relations, communication, organization, management, relationship, crisis, ethics, stakeholder, employee, internet, and corporate social responsibility. Taking "communication" as an example, there are three sub-themes under it, i.e., corporate communication, communication management, and integrated communication. For more detailed information, please refer to the Appendix.

Besides the most frequently appearing key term, "public relations," "communication" is second in frequency, "organization" is third, "management" is fourth, and "stakeholder" (an exchangeable concept of public) is eighth. The results involving the top key words mentioned above coincide with the definition of public relations spelled out by Grunig and Hunt (1984) as "the management of communication between an organization and its publics" (p. 6). Additionally, 93% of the total 932 key words appeared in the journal articles published in the second ten-year period (i.e., 2002–2011). If, as So suggests (2010, p. 232), journal publication represents the "actual work" done in a certain field, then these key themes provide a comprehensive picture of the influence of the Excellence Study on scholarship over the past decade.

Languages

There are 385 citations from non-English publications in 24 languages: Afrikaans, Bahasa Indonesian, Catalan, Chinese, Croatian, Danish, Dutch, Finnish, French, German, Italian, Japanese, Korean, Lithuanian, Malayan, Polish, Portuguese, Romanian, Russian, Slovene, Spanish, Swedish, Turkish, and Ukrainian. The first non-English publication citing the Excellence Study is a journal article published in the Spanish journal *Questiones Publicitarias* in 1994. To vividly illustrate the geographical locations of the 24 languages, a map (Figure 21.1) is drawn based on data from www.mapsofworld.com and Wikipedia.org.[1]

Of all the non-English publications, German takes up over one-fifth (21%), followed by Portuguese and Spanish. The publications in the top three languages account for more than half (52.1%) of the total non-English publications citing the Excellence Study. Languages spoken in Europe occupy nearly all the top ten positions, with Chinese, Korean, and Bahasa Indonesian being the exceptions. Chinese ranks eighth and is tied with Korean. Bahasa Indonesian ranks tenth. The findings involving Chinese and Korean as noticeable results in non-English citations should echo the previous finding that international research has emerged as the largest category of new studies as Chinese and Korean scholars have exerted their increasingly important influence in international PR research (Pasadeos et al., 2010). Moreover, the international studies particularly focus on East Asian regions, such as Taiwan, China, and South Korea (Huang & Zhang, forthcoming). Table 21.6 shows the details of the top ten languages.

Geographical Scope

This study also coded the countries of journal and book publishers. The data showed that *publishers of the journals* citing the Excellence Study operate out of 15 different countries, which include the US, the UK, the Netherlands, South Africa, Australia, Canada, India, Korea, Romania, Nigeria, Sweden, Denmark, Germany, Lithuania, and Malaysia. *Publishers of the books* are from 14 countries, including Canada, Germany, Australia, India, Finland, France, the Netherlands, New Zealand, Italy, Singapore, South Africa, Spain, apart from the US and the UK (see Table 21.7, Figures 21.2 and 21.3). The majority of the journals and books (including book chapters) citing the Excellence Study are published in the US and the UK. Canada is the third most active country in publishing studies that include such citations. Nevertheless, the gap between Canada and the US/UK is too large for comparison.

This study also recorded the countries in which the Excellence Study has been cited in graduate theses. Results showed 16 countries as sources of dissertations and theses that cite the Excellence Study: the US, Australia, the UK, South Africa, Finland, Switzerland, China, Singapore, Denmark, New Zealand, Sweden, Canada, Germany, South Korea, Taiwan, and Vietnam (see Figure 21.4). And 77%

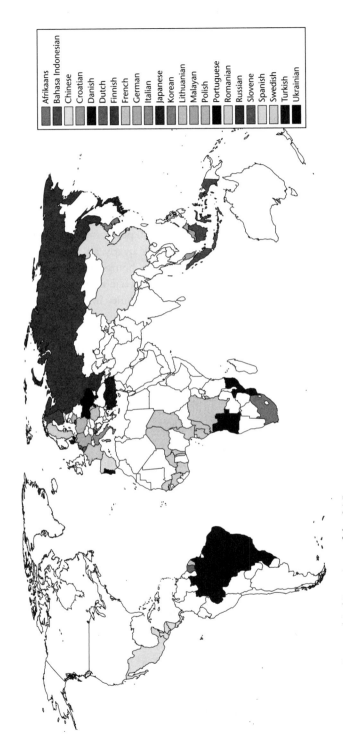

FIGURE 21.1 Geographical Locations of the 24 Languages

TABLE 21.6 Languages of the Non-English Publications

Rank	Language	Number of Times Cited	(%)
1	German	81	21
2	Portuguese	69	17.9
3	Spanish	51	13.2
4	Slovene	30	7.8
5	Swedish	26	6.8
6	Italian	20	5.2
7	French	19	4.9
8	Chinese	12	3.1
	Korean	12	3.1
9	Finnish	11	2.9
10	Bahasa Indonesian	6	1.6
	Danish	6	1.6
	Dutch	6	1.6

TABLE 21.7 Geographical Scope of the Study

Publishers of Journals		Publishers of Books		Excellence Study Cited in Graduate Thesis/Dissertation	
Country	Times	Country	Times	Country	Times
the US	343	the US	184	the US	203
the UK	283	the UK	78	Australia	12
the Netherlands	23	Canada	19	the UK	8
South Africa	21	Germany	15	South Africa	7
Australia	12	Australia	3	Finland	5
Canada	8	India	3	Switzerland	5
India	4	Finland	2	China	4
South Korea	3	France	2	Singapore	4
Romania	3	the Netherlands	2	Denmark	3
Nigeria	2	New Zealand	2	New Zealand	3
Sweden	2	Italy	1	Sweden	3
Denmark	1	Singapore	1	Canada	2
Germany	1	South Africa	1	Germany	2
Lithuania	1	Spain	1	South Korea	1
Malaysia	1			Taiwan	1
				Vietnam	1

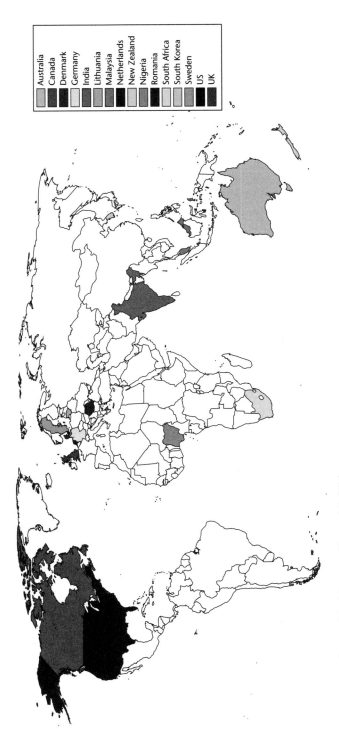

FIGURE 21.2 Geographical Scope of Journal Publishers

Australia
Canada
Denmark
Germany
India
Lithuania
Malaysia
Netherlands
New Zealand
Nigeria
Romania
South Africa
South Korea
Sweden
US
UK

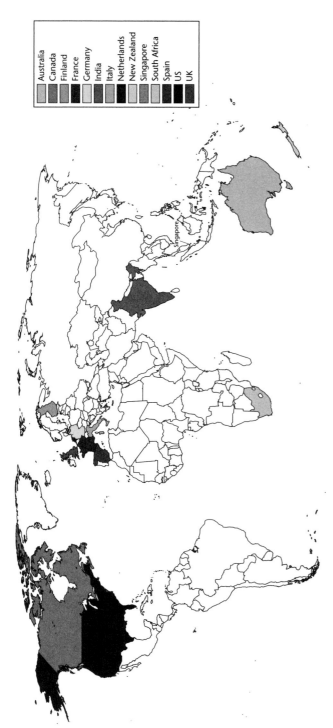

FIGURE 21.3 Geographical Scope of Book Publishers

	Australia
	Canada
	Finland
	France
	Germany
	India
	Italy
	Netherlands
	New Zealand
	Singapore
	South Africa
	Spain
	US
	UK

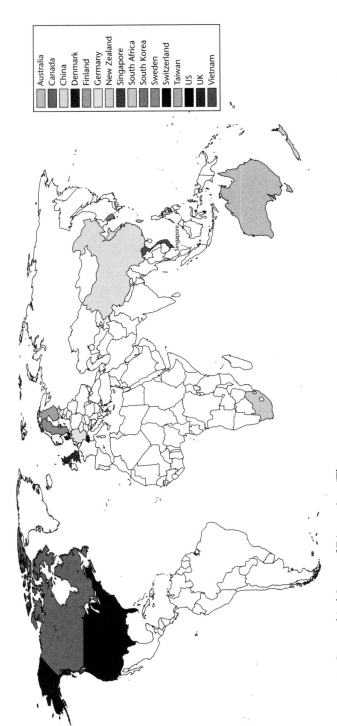

FIGURE 21.4 Geographical Scope of Dissertations/Theses

of total dissertations/theses citing the Excellence Study are from institutions in the US. Many Asian countries (China/Taiwan, Singapore, South Korea, Vietnam) also appear in the list, which in turn echoes the prior discussion involving international studies in China, Taiwan, and South Korea.

It should be noted, however, that in many countries, the dissertation/thesis could not be retrieved through online search functions in a database. Thus, the real results drawn from the dataset may be less than the actual number. It is reasonable to say that the real influence of the Excellence Study on higher education (including the prospective scholars) should be larger than the results in this study can show.

Conclusion

The data discussed in the previous sections clearly showed that the influence of the Excellence Study is significant in terms of the quantity of citations by various types of works. Furthermore, significant growth in scope of influence may be measured in categories such as geography and language, as well as in disciplines or fields applying the Excellence Theory.

Of the several types of academic works considered in this study, the constantly rapid rise in citations by journal articles and dissertations/theses is even more remarkable. Although this rise in citation of the Excellence Study may be explained as the result of the increasing numbers of journals, it essentially means that the Excellence Study remains an important part of the public relations literature. Moreover, it is also reasonable to conclude that increasing citations in dissertations/theses imply that the Excellence Study will continue to be influential for the next generation of scholars.

In addition, the surge between the second and third five-year periods is very impressive. Why has there been such phenomenal growth in citations of the Excellence Study since 2002? One reason may be the publication of the third book, *Excellent Public Relations and Effective Organizations: A Study of Communication Management in Three Countries*, thus making the Excellence Study literature more comprehensive. The rising influence of the Excellence Study may be related to the increasing academic interest in the Internet, which changed the communication environment. Phenomena such as interactivity (Hiebert, 2005), dialogic communication (Kent & Taylor, 1998), and relationship management conducted over the Internet (Stuart & Jones, 2004) are changing the contours of the profession not only for public relations practitioners but also for those who study public relations (Huang, 2012).

Furthermore, the data examined in the present study indicate the wide scope of the Excellence Study's influence in terms of geography. Journals published in 15 countries have cited the Excellence Study, and book publishers from 14 countries have published books citing the study. It should be noted that the publisher indicator is more of a reference to readership and distribution than a real geographical concept. For example, the *Asian Journal of Communication*, affiliated with the Asian Media Information and Communication Centre, Nanyang Technological University, is published in the UK. Furthermore, the Excellence Study, a theory developed out of a Western cultural context, has influenced higher education in at least 16 countries. Again, it should be noted that the results are likely underrepresented due to limited online distribution of dissertations/theses.

Another research objective pursued in this study concerns the application of the Excellence Study at the disciplinary level. Even given the limitations of the present study, and providing only the data derived from journal citations, the same pattern is unmistakable: Advertising and Public Relations, Business and Economics, and Communications are the major disciplines that routinely cite the Excellence Study. Also, the disciplines of Public Administration, Sociology, Law and Philosophy are increasingly citing the Excellence Study literature, which implies that the Excellence Study has drawn increasing attention from other disciplines outside public relations scholarship.

The final point to be made concerns the internationalization of the Excellence Study. A total of 385 non-English works in 24 languages have cited the Excellence Study over the past 20 years. Although English remains the dominant language in academic research, the disparity between English citations and non-English citations continues to decrease. This reduction is not caused by the decline of English works citing the Excellence Study, but rather by the rapid and constant increase in non-English citations, which to some extent predicts a continued increase in citations of the Excellence Study in non-English scholarship in the near future.

Appendix

TABLE 21.8 Key Themes in the Top 10 Journals

	Key themes	Including	Number of Times Cited
1	Public relations	Public relations, public relations and strategic management*, public relations in Gabon/Asia/Singapore, public relations message design, public relations area/autonomy/curriculum/education/effectiveness/ethics*/excellence*/measurement/models/perspective/practices/practitioners/roles/strategy/theory/value, multicultural public relations, transnational public relations, transition public relations, excellence in public relations*, excellent public relations*, professionalism in public relations*	121

TABLE 21.8 Continued

Key themes	Including	Number of Times Cited
2 Communi-cation	Communication(s), communication equality/competence/effectiveness/ethics*/management/models/strategy/systems/technologies/theory, communication management and planning*, symmetrical communication(s)*, two-way symmetrical communication*, development communication, ethical communication*, government communication, internal communication, intercultural communication, international communication, integrated communication*, marketing communication*, strategic communication, crisis communication*, website communication*, online communication*, stakeholder communication*	112
Corporate Communication	Corporate communication, corporate communication strategy	17
Communication Management	Communication management, communication management and planning	16
Integrated Communication	Integrated communication, integrated marketing communication, integrated marketing communications	10
3 Organization	Organizations, organization performance, organization structure, organization culture, organizational-public relationship, organizational culture*/development/learning/reputation/resources/trust*/effectiveness/communication*/mission and vision	37
4 Management	Management, management education, management roles, crisis management*, communication management, communication management and planning	35
5 Relationship	Relationship, relationships, relationship building/cultivation/decline/development/management/marketing/principles/theory, relationship between marketing and public relations, employer–employee relationships*, employee relationships*	34
6 Crisis	Crisis, crisis communication*, crisis leadership, crisis plans, crisis management*, crisis communication and management, and form of crisis response	26

TABLE 21.8 Continued

	Key themes	Including	Number of Times Cited
7	Ethics	Ethics, ethical communication*, ethics training, communication ethics*	17
8	Stakeholder	Stakeholder(s), stakeholder relationship building, stakeholders analysis/communication*/ management/theory	14
9	Employee	Employee attitudes/communication*/ empowerment/motivation/relations/relationships*, employer–employee relationships*	11
10	Internet	Internet, online communication*, online community, website communication*	10
	Corporate Social Responsibility	CSR, CSR programmes, CSR risks	10
11	Culture	Culture, cross-culture, cross-cultural, cultural intermediary, national cultures, organization culture*, organizational culture*	17
	Excellence	Excellence in public relations*, Excellence Study, Excellence Theory, excellent public relations*, public relations excellence	9
12	Marketing	Marketing public relations, marketing communication(s)	8
	Professional	Professionalisation, professionalization, professional roles, professionalism, professionalism in public relations*	8
	Trust	Trust, trust building, trustworthiness, interpersonal trust, organizational trust*	8
13	Symmetry	Symmetrical communication(s)*, two-way symmetrical communication*	6

Note: * means that the term was categorized as containing more than one key theme and was counted more than once.

Note

1   Data on the areas of the world speaking the following languages are based on www.mapsofworld.com: Chinese, Dutch, English, French, German, Japanese, Korean, Portuguese, Russian, Spanish, Swedish, Turkish, Ukrainian and Finnish. Data on the areas of the world speaking the following languages are based on Wikipedia.org: Afrikaans, Bahasa Indonesian, Croatian, Danish, Italian, Lithuanian, Malayan, Polish,

Romanian and Slovene. Only languages spoken by more than 50% of the population are included.

References

Barnett, G., Huh, C., Kim, Y., & Park, H. W. (2011). Citations among communication journals and other disciplines: A network analysis. *Scientometrics, 88,* 449–469.

Bayer, A. E., & Folger, J. (1966). Some correlates of citation measure of productivity in science. *Sociology of Education, 39,* 381–390.

Beel, J., & Gipp, B. (2009). Google Scholar's ranking algorithm: An introductory overview. In B. Larsen & J. Leta (Eds.), *Proceedings of the 12th International Conference on Scientometrics and Informetrics, 1,* 230–241.

Borgman, C. L., & Furner, J. (2002). Scholarly communication and bibliometrics. *Annual Review of Information Science and Technology, 36,* 3–72.

Botan, C. H., & Taylor, M. (2004). Public relations: State of the field. *Journal of Communication, 54*(4), 645–661.

Broom, G. M. (2006). An open-systems approach to building theory in public relations. *Journal of Public Relations Research, 18,* 141–150.

Craig, R. T. (1999). Communication theory as a field. *Communication Theory, 9*(2), 119–161.

Cronin, B. (1984). *The citation process: The role and significance of citations in scientific communication.* London: Taylor Graham.

Cole, J, R., & Cole, S. (1973). *Social stratification in science.* Chicago: The University of Chicago Press.

Dozier, D. M., Grunig, L. A., & Grunig, J. E. (1995). *Manager's guide to excellence in public relations and communication management.* Mahwah, NJ: Lawrence Erlbaum Associates.

Fleisher, C. S. (1995). *Public affairs benchmarking.* Washington, DC: Public Affairs Council.

Garfield, E. (1979). *Citation indexing: Its theory and applications in science, technology and humanities.* New York: Wiley Interscience.

Gordon, M. D. (1982). Citation ranking versus subjective evaluation in the determination of journal hierarchies in the social sciences. *Journal of the American Society for Information Science, 33*(1), 55–57.

Grunig, J. E. (1989). Symmetrical presupposition as a framework for public relations theory. In C. Botan & V. Hazleton (Eds.), *Public relations theory* (pp. 99–110). Hillsdale, NJ: Lawrence Erlbaum Associates.

Grunig, J. E. (Ed.). (1992). *Excellence in public relations and communication management: Contributions to effective organizations.* Hillsdale, NJ: Lawrence Erlbaum Associates.

Grunig, J. E., & Grunig, L. A. (1992). Models of public relations and communication. In J. Grunig (Ed.), *Excellence in public relations and communication management* (pp. 503–550). Hillsdale, NJ: Lawrence Erlbaum Associates.

Grunig, J. E., & Grunig, L. A. (2002). Implications of the IABC Excellence Study for PR education. *Journal of Communication Management, 7*(1), 34–42.

Grunig, J. E., & Hunt, T. (1984). *Managing public relations.* New York: Holt, Rinehart & Winston.

Grunig, L. A., Grunig, J. E., & Dozier, D. M. (2002). *Excellent public relations and effective organizations: A study of communication management in three countries.* Mahwah, NJ: Lawrence Erlbaum Associates.

Harzing, A. W., & van der Wal, R. (2008). Google Scholar as a new source for citation analysis? *Ethics in Science and Environmental Politics, 8,* 61–73.

Hiebert, R. E. (2005). Commentary: New technologies, public relations, and democracy. *Public Relations Review, 31*, 1–9.

Huang, Y. H. (2012). Internet public relations: A review of research articles and the construction of a theoretical model. *Communication & Society, 19*, 181–216.

Huang, Y. H., & Zhang, Y. (forthcoming). Organization–public relationships (OPR): A meta analysis. In J. Ledingham, E. J. Ki, & J-N. Kim (Eds.), *Public Relations as Relationship Management.*

Kent, L. M., & Taylor, M. (1998). Building dialogic relationships through the World Wide Web. *Public Relations Review, 24*(3), 321–334.

Koenig, M. E. D. (1983). Bibliometric indicators versus expert opinion in assessing research performance. *Journal of the American Society for Information Science, 34*, 136–145.

Lewison, G. (2001). Evaluation of books as research outputs in history of medicine. *Research Evaluation, 10*(2), 89–95.

Meho, L. I. & Yang, K. (2007). A new era in citation and bibliometric analyses: Web of Science, Scopus, and Google Scholar, *Journal of the American Society for Information Science and Technology, 58*(13), 2105–2125.

Noruzi, A. (2005). Google Scholar: The new generation of citation indexes. *Libri, 55*, 170–180.

Pasadeos, Y., Berger, B., & Renfro, R. B. (2010). Public relations as a maturing discipline: An update on research networks. *Journal of Public Relations Research, 22*(2), 136–158.

Pasadeos, Y., & Renfro, R. B. (1992). A citation study of public relations research, 1975–86. *Public Relations Review, 15*, 48–50.

Pasadeos, Y., Renfro, R. B., & Hanily, M. L. (1999). Influential authors and works of the public relations scholarly literature: A network of recent research. *Journal of Public Relations Research, 11*, 29–52.

Reed, K. L. (1995). Citation analysis of faculty publications: Beyond Science Citation Index and Social Science [*sic*] Citation Index. *Bulletin of the Medical Library Association, 83*(4), 503–508.

Sadeh, T. (2006). Google Scholar versus metasearch systems. *High Energy Physics Libraries Webzine,* issue 12, February 2006. Retrieved from: http://testing-library.web.cern.ch/testing-library/Webzine/12/papers/1.

Seglen, P. O. (1998). Citation rates and journal impact factors are not suitable for evaluation of research. *Acta Orthopaedica Scandinavica, 69*(3), 224–229.

So, C. Y. K. (1988). Citation patterns of core communication journals: An assessment of the developmental status of communication. *Human Communication Research, 15*, 236–255.

So, C. Y. K. (2010). The rise of Asian communication research: A citation study of SSCI journals. *Asian Journal of Communication, 20*(2), 230–247.

Stuart, H., & Jones, C. (2004). Corporate branding in marketspace. *Corporate Reputation Review, 7*(1), 84–93.

Summers, E. G. (1984). A review and application of citation analysis methodology to reading research journal literature. *Journal of the American Society for Information Science, 35*, 332–343.

Van Raan, A. F. J. (1996). Advanced bibliometric methods as quantitative core of peer-review-based evaluation and foresight exercises. *Scientometrics, 36*(3), 397–420.

Van Raan, A. F. J. (2005). Fatal attraction: Conceptual and methodological problems in the ranking of universities by bibliometric methods. *Scientometrics, 62*(1), 133–143.

AUTHOR INDEX

SUBJECT INDEX

Page indicators in bold refer to figures; page indicators in italics refer to tables.